RAMSEY

English in Its Social Contexts

May, 1992

Sheila –

Glad to know you'd
like to have a copy.
Love,
Dad

Microfche   310-9470 $15 ?

Oxford Studies in Sociolinguistics

Edward Finegan, General Editor

Editorial Advisory Board

Locating Dialect in Discourse
The Language of Honest Men and Bonnie Lasses in Ayr
Ronald K. S. Macaulay

English in Its Social Contexts
Essays in Historical Sociolinguistics
Tim William Machan and Charles T. Scott

English in Its Social Contexts

Essays in Historical Sociolinguistics

Edited by

TIM WILLIAM MACHAN

CHARLES T. SCOTT

New York Oxford
OXFORD UNIVERSITY PRESS
1992

Oxford University Press

Oxford   New York   Toronto
Delhi   Bombay   Calcutta   Madras   Karachi
Petaling Jaya   Singapore   Hong Kong   Tokyo
Nairobi   Dar es Salaam   Cape Town
Melbourne   Auckland

and associated companies in
Berlin   Ibadan

Library of Congress Cataloging-in-Publication Data
English in its social contexts : essays in historical sociolinguistics
edited by Tim William Machan and Charles T. Scott.
p. cm.—(Oxford studies in sociolinguistics.)
Includes bibliographical references and index.
ISBN 0-19-506499-2
ISBN 0-19-506500-X (pbk.)
1. English language—Grammar, Historical.
2. English language—Social aspects.
3. Sociolinguistics.
I. Machan, Tim William.
II. Scott, Charles T., 1932–
III. Series.
PE1101.E55   1992   306.4'4'0917521—dc20
91-19190

9 8 7 6 5 4 3 2 1

Printed in the United States of America
on acid-free paper

Series Foreword

Sociolinguistics is the study of language in use. Its special focus, to be sure, is on the relationships between language and society, and its principal concerns address linguistic variation across social groups and across the range of communicative situations in which men and women deploy their verbal repertoires. In short, sociolinguists examine language as it is constructed and co-constructed, shaped and reshaped, in the discourse of everyday life, and as it reflects and creates the social realities of that life.

While some linguists study the structure of sentences independent of their contexts of use (independent of who is speaking or writing, about what, and to whom, of what has preceded and what will follow, and of the setting and purposes of the discourse), sociolinguists investigate language as it is embedded in its social and situational contexts. Not surprisingly, among people who are not professional linguists virtually all linguistic interest likewise focuses on language in its contexts of use, because the patterns of that use reflect the intricacies of social structure and mirror the situational and strategic influences that shape discourse.

In offering a platform for studies of language use in communities around the globe, Oxford Studies in Sociolinguistics invites significant treatments of discourse and of social dialects and registers, whether oral, written, or signed, whether synchronic or diachronic. The series will host studies that are descriptive and theoretical, interpretive and analytical. While most volumes will report original research, a few will synthesize or interpret existing knowledge. All volumes will aim for a style accessible not only to linguists but to other social scientists and humanists interested in language use. Occasionally, a volume may appeal beyond scholars to students and to educated readers keenly interested in the everyday discourse of human affairs—for example, of doctors or lawyers trying to engage clients with their specialist registers, or of women and men striving to grasp the sometimes baffling character of their shared interactions.

With *English in Its Social Contexts,* Oxford Studies in Sociolinguistics presents its second volume. As editors of this volume, Tim William Machan and Charles T. Scott have commissioned essays in historical sociolinguistics that highlight the diverse social contexts in which varieties of English—Old, Middle, and Modern—have developed, from early Britain to present-day Papua New Guinea.

Despite extensive scrutiny of Old, Middle, and Modern English in scholarly works abundant enough to fill shelves of bibliographical tomes, sociolinguistic histories are scarce. Recent understanding of social dialects, registers, and the processes of standardization, coupled with critical reappraisal of the role of language in brokering social power and promoting solidarity, have stimulated intense interest in the social history of English. *English in Its Social Contexts* makes a valuable contribution to this renaissance of sociolinguistic history, particularly by synthesizing and interpreting the latest scholarly thinking. Themselves showing respect for the diverse forms of English around the world, and with a nod to varying editorial practices, the volume editors have assembled, in the chapters that follow, a diversity of topics and approaches to language, and to its organization, citation, forms, and usage. While not attempting to cover all significant aspects of social history nor the contributions of every important social group, the diversity represented in this volume points to the need for continuously emerging social histories of English—not of *the* English language, but of "Englishes" worldwide. Even the volume's table of contents reflects the diversity and vitality of English in spelling the very word for linguistic uniformity in two ways: The spellings "standardisation" and "standardization" are ironic emblems of the diversity represented in these chapters and the irrepressible independence of Englishes around the world.

In the decade ahead, Oxford Studies in Sociolinguistics will provide a forum for innovative and important studies of language in context. In so doing, it hopes to influence the agenda for linguistic research in the next century and to provide an array of insightful, provocative, and useful analyses to help launch that agenda.

Edward Finegan

Preface

As teachers of the history of the English language, we have long felt a need for a book such as this. The most commonly used textbooks, we believe, tend to emphasize internal history at the expense of external context, or to treat the latter in a way that does not fully utilize the advances in sociolinguistics in the past quarter century. We hope that the diverse essays contained herein will help to rectify this situation by demonstrating the ways in which specific varieties of the English language have always been utilized by specific individuals or groups for specific reasons. It is this use of the language to serve a broad range of communicative functions that both sustains and changes the language and that links speakers of English today with those from the past.

The primary audience of this book, then, is the student new to the study of linguistics in general and the history of English in particular. By this we mean only that the essays have not been written with the assumption that the reader will have a great deal of familiarity with the facts and concepts under discussion. Such a student may well be enrolled in a class on the history of English, but the issues of this book, we think, will also be important to those studying sociolinguistics, sociology, anthropology, and history.

Something should be said here about the style and content of these essays. Given the focus of the collection, as editors we did not prescribe a set list of topics to each contributor; the contributors decided on their own which issues were most relevant in the areas they examine. If the advantage of a more systematic approach is the sense of comprehensiveness it implies, the disadvantage, for this collection, is that systemization might obscure the dynamics of different critics using different methods to examine different issues; and such dynamics are characteristic of sociolinguistic inquiry. In the same vein, the distinctive English voices of the contributors—American, Australian, British, Indian—have not been copy-edited into a deceptive homogeneity. The contributions here reflect the variant orthographic practices and styles of the English language.

In compiling this book we have had the good fortune to benefit from the suggestions of a number of individuals. We would first like to thank the contributors for sharing their expertise in their respective areas. Edward Finegan was especially helpful and encouraging at an early stage in this project, and Cynthia Read, our editor at Oxford, has been both patient and resourceful. We would also like to thank Frederic G. Cassidy, Geoffrey Leech, and Peter Trudgill for their advice and interest.

Madison, Wisconsin   T.W.M.
June 1991   C.T.S.

Contents

    John Gunn

9. The Second Diaspora of English, 230
    Braj B. Kachru

    Afterword: English: From Village to Global Village, 253
    Suzanne Romaine

    Index, 261

Contributors

John Algeo
Department of English
The University of Georgia
Athens, Georgia

Craig M. Carver
Dictionary of American
  Regional English
University of Wisconsin
Madison, Wisconsin

Edward Finegan
Department of Linguistics
University of Southern California
Los Angeles, California

John Gunn
Department of English
University of Sydney
Sydney, Australia

Braj B. Kachru
Department of Linguistics
University of Illinois
Urbana, Illinois

Tim William Machan
Department of English
Marquette University
Milwaukee, Wisconsin

Judith Rodby
Department of English
California State University–Chico
Chico, California

Suzanne Romaine
Merton College
Oxford University
Oxford, England

Charles T. Scott
Department of English
University of Wisconsin
Madison, Wisconsin

Jeremy J. Smith
Department of English Language
University of Glasgow
Glasgow, Scotland

Thomas E. Toon
Program in Linguistics
University of Michigan
Ann Arbor, Michigan

Joseph M. Williams
Department of English
University of Chicago
Chicago, Illinois

The Phonemes of Present-day English

Phonemes

		BILABIAL	LABIODENTAL	INTERDENTAL	ALVEOLAR	ALVEOPALATAL	VELAR	GLOTTAL
Nonsyllabic								
Stops	vl	p			t		k	
	vd	b			d		g	
Affricates	vl					č		
	vd					ǰ		
Fricatives	vl		f	θ	s	š		h
	vd		v	ð	z	ž		
Nasals		m			n		ŋ	
Liquids					l	r		
Glides						y	w	

Syllabic *Monophthongs*

High	tns	i	u
	lax	I	U
Mid	tns	e	o
	lax	ε	ʌ
Low	tns	æ	ɔ
	lax	a	ɑ

Syllabic *Diphthongs*

Fronting	ay	(or aI)
	ɔy	(or ɔI)
Backing	aw	(or aU)

1. Dialects that distinguish *merry, Mary, marry* have [ε æ a] respectively; these are homophonous in many dialects, the vowel usually being [æ]. Most dialects have only one low front vowel, usually represented as [æ].

2. Many dialects do not distinguish [ɔ] and [ɑ], usually having only the latter in pairs like *caught, cot; naughty, knotty;* and so on.

3. In unstressed syllables, lax vowels are usually pronounced with the reduced vowel [ə] (compare the first vowels of *atom, atomic* or the second vowels of *telegraphy, telegraph*), or the reduced vowel [ɨ] (compare the final vowels of *roses* (with [ɨ]) and *Rosa's* (with [ə]).

4. The tense vowels [i e u o] are phonetically diphthongal, usually pronounced [iy ey uw ow], respectively.

5. In Southern American English, [ay ɔy] are monophthongized to [ɑː ɔː], respectively (e.g., in *time, oil*); many dialects have [æw] for [aw] (e.g., in *down, house*).

6. A colon (:) after a vowel indicates that the vowel is long, and an umlaut (¨) above a vowel indicates that it is fronted.

Contrastive Pairs

/p/	pail	staple	cop
/b/	bail	stable	cob
/t/	tear	metal	cot
/d/	dear	medal	cod
/k/	cane	hackle	tack
/g/	gain	haggle	tag
/č/	chin	lecher	etch
/ǰ/	gin	ledger	edge
/f/	fine	shuffle	leaf
/v/	vine	shovel	leave
/θ/	thigh	ether	teeth
/ð/	thy	either	teethe
/s/	seal	muscle	loose
/z/	zeal	muzzle	lose
/š/	shop	Aleutians	leash
/ž/	——	allusions	liege
/m/	met	simmer	sum
/n/	net	sinner	sun
/ŋ/	——	singer	sung
/l/	load	belly	shawl
/r/	road	berry	shore
/y/	yacht	tire	buy
/w/	what	tower	bough
/h/	hot	——	——

/i/	keen	/u/	cooed	/ay/	file
/ɪ/	kin	/ʊ/	could	/aw/	foul
/e/	cane	/o/	code	/ɔy/	foil
/ε/	Ken	/ʌ/	cud	/yu/	fuel
/æ/	can (n.)	/ɔ/	cawed		
/a/	can (v.)	/ɑ/	cod		

English in Its Social Contexts

INTRODUCTION

Sociolinguistics, Language Change, and the History of English

CHARLES T. SCOTT AND TIM WILLIAM MACHAN

Some fifty years ago, when Latin was a required subject of study in many American high schools, students often expressed their attitude toward this academic exercise with the little ditty:

> Latin is a language
> As dead as it can be
> First it killed the Romans
> And now it's killing me.

Without benefit of any technical expertise or linguistic sophistication, the students who sang this song—most with considerable conviction—knew clearly what was meant by a "dead" language. It was a language that existed only in its texts. No one spoke Latin, or wrote it to exchange greetings, to ask for directions, to complain about the weather or the increase in taxes, to interview sports heroes, to report the news of the day, to seek voter support in the next election, to declare that a state of war existed between the United States and Germany—in short, to do the myriad things, whether trivial or grave, that a "living" language is ordinarily, and extraordinarily, used for. Latin was (and is) no longer a language of everyday communication among people, young and old, as they carry out their daily affairs. Even the Catholic priest, who then used Latin as the language to celebrate the Mass, did not use it to confer with his parishioners, thereby confirming that the language had only a ritual, not a social, function. And without this social function, this *use* of the language to accomplish the deeds that make up much of the everyday life of a community, there was little real motivation to learn Latin.

In contrast, students of those days (and perhaps today's students) often complained that, *if* they were to be *required* to study a foreign language, why could it not be Spanish? Spanish, after all, was the first language of a majority of the people living in the Western Hemisphere: in Mexico, in Central America, in Puerto Rico, in most of the countries of South America. Spanish, too, was the first language of an increasing number of people settling in the United States. Spanish, therefore, was a language to be reckoned with, a language that might be

3

used for practical, everyday purposes and it would surely be important for trade and commerce. Besides, Spanish was "easier" than Latin. So it was commonly thought.

If there was no clear practical motivation to study the Latin language, there were, however, imagined ones (though these were often held with firm conviction only by curriculum designers, school administrators, and some teachers): The study of Latin would provide a base for expanding one's English vocabulary; the study of Latin would offer the student a proper introduction to the principles of "grammar"; the study of Latin would encourage orderliness of thinking; the study of Latin would ensure discipline of the mind. From such a line of reasoning it was an easy next step to begin to believe that the study of Latin might also contribute to moral rectitude. Indeed, the arguments offered for making Latin a required school subject almost exactly paralleled the arguments adduced for making plane geometry a required subject as well, another course in the curriculum that appeared to have little practical application but was deemed valuable for instilling the powers and virtues of deductive reasoning. Together, Latin and plane geometry were widely regarded, though seldom overtly described, as cornerstones of the school curriculum: Without the exceptional discipline of study that these subjects supposedly demanded, how could students have their minds and characters properly molded during their school experience?

From this brief, and only slightly exaggerated, description of the view of students and officials toward part of the typical school curriculum of half a century ago, we can derive a number of observations, some true, some false, about social aspects of language relevant to the central theme of this book. From our little scenario, we can deduce that students were intuitively aware of propositions like the following:

1. A language is "dead" when there no longer is a community of people who speak or write it to carry out everyday social interactions. American students of fifty years ago rightly concluded that the Latin of their texts was "dead," since (a), unlike Spanish, they knew that Latin was not used in its spoken form except ritualistically in the Catholic Mass and (b) they knew that Latin was rarely, if ever, used to create new written texts, that in fact it existed for them only in grammars and in surviving ancient texts (e.g., Julius Caesar's account of the military expeditions in Gaul, the orations of Cicero, and Vergil's epic poem *Aeneid*).

2. A language is "living" when there are people who speak it, and perhaps write it, to communicate with one another and to carry out the affairs of everyday life. Americans living in southern California, in the Southwest, and in Florida had long been well aware of Spanish-speaking communities in their midst. In the years immediately following World War II an influx of Spanish speakers into Northern cities of the United States, particularly Puerto Ricans in New York City, gave more Americans a heightened awareness of another "living" language besides English, and, further, suggested to the more entrepreneurial-minded the possible economic advantage of learning Spanish as a second language.

3. A language is "hard" (i.e., difficult to learn) if one is required to memorize numerous variant forms of nouns, adjectives, pronouns ("declensions") according to whether the word is part of a subject noun phrase or an object noun phrase in a sentence, or variant forms of verbs ("conjugations") according to the mood, tense, number, and person categories to be expressed by the verb of the sentence. Students tended to think that a language that exhibited such variation in word forms was inherently "difficult," forgetting that, from the point of view of a non-native English speaker, English, with its constraints on word order and its high incidence of function words (e.g., articles, prepositions, auxiliary verbs), might be regarded as "difficult" too. In short, the idea that one language is more difficult to learn than another was seldom understood as a relative concept: Relative to one's native language, other languages might be seen as more or less difficult to learn. Thus, because Spanish and English show some major similarities in word order, Spanish was deemed by Americans to be "easier" to learn than Latin, even though Spanish also exhibited some of the variation of forms that was regarded as such a difficult feature of Latin.

4. One should be required to learn a second language only if there is a demonstrable need to use that second language for practical communication. Recall that American students generally felt that *if* a foreign language was to be required study in the schools, it should be a language like Spanish, rather than Latin, because there was a greater chance of practical use of Spanish. By implication, though, the general attitude was one that rejected the study of *any* foreign language unless there was an immediate practical value to knowing it. Most students rightly concluded that, as English-speaking citizens of the United States, separated from the continents of Europe and Asia by vast oceans, the probability of ever having to use another language was so negligible that it could be safely dismissed. In short, linguistic isolation was widely considered to be a logical and acceptable concomitant of geographic isolation.

From the same little scenario sketched earlier, we can also deduce certain propositions held by school officials and other persons of social authority:

1. The study of classical languages like Latin or Greek should be required in the schools for reasons that transcend practical and utilitarian objectives. A host of reasons was given, as indicated earlier, some of which reveal more about attitudes toward language and learning than about relevance in the curriculum. For example, the view that studying Latin would enhance one's English vocabulary, although it has some merit, appears to rest on the false presumption that the meanings of Latin word components have remained unchanged to the present day—the "etymological fallacy." The view that studying Latin would contribute to orderliness of thinking seems to derive from an assumption that languages that contain a lot of inflectional apparatus (prefixes, suffixes) are best learned through processes of memorization and classification and that these mental processes, in turn, are valuable in their own right. However, that such mental processes might be thought to contribute ultimately to moral rectitude requires such a leap in fanciful judgment as to be absurd.

2. The languages available for study in the schools, whether required or

optional, should be the languages of "admired" societies. The cultural snobbism, perhaps even racism, lurking behind this view was never voiced publicly, of course, but was justified obliquely by reference to such notions as "our Western heritage," "the foundations of Western civilization," and so on. Classical Latin, the language of the texts of the Roman Empire, was the foremost candidate for required study in the schools, but the only Romance language that was an acceptable alternative was French, the form of Vulgar Latin (the colloquial speech of the Romans) that emerged as a result of contact with the Germanic-speaking Franks in Gaul. French was an acceptable foreign language for school study, presumably because a suitable culture for emulation had evolved in France, though one may wonder why the cultures of Italy, Spain, and Portugal were not equally thought worthy of emulation. Thus, it should be no surprise that Classical Latin (sometimes Classical Greek) was the expected foreign language required for study in the schools, that French was regarded as an appropriate second choice, and that Spanish—then—was scarcely available for school study at all.

The scenario of fifty years ago in the United States that we have sketched here is meant to highlight certain social aspects of language use and the study of languages. These social aspects concern attitudes and myths—attitudes toward languages themselves (and, implicitly, the people who speak, or spoke, those languages natively), attitudes toward varieties of English itself, and myths about the ease or difficulty of learning particular foreign languages and the presumed salutary effects of studying a classical language like Latin. It is reasonable to suppose that matters of attitude and matters of myth concerning foreign languages and their study, and concerning English in its manifold varieties, have played a role in the social contexts of English throughout most of its history. This supposition, in turn, raises a number of questions.

Was there ever a moment in the history of the English-speaking community when studying Latin was *not* regarded as studying a "dead" language? If so, when was that moment and what were the circumstances that allowed students to view Latin differently from the way they view it now? What were the circumstances in which French was studied as a second language, and how was it viewed as a school subject? Did our earliest English-speaking ancestors of the fifth century find the Celtic language of the native Britons to be "difficult" or "easy" to learn? What was their attitude toward learning it at all? At what point in the history of schooling in England did foreign language study become required? And what language, or languages, were chosen for the curriculum? Was there ever a time when the study of foreign languages came to be regarded as unnecessary or irrelevant? When was that, and why?

How mutually intelligible was English and the North Germanic speech of the Scandinavian settlers in the period just before the Norman Conquest? When, and under what circumstances, did speakers of French living in England begin to recognize that the future belonged to those who spoke English? When, and under what circumstances, did English speakers begin to recognize that some forms of English were more prestigious than other forms? How influential was the emergence of a standard written English for the development of a socially preferred spoken English? When, in a social psychological sense, did English really become the national language of England, and what were the conditions that brought this about?

Such questions touch upon the social contexts of English through its history in at least two ways: the societal functions of the language at different points from its beginnings to the present day and the attitude of its speakers toward other languages with which they came into contact at different points in this history. In the first instance, the question is: What functions did English speakers expect their language to perform at various stages in the development of the society? The answer to this question is partly determined by what other linguistic options were available in coexisting languages at various historical moments. In the second instance, the question is: To what extent did English speakers learn the language of the Romans, or the Britons, or the Danes, or the Normans, or other speech communities in close contact with English speakers, for the conduct of everyday affairs of business and social interaction? The answer to this question is determined in large part by the attitudes of English speakers toward those other languages and toward the speakers of those other languages.

When we ask questions like these, we attempt to understand historical change in the English language from a sociolinguistic perspective. Indeed, we may speak of the sociolinguistic profile of a language when we seek to characterize the societal functions expected of it at various moments in its history (Leith, 1983). When we try to explore the attitudes and myths that people hold about language and languages—English and the other languages with which it has vied—we engage in the study of an important sociolinguistic aspect of the development or the decline of these languages, including English. But the sociolinguistic approach to the study of languages, their functions, and their speakers encompasses much more than we have so far suggested. Let us turn, therefore, to what we mean by sociolinguistics and then ask how such a view of language and languages is relevant to our understanding of how a language may change over time and to our understanding of changes in the English language in particular.

SOCIOLINGUISTICS

What is sociolinguistics, and what perspective does it bring to the study of human language and languages? The term itself suggests some special interrelationship between linguistics (the field that takes the scientific study of language as its domain) and society or sociology, just as psycholinguistics suggests a special interrelationship between linguistics and psychology, or language and mind. By implication at least, linguistics is to be distinguished from sociolinguistics. But this distinction has troubled many sociolinguists, who insist that the study of "language as it is used in everyday life by members of the social order, that vehicle of communication in which they argue with their wives, joke with their friends, and deceive their enemies" (Labov, 1972:xiii), is exactly the subject of linguistics, and that, therefore, the term *sociolinguistics* is redundant. Most introductory linguistics texts define language as a system of arbitrary symbols, normally vocal, by means of which members of a society communicate with each other, noting further that *linguistics* is the term used to identify the discipline that takes language as its central object of study. Since this is the case and since there appears to be no realistic interpretation of language apart from its *use* as a communication system for members of a society, sociolinguists have argued that what they do is linguistics. That is, there is no significant difference between linguistics and sociolinguistics.

The point is a strong one, but it has not succeeded in eliminating the term *sociolinguistics,* which means that students and scholars in the field continue to find some value in making the distinction. In practice, the difference between linguistics and sociolinguistics appears to be one of emphasis: linguistics emphasizes the description of the formal elements of language, and their combinations, which constitute the "code" (called English, Latin, Swahili, Chinese, etc.) known and employed by members of a speech community. Sociolinguistics, on the other hand, emphasizes variation in the forms of the code according to such widely recognized sociological categories as age, sex, ethnicity, and socioeconomic class, and the uses of that code in accomplishing the everyday affairs of the community.

Linguistics has traditionally focused on the identification, classification, and distribution of the elements of language form, as these manifest themselves in sounds, morphemes, words, phrases, and sentences, and as these forms are used in the "code" to convey referential meaning. Thus, linguistics has traditionally been concerned with the analysis of the sound system of a language (its phonology), its inventory of grammatical and lexical form units (its morphology), the rules that govern the combination of words and phrases into grammatical sentences (its syntax), and the description of how linguistic forms refer to objects, events, qualities, actions, and states of being in the world about us (its semantics). In sum, linguistics has emphasized the structure of language, the systematic and predictable patterns that govern the combinability of linguistic elements to construct larger units such as words, phrases, and sentences.

Sociolinguistics has traditionally been concerned with a variety of matters, all having to do with what we have called social aspects of language. These may be matters of correlation between language form and social group identification— the typical occurrences of sounds, words, or constructions that serve to mark the speaker as a member of some sociological category (e.g., "teenager," "woman," "working class," "Chicano"). Or they may be matters of language use [i.e., the ways in which language is actually used by its speakers to create discourses, to negotiate social meanings (in contrast with referential meanings), to participate linguistically in multiple subgroups within the society at large]. Thus, sociolinguistics is concerned primarily with heterogeneity and variation within the speech community and within the speaker.

Heterogeneity refers to the fact that, in any given speech community, we find differences in the speech behavior of its members according to such social variables as age, sex, occupation, education, and ethnic background. We are well aware that children and adults do not normally speak alike, that there are typical differences in the speech of men and women, that college professors and plumbers usually speak quite differently, and that many (but not all) English speakers of Afro-American, Chinese-American, Jewish-American, Mexican-American, and West Indian–American ancestry, as well as the "white Anglo-Saxon" majority, exhibit characteristic features of speech. In other words, we belong simultaneously to a number of different and intersecting subgroups within our community and we are capable of modifying our language patterns according to these multiple memberships. Variation refers to the fact that individual speakers characteristically modify their language patterns according to such factors as topic of discourse, social relationship to addressee, channel of communication (e.g., whether written or spoken, face to face, or over the telephone), and size and nature of audience and setting, among other considerations. "Style-shifting" for the purpose of meeting these varying circumstances appropriately is, therefore, very much a normal and expected characteristic of our linguistic capability. When we use the term *heterogeneity,* we refer to variation in the language as a whole; that is, as a shared code. We mean variation according to the users of the language, and the variant manifestations of the language identified in this way are usually referred to as social dialects. When we use the term *variation* in the sense suggested earlier, we refer to variation in the repertoires of individual speakers (i.e., variation according to circumstances of use); the variant manifestations of the language identified in this way are usually referred to as registers. In sum, sociolinguistics has emphasized the use of language as the principal vehicle for the communication of emotions, directives, beliefs, conjectures, and information in the daily interactions of members of the speech community, and the users of the language insofar as language features serve to mark the social status and categories of speakers.

Sociolinguists assert that such heterogeneity and variation in both the speech community at large and the linguistic behavior of individual members of the community are normal and that, therefore, linguistics, as the "science of language," must have both a methodology and a descriptive notation for representing this normal absence of homogeneity and uniformity. The point is crucial, because it contrasts with a widely held methodological assumption of much formal linguistic description—the assumption that the language (or dialect) being described characterizes a homogeneous and invariant population of speakers. This assumption is often spoken of as the idealization principle, the methodological fiction that the grammar of a language (the result of linguistic analysis and description) represents the knowledge of an "ideal speaker-listener, in a completely homogeneous speech-community" (Chomsky, 1965:3), that is, speakers who have full and errorless command of the language they use in speech and writing. It is important to recognize that the principle of idealization is a purely methodological one, considered to be a necessary procedure in formulating a correct descriptive account of a language. No one who holds to this principle denies what any observer of actual speech behavior recognizes without question—that speakers often "misspeak" inadvertently (i.e., produce utterances that contain false starts, revisions, random errors, ungrammaticalities, and various other "violations" of the rules that govern sentence formation) and sometimes "misspeak" deliberately for purposes of special effect or solidarity with someone from a different social class. But it is commonly asserted that such "misspeakings," such instances of actual speech performance, cannot properly be accounted for without reference to an idealized linguistic form. Even so, sociolinguists object to this methodological principle on the grounds that it promotes the view that an acceptable object of linguistic description is language in isolation (i.e., language apart from social context). At issue are fundamentally divergent interpretations of the proper goal of linguistic theory, one seeing human language as an inherently social activity, the other seeing it as an inherently cognitive faculty. Both interpretations are valid, of course, and a number of scholars have offered proposals to reconcile the two positions (see especially Labov, 1972).

There are two main strands of the field of study that has come to be referred to generally as sociolinguistics. One strand is perhaps more accurately labeled the *sociology of language;* the other is sometimes called the *ethnography of speaking* (Labov, 1972:183–184). The first deals mainly with broad issues concerning the relationship of languages to society, particularly political states (e.g., bilingualism and multilingualism; language planning for developing nations; official languages, national languages, standard languages, and languages of widest communication; and written languages). The second focuses on systematic features of language use by speakers in specific contexts, and thus centers on individuals rather than on society at large. But in concentrating on individuals, this approach never forgets that the overarching function of language is communication, and communication presupposes listeners as well as speakers, and a context of circumstances within which communication takes place. Both of these main strands of inquiry bear importantly on change in the history of English. The first allows us to construct a sociolinguistic profile for the English language as a whole at various stages in its external history, and thus to calculate the extent to which the language has served, and is serving, to fulfill the range of societal functions that might be imagined for it. The second gives us a valuable perspective from which we can try to understand heterogeneity and variation in English through its history and the probable conditions for initiating and propagating those specific linguistic changes in pronunciation, grammar, and lexicon. Taken in their totality, these changes have resulted in a form of English today that would be incomprehensible to our earliest linguistic forefathers, just as their texts of, say, the tenth century are effectively, for us today, examples of a "foreign language."

SOCIOLINGUISTICS AND HISTORICAL CHANGE IN LANGUAGE STRUCTURE AND USE

No one has ever seriously doubted that languages change over time. Indeed, when the historical record reaches back just over 1000 years, as is the case for English, the apparent contrast between the earliest and most recent stages of the language can be so great as to make us wonder if we are not really dealing with two entirely different languages, rather than earlier and later stages of one language. In such a case, it is only on close inspection of the early textual evidence, including the setting aside of many superficial details, that we may finally recognize certain structural features that convince us that we are in fact dealing with an earlier form of one language.

Once we have learned to examine the textual evidence carefully and can distinguish between superficial and significant differences in the earlier and later stages of the language, we seek explanations for the changes that have occurred over the centuries. We try to construct a history of English. Until recently, it was customary to separate "external history" from "internal history." External history designated all the political, cultural, and social events associated with the community of English speakers from the time of their first arrival in Britain to the present day that seemed to have some bearing on the development of the English language. For example, such events would include the Norman Conquest of 1066, the devastation of the Black Plague in 1348, and William Caxton's introduction of printing in 1476. Internal history designated certain major changes or processes that had the effect of modifying forms of the language itself. For example, such changes would include the loss of numerous inflectional endings on nouns, adjectives, and verbs in the late Old English and early Middle English periods; the rhythmical balancing of syllables in historically disyllabic words known as "Thirteenth Century Lengthening in the Open Syllable"; and the "Great English Vowel Shift" of the Early Modern English period. Since the focus of attention is on the history of the English *language,* and not the history of the English *people,* it was thought, until recently, that primary attention should be given to internal history. How should we best describe the change of English pronunciation from its beginnings to the present day? How should we best describe the change of English grammar from its beginnings to the present day? How should we best describe the change of English word meanings from their beginnings to the present day? How should we best describe the change of English dialect variation from its beginnings to the present day? In general, these were the areas of focus for those who sought to construct an internal history of the English language.

The notion of a coherent internal history of English (or of any language), which has been presumed to be an appropriate goal of historical linguistics, presupposes a view of any language as a homogeneous structure that can be described independently of external, social influences. In this view, a language is a system of systems (phonology, inflectional and derivational morphology, syntax, semantics) that can undergo change as a result of a number of different systemic pressures. Such pressures include an apparently inherent tendency toward simplification of linguistic patterns by increasing symmetry of patterning or by leveling irregularities of patterning while still maintaining communicatively important oppositions within the system. (It is not at all clear that this tendency toward simplification is an inherent property of a linguistic system, or why this should be the case if it is.) This mechanistically oriented perspective on linguistic change was encouraged by an intensive focus on those aspects of any language system that lend themselves easily to such analysis, specifically the phonological system and the inflectional system.

Table I.1. English Consonant Systems

Old English					New English					
p		t	č	k	p		t	č	k	
b		d	j	g	b		d	j	g	
f	θ	s	š	x	f	θ	s	š		h
					v	ð	z	ž		
m		n			m		n		ŋ	
		l	r				l	r		
			y	w				y	w	

For example, in the history of change in the English consonant system two important modifications have taken place between the classical Old English period (tenth century) and the present day: (1) velar fricatives ([x, ɣ]) have been lost and (2) voiced fricatives have become distinct phonemes. A comparison of standard "articulatory displays" of the English consonant system for then and now points up this change (Table I.1). In Old English, the phonemes /f θ s/ were pronounced [v ð z], respectively, when they occurred between voiced sounds. Otherwise they were pronounced [f θ s], respectively. Thus, OE *wif* (NE *wife*) was pronounced [wiːf], but *wifas* (NE *wives*) was pronounced [wiːvas]; OE *bæþ* (NE *bath*) was pronounced [bæθ], but OE *baðian* (NE *bathe*) was pronounced [baðian]; and OE *cyssan* (NE *kiss*) was pronounced [küssan], but OE *risan* (NE *rise*) was pronounced [riːzan]. Thus, the OE consonant phonemes /f θ s/ had voiced and voiceless allophones, with the voiced allophones occurring between voiced sounds and the voiceless allophones occurring otherwise. Only when conditions changed such that voiceless fricatives came to be pronounced between voiced sounds, or voiced fricatives came to be pronounced in positions other than between voiced sounds, did the contrast between voiced and voiceless fricatives arise, thus leading to the emergence of the two series of fricatives in present-day English. What initiating change in condition brought about this split of allophones? Hans Kurath (1956) argued that it was the loss of "long consonants" (i.e., doubled, or geminated, consonants) in Middle English that resulted in a new opposition of voiced and voiceless fricatives in intervocalic position in words. For example, when the geminated [-ff-] of OE *pyffan* (NE *puff*), pronounced [püffan], came to be pronounced as a single [-f-], or [püfan], this single intervocalic [-f-] was then in contrast with the single intervocalic [-v-] of a word like OE *drifan* (NE *drive*), pronounced [driːvan]. Similarly, when the geminated [-ss-] of OE *cyssan* came to be pronounced as a single intervocalic [-s-], it came into contrast with the single intervocalic [-z-] of a verb like OE *risan*. Subsequently, these new contrasts were reinforced and expanded to word-initial and word-final positions as a result of newly borrowed words from French (e.g., *veal, zeal*). In the case of [θ] and [ð], it was the apparent weakening (voicing) of the initial consonant of such *function* words as OE *þu* (NE *thou*), OE *ðæt* (NE *that*), OE *þus* (NE *thus*), presumably because of reduced stress on such words, that led to the contrast between /θ/ and /ð/ in word-initial position in present-day English (e.g., *thigh* and *thy*). In word-final position it was the eventual loss of the unstressed final -e vowel of verbs like *bathe* (OE *baðian*) that brought [-ð] into contrast with word-final [-θ], as in *bath*.

Old English also had voiced and voiceless velar fricatives in words like *fugl* (NE *fowl*) (pronounced [fuɣl]), *bodig* (NE *body*) (pronounced [bodiɣ]), *truht* (NE *trout*) (pronounced [truxt]), and *niht* (NE *night*) (pronounced [nIxt]). Following front vowels, these sounds lost their fricative quality and merged with the postvocalic glide [y]; following back vowels, these sounds lost their fricative quality and merged with the postvocalic glide [w]. The "loss" of these sounds, then, is seen as a process of merger with the semivowels (glides) /y w/, which have been in the language from its earliest stage.

Note finally that modern English has a phoneme /ž/, which is found as the medial consonant of words like *treasure, pleasure,* and *leisure* and of words like *explosion, allusion,* and *vision.* In these cases, [ž] developed as a result of palatalization of /z/ before such suffixes as -*ure* and -*ion.* But in word-final position [ž] occurs only in such words as *beige, rouge, barrage,* which are clearly identified as relatively recent borrowings from French. And in word-initial position [ž] occurs only in such personal names as *Gigi* and *Zsa Zsa.* Although Old English of about the tenth century most probably had a voiceless palatal fricative /š/ [e.g., in words like *scip* (NE *ship*) and *fisc* (NE *fish*)], there was no voiced counterpart to this fricative. How, then, do we account for its emergence in English? By the end of the Middle English period, as a result of the allophonic split of /f θ s/ mentioned earlier, the set of English fricative consonants was the following:

    f   θ   s   š   h
    v   ð   z

It is easy to see that concepts such as "structural pressure" or "tendency toward symmetry" appear to offer a reasonable explanation for the relatively easy introduction of the /ž/ phoneme into the English system in the Early Modern English period. By extending the paired opposition of voiceless and voiced fricatives, a "hole in the pattern" has been filled.

Notice that in this account of change in one part of the consonant system of English, the "explanations" offered are all in terms of mechanistic modifications of the original system: (1) The sounds [v ð z] have been in the English system all along but in the Middle English period their "status" changes from allophones to phonemes as a result of a process of phonemic split. (2) The sounds [ɣ x] were present in Old English but no longer occur in standard modern English (though the voiceless velar fricative [x] can be heard in some varieties of Scottish English); they are "lost" in the history of English as a result of merger with the glides /y w/. (3) The "newest" consonant phoneme of English, /ž/, enters the system as a result of a general process of simplification that favors "balance" over "imbalance" in the subsystem of fricatives.

Viewed in this way, change in the sound system of a language appears to be system-driven, independent of any biases, preferences, and involvements of speakers. Such a perspective fits well with the nineteenth-century Neogrammarian position on the "lawlike" regularity of sound change and with the twentieth-century Structuralist preoccupation with systematic adjustments in networks of phonological oppositions.

Any persuasive indication of why these changes led to structural modifications in the phonological system is absent from such explanations. We are told *how* these changes may have started, but not *why* they were propagated and accepted. For example, if the rise of the voiced fricatives /v ð z/ was triggered by the loss of geminated consonants in the Middle English period, why did speakers of English begin to change their pronunciation of a word like *cyssan, kisse* from [kɪssɑn, kɪssə] to [kɪsə] and eventually [kɪs]? What motivated the preservation of a voiceless fricative in intervocalic position in this word, thus setting up a contrast between voiceless and voiced fricatives in this environment? If the merger of the velar fricatives with the glides /y w/ was triggered by loss of audible friction, why did speakers of English begin to pronounce words like *fugl* and *niht* without this friction in the postvocalic consonant? And if the introduction of /ž/ into the English consonant system was facilitated by the pressure for symmetry or balance, why does any occurrence of this phoneme in word-final or word-initial position automatically still mark the pronunciation of such a word as "foreign" or "French-based"? In short, a role of social motivation appears to be absent from historical accounts such as those offered earlier.

In addition to systematic sound change, analogy was regarded as a major mechanism of linguistic change within the internal history paradigm. Put simply, analogy proceeds from the recognition that some structural patterns of the language system are dominant and that, unless some other factor intervenes, minor or irregular patterns will typically adjust to the major pattern. Thus, by analogy with the principal means of marking the past tense of English verbs (by affixing a dental suffix -*ed* to the verb base), the modern English verbs *help, bellow, swallow,* and *melt,* which originally formed the past tense by internal vowel change (like *dig–dug*), now have the "regular" past tense forms *helped, bellowed, swallowed,* and *melted.* The dominant pattern for marking the plural of count nouns in modern English is attachment of the suffix -(*e*)*s* to the noun base (the reflex of the nominative–accusative plural case ending -*as* of so-called masculine *a*-stem declension nouns of Old English). Nouns such as *ship, sheep, glove, deed, eye, name, tongue, ear, church, book, cow,* and many others, which formed their plurals in other ways, now use the -(*e*)*s* ending by analogy with the historical "masculine declension" nouns (e.g., the OE ancestors of *king, stone, loaf, baker,* and *day*). Sometimes analogical reformation seems to be the appropriate explanation for the "leveling" of variant base forms in certain grammatical paradigms. For example, the OE adjective *eald* (NE *old*) had the comparative and superlative forms *yldra* and *yldest* (NE *elder, eldest*) as a result of an earlier sound change that affected the stem vowel. Thus, the more commonly used forms *older* and *oldest* in modern English are forms that have been reshaped on the model of the base form *old.* A similar remodeling has affected the modern English adjectives *young, great, high, long, short,* and *strong.*

Analogy, as a mechanism of linguistic change, normally operates in such a way as to bring less dominant forms into conformity with dominant forms. In this way, variation is eliminated in favor of regular patterning. Thus, the OE paradigm *dæg–dagas* should have yielded modern English *day–dawes* by normal systematic sound change if analogy had not operated to remodel the base of the plural form to conform to the singular form. But before the form *days* had become the accepted form of the plural of *day,* there undoubtedly was a period when the historically regular form *dawes* and the analogically created form *days* were both in use, competing for survival, as it were. We assume this to be the case on the evidence of similar variation observed in modern English. For example, some speakers use *dove* as the past tense of the verb *dive;* others use *dived.* In general, they appear to be mutually exclusive. That is, speakers who use *dove* do not use *dived,* and vice versa. It is important to note that neither of the forms appears to be "stigmatized" in present-day English, as, for instance, *ain't* is a stigmatized variant of *am not, aren't,* and *isn't.* In both cases, the variant forms are still current, but categorized differently in terms of social acceptability. Similarly, the past tense of the verb *awake* is sometimes *awoke,* sometimes *awaked.* In this case, many speakers seem to use both forms interchangeably but with a certain lack of confidence as to which of the forms is "acceptable." *Bring* has *brought* as its past tense form in standard English, although there are speakers who use *brang* as the past tense form (obviously by analogy with *sing–sang, drink–drank, swim–swam,* and so on). But *brang* is widely regarded as nonstandard, although tolerated as "country speech," and therefore not stigmatized in the way that *ain't* is. All these examples involve variant, competing forms. In some instances, one of the variant forms eventually disappears entirely from the language. In other cases, both forms survive but usually get categorized differently: One form is standard; the other is nonstandard; or, both forms are standard, but one is more limited than the other in its distribution (e.g., *the elder son* but *the older boy*). The survival, or recategorization, of variant forms seems to be determined by social considerations. Thus, just as the contemporary view of language history seeks the social motivation for sound changes, so also social motivation is required to explain the operation of analogy as an important mechanism of linguistic change.

One of the characteristic features of the Germanic languages, of which English is one representative, is that word stress is predictably located on the root syllable (usually the first) of a word. Thus, the following Old English words had stress on the first syllable: *fæder, heofon, nama, rice, yfele.* Stress is located on the second syllable of the following words because the first syllable is a prefix: *gehalgod, becume, gewurðe, forgyf, gelæd.* Many words that have been borrowed into English from other languages have been repronounced in accordance with this principle (*balcony* from Italian, *chauffeur* from French). There is contemporary evidence that this process of stress shifting is still taking place: Many speakers of British English have strongest stress on the first syllable of *garage* and *ballet,* although speakers of American English preserve the French origin of these words with stress on the last syllable. Many speakers of Southern American English place strongest stress on the first syllable of words like *police* and *insurance,* although speakers from other dialect areas have not followed suit. But the early principle of locating stress on the root syllable of a word has been replaced by one that assigns stress in accordance with certain phonological and morphological features of words. Thus, although the location of stress on *atom* appears to follow the early Gemanic pattern, the location of stress on *atomic* reveals that the Germanic principle is no longer the dominant pattern. Similarly, sets of derivationally related words like *harmony, harmonious, harmonic* or *telegraph, telegraphic, telegraphy* demonstrate that some principle other than the Germanic pattern is now at work. This newer principle governing stress assignment on words was evidently introduced into English along with the massive borrowing of words from French in the period from 1250 to the end of the fourteenth century. Rather than being replaced, the Germanic pattern was subsumed as a particular case of the more comprehensive Romance Stress Rule (Halle and Keyser, 1966). If this interpretation is correct, then we may attribute change in this aspect of the internal history of English to borrowing.

Tenth-century Old English had a word *fæt* ("vessel"). In the southwestern dialects, word-initial [f θ s] were characteristically voiced. As a result, this word was pronounced [væt]. It survives with this pronunciation in standard English today: *vat*. We account for its occurrence in modern standard English as an instance of dialect borrowing, which is the adoption of a linguistic feature (in this case, a particular pronunciation of a word) from some regional or social dialect that was not the standard dialect at the time of adoption. Because of a pre–Old English sound change, the diminutive (and feminine) form of standard Old English *fox* (NE *fox*) was *fyxen*. From the same southwestern dialect, with its pronunciation [vɪksən], we have the modern standard English form *vixen* (with semantic change as well). Historical doublets such as *skirt–shirt, dike–ditch, baker–batch,* as well as the variant pronunciations of the second element of the place names *Doncaster, Lancaster* vs. *Winchester, Westchester,* attest to dialect borrowing for their presence in modern standard English. Even grammatical features like the third-person plural pronouns *they, them, their* and the third-person singular present tense -*s* inflection on verbs are attributed to borrowing from the northern dialects (Scandinavian influenced). In instances such as these, and many more, the notion of borrowing (whether from another language or another dialect) as a mechanism by which we account for otherwise unexplainable forms in present-day English has little meaning unless it is tied to the notion of social motivation (i.e., unless the borrowed feature is perceived as contributing to some social advantage for those who adopt it).

When we look for the social motivation for a particular sound change, for a change brought about by analogical reformation, or for the adoption of some feature from another language or dialect, we introduce the sociolinguistic perspective into our history of English. Of two or more variant features competing for acceptance and adoption, typically one is favored and enters the standard language as the feature to be passed on to later generations of speakers. But the sociolinguistic perspective assures us that at any given period in the history of a language, there are many varieties of that language, differing more or less from one another according to the social groups using the language—groups defined by age, sex, occupation, ethnicity, socioeconomic class, and so on. Thus, the relevant and interesting questions are (1) whether linguistic changes are introduced by any or all of these social groups, and (2) what their motivations are for doing so (Guy, 1988).

Since the standard language is that social variety of the language used by those who have power and status in the society and since power and status are most closely identified with socioeconomic class (at least in industrialized societies), it has generally been assumed that linguistic changes are typically initiated by one or more subgroups within the socioeconomic categorization of the community. Determining what these subgroups are in some reasonably objective way is not easy, and a number of different subcategorizations have been used by sociologists and sociolinguists. Typically, these are more or less finely stratified groupings along a scale from "lower class" to "working class" to "lower middle class" to "upper middle class" to "upper class." In theory, we might expect linguistic changes to be initiated by any one of these subgroups, or by all of them indifferently. In practice, several major studies of social stratification in language use (Labov, 1966; Sankoff and Cedergren, 1971; Trudgill, 1974; Horvath, 1986) generally confirm the position that untargeted changes (i.e., modifications attributable to either sound change or analogical change, not borrowing) are initiated by the working class or the lower middle class, whereas targeted changes (due to conscious borrowing from a more prestigious speech community) are initiated by the upper middle class (sometimes referred to simply as the middle class).

Accounting for these changes in terms of their motivation is an even more difficult matter, though a social psychological basis seems inescapable. For example, much linguistic change appears to be associated in an important way with upward social mobility. Certain linguistic features, which are characteristic of the speech patterns of those who wield power in the society, are perceived to be emblematic of social class and thus become social markers (not unlike the perceived correlation of status with the make of automobile one owns). Those who aspire to a position of higher status in the society tend to "correct" their speech toward the prestige norms, sometimes even exhibiting hypercorrection. This is especially true when a speaker is engaged in the kind of discourse that heightens self-consciousness about speech, such as reading aloud. "Style shifting" of this sort is normal and is characteristic of all stratified social groups, though hypercorrection appears to be most characteristic of those who are insecure about their speech patterns, usually because they are concerned about the social image their speech projects. Clearly, such considerations make sense only in societies where upward social mobility is possible, as, for example, in England of the mid-fourteenth century, when the old feudal structure finally collapsed and the rising mercantile economy, with its opportunities for financial success, led to a dramatic expansion of the middle class. But not everyone in such a society shares equally in opportunity or success: The lower class, faced with no real prospects for advancement, is typically not concerned with projecting an upscale social image through speech patterns, and thus separates itself linguistically even more from the working class and the lower middle class.

Indeed, it is often the case that social markers of speech are used for their reverse value—as deliberately persistent identifiers of membership in some subgroup (a particular ethnic identification, "one of the good ol' boys," and so on).

In short, the social psychological motivation of establishing solidarity with an identifiable social class can sometimes explain the conservation of certain linguistic features, thus widening the gap between social groups. For this reason the upper class, those who are comfortably sure of their power and status in the society, is also typically conservative linguistically. The recognition today of BBC (British Broadcasting Corporation) English, on the one hand, and BEV (Black English Vernacular) English, on the other, two social varieties of present-day English that are probably perceived to be at opposite ends of any social class scale, each with markedly different linguistic and discoursal features, is probably made possible as much by the subtle operation of the solidarity principle as by any other factor. Class identification can be a powerful, even if disenfranchising, phenomenon. In the meantime, it is the middle class generally that forges ahead, setting the trend linguistically as well as in other domains of social behavior. This establishes what Labov has termed a curvilinear pattern, a pattern of change in which innovation is precipitated by the inner social classes (working class, lower middle class), not by the outer classes (lower class, upper class).

Perhaps the social class that is most crucial to the eventual acceptance and solidification of a linguistic innovation is the (upper) middle class. This is the class that sometimes initiates change, though only the targeted change mentioned earlier. For example, this class is presently leading a major change in the dialect of Metropolitan New York City: the shift from an "*r*-less" dialect (absence of postvocalic, preconsonantal [r] in words and phrases like *car, park, York,* and *the water was cold*) to an "*r*-ful" dialect, even increasingly in casual speech styles. In this case, the "*r*-ful" feature of General American speech has become socially prestigious, and therefore the model to be imitated. More important, however, this is the class that ultimately determines whether an untargeted change will survive as an accepted feature of the standard language (i.e., whether, by adopting a change initiated by working-class or lower-middle-class speakers, it gives tacit approbation to the change).

SOCIOLINGUISTICS AND THE HISTORY OF ENGLISH

The focus of this book is what a sociolinguistic perspective can contribute to our understanding of the changes the English language has undergone in the past 1500 years. Consequently, with our remarks about sociolinguistics and the mechanisms of linguistic change in mind, we turn to a brief overview of the history of English, both to sketch out the scope of the essays and to indicate some of the more important ways in which diachronic and synchronic sociolinguistic relations have shaped this history. In a sense, these relations are our themes.

It is important to note at the outset, however, that any sociolinguistic perspective on the history of the English language is necessarily a function of both the critic's attitudes and the indications we have of the attitudes held in the various historical periods. This latter point is an important but complicated one, for what some members of a culture may say about the culture or its language need not reflect the views of everyone in that culture. Moreover, the information that survives the ravages of centuries or millennia need not be a typical or even important indication of the nature of the culture that produced that information. How accurate would our view of nineteenth-century American English be, for instance, if we were to assume that the language of Mark Twain's *Adventures of Huckleberry Finn* was the linguistic norm? Or how accurate would our view of twentieth-century attitudes toward English be if it were based solely on Otto Jespersen's *Language,* which maintains that "women much more often than men break off without finishing their sentences, because they start talking without having thought out what they are going to say" (1922:250)? In the former instance, it is only the existence of a great number of other documents that tells us the book is written in an intentionally nonstandard style. In the latter, it is our own experience that tells us that the ideas and mores of the 1920s are not those of today and that at any time period, including the 1920s, the views of the privileged, dominant group are not likely to agree with those of the dominated one, at whose expense the privileged views have in fact developed. It is, in short, the proliferation of documentation that helps to corroborate and correct any linguistic views expressed about the past two centuries, whether by contemporary critics or by persons living at a given time.

Consequently, sociolinguistic analysis of English becomes increasingly problematic for the years before 1800, for the farther back in time we go, the less documentation we have. To be sure, there are firsthand remarks about the social function of language. But we cannot be sure how representative such remarks are. Are there so few remarks because few were ever made? And were few made because people did not consider the matter important or because they wanted to suppress potentially destabilizing trends? Or were many made, and did the few that survived do so through chance? Or were a great many remarks of potentially sociolinguistic importance destroyed for political or religious reasons?

It is clear that the efficient cause of the beginning of what we call the English language was arguably a sociolinguistic phenomenon: the invasion of England in the fifth and sixth centuries by Germanic tribes who brought with them their own culture, customs, and language. The society that these tribes initiated in England, influenced as it was by the remnants of the Roman occupation, by the scattered indigenous Celtic peoples, and by the geographic and political exigencies of the new environment, necessarily placed demands on communication different from those experienced on the Continent. These exigencies concomitantly shaped the form and function of the dialects of Old English. Such sociolinguistic factors, indeed, contributed to English for the first time notions of linguistic prestige and the power of *written* language.

The end of this first period in the history of English can also be considered sociolinguistic. Thus, if the conclusion of the Anglo-Saxon epoch for historians is the Battle of Hastings, and if for linguists it is the loss of inflections and grammatical gender, for sociolinguists it is a fundamental shift in language attitudes and the function of language that initiates Middle English. In this period, when French was the language of law and the court and Latin was the language of the Church and education, the English language, even though it remained the first and only language of the vast majority of people in England, held nonprestigious status. Linguistic self-consciousness, moreover, increased throughout this period. In the fourteenth century, for instance, the southerner John Trevisa noticed wide differences between the ways English was spoken throughout England, so that, according to him, southerners could scarcely understand northerners. Similarly, Chaucer, in his *Reeve's Tale,* was the first English writer to use dialect as a method of characterization.

Chaucer's use of spoken forms—pronunciations and lexis—in his written poetry points to another central quality of Middle English that is accessible only from a sociolinguistic perspective: its embodiment of the qualities of both orality and textuality. Anglo-Saxon culture was essentially oral; although written Old English certainly was produced, it was a relatively recent phenomenon, and only a tiny percentage of English speakers was literate. It was a time, consequently, when writing generally played an insignificant role in daily life and when word of mouth was the common medium of history, poetry, and politics. In the modern period, conversely, the written word is everywhere, and we are almost overwhelmed not only by texts but also by textual metaphors. The spread of compulsory education and the development of cheap methods of printing in English-speaking communities since the nineteenth century have in fact made command of written language one of the most powerful social determinants in modern societies. Middle English, then, is situated between these extremes: an increasing (although still small) number of individuals was literate in English, and written language, in the form of charters, wills, and letters, was beginning to permeate daily life. Nonetheless, primary orality had been a dominant feature of English culture in the very recent past, and so a sometimes uneasy compromise between orality and textuality is one of the distinctive features of language use in the years 1100 to 1500. At the beginning of his ribald *Miller's Tale,* for instance, Chaucer offers a curious blend of the oral and textual by warning the fastidious reader (Benson, 1987:67):

> . . . whoso list it nat yheere,
> Turne over the leef and chese another tale.

> [whoever doesn't want to hear this, turn over the page and choose another tale]

The shift from primary orality to primary textuality has in fact been one of the most profound sociolinguistic alterations in the history of the English language. It was the advent of print in particular that facilitated this shift and that provides a useful sociolinguistic reference for the transition from Middle to Modern English of the Renaissance. When Caxton set up his press in the city of Westminster in 1476, he did so primarily for pragmatic reasons. Foremost a merchant, he had gained experience in the book trade while on the Continent, and he recognized that the English market was ripe for the introduction of printed books. His choice of Westminster for his press shop was equally pragmatic; he was thereby near the ever-growing London metropolis and the influential, wealthy, and literate courtiers, ecclesiasts, and government officials who lived there. They provided an eager audience for whose tastes he shaped his catalogue, which was in fact dominated by histories, moral handbooks, and courtly poetry, particularly that of Chaucer.This early sociolinguistic identification of written, printed language with an affluent and influential sector of society not only solidified the prestige and power of writing but also significantly shaped the course of attitudes toward language right up to the present day. The introduction of print also had psychological consequences, for in fixing the contents and structure of written works in a way not possible in a manuscript culture, print shaped the nature of written texts, individual authors, and, it has been argued, thought itself (see Ong, 1982).

Although we can trace such gross sociolinguistic changes with some confidence, more delicate shifts are harder to detect, partly because of inadequate documentation and uncertain interpretation, as noted earlier. How, for instance, did language in the Renaissance serve as a medium between men and women, or between English speakers and those of other countries? As a partial answer to these questions, we can point to passages that reflect or identify for the first time in the history of the language differences dependent on the different genders or social classes of the speakers. In the middle of the fifteenth century, for example, Sir John Paston of Norfolk, in one of his many letters to his wife Margaret, shifts registers when the subject turns to love and adopts the words and phrasing of courtly romances: "Mine own dear sovereign lady, I recommend me to you, and thank you of the great cheer that ye made me here" (Davis, 1983:132). And in Shakespeare's *Henry IV, Part I,* when Lady Percy declines to sing a song by saying "Not mine, in good sooth," Hotspur mocks her for the mild nature of her oath:

> Not yours, in good sooth? Heart! you swear like a
> comfit-maker's wife. 'Not you, in good sooth!' and 'as
> true as I live!' and 'as God shall mend me!' and 'as
> sure as day!'
> And givest such sarcenet surety for thy oaths
> As if thou never walk'st further than Finsbury.
> Swear me, Kate, like a lady as thou art,
> A good mouth-filling oath, and leave 'in sooth'
> And such protest of pepper gingerbread
> To velvet guards and Sunday citizens.
>   [III.i.244–254]

Although John Paston's letter reflects an awareness of how context conditions register, Hotspur's outburst bespeaks a recognition of how social rank conditions (or should condition) usage.

For a partial answer to our question about the sociolinguistic relations in the Renaissance between speakers of different languages, we can look briefly to the Celtic languages. It has been characteristic of English that throughout its existence it has been used in close social and geographic proximity to other languages. In the Anglo-Saxon period, English coexisted with Latin, and in the Middle English period it coexisted with both French and Latin. Throughout both periods, however, speakers of a number of Celtic languages—Cornish, Welsh, Cumbrian, Gaelic, Manx, and Irish—were also in close contact with English speakers. For a variety of reasons, contact between these Celtic speakers and English ones was minimal until the thirteenth century. Afterward, and with increasing frequency during the Renaissance, the speakers did interact, and the consequences of these interactions have proved fatal for Celtic speakers: Cornish, Cumbrian, and Manx are no longer spoken as living languages, and Irish and Gaelic as first languages are limited to very few speakers indeed. Only Welsh may be said to be vital, although it certainly is not thriving.

We mention this example here because it illustrates how the English language, like all languages, can be used as a social and political tool and how the efficacy of this tool can affect the course of language development. That is, early in its history English had held nonprestigious status among intellectuals, and command of English alone (without Latin or French) was an impediment to social advancement. By the Renaissance, however, such nonprestigious status had been transferred to the Celtic languages. Moreover, to reside in England and not speak English, or to speak it with the accent of a nonnative speaker, had become socially stigmatized. The 1536 Act of Union of England and Wales, for instance, stated that "from hensforth no personne or personnes that use the Welsshe speche or langage shall have or enjoy any maner office or fees within the Realm of Englonde Wales or other the Kinges dominions upon peyn of forfaiting the same offices or fees onles he or they use and exercise the spech or langage of Englisshe" (Price, 1984:106–107). Indeed, language had become an active political weapon. One way to break down the allegiances of the Celtic speakers and to increase a sense of English nationalism, it was recognized, was to repress, if not exterminate, the non-English languages. Hence, policies were adopted that instituted compulsory education in English and that restricted use of non-English languages in school. As is often the case, religion was a significant factor in this sociolinguistic struggle. On the one hand, the Reformation institutionalized English as the language of the Church and thus contributed to the prestige of the language. The King James Bible in particular, by demonstrating that, as a literary language, English could be both elegant and sophisticated, reveals how translation of the Bible can provide a bulwark for both language and culture. On the other hand, the substitution in church services of the vernacular did not include the Celtic languages. Indeed, efforts to practice religion in these languages were actively resisted by the dominant English class; a partial Welsh translation of the New Testament was published in 1567, and a Gaelic translation first appeared in 1769. Not coincidentally, although certainly not entirely because of the earlier date of its Bible translation, Welsh today is far stronger than Gaelic. This example shows most clearly the intimate and potentially powerful connections between language and the society in which it is used: The English–Celtic clash reveals both how language can negotiate social relations and, concomitantly, how external social relations can influence internal linguistic history.

For the centuries since the English Renaissance, sociolinguistic analysis is facilitated by the diversification and spread of written documents. Problems remain even here, however. One of the most prolific branches of sociolinguistics in the past century, for instance, has been dialectology: the identification and analysis of regional or social subgroups of the speakers of a given language. Dialectology has been especially concerned with the words different dialects use to describe the same phenomenon. (Does a given region use *wasp, yellow jacket,* or *hornet,* for instance, to designate the annoying beelike insect found in much of the United States?) But the validity of this important and extensive research has recently become uncertain with the recognition that many dialect studies utilized far more men than women for informants (Coates, 1986:41–51). Furthermore, as insightful as these studies may be about lexis, they typically reveal little about other, equally important and distinctive linguistic features like syntax and intonation. The results of such work, therefore, certainly remain meaningful, but only as characterizations of part of half a given region's language. Even these speakers, moreover, may differ significantly in language use in ways *not* revealed by the dialect tests, so that the identification of any speech community—a group of speakers who share both language use and language attitudes—is always open to question, for it always obscures the individuality of its members (see Romaine, 1982).

Moreover, as the importance of writing and the geographic diversity of English have increased since the Renaissance, so have the sociolinguistic complexities of gender, social class, and language contact. In patterns familiar from the early history of English, language use has become an integral part of social identity and interaction, and social factors have in turn conditioned the development of English. For instance, the spread of English to the North American continent, Australia, and elsewhere—itself a sociolinguistic act—has led to the reenactment of the English–Celtic sociolinguistic conflict between speakers of indigenous languages and the newly arrived, and socially dominant, if not always prestigious, English speakers. The conflict is played out yet again with the immigration of West Indians into England and Hispanics and Asians into the United States. But dialect as well as language remains an omnipresent aspect of the sociolinguistics of English since the Renaissance, with certain accents being equated with social standing, success, and identity. In *Huckleberry Finn,* for example, the vagabond "king" attempts to disguise his identity by adopting British pronunciation. But when the person he is impersonating suddenly appears, it is language that partially undoes the "king": "That old gentleman that had just come, looked all puzzled to death. Pretty soon he begun to speak, and I see, straightoff, he pronounced *like* an Englishman; not the king's way, though the king's *was* pretty good, for an imitation" (Twain, 1985:249).

In fact, the geographic and social diversity of spoken English today—and to a lesser extent written English as well—forces us to reconsider traditional definitions of language and dialect. Is British English, for instance, to be considered "proper English," since Britain was the homeland of the original English speakers? If so, which dialect of British English—the socially prestigious Received Pronunciation, which is in fact the pronunciation of "only 3 to 5 percent of the English population" (Finegan and Besnier, 1989:504)? Or should Indian or Melanesian English be considered "proper English," since the number of speakers vastly exceeds the number of speakers for other English dialects? In this case, British preservation of certain historically correct morphological features would

then mark British English as nonstandard. Or since language is so closely identified with culture and identity, should the various forms of English be considered not dialects but separate languages? As the cultures and languages of English
speakers increasingly diverge, so may the desire of these speakers to identify with
one another. Indeed, such was the case in nineteenth-century America, when
reformists like Noah Webster sought ways of better representing American usage
and pronunciation.

Emotions run high when language and identity are at issue. A good example
of the most emotional extension of reformist thought is the suggestion of Elias
Molee, who in 1888 proposed replacing English in America with a truly "American" language:

> The only ones in this large population that can be expected to have a special love for
> the English language . . . is the English element. . . . The proposed language being an
> extract and coalescence of the best principles found in the leading languages of the
> United States, must be considered as a good illustration of true Americanism.
>
> [92–93]

The racial and ethnic biases of Molee, who believes that, because of the Norman
Conquest, the "Englishman speaks as a conquered man" (85), are easy to detect:
"I think, however, that the best of all would be for the whole Germanic or Gothic
race to unite upon one good Germanic language, and let other related peoples
do the same" (121). These biases usefully underscore how emotional the connection between language and identity can be, and such emotions can intrude
into any sociolinguistic discussion. The current popular discussion about the
largely symbolic act of making English the official language of the United States,
for instance, is often conducted at an emotional, rather than a logical, level. Any
argument today about the social and financial benefits of acquiring English is
necessarily complicated by the pride nonnative speakers rightly have in their
own languages.

Today social factors are among the most powerful determinants of language
use. In the United States, the slave trade created a social underclass by bringing
together black Africans of diverse linguistic backgrounds. Unable to speak the
language of the slave traders and often thrust together with speakers of a language they did not know, the slaves of necessity developed a pidgin. This pidgin
creolized and ultimately gave rise to what is today called Black English Vernacular, a dialect with its own distinctive phonological, morphological, and lexical
features. In turn, speakers of this dialect, like speakers of social or geographical
dialects throughout the English-speaking world, may alter their language for
social reasons. As Labov showed in his pioneering studies, and as we noted earlier, a desire to identify with another sociolinguistic group will lead to the adoption of preferred speech patterns, whereas a desire to underscore separation from
some social group will cause speakers to overemphasize the distinctive pronunciation or word choice of their native dialect. And such has proved to be the case
whether the linguistic group is based on ethnicity, geography, class, or gender.
But if awareness of this fact is one of the sociolinguistic achievements of the
modern period, so has been recognition of the difficulty of studying many such

sociolinguistic relations. Recent work on gender and language, for example, has affected how we understand the role of language in shaping social relations and, concomitantly, has demonstrated that sociolinguistic methodology itself cannot be value-free but must always be constrained by social relations and the linguistic observer's understanding of them. Uncontestable identification of gender-specific linguistic features has in fact proved difficult, and some of the truisms of female-male language use (e.g., males are more given to vulgarity) have been called into question (see Coates, 1986). Similarly, even when features have been identified—such as the fact that women interrupt men in conversations less often than men interrupt women—their interpretation is far from clear (see Cameron, 1985). Critical self-consciousness about one's views on gender—or ethnicity, or social class, or geographical position—is therefore necessary in the study of any sociolinguistic phenomena.

In all this complexity one thing remains clear: English, like any natural language, was, is, and will be a social phenomenon. Throughout its history the language has constituted social relations in such a way as to further or repress the interests of specific social groups. When the grammatical structure of the language has changed, moreover, it has changed as much for reasons of social function as for any qualities inherent in its grammar. And as long as there are speakers of English, the language will be an integral part of social relations and will, in turn, be subject to them, as Russell Hoban shows in his futuristic novel *Riddley Walker*. Set sometime after a nuclear holocaust has returned modern society to isolated, primitive tribes, the first-person novel is told in the form of English as it has developed at that time. Evident in the opening sentence are changes such as metathesis, apocope, and syncope, which are common in the observable past of English language history: "On my naming day when I come 12 I gone front spear and kilt a wyld boar he parbly ben the las wyld pig on the Bundel Downs any how there hadnt ben none for a long time befor him nor I aint looking to see none agen" (1980:1).

CONCLUSION

In this book we have divided the history of the English language into nine periods, derived partly from chronological considerations and partly from social ones. As each of the essays indicates, these periods were scarcely monolithic and static. But they are moments of varying length for which it is possible to construct a coherent (albeit idealized) account of the social functions of the English language and in which these social functions differed significantly from those of other, sometimes contemporaneous moments. From a historical perspective, what is intriguing is that sociolinguistic factors can provide a useful way for categorizing and analyzing the history of English and that the categories so devised sometimes, but not always, coincide with categories predicated on grammatical change.

How one chooses to divide the history of English (or any history), of course, has a great influence on how that history will be perceived by others and on what that history will be. For the early periods of the language's history, the limited amount of material and the limited areas in which English was used make the definition of epochs relatively straightforward. But, especially since the eighteenth century, as English has spread across Europe, North America, and Asia and as the proliferation of documentation facilitates broader sociolinguistic analysis, the linguistic epochs become broader and more complex. We certainly make no claim to have exhausted the sociolinguistic relations of English throughout its history. There could well be as many sociolinguistic relations as there are speakers of a language. Thus, the latter chapters of this book in particular can only scratch the surface of the many complex sociolinguistic issues and relations. In offering an essay on Australia, for example, we want to illustrate the language relations in a large and complex native-speaking community outside of the two largest centers of English use, England and the United States; essays might be written equally on South Africa or Canada. Similarly, the complex social status of English in Nigeria could have been emphasized more than the equally complex status of the language in India. Even such omissions, however, contribute to one of the objectives of this collection: to illustrate the diversity of language use and language attitudes that is sometimes homogenized by broad labels like "Old English," "Middle English," and "Modern English." As James Milroy asks in a study of the phonological variation of contemporary Belfast English: "If twentieth-century speakers observe great complexity of regular variation in /a/, then what is the status of characteristic historical 'findings' of the kind that say 'E[arly] Mod[ern] E[nglish] /a/ was fronted to [æ] in the seventeenth century'?" (1982:46–47).

A sociolinguistic perspective will thus not clarify all the issues in the history of the English language. If it is reasonable to suppose that sociolinguistic motivations of the sort Labov studied underlie the Great Vowel Shift, for example, we still have very little way of determining the precise nature of those motivations. But the relations between society, language, and language change remain as profound as they are unavoidable, and consequently the insights of sociolinguistics are essential to any informed understanding of language use, past, present, or future. This book aims at providing such insights. We hope that, through these essays, both the complex social issues confronting speakers of English today and the complex history in which these issues have developed will become clearer.

WORKS CITED

Baugh, Albert C., and Thomas Cable. 1978. *A History of the English Language,* 3rd ed. Englewood Cliffs, NJ: Prentice-Hall.
Benson, Larry D., ed. 1987. *The Riverside Chaucer,* 3rd ed. Boston: Houghton Mifflin.
Bloomfield, Leonard. 1933. *Language.* New York: Holt.
Bynon, Theodora. 1977. *Historical Linguistics.* Cambridge, England: Cambridge University Press.
Cameron, Deborah. 1985. *Feminism and Linguistic Theory.* London: Macmillan.

Chomsky, Noam. 1965. *Aspects of the Theory of Syntax.* Cambridge, MA: MIT Press.

Coates, Jennifer. 1986. *Women, Men and Language.* London: Longman.

Davis, Norman. 1983. *The Paston Letters: A Selection in Modern Spelling.* Oxford, England: Oxford University Press.

Finegan, Edward, and Niko Besnier. 1989. *Language: Its Structure and Use.* New York: Harcourt Brace Jovanovich.

Guy, Gregory R. 1988. "Language and Social Class." In Frederick J. Newmeyer, ed., *Language: The Socio-cultural Context,* Vol. IV, *Linguistics: The Cambridge Survey.* Cambridge, England: Cambridge University Press. Pp. 37–63.

Halle, Morris, and Samuel Jay Keyser. 1966. "Chaucer and the Study of Prosody." *College English* 28:187–219.

Harbage, Alfred, ed. 1969. *William Shakespeare: The Complete Works.* London: Penguin.

Hoban, Russell. 1980. *Riddley Walker.* New York: Summit Books.

Horvath, B. 1986. *Variation in Australian English: A Sociolinguistic Study of English in Sydney.* Cambridge, England: Cambridge University Press.

Hymes, Dell. 1974. *Foundations in Sociolinguistics.* Philadelphia: University of Pennsylvania Press.

Jespersen, Otto. 1922. *Language: Its Nature, Development and Origin.* London: Allen & Unwin.

Kurath, Hans. 1956. "The Loss of Long Consonants and the Rise of Voiced Fricatives in Middle English." *Language* 32:435–445.

Labov, William. 1966. *The Social Stratification of English in New York City.* Washington, DC: Center for Applied Linguistics.

———. 1972. *Sociolinguistic Patterns.* Philadelphia: University of Pennsylvania Press.

Lavandera, Beatriz R. 1988. "The Study of Language in Its Socio-cultural Context." In Frederick J. Newmeyer, ed., *Language: The Socio-cultural Context,* Vol. IV, *Linguistics: The Cambridge Survey.* Cambridge, England: Cambridge University Press. Pp. 1–13.

Leith, Dick. 1983. *A Social History of English.* London: Routledge & Kegan Paul.

Milroy, James. 1982. "Probing under the Tip of the Iceberg: Phonological 'Normalization' and the Shape of Speech Communities.' In Suzanne Romaine, ed., *Sociolinguistic Variation in Speech Communities.* London: Edward Arnold. Pp. 35–47.

Molee, Elias. 1888. *Plea for an American Language, or Germanic-English.* Chicago: John Anderson.

Ong, Walter. 1982. *Orality and Literacy: The Technologizing of the Word.* London: Methuen.

Price, Glanville. 1984. *The Languages of Britain.* London: Edward Arnold.

Quirk, Randolph, and C. L. Wrenn. 1955. *An Old English Grammar.* London: Methuen.

Romaine, Suzanne, ed. 1982. *Sociolinguistic Variation in Speech Communities.* London: Edward Arnold.

Sankoff, G., and H. Cedergren. 1971. "Some Results of a Sociolinguistic Study of Montreal French." In R. Darnell, ed., *Linguistic Diversity in Canadian Society.* Edmonton, Canada: Linguistic Research.

Trudgill, Peter. 1974. *The Social Differentiation of English in Norwich.* Cambridge, England: Cambridge University Press.

Twain, Mark. 1985. *Adventures of Huckelberry Finn.* Berkeley: University of California Press.

1

The Social and Political Contexts of Language Change in Anglo-Saxon England

THOMAS E. TOON

Everyone who has stopped to consider the fact realizes that written English is very different from spoken English. Probably few, however, have considered in depth the ways in which writing English is different from speaking English or have thought much about the consequences of those apparently simple facts. On first examination the important difference seems to be simply one of medium or form—on the one hand, sounds; on the other hand, letters that are written, printed, or have more recently become images on computer or video screens. Further reflection reveals major differences in function as well: We use the spoken language and the written language for different things. In the last decade, a number of literary critics, linguists, anthropologists, sociologists, and psychologists have begun to examine the ways in which the forms and functions of written and spoken language interact. Such studies of orality and literacy examine how individuals and societies use these two different forms of languages.

This essay examines the period in which the parent of Modern English became a separate language, distinct from other continental Germanic languages. That process began around A.D. 450, when Germanic tribes first settled in England. Because those people were isolated from their kindred on the continents, British varieties of the Germanic tongue slowly changed and developed into recognizably different species. Within a few hundred years, Anglo-Saxon was substantially different from continental Saxon or Norse, though speakers of these varieties could clearly understand each other. The processes of independent change continued during the intervening centuries, so that speakers of modern English, Danish, Dutch, and German can no longer understand each other's native tongues. Two kinds of facts will be of particular interest. First, the records from this period give us a glimpse of the processes that occurred as a number of subtly different varieties evolved into a single national variety. Since this was also the period during which speakers of English first became writers of English, we can also become informed about the role writing can play in the development of a national variety.

Since all readers of this book are already familiar with contemporary spoken and written English and few have studied Old English, we should start with a few observations about modern English that will highlight some of the phenomena we later examine for the Old English period. If we are in an airplane and overhear a conversation in the row behind us, we can make some predictions about the speakers. We might notice a "Southern accent"; we probably would form mental images of their age, gender, or race; we might guess something about their profession, economic status, or ethnicity; and we could conjecture about how well the people know each other. We would be picking up on such cues as pronunciation, choice of words, levels of formality, choice of topics, and the like. We would be responding to the ways in which the form of language is determined by the function of language.

We do all this more or less naturally. Being able to make such (usually unconscious) assessments is a direct consequence of being native speakers of English. Although we might think less about it, we constantly broadcast such information about ourselves. We might notice in addition how the demands of immediate use of spoken language determine such choices. We know that we speak more carefully to strangers, watch our language, and know the topics that are possible and those that are taboo. Even reflection on such a trivial and hypothetical scene leads us to observe something paradoxical about the situation. Although we feel uncomfortable "speaking to strangers," we feel a strong obligation to do so. We find ourselves closer than we usually get to people we do not know. Closeness results in eye contact, and we feel powerfully the need to acknowledge those with whom we have such contact. In fact, we find ourselves obliged to talk with these "neighbors" unless we pretend to fall asleep, pretend to be engaged with a book or headphones, or stare out the window. All of this is only to observe that speech situations are very complex and involve a number of competing influences.

Consider how different the situation would be if we noticed a group of people exchanging written notes. First of all, we would assume some compelling reason forced them to write rather than to communicate "naturally." The plane might be noisy, or they could be deaf. Even if they were deaf, alternative forms of sign language would seem more natural than writing. That is, everyone naturally speaks, but writing is somehow less natural. For most of us, talk is easy and free-flowing, but writing is a job that requires more conscious attention. After all, we learn to speak almost with no bother at all, but we have to go to school and be taught how to write. A similar set of facts is true of the languages of the world. All languages are spoken, but relatively few are written. There are thousands of different spoken languages, but only a few systems have developed for representing them in writing. Spoken language is found wherever humankind has developed. But writing systems do not develop spontaneously. They are spread by such social forces as conquest, education, political influence, religious conversion, and trade. That means that written language has a separate, official status—an authority—that most spoken varieties lack.

The written exchanges might be motivated by special pragmatic needs (e.g., for privacy). Even if we were allowed to read the messages, notice how much less we would be able to infer about these people than we could for exchanges that are overheard. Written language greatly masks individuality. We might guess age by encountering either a childish scrawl or the well-formed handwriting now to be associated with older generations. Few of us speak without revealing something of our origins, but the typeset, written English of people all over the world is amazingly homogeneous. The more formal the writing, the fewer distinguishing characteristics remain. Scholarly books and articles reflect less of the origin of their authors than do mystery stories written by Britons, Australians, or South Africans. And those works show less native flavor than does the English found in local newspapers, say, in Sierra Leone, Sri Lanka, or Singapore. The consistency of written academic English is a truly remarkable fact that most of us accept as commonplace. English has been written for over 1000 years, and the literate traditions of that millenium have slowed dramatically the rate at which the written language has changed. We read turn-of-the-century English with hardly any trouble. Even late-seventeenth-century works are hardly a problem. Only when we reach as far back as Shakespeare do we begin to encounter significant difficulties, and hearing a Shakespearean play is easier than reading one. We need elaborate assistance to work through Chaucer's *Canterbury Tales,* but we approach *Beowulf* as if it were written in a foreign language. One reason the rate of change of written English has slowed is that it has simply become too powerful a device for communication to allow individual differences to get in the way of that communication. But as we have already observed, simple communication of facts is just one of many uses to which we can put language. Written language is not only a powerful instrument, but an instrument of power and of the powerful.

This essay explores the origins of the historical dimensions of the uniformity and use of written language by examining the political and social contexts within which speakers of English first learned to give written form to their spoken varieties. The study of the oldest surviving texts written in English has a long and distinguished tradition. What follows is an attempt to offer a contemporary, sociolinguistic perspective to that tradition. Because most current work in the relationships between language variation and social factors is done as very carefully controlled social science, a caveat is in order. Historical linguists cannot go out and collect new data using the rigorous methods of such modern sociolinguists as William Labov or Peter Trudgill. Historical sociolinguists are forced to make do with the records that have managed by chance to survive through the centuries. Since modern sociolinguistics has so dramatically changed our understanding of the processes of variation and change, it is very important that contemporary attempts to reassess historical data be informed by current analytic methods. We can, as Labov suggested, "use the present to explain the past." Customs and traditions are transitory and change easily until they become written; the work of such contemporary anthropologists as Goody (1977) documents the profound effects of the development of writing on human societies. Certainly, as modern speakers and/or writers of standard English, we can recognize how powerful the written language is and how difficult it must be to live in contemporary society without knowing how to read or write. A comparative look at the rates of literacy across our pluralistic society quickly reveals how closely economic and social status is related to education and the ability to read and write our language. When, as speakers of Old English, our ancestors learned to write their speech, they also learned a powerful way of establishing and maintaining social structures.

The great Anglo-Saxon scholar who is popularly known as the Venerable Bede is an appropriate place to begin a discussion of literacy in this period. Although he was English, Bede had no choice but to write in Latin, since only the classical languages were regularly written until his time. Bede was an innovator in many regards. In the first place, he was the first writer of history in the modern sense, because he thought it important to base his accounts on written, rather than oral, traditions. He assembled documents as widely as he could and wrote a history that is especially rich in well-documented Old English personal names, as well as in the English equivalents for Roman and Celtic place names. Just as important, Bede, who was the greatest Latin scholar of his time, pioneered the practice of translating major texts into English, although unfortunately none of them survives. He further urged that the clergy be able to teach the rudiments of Christian doctrine in English. The principle was so important to him that he spent his waning energies in dictating from his deathbed an English translation of St. John's Gospel. His students felt it worth reporting that Bede chose to sing his death song in our English speech.

As in the example of Bede's *History,* the earliest attestations of written Old English are English names in Latin texts, in legal documents, or on coins. Soon English equivalents of difficult Latin words made their way into texts, extending a practice of glossing difficult Latin words with more common Latin words— much in the manner of modern students who write a word from their own language next to the word it is meant to translate. Later, scribes began to insert more extensive English glosses in the spaces between the lines of Latin texts. In the eighth and ninth centuries, these occasional glosses were assembled and large Latin–Latin glossaries were compiled. Three of these earliest glossaries are of particular interest because they contain substantial numbers of English words. The first extended examples of written Old English are complete interlinear, word-for-word glosses added in the ninth and tenth centuries to manuscripts of the Gospels or Psalms. As this practice became fairly frequent, some Latin texts were written with wide spaces between lines, apparently so that they could easily accommodate the interlinear glosses. Not until the educational reforms of King Alfred do we find independent translations of Latin works into idiomatic Old English.

Since the first attempts to write English involved applying Latin and its foreign alphabet (with well-established sound–spelling correspondences) to our native speech, those experiments contain valuable data from which historical linguists are able to reconstitute the pronunciation patterns of early Old English. Even though these earliest English texts are critical for understanding the history of the development of the language, that is not their greatest importance. To restrict ourselves to studying the origins of alphabetic literacy from such a limited perspective would be unnecessarily short-sighted in its own way. It would focus too narrowly on the form of language, while overlooking the study of the functions, the uses of language. The scribes who left us the first English texts did not intend to write linguistic history; they were conducting the businesses of their daily lives. Therefore, any study based on the products of a literate tradition ought to begin as a study of literacy, its uses, and its effects. We shall understand better why and how the form of Old English changed when we have come to a better understanding of the uses to which the Anglo-Saxons put their written language. To understand the importance of Old English texts, we need to understand the contexts in which they were written. Consequently, a first concern of the study of the texts of early Anglo-Saxon England is to offer a historical sketch of the political, social, and economic situation in which literacy became a functional part of English life. We shall see in the following pages how the experiment of writing English had a result that went far beyond simply giving a new written form to English. Writing had broad political and social consequences. Before the Anglo-Saxons began to write the varieties they spoke, they were a heterogeneous amalgamation of small and disparate tribes. These tribal people began to be (and to think of themselves as) an English nation just when they began to be writers of our English language. That the early English could, and did, write their language is related not only to their linguistic habits and abilities, but also to their social and political habits and abilities. Until recently, the language of these earliest texts had not been studied systematically, partly because the earliest texts do not exhibit the sort of regular spelling that we expect of modern English and that we do find in the late Anglo-Saxon texts. Such variety, we argue, is typical of oral language, especially in a society that lacked the powerful forces that foster language standardization—centralized government and education. In fact, we shall see that standardization of the written language occurred just as those political and social institutions developed.

Although no full contemporary accounts survive, Anglo-Saxonists are able to piece together from a variety of fragmentary sources a general account of the process by which the Germanic invaders of post-Roman Britain became an English nation. Details are few and only fortuitously attested. Although they provide a clear outline of widely accepted facts, much is still left to speculation and scholarly debate. All students of the period do, however, agree that the early settlement and conquest of Britain were essentially a piecemeal, tribal affair. By A.D. 600, the larger, more powerful tribes had consolidated themselves into the seven kingdoms of the so-called Anglo-Saxon Heptarchy—Northumbria, Mercia, East Anglia, Wessex, Essex, Sussex, and Kent. The "kings" of these tribal groups were locally powerful warlords who managed temporarily to secure a tenuous influence over their eventual usurpers. Few died of old age; fewer still passed their title on to an immediate heir. According to Bede, an overlord was occasionally able to extend his political influence over neighboring kingdoms and to establish the sort of stability we take for granted. Even though the traditional view of seven early Anglo-Saxon kingdoms is an oversimplification, it is a useful starting point. In fact, three kingdoms, each with successively greater influence, were able to establish widespread influence. First, the Northumbrians

(A.D. 625–675), about whom Bede is a local resource, were a dominant influence that gave a period of peace to the whole nation. Later, the Mercians (A.D. 650–825) of western and central England were able to consolidate power over all the southern English. The West Saxons (A.D. 800–1050) were the most successful, and Alfred the Great could truly claim to be king of England in something approaching the modern sense. Although these periods were marked by significant, though relative, political and social stability, it would be a mistake to suggest absolute continuity in succession of authority. Still, the fact of successful hegemony by one powerful overlord, and especially by a series of them, made the chances for future stability dramatically higher.

Of particular interest is the fact that in each case some degree of political stability occasioned a flowering of learning. The Northumbrian kings, for example, established the monasteries of Wearmouth and Jarrow and the intellectual climate that ultimately produced the famous school at York, the most extensive library in Europe, and such students as Bede and Alcuin. So great was their achievement that Charlemagne looked to the Northumbrian wealth of learning when he invited Alcuin to establish a school in his court. Indeed, the Bible as we know it owes much to Wearmouth and Jarrow. The most authoritative version of the Latin Vulgate text is preserved in the Codex Amiatinus. That manuscript was one of three complete Bibles produced around A.D. 715 in Northumbria—each one over 1000 leaves of quality vellum (27.5 inches by 20.5 inches), weighing in excess of 75 pounds. The immense cost of such a production is a poignant measure of Anglo-Saxon dedication to the Word and hence a direct indication of the importance of literacy to Anglo-Saxon kings. King Ceolwulf of Northumbria paid personal attention to the production of Bede's *Ecclesiastical History;* he read and criticized a draft of it. We ought not to be surprised to see Bede pay full tribute to the power of Northumbrian kings as rulers of all England, while at the same time politically ignoring the supreme Mercian ruler of southern England. King Ceolwulf and Bede knew the powers of the written word. They would not be surprised to learn that even modern historians have too uncritically accepted Bede's clearly northern perspective. Later Anglo-Saxon kings read their Bede and learned their lesson: an educated clergy can be more than a mere luxurious adornment to a dignified court.

Hegemony was developed into something more like genuine kingship during the West Saxon period; in fact, William conquered England in A.D. 1066 by subduing one English king. The period of political stability under the West Saxons typically fostered its own development of learning and resulted in a wealth of written products that reflect, because of already well-established traditions, the native language of the people and their king. In fact, the very success of the West Saxon hegemony has made studying earlier periods more difficult. Because almost all the surviving Old English texts date from the West Saxon period and because they are written in a very regular, standardized literary language, "West Saxon" is often treated as a synonym for Old English. Even those who avoid that oversimplification continue to expect of earlier Anglo-Saxon texts the same linguistic homogeneity that is typical of the West Saxon productions. Further, it is easy to forget that the contents of the West Saxon texts reflect a southwestern view of reality just as certainly as Bede's history reflects the northern, North-umbrian perspective. For example, the earliest extant chronicle is the West Saxon version of the *Anglo-Saxon Chronicle*. Its writers chose, for perfectly understandable reasons of their own, to parallel Bede in ignoring the extent of Mercian domination. They were in fact using Bede as one of their own major sources of information and may simply have absorbed his view of history uncrit-ically. More probably, they were providing an account of early history for the satisfaction and use of West Saxon kings. Since the West Saxons were the imme-diate conquerors of the Mercians, the exigencies of hegemony would encourage neither a faithful assertion of Mercian strength nor an accurate account of the glories of the Mercian political and social achievement.

The Mercian hegemony bridges the gap between Northumbria's first attempts at the political unification of what is now England and the West Saxon accom-plishment of that fact. Clearly, the Mercian period was one of continuing con-solidation of power; it was also the period that produced the first surviving texts written in the language of its people. As such, the Mercian period is necessarily the focus for a study of the origins of English vernacular literacy. Unfortunately, such a study is made more difficult by the fact that the Mercians failed to produce either a local historian of Bede's stature or a surviving independent chronicle tradition such as that which aids the reconstruction of West Saxon history. Thus, the texts that do survive, even though they are fairly extensive in themselves, form a forbidding mass of secondary sources that needs to be gleaned painstak-ingly for fragments of evidence. As a result, the period that is so critical for under-standing the beginnings of English literacy has been understudied, and the con-tributions of the Mercians to the development of English political and literate culture have been undervalued (Vleeskruyer, 1953:39–42). For example, histo-rians have generally misunderstood the role that King Alfred the Great of Wes-sex (A.D. 871–899) played in the development of English letters when they have viewed him as the originator of the tradition. The position of a teacher-king as a force in the establishment of a standard written variety is not to be underesti-mated, but Alfred functioned as a reviver and innovator of literate traditions rather than as their source. The frequently quoted comment with which he begins his translation of Gregory's *Pastoral Care* is the comment of a reformer. As such, he naturally overstated the decay of learning in England. Although he complains of the poor state of Latin literacy, it is important to observe that he is affirming a higher standard of English literacy: "yet many could read English writing" (Sweet, 1871:7). That level of native literacy could only have been a Mercian achievement. In fact, we have direct evidence that Alfred was able to build on a strong base of Mercian scholarship in his efforts to further extend ver-nacular literacy. Four of his seven chief aides in that task were learned Mercians, and the balance had no doubt been trained in centers founded by Mercians or where Mercian influence would still have been strong. This example reinforces the need for a reappraisal of whatever data can be collected and for a fresh reworking of those bits of evidence. We can then begin to appreciate the social and political context that informed the processes by which the English became a literate nation.

The *Tribal Hidage* is one of our single most important resources for understanding the political and social structure of early Anglo-Saxon England. This document is a listing of the names of tribal groups (generally found in the possessive plural), each of whom is assigned a numerical assessment in hides. Since the term *hide* originally designated a nuclear family or the land needed to support a nuclear family (fixed in the later medieval period at 120 acres), it is clear that this document is some sort of census list. No one has ever doubted that the list was drawn up from a Mercian perspective, even though the largest number of hides is associated with the West Saxons (100,000 hides). First, the fact that none of the folk north of the Humber River are included is a strong indicator that the text was a southern production. Further, the opening entry [*Myrcna landes is thrittig thusend hyda thær mon ærest myrcna hæt* (the Mercian's land, that is, of those first called Mercians, is 30,000 hides)] establishes the focus of the list while implying that the current influence of the Mercians had spread. "No one in the seventh or eighth century can be imagined compiling such a document out of mere curiosity. It only becomes intelligible when it is regarded as an attempt to guide a king's ministers in the exaction of his dues from subject provinces" (Stenton, 1971:297). That king was no doubt an early Mercian overlord, and internal evidence points to an early date—probably to Wulfhere (A.D. 657–674) or Æthelred (A.D. 674–704). Clearly, the potential for political stability and the ability to levy tribute were intimately interwoven.

It is notable that the census is organized not according to strict geographical divisions but tribally; territory is viewed in terms of inhabitants and traditional tribal loyalties rather than of geographical boundaries. Three major classifications of peoples emerge: the very large [such kingdoms as those of the Mercians themselves (30,000), the Kentish (15,000), and the West Saxons (100,000)], the medium-sized [the Hwicce (7000), the Chilterns (4000), and so on], and the small, often as yet unidentified and unlocalized (in multiples of 300). The largest are easily identified as the major tribal groups that vied for control of southern England during this period, whose kings were powerful enough to grant land and privilege in their own right. The middle groups were still substantial, but dependent. Their leaders might call themselves kings, but they are known to us in documents in which they are designated as *ministri* to or *subreguli* of their Mercian overlords. The leaders of the smallest tribes constitute the *comites*, the *principes*, the *duces*, and the *ealdormen* of the contemporary documents. An administrative hierarchy is clear when the data of the charters and the *Tribal Hidage* are taken together. One of the major kingdoms (in this case, that of the Mercians) would be in control, with the middle groups subject directly to them. "By contrast, the *Tribal Hidage* small groups form *no* part of a larger unit; between them and their Mercian overlord there is no larger negotiating power" (Davies and Vierck, 1974:240). The power of one kingdom might extend over its peer kingdoms for a time, but the basic fabric of Anglo-Saxon society during the Mercian period was still tribal in nature. Political unification would depend on an overlord's ability to effect and maintain a confederation of large and small tribal groups. Tribal organization obviates a strict territorial division of the south of England into just those kingdoms of the heptarchy, since the smaller groups maintained their own identity while clearly playing an important role in an over-lord's economic (hence political) base. Further, two standard assumptions of English historical linguistics need to be challenged: The dialectology proposed for early English has been geographical in its orientation and has, in addition, emphasized unduly the four major powers of early England (Kent, Northumbria, Mercia, and Wessex). Old English dialectologists have, moreover, assumed that each of these four regional varieties was represented by a single, homogeneous speech variety. Tribal organization of the sort reflected in the *Tribal Hidage* is not a likely foundation for widespread linguistic homogeneity.

Just as a consideration of the data of the *Tribal Hidage* alters our perspective on, and expectations of, the nature of language change and literacy in the early Anglo-Saxon period, the data from the earliest Anglo-Saxon charters also aids us in further defining the sociolinguistic context. The Mercian kings rose from the obscurity of preliterate times just as they were first converted to Christianity (and thus had recourse to the benefits of a literate clergy). Penda (A.D. 632–655) was the first of the strongest (and the last of the pagan) Mercian overlords, but we would know little beyond his name had he not attracted Bede's attention as being among Northumbria's most formidable enemies. Although it is unclear whether the other kings of the south were strictly subject to him, he was certainly the foremost among them and their leader in the battles against Northumbia. By virtue of defeating Penda, Oswiu of Northumbria could claim the title of over-lord of the Mercians and the rest of the southern English.

Penda's son Wulfhere (d. A.D. 674) was able, after a brief reversal of Mercian fortunes, to reconsolidate and then extend his father's influence. He began his career by conquering his southern neighbors, the West Saxons. He immediately demonstrated his supremacy by making a grant of traditionally West Saxon territory to Æthelwalh, the king of the South Saxons. The unusual occasion at which this grant was made is recorded by Bede: "Æthelwalh, king of that people, shortly before had received baptism in Mercia, owing to the prompting and the zeal of the Mercian king Wulfhere . . . he took him as god-son, and in token of amity made over to him two provinces" (Miller, 1890:303).

Wulfhere is not simply using his authority to help spread the faith; he is just as clearly also using his position as the guardian of the faith to demonstrate the extent of his political control. In the same act, he is taking land (power base) away from a strong, and nearby, opponent and using it to create a friendly dependent. This strong warlord added new dimensions to his secular authority as he began to act regularly in a fashion befitting a Christian king: he gave land (in far off Lindsey, a previously Northumbrian province) to Chad for the founding of a monastery; he sold the episcopal see of London to a bishop whom Wulfhere's enemy, King Cenwahl of Wessex, had expelled; he sent his own bishop to Essex to quell a reversion to paganism. To notice that these acts enhanced Wulfhere's political position is not to question his piety, but to emphasize the interdependence of the development of early Mercian concepts of Kingship and the involvement of the kings in the affairs of the church. Wulfhere apparently also knew how to make use of a literate clergy, since it was probably he who commissioned the writing of the *Tribal Hidage*.

The coalition between church and state was genuinely synergistic in that it produced written documentation of its effects. Kings could grant land and privileges; clerics could record and witness the act. Working cooperatively, however, both parties could produce a written document, a charter that manifested elements of authority that neither party could effect independently. Overlords and their scribes might make charters, but charters made kings and kingship official in a dramatically new way. They constituted, in the new substance of written words, concrete and permanent evidence of political structure. One might argue whether "the pen is mightier than the sword," but their combined might is not debatable. We have already seen the evidence of Wulfhere's expanding authority and might wonder, as his contemporaries must have wondered, if he deserved a title that better described the expanding role of Mercian kings. We recognize a new element in Mercian hegemony when we find a charter recording a land grant by King Frithuwold of Surrey, "subking of Wulfhere," confirmed by Wulfhere and witnessed by four other subkings. Such a charter substantiated in the permanent medium of the written word both Frithuwold's submission and Wulfhere's claims to kingship; it literally gave substance to the kingly state.

Precisely because the first written documents are more than a simple record of a king's activities, the earliest charters are the major source of information about the process by which the Mercian kings made a political institution out of a military hegemony. A close study of the charters reveals an evolution of royal prerogative structures needed to execute that prerogative. The titles of respect that individual kings employed record the extravagant terms in which those kings could insist they be viewed. These were the very terms by which they stated the nature of their right to rule and defined the relationship of their client subkings to themselves. Place names within the charters attest the geographical extent of a king's influence and inform us where he regularly held court. The names in the witness lists give an indication of the extent of a king's reputation among the secular and religious nobles of his time; these were the elite who gravitated to his court, or those whose presence he could command. Such conclusions as these must have been just as readily evident to the makers and readers of the Anglo-Saxon charters as they are to us. It is not likely to be mere coincidence that royal authority increased concomitantly with the development of the resources enabling the official documentation of that authority.

The full potential of Wulfhere's experiment in the institutionalization of political control was realized during the reigns of Æthelbald (A.D. 716–757) and Offa the Great (A.D. 757–796). This eighty-year period of relative political unification and stability was a remarkable first in early Anglo-Saxon history. Even Bede, who elsewhere had been able to ignore the Mercian dynasty, ended his history with a political survey of England for A.D. 731 in which he was forced to recognize the extent of the rising influence of Mercia: "And all these provinces and also other southern provinces, so far as the boundary of the river Humber, with their kings also, are subject in obedience to Æthelbald, king of Mercia" (Miller, 1890:479). The charters that survive from this period record a self-conscious attempt to make formal, to document, the unambiguous control that the Mercian kings exercised over submissive local subkings.

A charter of A.D. 736 confirms Bede's statement and describes Æthelbald as "king not only of the Mercians but also of all the provinces which are called by the general name 'South English.'" The witness list makes the assertion even more boldly: *Æthelbald rex Britanniae*, "Æthelbald, king of Britain." The local King Æthelric of the Hwicce, within whose territory this grant of land was made, is rendered "underking and companion of the most glorious prince Æthelbald." A Wiltshire charter (conveying land within the boundaries of Wessex) was witnessed, but not authored, by King Cynewulf of Wessex and several West Saxon nobles and bishops; such deference to Æthelbald is clear indication of his control over his most powerful neighbors. Æthelbald's authority at London is clear from the fact that he regularly collected tolls from ships in this the major city of his realm. That toll may well have been collected in the very coinage recently attributed to Æthelbald's reign (Metcalf, 1977). (Offa had previously been held the only Mercian coiner of note.) The iconography of the coins is telling: The *cynehelm*, "crown-helmet" of the Anglo-Saxon warrior-kings, and the cross—the two major instruments of Æthelbald's successful ascendancy—figure prominently.

Æthelbald's confederacy dissolved during a period of civil war in Mercia that followed his murder, but his distant cousin Offa was able to restore peace so quickly that the years of his reign nominally begin with the year of Æthelbald's death. Offa's ability to recoup and then to extend Æthelbald's authority reminds us of how dependent the success of early kingship was upon the strong personality of kings, but certainly the security that a strong king offered also had its own attractions: After having enjoyed the benefits of Æthelbald's long and peaceful reign, subkings must have seen the advantages of trading a title, vacuous in anarchy, for the protection of a strong overlord. The kings of the Hwicce acknowledged officially their status as underkings of Offa, *rex Merciorum*, within two years of Æthelbald's death (by A.D. 759). By A.D. 764, Offa had reestablished some measure of control in the southeast, as the following facts evidence: He confirmed Æthelbald's remission of toll at London for the minister at Thanet, with the king of Kent and the archbishop of Canterbury attesting; and in the same year, he confirmed grants of land in Kent. The Kentish kings, in the next year, sent a grant of land at Rochester to Peterborough for Offa's confirmation. In A.D. 767, Iænberht, of Canterbury, and the bishops of Leicester and Lichfield were willing to witness Offa's grant of land in Middlesex. Osmund, king of the South Saxons, witnessed one of Offa's charters (A.D. 772) as *dux* (in Old English simply *ealdorman).*

Two dealings with subkings demonstrate clearly both the expansion of Offa's powers and the means by which he was able to effect that expansion. Not only was he granting lands throughout England at will, but he was able to annul one of Egbert of Kent's grants and confiscate the subject lands. A subking, he argued, could not give to another what was given him by his overlord except with his overlord's permission. A charter (A.D. 780) of Oslac, an ealdorman of Sussex, constitutes the first "direct evidence that an Anglo-Saxon king has writers in his employment whom he can use for official business. The charter itself is written in a crude and apparently unpracticed hand. . . . Offa's endorsement is written in a typical insular hand of the period" (Stenton, 1955:37). Offa's personal royal *scriptorium* marks the creation of a professional learned class whose express concern it was to record "the king's English."

It is at first surprising that a king of Offa's stature would choose as his most frequent title *rex Merciorum,* "king of the Mercians." It may well be that, after Æthelbald, *rex Merciorum* implied *rex Britanniae,* since Offa did occasionally have his title recorded in the fuller form, *rex Merciorum simulque aliarum circumquaque nationum,* "king of the Mercians and surrounding nations." After all, Egbert of Wessex, only thirty years after Offa's death, called himself *rex Merciorum,* apparently to express the fact that he was supreme in the south. Two Kentish grants to Archbishop Iænberht refer to Offa in the most extravagant terms that had ever been applied to an Anglo-Saxon king—*rex Anglorum,* "king of all the English," and *rex totius Anglorum patriae,* "king of all England." Although these last two titles appear in tenth-century copies of contemporary documents, no less an Anglo-Saxonist than Stenton accepted them as faithful to the language of their eighth-century originals: "The phrase is important as a contemporary gloss upon the most important of English regnal styles at the moment of its first appearance" (Stenton, 1918:60, n. 6).

Anglo-Saxon notions about kingship were closely tied to other literate products.

> Genealogies and king-lists are . . . associated with early medieval royal legislation. . . .
> The ecclesiastical connections of the early Germanic law-codes suggest that churchmen felt king-lists and royal genealogies to be important mirrors of a king's right to rule. A king had a long line of royal predecessors: he belonged to a royal tradition. A king possessed an appropriately royal pedigree, therefore he was of royal blood. A king legislated; therefore he was a king [Dumville, 1977:75].

We have evidence that Offa used his professional *scriptorium* to help him assert his kingship through the production of genealogies and laws (in addition to charters). Offa substantiated the claim of an early charter that described him as "sprung from the royal stock of the Mercians and made king by appointment of Almighty God" by having his own genealogy compiled from available (probably Northumbrian) sources. The survival of that genealogy in a number of different manuscripts is strong indication that it was considered a very important document. Further, we have the testimony of contemporary authors that Offa was a lawmaker of note. Alfred, who drew so heavily on Mercian learned achievements, specifically acknowledges his debt to Offa's laws, the same laws Alcuin praised as good, moderate, and chaste.

Offa also manipulated social convention to make good his claim to being king of all the English people. He increased his own dignity by making royal personages of his wife and son, both of whom joined him as witnesses to charters. His wife, Queen Cynethryth, was further dignified with her own coinage; she is the only consort ever to appear on an English coin. Through a great deal of bloodshed and coercion, Offa was able to secure the succession of his son Ecgfrith (who was to reign for only 141 days). He went so far as to have Ecgfrith consecrated king in his own time; the first recorded anointing of an English king added the official sanction of the church to the Mercian hegemony. Offa maximized his own security by giving his daughters in marriage to the kings of Wessex and Northumbria.

An important measure of Offa's greatness was the respect he was afforded outside England. He carried on an extended, friendly correspondence with Charlemagne, and Charlemagne was ever careful to treat Offa as a peer, even suggesting the marriage of his son Charles to one of Offa's daughters. "Even at Rome Offa seemed a real, though inscrutable, force in the international world" (Stenton, 1971:215). Offa was able to attract the first papal legation to England since the formation of the English church and presided personally over the synod of southern bishops who welcomed the legation. Although it is possible that it was the papal legates who anointed Ecgfrith, it is certain that Offa took the occasion of their visit to argue for a Mercian metropolitan see.

As extensive as Offa's power was, rebellion in some portion of his kingdom was an inevitable aspect of hegemony. Periodic challenges to an overlord's authority were a certainty of early Anglo-Saxon politics. Trouble in Kent would present a further complication: The archbishop of Canterbury, the head of the southern church, might join, or at least be sympathetic toward, a challenge against the Mercian king. Opposition from the church, even lack of cooperation, would make an overlord's position untenable. Iænberht, Archbishop of Canterbury, did in fact constitute such a real threat and apparently knew how to make his opposition felt. His signature is conspicuously absent in some charters where it might have been expected and was certainly desired. At any rate, Offa was successful in arguing that the southern church had grown too large to be administered efficiently by a single archbishop. Pope Hadrian acceded reluctantly, and in A.D. 788 Hygeberht received the *pallium*, which made him archbishop of Lichfield—the peer of Canterbury and York and Offa's own archbishop. In the same year Hygeberht witnessed a grant by Offa *in Kent*, something which Iænberht had been reluctant to do.

Cultural achievement during the period of Mercian supremacy reflected the cumulative effect of eighty years of relative peace under Æthelbald and Offa, although there is understandably greater evidence of such achievement during Offa's reign. Archaeological excavations indicate that this was a period of extensive fortification and development of towns. For example, Offa defined the western frontier of his kingdom by initiating the construction of a 70-mile-long defensive earthwork, which has been compared to the pyramids in terms of expenditure of effort. At about the same time, *Tomtun,* the ancient royal residence of Mercian kings, was protected by a dyke, making it what the Anglo-Saxons termed a *worthig.* Beginning in Offa's reign, Mercian kings held court in the royal city of *Tomworthig* (modern Tamworth) at Christmas and Easter. The several hundred coins that survive from Offa's reign evidence an administrative structure that was both extensive and profitable. Their beauty and integrity proclaim a king of substance.

The synod of Clovesho in A.D. 747 had required that priests know the mass, the rite of baptism, the creed, and the Lord's Prayer in *English.* That requirement helps account for the impulse among the Anglo-Saxon *literati* to compile

Latin–Old English glossaries (such as the Epinal, Erfurt, and Corpus glossaries) and to make interlinear glosses to religious texts (such as the gloss to the Vespasian Psalter). Those glosses and glossaries are, of course, our principal source of data from which we can reconstitute Mercian varieties of Old English. These texts are, in addition, art historical monuments of exquisite beauty. Although they were written at a time when book production was costly indeed, we unfailingly find the best of materials, wide margins, spacious and uneconomical hands, and illuminated capitals of subtle and intricate design. The presence of English glosses in these texts further indicates that the addition of the vernacular was considered an adornment to these deluxe productions—powerful testimony of the privileged position of the written English word in Anglo-Saxon culture. Such books could only be produced at times of plenty and relative social and political stability. Because of the costs of production, they were almost certainly produced at centers that enjoyed royal patronage, where, of course, political influences would be most strongly felt. These books may even have been produced at royal command or as presentation copies to royal persons. After all, a psalter is a quintessentially royal book; the songs of a king make a fitting prayer book for a king. In the Vespasian Psalter painting of King David playing his conspicuously Anglo-Saxon harp, we may be invited to see the type of a perfect Anglo-Saxon king. Also interesting in this vein is a late-ninth-century charter that specifies the way in which royal patrons are to be remembered: "At every matins and at every vespers and at every tierce, the *De profundis* as long as they live, and after their death *Laudate Dominum;* and every Saturday in St. Peter's church thirty psalms and a Mass for them . . ." (Whitelock, 1955:598). A deluxe psalter would be an appropriate production for such a community as received this charge.

Since the church played such a crucial role in the establishment of the Anglo-Saxon monarchy, kings would understandably commission the production of deluxe Bibles and psalters for use at state occasions. Any Mercian king would also want to have his own copy of Bede's *Ecclesiastical History,* the text that proclaims the ascendancy of the Mercian dynasty by A.D. 731. One copy (British Library MS Cotton Tiberius C. ii), with its conspicuous Mercianization of proper names and its Mercian glosses, is a manuscript of Bede known to have been copied in the south within the reigns of Æthelbald and Offa. It is unique among the earliest Bede manuscripts for its lavish decorative initials, which strongly suggest that it was produced for a royal person. In one of his letters, Alcuin sent Offa off to look up a passage in his own copy of the history; Offa was an interested user of books, not a mere patron of literacy.

Secular literature also flourished at this time. The bulk of Anglo-Saxon poetry, although it survives in late West Saxon copies, was composed in Mercian times. The poetic *koine* has a distinctly Mercian substratum. Cynewulf, the only major Old English poet we know by name, has long been accepted as a Mercian, probably from Lichfield. The interest that the authors of the *Beowulf* and *Widsith* poems showed in the continental King Offa (from whom Offa the Great labored to demonstrate descent) prompted Whitelock to suggest that they were composed during Offa's reign, if not at his court. Every aspect of Mercian cultural development was used by the Mercian kings to celebrate the glory of the social institution of a kingship. Powerful kings enabled the Anglo-Saxon peoples to build a society and culture based on peace rather than on constant intertribal hostility. Since culture and its benefits derived from the overlords, eighth-century culture, through all of southern England, was Mercian culture. Eighth-century literacy was an especially Mercian literacy. Eighth-century texts were Mercian texts no matter where in southern England they were produced. Since Mercian kings made bishops and founded monasteries, the religious establishment—the source of the literate, scribal class—was dependent upon royal patronage. Those scribes and their patrons created the political, social, and intellectual context for the rise of English literacy, as summarized in Figure 1.1.

The construction of the *Tribal Hidage* was among the first Mercian acts of literacy. The text formalized the economic base for the Mercian hegemony. The revenue derived from the *Hidage* made possible the construction of Mercian defensive dykes along the western frontier; the ability to assess taxes no doubt encouraged the production of coins and the regulation of their integrity. The resultant political stability enabled the solidification of the powers of the Mercian kings, and the charters were drawn up to define and confirm royal prerogatives. Royal support for the major religious houses made possible the extensive production of fine manuscripts. The expansion of libraries reinforced the Mercian renaissance of Latin and English learning. As literacy flourished in the Roman mode, attention was directed to the writing of genealogies and the codification of laws. With the establishment of a royal Mercian *scriptorium*, peculiarly Mercian orthographic practices developed while the production of charters mushroomed. (Notice the dramatic hiatus in charters that resulted from the quarrel between Cenwulf and the archbishop of Canterbury.) From the same period in which all charters exhibit Mercian letter forms, we find the Vespasian Psalter gloss, also with its own Mercian letter forms. The writing of what is universally accepted as the most thoroughly Mercian text coincides with the apex of Mercian influence on literacy. The consolidation of Anglo-Saxon politics and culture was the development of English politics and culture largely because of the act of English kings writing their own English language. What must loom large in our attention is this fact: From earliest times, writing the English language has been a political act.

Our modern expectation is for uniformity in standard written English. Perhaps because of reasons like that, the linguistic heterogeneity of the earliest glosses and glossaries caused language historians to think it impossible to do a systematic analysis of the language of these texts. Since it was impossible to identify perfectly regular changes, the data were dismissed as nonanalyzable. If, however, we take the manuscript data seriously and put them into their historical context, two things happen. First, we expect that a heterogeneous, tribal culture on the verge of making the transition from orality to literacy would produce documents that reflect a range of spoken varieties. That is, our knowledge of Anglo-Saxon society should lead us to expect heterogeneity in the first attempts to write Old English. Without the weight of traditional spellings, written varieties would be expected to vary as much as spoken varieties do. Second, when the linguistic

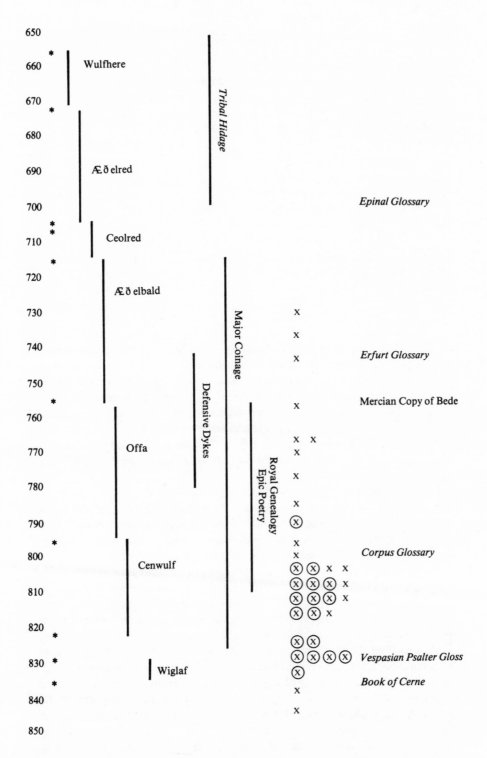

Figure 1.1. The products of literacy in their political context. (The x's are individual charters; ⊗'s are charters that contain Mercian letter forms.)

43

Table 1.1. Sound Changes Showing Mercian Influence.

	Epinal c. 700	Erfurt c. 750	Corpus c. 800	VP c. 825
Smoothing of [i:o]	+	+	+	+
Smoothing of [io]	+	+	+	+
Gmc. [æ:] to [e:]	0.8	0.9	0.9	+
Smoothing of [eo]	0.8	+	+	+
Smoothing of [æa]	0.6	+	+	+
Smoothing of [æ:a]	0.6	0.8	+	+
Smoothing of [e:o]	0	0	0.7	+
Prim. OE [a] to [æ]	0.3	0.3	0.3	+
Velar umlaut of [æ]	0.5	0.5	0.8	+
Confusion of [io], [eo]	0.5	0.5	0.6	+
[æ]/___N to [e]	0.3	0.3	0.9	+
Second fronting [æ]	0.2	0.4	0.2	+
Confusion of [i:o], [e:o]	0.2	0	0.2	+
Raising of nasal [a]	0	0.5	0.7	+
Velar umlaut of [i, e]	0	0	0.9	+

variation in the texts is compared chronologically, distinct patterns of historical development emerge within data that had first seemed chaotic. Table 1.1 summarizes the rates of development of several sound changes that occurred during the Old English period. Using as an example the Anglian development of a raised and rounded vowel before nasal consonants (Anglian *lond* vs. non-Anglian *land*), the table indicates that the sound change is not evident in the Epinal Glossary, where we find only *a* spellings. We find *o* 50 percent of the time in the Erfurt Glossary and 70 percent of the time in the Corpus Glossary. The Vespasian Psalter has only *o* spellings.

The language of the Vespasian Psalter represents a standard written variety that can be associated geographically with the west midlands of England, politically with the Mercian kings, and chronologically with the ninth century. This is not to suggest that all speakers of Mercian Old English had pronunciations mirrored in the spelling systems of the texts associated with this period and these kings. The suggestion, rather, is that writing was a politically important activity that looked to the Mercian political and intellectual institutions for authority. The written standard reflected the geographical dialect of the politically powerful. Using again the example of the development of [a] before nasals, it is noteworthy that political documents written in Kent, a non-Anglian area, exhibit the Anglian spelling of *o* only during the period in which Mercia dominated political affairs in the south of England and when in fact Offa the Great had installed his younger brother as the King of Kent. Documents written before this period reflect the local variety (*a* spellings), as do the documents written during the period of West Saxon political domination. It is unlikely that the Kentish changed their pronunciation of these words, and it is remarkable that they accepted as standard a spelling that reflected Mercian pronunciation in a way that parallels the modern divergence of the written and spoken languages.

It is commonplace for Anglo-Saxonists to lament the fact that the early

English built almost exclusively in wood. As a consequence, so the argument goes, we do not have available for modern study the same kind of enduring monument of stonework that the Romans left as a more permanent record of their involvement in early British history. Similarly, even those of us who are the cultural descendents of the early English seem to find little in our social, cultural, and temperamental make-up that we owe directly to our Germanic forebears. Even though we might know that we speak a language that is a lineal descendant of Old English, we also know that the language has changed—just as dramatically as the nature and needs of its speakers have changed.

All these statements are true enough; they are less a testimony to historical myopia than an acknowledgment of historical fact. However, they ignore a real, if less obvious, accomplishment of the early Anglo-Saxon period: learning to write the English language. A nearly universal, vernacular literacy so pervades our lives, our culture, our social and political structures that we speakers of English can take for granted our ability to write the language. Surely, the idea of vernacular literacy did not originate in England, but the impulse of our forebears to experiment with writing their own speech greatly affected the development and discrimination of Western European modes of thought. Like Bede and Alcuin, we too love learning and write our intellectual histories. Unlike them, but because of them and their time, we need not write our histories in another's language. We pay unconscious tribute to them as we conduct the business of literacy in our mother tongue, which they knew only how to speak. We learned to build our most permanent monuments during the Old English period. It is our Anglo-Saxon heritage that we chose as building material—neither wood nor stone, but the ink and parchment of the written word.

WORKS CITED

Campbell, A. 1959. *Old English Grammar.* Oxford, England: Oxford University Press.

Colgrave, B., and R.A.B. Mynors. 1969. *Bede's Ecclesiastical History of the English People.* Oxford, England: Oxford University Press.

Davies, Wendy, and Hayo Vierck. 1974. "The Contexts of Tribal Hidage: Social Aggregates and Settlement Patterns." *Frühmittelalterliche Studien* 8:223–293.

Dumville, David N. 1977. "Kingship, Genealogies and Regnal Lists." In P. H. Sawyer and I. N. Wood, eds., *Early Medieval Kingship.* Leeds, England: The University of Leeds Press. Pp. 72–104.

Goody, Jack. 1977. *The Domestication of the Savage Mind.* Cambridge, England: Cambridge University Press.

Labov, William. 1972. *Sociolinguistic Patterns.* Philadelphia: University of Pennsylvania Press.

———. 1974. "On the Use of the Present to Explain the Past." In Luigi Heilmann, ed., *Proceedings of the Eleventh International Congress of Linguists.* Bologna: Società editrice il Mulino. Pp. 825–851.

———, M. Yaeger, and R. Steiner. 1972. *A Quantitative Study of Sound Change in Progress.* Philadelphia: U.S. Regional Survey.

Metcalf, D. M. 1977. "Monetary Affairs in Mercia in the Time of Aethelbald." In A. Dornier, ed., *Mercian Studies.* Leicester: Leicester University Press. Pp. 87–106.

Miller, Thomas. 1890. *The Old English Version of Bede's Ecclesiastical History of the English People,* Part I. Early English Text Society o.s. 95, 96. London: Trübner.

Stenton, Frank M. 1918. "The Supremacy of the Mercian Kings." *English Historical Review* 33:433–452. Reprinted in Doris Mary Stenton, ed., *Preparatory to Anglo-Saxon England, Being the Collected Papers of Frank Merry Stenton.* Oxford: Clarendon Press, 1970. Pp. 48–66.

———. 1955. *The Latin Charters of the Anglo-Saxon Period.* Oxford: Oxford University Press.

———. 1971. *Anglo-Saxon England,* 3rd ed. Oxford, England: Oxford University Press.

Sweet, Henry. 1871. *King Alfred's West-Saxon Version of Gregory's Pastoral Care,* Part I. Early English Text Society o.s. 45. London: Trübner.

Toon, Thomas E. 1983. *The Politics of Early Old English Sound Change.* New York: Academic Press.

Trudgill, Peter. 1986. *Dialects in Contact.* Oxford, England: Blackwell.

Vleeskruyer, R. 1953. *The Life of St. Chad.* Amsterdam: North-Holland.

Weinreich, Uriel, William Labov, and Marvin Herzog. 1968. "Empirical Foundations for a Theory of Language Change." In W. P. Lehmann and Yakov Malkiel, eds. *Directions for Historical Linguistics.* Austin: University of Texas Press. Pp. 95–105.

Whitelock, D. 1955. *English Historical Documents c. 500–1042.* London: Eyre and Spottiswoode.

2

The Use of English: Language Contact, Dialect Variation, and Written Standardisation During the Middle English Period

JEREMY J. SMITH

THE ECLIPSE OF ENGLISH

> At nine in the morning of Thursday, 28 September, the fleet entered Pevensey bay, and the army disembarked at leisure on an undefended shore.
>
> [Stenton, 1971:591]

Thus Sir Frank Stenton described the arrival in England of William, Duke of Normandy, and his followers in 1066. Of illegitimate birth, William was an adventurer who had carved out a state for himself in northern France. Nominally a vassal of the French king, by the eve of his conquest of England he had achieved an independent position and had few constraints on his actions. His people, the Normans, were—as their name suggests—originally Scandinavians who had landed in France in the ninth century and had settled there in the early 900s. However, they had quickly been assimilated to French culture and had come to speak a variety of the French language. The Normans excelled in the military arts, notably castle building, but were not otherwise especially sophisticated in their culture.

In contrast, late Anglo-Saxon England was a complex and relatively highly developed society, with an established tradition in the arts, notably in church architecture, metal work, embroidery, and manuscript illumination. It had comparatively sophisticated systems of government, based on established law codes and a secure coinage. Latin learning in England on the eve of the Conquest may not have matched that achieved in parts of the continent of Europe, but there was a strong tradition of vernacular literacy, albeit largely confined to monastic houses. One variety of Old English, West Saxon, had achieved the status of a literary standard copied outside its area of origin. Fatally, this sophistication did not extend to national defence (for details, see Whitelock, 1952, and Wilson, 1981).

The details of William's claim to the English throne and his victory over Harold II, last king of Anglo-Saxon England, need not concern us here. It is sufficient to say that the battle of Hastings at which Harold was killed was followed by the imposition of Norman earls and churchmen in positions of power throughout the country. This pattern of replacement was so extensive that, by the end of William's reign in 1087,

> all directive power within the English state had passed from native into alien hands. In 1087, with less than half-a-dozen exceptions, every lay lord whose possessions entitled him to political influence was a foreigner. The English church was ruled by men of continental birth and training. No Englishman had been appointed by the Conqueror to any English see and, when he died, Wulfstan of Worcester and Giso of Wells alone survived from the episcopate of King Edward [the Confessor, last Anglo-Saxon king]'s day . . . the leading members of the king's household were all Frenchmen; a French clerk presided over his chancery, and French sheriffs controlled the administration of all but an insignificant number of shires.
>
> [Stenton, 1971:680]

These men spoke Norman French, which later developed in England into what modern scholars call Anglo-Norman. Since the Conquest is also associated with a revival of Latin learning in England, brought about through the appointment of continental ecclesiastics to positions of power, it is evident that Old English was now under pressure from both French and Latin in terms of prestige.

The relationship between these three languages in England during the twelfth and thirteenth centuries is complex and can only be treated briefly here. (See Clanchy, 1979, Chapter 6, and references there cited, for a useful survey.) It seems that each language had a different social function; moreover, these functions changed over time.

The role of Latin might be considered first. Clanchy (1979:165) has drawn attention to a bilingual writ, dating from the 1070s, addressed by the Conqueror's half-brother, Bishop Odo of Bayeux, to Archbishop Lanfranc and the sheriff of Kent. All three men would have spoken varieties of French as their first language. This document, probably written by an Anglo-Saxon scribe of Christ Church Canterbury, has a Latin text at the top and a translation into Old English beneath it. As Clanchy points out, perhaps "Odo wanted Latin used because it seemed absurd to address Lanfranc in a language which neither of them knew, while the Christ Church scribe favoured Anglo-Saxon because that was the traditional language of Anglo-Saxon writs" (1979:165). The document represents the transition from one language of government record to another. Subsequently, Latin became the usual language of government documents in England during the twelfth and early thirteenth centuries, used for such major texts as Domesday Book (1086) and Magna Carta (1215); it was also the literary language used by major writers like John of Salisbury, Geoffrey of Vinsauf, Alexander Neckham, Edmund of Abingdon, Walter Map, and Robert Grosseteste— all of whom lived and worked in England. John of Salisbury may be taken as representative. "The most learned man of his time" (Poole, 1951:234), he was educated at Paris but became a key figure at the court of King Henry II of England (ruled 1154–1189). Latin, the written language used by these men, remained the language of international scholarship and diplomacy throughout the Middle Ages and the Renaissance.

French, though the language of the invading elite, could not at first compete with Latin as the language of written record. It may even be, as Clanchy points out, that "contact with England, with its long tradition of non-Latin writing, may have helped to develop French as a written language" (1979:168). However, an extensive written literature in Anglo-Norman developed during the twelfth and thirteenth centuries (see Legge, 1963), and French became much more widespread as the written language of government transactions from the middle of the thirteenth century. The earliest indication of this is the French translation of Magna Carta made soon after 1215 (Clanchy, 1979:170).

Finally, there was English. [Not discussed here are minority languages in medieval England, such as Hebrew, Cornish, and so on, whose influence on English was minimal. For an interesting discussion of Hebrew in England during the Middle Ages, however, see Clanchy (1979:154–156).] Until the fourteenth century at the earliest, English was eclipsed as the language of written record and of prestige. In the years immediately after the Norman Conquest, Old English texts continued to be copied in monastic scriptoria, especially in the southwest Midlands, where Anglo-Saxon clerics such as Wulfstan of Worcester maintained older traditions. Even as late as the beginning of the thirteenth century, the old scriptorium system in this area was still producing new works in a "standardised" form of English, albeit one different from the late West Saxon of Anglo-Saxon times: the texts of the *Ancrene Wisse* group, written in a conservative form of the Herefordshire dialect (see the section entitled "Orthography").

In general, however, written English of the period up to about 1250 is peripheral to literary culture. As the prestige linguistic models of the Anglo-Saxon past cease to be used, so what written English there is begins to break free from the artificial constraints of a standardising spelling system. In such texts as the *Peterborough Chronicle Continuations* we see a steady drift away from late West-Saxon to a kind of written language that reflects linguistic changes and dialectal variation that had hitherto been hidden from view (see Clark, 1970).

Of key importance here is the difference between the written and spoken modes of language. The two are often confused, especially by the beginning student; but a little thought soon indicates the validity of the distinction (see McIntosh, 1956; Samuels, 1972, Chapter 1). Nowadays, a standard spelling system for English is used around the world, with certain very minor regular differences (e.g., American usage, based in part upon the principles of Noah Webster's 1828 *American Dictionary of the English Language,* and British usage, exemplified by the *Oxford English Dictionary*). Thus (to use examples from the United Kingdom alone), a Glaswegian, a Liverpudlian, a Londoner, and a native of Belfast would all use the same spellings, even though their accents would differ markedly.

In short, it is not possible in present-day English to perceive spoken accent from the written language. However, for much of the Middle English period, such an authoritative spelling norm did not exist, and orthographic systems varied from locality to locality, much as spoken accents vary today. For this reason

Middle English has been referred to as "*par excellence,* the dialectal phase of English, in the sense that while dialects have been spoken at all periods, it was in [Middle English] that divergent local usage was normally indicated in writing" (Strang, 1970:224).

The ancestors of these Middle English dialects, of course, existed in Anglo-Saxon times but are only fragmentarily indicated in the written record—for, as has already been pointed out, a literary standard did exist for Old English, and this hides from our view the natural variation of the spoken mode. Moreover, the Old English dialect map had undergone a major disturbance in the ninth and tenth centuries as large parts of the country were settled by Scandinavian peoples. These folk had been integrated into the Old English–speaking community fairly easily—"Norse" and "English" in late Anglo-Saxon times seem to have been more or less mutually intelligible—but it is only during the Middle English period that the full effect of the Scandinavian influence on the history of English becomes clear. (For the place-name evidence for peaceful Scandinavian settlement, see Cameron, 1975; Samuels, 1985.) As a result of this contact, there were many parts of the country where English had become thoroughly "Scandinavianised."

This dialectal English continued to be spoken, after the Norman Conquest, by the majority of people in England, the peasantry; but this class of society remained generally illiterate throughout the Middle Ages. (This has been overstated, however; see Parkes, 1973, who detects a degree of "pragmatic literacy" in the higher echelons of this social class—e.g., the ability to read accounts.) As a result, we can only infer and extrapolate from other evidence as to linguistic developments in this "estate" of society (to use the medieval term).

For the higher social classes we have more evidence, but its interpretation is controversial. Jocelin of Brakelond, writing his Latin *Chronicle* at the end of the twelfth century, gives us some information about the priesthood, the "second estate" of medieval society. He records how Samson, abbot of Bury St Edmunds (1182–1211), was a graduate of the University of Paris, "eloquent in French and Latin." In addition, he knew "how to read literature in English most elegantly, and he used to preach in English to the people, but in the speech of Norfolk *(lingua Norfolchie)* where he was born and bred" (Clanchy, 1979:159; Greenway and Sayers, 1989). The "literature written in English" was probably Old English. Clanchy suggests that texts such as Ælfric's *Life* of King Edmund would have been especially suitable for such an abbot's holy reading.

Such abilities are perhaps not surprising in a churchman whose tasks included popular preaching, although it is perhaps interesting that Jocelin can assume a degree of "elegance" to be possible in English. The minor nobles are another matter. It is often pointed out that the social status of English at this time in relation to French is indicated in the production of meat: *pigs, cows,* and *sheep* are tended by English speakers and, while alive, are distinguished by names of Old English derivation. However, these animals become *pork, beef,* and *mutton*—terms derived from French—on the dinner table and are eaten by French speakers. The implication for the social status of the two languages is clear.

However, there is evidence that the Norman aristocracy learnt English fairly

quickly. William of Canterbury, in his Latin *Life of Thomas à Becket,* tells a
story of the mother of one of the archbishop's murderers:

> Overcome with an unrequited passion for a youth, she induced the latter to appear
> before her husband in play with a drawn sword. He is said to have been condemned
> and boiled to death. The chief interest of the tale lies, however, not so much in its
> lurid details as in the fact that the warning cry of the woman was in English: "Huge
> de Morevile, ware, ware, ware, Lithulf heth his swerd adrage."
>
> [Poole, 1951:252–253]

It would seem, therefore, that English was spoken in at least some noble house-
holds in the early twelfth century, and there is good evidence that, although
French was prestigious, English was widely used amongst the nobility in the centuries following the Conquest. Walter of Bibbesworth's *Treatise* on French,
composed some time in the middle of the thirteenth century for "my lady Denise
de Montchensy," makes clear that, for both the lady Denise and Walter, English
is the mother tongue, but French is a necessary accomplishment for cultivated
people, the *gentils hommes.* It would seem that, by Walter's time, the relationship between English and French was much the same as that between Russian
and French as described in Tolstoy's *War and Peace:* French was still the language of prestige and sophistication, but used as a conscious affectation rather
than for normal social intercourse. "For unless a man knows French, he is
thought of little account" writes "Robert of Gloucester" in his metrical *Chronicle,* roughly contemporary to Walter's *Treatise.* It seems somehow significant
that "Robert" writes in English (Clanchy, 1979:152ff). ("Robert"'s words in the
original Middle English are as follows: "Bot a man conne Frenss, me telth of him
lute.")

Precisely when the change from French to English as the mother tongue of the
ruling classes of the period took place is uncertain; it may well have happened
comparatively quickly after the Conquest. In Poole's words, "We may suppose
that succeeding generations would pick [English] up in youth from nurses, servants and rustics about their estates" (Poole, 1951:252), although, of course, this
does not always happen when a conquering force subjects a people to foreign
domination (e.g., the Conquistadores continued to speak Spanish in colonial
Mexico and did not adopt the Nahuatl language of the Aztecs). But the change
must have been particularly encouraged by the events of 1204, when the rulers
of England lost control of Normandy and those barons who owned land in both
countries—as many did—had to choose between their estates. Those who
elected to stay in England, in Poole's words, "devoted themselves to English
affairs and English interests untrammelled by continental complications"
(Poole, 1951:433).

THE TRIUMPH OF ENGLISH

Despite this new emphasis on "Englishness" after 1204, French culture
remained dominant throughout the thirteenth century and for most of the four-

teenth. To use French during this period is to mark social difference, to assert social superiority over those who could not. Even in the late fourteenth century, in his modified English version of Higden's *Polychronicon,* John Trevisa records how country people busied themselves "to speke Freynsh" in order to sound like "gentil men" (cited in Leith, 1983:30).

This French-based culture was not that brought over by the Conquest. "Anglo-Norman" rapidly became stigmatised as provincial during this period (such a stigma lies behind the joke about Chaucer's Prioress speaking French "after the scole of Stratford atte Bowe"); the new prestigious model was Parisian French. The fourteenth century sees the dominance of this Central French culture throughout Europe, and it is not surprising that its effect is seen so strongly in England, where a sociolinguistic role had already been established for it. As will be seen in the "Lexis" section, the nobility of England from about 1250 appear to have developed the habit of studding their English mother tongue with Central French words to express their social distance from people of lower social status.

During the fourteenth and fifteenth centuries, however, a number of historical events took place that disturbed the established social order and that had a profound effect on the role and status of English (see Myers, 1971, *passim*). The Hundred Years' War between France and England continued a state of chronic warfare that had begun in the thirteenth century and that existed throughout Western Europe, causing a slump in the agrarian economy of England and draining its financial resources. Population growth during the period was not accompanied by growth in the means of subsistence, leading to intermittent famine and susceptibility to disease. Although the vast mortality caused by the Black Death of the middle of the fourteenth century meant a drop in the population, that drop was so massive and so sudden that a serious labour shortage resulted, and economic stability was not achieved. There would seem to be a causal link between the Black Death and the Peasants' Revolt of 1381.

Despite these massive economic problems, the late Middle Ages throughout Europe saw the growth of towns; and it is largely in towns, and in the civic institutions (such as guilds) that arose to govern them, that we can see the emergence of an identifiable middle class. Above all in England, this is the period of the rise of London as the major—and magnetic—urban centre of the country. The story of Dick Whittington, staple of English pantomimes today, is from the end of the fourteenth century (he died in 1423); and there is a good deal of evidence to show that his rise from poor provincial youth to Lord Mayor of London was paralleled by many others, if in a less spectacular fashion.

When these points are taken in combination, it is apparent that the superficially fixed picture of the English social scene in the later Middle Ages conceals a ferment of social mobility. This was not something that contemporary writers felt generally happy about. Langland's *Piers Plowman* is about many things, but its emphasis on each "estate" in society playing its allotted part in an ideal body politic is essentially a conservative one; for Langland, the decay of this structure is a sign of the imminent end of the world. Gower's (Latin) *Vox Clamantis,* with its attack on the Peasants' Revolt, is similarly backward-looking.

Despite such contemporary complaints, these revolutionary tendencies continued into the fifteenth century. Civil strife and dynastic struggles, such as the Wars of the Roses between the great houses of York and Lancaster, did not prevent the continuing rise of the middle classes; and William Caxton, who set up the first English printing press at Westminister in 1476, was one of their number, with a background in the prosperous English wool trade. He and his successors, men like Wynkyn de Worde and Richard Pynson, met the increasing demand for books from the rising middle class.

The books Caxton printed were in English, and the rise of the middle class is accompanied by a rise in the status of English. Middle-class boys were educated in grammar schools, which begin to appear in England during the thirteenth century, and Trevisa at the end of the fourteenth century recorded how innovative schoolmasters like John Cornwal and Richard Pencrych taught their pupils in English, not French, "so that now, the yer of oure Lord a thousand thre hondred foure score and fyue, of the secunde kyng Richard after the Conquest nyne, in al the gramerscoles of Engelond childern leueth Frensch, and construeth and lurneth in Englysch . . ." (quoted from Sisam, 1921:149). It is not surprising that the literacy rate seems to have increased from the thirteenth century onward.

In some ways the key date is 1362, from which time Parliament was conducted officially in English; but there is good evidence that vernacular literacy was fairly widespread well before that date. By the end of the fifteenth century, Caxton had come to feel that, despite its dialectal diversity, English had acquired dignity, especially through the great poets of the late fourteenth and fifteenth centuries, such as Geoffrey Chaucer, John Gower, and John Lydgate. The parallel with fourteenth-century Italy and its poetic pantheon of Dante, Petrarch, and Boccaccio is plain, but it is not just a matter of copying foreign habits; Caxton exhibits a great confidence about the possibilities of the vernacular. It is in the fifteenth and sixteenth centuries that we can speak of the "triumph" of English as a language fit for the discussion of serious matters. Thus, at the end of the fifteenth century, the great humanist writers like Sir Thomas More can write in English as well as in Latin. (Latin remained the language of international learning into the seventeenth century, to be displaced by French in the eighteenth century; see Hampson, 1968:35).

It is in the light of this social history that we must see the various changes that English underwent during the Middle English period. In what follows, each "level" of language—orthography, phonology, grammar, and lexis—will be examined in turn to see how the impact of social history manifested itself linguistically.

ORTHOGRAPHY

Orthography is sometimes separated by scholars from "language proper," but this is a mistaken attitude. The written mode, though intimately related to the spoken medium, is nevertheless distinct and—at least methodologically—should be treated as a separate manifestation of human language (see McIntosh, 1956; Scragg, 1974).

A complete history of Middle English orthography would be a formidable undertaking, not least because a huge body of material has lately become available to scholars, namely, that contained in the *Linguistic Atlas of Late Medieval English* (McIntosh, Samuels, and Benskin, 1985). Scragg (1974, Chapters 2–4) provides the beginning student with a useful general outline. For our purposes, we might examine two areas that demonstrate the importance of historical context for understanding linguistic change:

1. The survival of "standard" Old English from late Old English to early Middle English times, with special reference to a literary dialect developed in the southwest Midlands.
2. The growth of "standard" written English during the fourteenth and fifteenth centuries.

The continuity of Old English traditions in the west Midlands has been referred to already (see p. 49). This continuity found its strongest expression in the *Ancrene Wisse,* a handbook for female recluses written at the Victorine abbey of Wigmore in Herefordshire. The Corpus manuscript of this text (MS Cambridge, Corpus Christi College 402 = "A") and a manuscript of saints' lives and homilies (MS Oxford, Bodleian Library, Bodley 34 = "B") were written by different scribes but in the same spelling system. There are traces of this spelling system in a large number of related manuscripts containing copies of the same or associated texts. Since Tolkien (1929), this spelling system has been called "AB-language" after the two manuscripts that display it most clearly.

This "AB-language" has often been described (see Tolkien, 1929; d'Ardenne, 1961; Dobson, 1972). Its relationship to late Old English is not straightforward; it descends not from "standard" late West Saxon, but from a literary dialect of West Mercian that is only fragmentarily represented in the surviving Anglo-Saxon written record [e.g., the gloss to the *Vespasian Psalter,* and the *Life of St Chad* (d'Ardenne, 1961; Vleeskruyer, 1953)]. Nevertheless, in a number of its features it resembles the products of a late Anglo-Saxon scriptorium. Thus, its orthographic system is a conservative one; a conscious effort has been made to retain forms that must have been archaic at the time of writing. This is indicated by occasional scribal "errors," such as *o* for OE [ɑ:] (usually spelt *a* in AB-language). Such slips indicate that the scribes, left to their own devices, would doubtless have introduced the advancing form *o*. Apart from these occasional "errors," AB-language—unlike the language of many Early Middle English texts—is orthographically regular, and "conventionalised" distinctions are commonly used [e.g., *oþer* ("other") versus *oðer* ("or"), even though þ and ð seem to have had identical "phonic" significance in AB-language.]

The discipline needed to sustain such an orthographic system within the fluid conditions of the early Middle English period must have been very strong, and recalls the discipline exercised in late Anglo-Saxon scriptoria. In that sense, texts in AB-language are traditional, looking back to the Old English past.

However, *Ancrene Wisse* achieved something of a vogue beyond its original audience, the anchorite sisters for whom its author was spiritual director. During the thirteenth and fourteenth centuries a number of copies of the work appear, referred to collectively by the Victorian title of *Ancrene Riwle.* The developing orthography of these other texts of the work demonstrates effectively how the old-style scriptorium disciplines broke down. Two texts roughly contemporary with the Corpus manuscript are of special interest for our purposes: "Cleopatra" (MS London, British Library, Cleopatra C.vi) and "Nero" (MS London, British Library, Nero A.xiv) (see Dobson, 1972, and Day, 1952, respectively).

The Cleopatra and Nero manuscripts are closely related textually to Corpus, but linguistically they are distinct and show the kind of dialectal variation that is characteristic of the later Middle English period. Dobson (1972) examines all the available evidence with regard to the Cleopatra manuscript and concludes that the demand for the book during the thirteenth century was such that the old scriptorium system, satisfactory enough for a period of restricted literacy, was simply unable to cope with a wider readership. Outworkers had to be hired to increase the speed of copying texts, and these scribes were not within the range of the close discipline that produced the Corpus manuscript. As a result, they introduced in the Nero and Cleopatra manuscripts their own spelling systems, carrying out a scribal "translation" from one dialect into another.

There is evidence that such scribal "translations" became more common as the Middle English period progressed; and the reasons are not hard to find. As indicated earlier in the section "The Triumph of English," literacy in the vernacular was becoming much more widespread in the thirteenth and fourteenth centuries. In such circumstances, the old monastic orthography and the discipline associated with it must have been impossible to sustain. New spelling systems, based upon practices developed in individual schools and parishes rather than on those of a few monastic centres, came into use. Given the continuing lowly status of English during this period, however, there could have been no spelling "norm" to imitate—certainly not AB-language, which was the written manifestation of the language of a peripheral part of the kingdom. In short, the decay of AB-language and of the Anglo-Saxon traditions that produced it relates closely to changes in English society. [For interesting codicological developments during the same period that correlate with this, see Parkes (1979), Benskin and Laing (1981:90–93), and Dahood (1988).]

With the rise in the status of English during the latter years of the Middle Ages, it is not surprising that standardisation of orthography begins to emerge during the late fourteenth and fifteenth centuries. Given the social developments outlined earlier, the basis of this standardisation had to be the form of the language current in London. The prestige of the capital had a linguistic effect of the kind commonly recorded in modern sociolinguistic surveys (see Hudson, 1980:33).

The growth of written standard English has been studied most notably by M. L. Samuels (1963, 1972), and this section derives its orientation from his work. [See also Fisher (1977, 1979), although these articles should not be read without reference to Davis (1983) and Sandved (1981).] Samuels has detected four "types" of incipient standard English emerging during the course of the fourteenth and fifteenth centuries:

Type I stands rather apart from the other types. A *lingua franca* of the written mode, centred upon spellings commonly found in the central Midlands, it is thus sometimes referred to as Central Midlands Standard. Characteristic forms are: *sich* ("such"), *mych* ("much"), *ony* ("any"), *silf* ("self"), *stide* ("stead"), ȝouun ("given"), *siʒ* ("saw") (Samuels, 1963:67). It finds characteristic use in texts associated with the Wycliffite movement, and although imitated outside its area of origin [e.g., by the Welshman Reginald Pecock, see Samuels (1963:68)], it had generally died out by the end of the fifteenth century.

Type II, or early London English up to about 1380, is best represented by the language of a number of hands in the famous "Auchinleck" manuscript, now in the National Library of Scotland in Edinburgh. (This manuscript is probably best known to students for its collection of Middle English romances, such as *Sir Orfeo*.) Type II contains a number of East Anglian features, reflecting immigration into the capital from that part of the country; it does not seem to have been used outside London. Characteristic forms include *nouʒt/no* ("not"), *eld(e)* ("old"), *werld/warld* ("world"), *þai/hij* ("they"), *þei(ʒ)* ("though"), *-ande/-ende/-inde* (pres. part. inflexion), *noiþer/noþer* ("neither"), *schuld* ("should"), *wil* ("will") (see Samuels, 1963:70).

Type III, or London English of the period from about 1380 to about 1425, is often identified with Chaucerian English; but it might be identified more correctly with the language of the Ellesmere manuscript of the *Canterbury Tales* (Samuels, 1983). It shows the signs of a shift in the pattern of immigration, this time from the central Midlands to London; this linguistic deduction is confirmed by the demographic evidence. Characteristic forms include *nat* ("not"), *old(e)* ("old"), *world, they, though, -yng* (pres. part. inflexion), *neither, sholde* ("should"), *wol(e)/wil(e)* ("will"), *yaf* ("gave"), *bot* ("but"), *swich(e)* ("such"), *hir(e)* ("their"), *thise* ("these"), *thurgh* ("through") (see Samuels, 1963:70; 1972:169).

Type IV is often referred to as "Chancery Standard," since it appears in government documents from about 1430. Its linguistic features show the impact of a further wave of immigration from the Midlands, including features hitherto regarded as northern [e.g., *gaf* ("gave"), *theyre* ("their")]. Other characteristic forms include *not, but, such(e), thes(e), thorough/þorow(e)* ("through"), *shulde* ("should") (Samuels, 1972:169).

Of these four types, only types I and IV were used outside their area of origin, and only type IV maintained this position, becoming the basis of modern English spelling. During the course of the fifteenth century, the local dialect usages of individual parishes characteristic of fourteenth-century spelling became gradually displaced by standardised forms. The best-known example of this kind of behaviour is that demonstrated in the Paston Letters (Davis, 1954), but similar patterns can be observed in many texts (e.g., in the letters of Cardinal Wolsey) (Samuels, 1981, and references there cited).

Hudson (1980:32–34), following Einar Haugen, has listed four criteria for a "standard" form of language:

1. Selection: "somehow or other a particular variety must have been selected as the one to be developed into a standard language" (1980:33).
2. Codification: "some agency such as an academy must have written dictionaries and grammar-books to 'fix' the variety, so that everyone agrees on what is correct" (1980:33).
3. Elaboration of function: "it must be possible to use the selected variety in

all the functions associated with central government and with writing"
(1980:33).

4. Acceptance: "the variety has to be accepted by the relevant population as
   the variety of the community—usually, in fact, as the national language"
   (1980:33).

It will be evident that none of the preceding types fulfills all the criteria identified
by Hudson. Type IV comes nearest to it, fulfilling criteria (1), (3), and (4), but
there is no explicit codification of forms, and certainly type IV admitted of a
much greater variation in spelling than is allowed in modern English orthography. It is therefore premature to write of a fixed standard written language in the
fifteenth century. [For the confused situation that existed then, see Samuels
(1981).] Only in the sixteenth century, after printing had provided authoritative
norms for private usage, can we speak of standard written English in the modern
sense—and, even then, a certain (if very trivial) degree of variation remained
acceptable. This is indicated by the historian William Camden (*Remaines concerning Britaine,* 1605): "it hath beene seene where tenne English writing the
same sentence, have all so concurred, that among them all there hath beene no
other difference, than the adding, or omitting once or twice of our silent E, in the
end of some wordes" (quoted by Scragg, 1974:70).

   The parallel would seem to be not so much with modern written standard
English as with the spoken "standards," or socially prestigious varieties, which
have developed in English-speaking communities. The best known of these is
R.P., or "Received Pronunciation," a spoken accent of English associated with
the ancient English universities of Oxford and Cambridge, "public" (i.e., private,
in British parlance) schools, and the British Broadcasting Corporation. The term
was first coined by the nineteenth-century phonetician A. J. Ellis (1869–89,
pt.I:13). R.P. has often been treated as a monolithic entity, but Ellis himself saw
it as a "kind of mean" (1869–89, pt.I:18), an abstract goal toward which individual speakers approximate—a prestigious "magnet" or (a better analogy)
"black hole." [For an interesting discussion of such issues, see Crowley (1989).]
Such patterns of pressure can, of course, be very uncertain [for instance, in modern Scotland, where speakers aspiring to a prestige accent can choose between
R.P. and the accent of Scottish Standard English (Aitken and McArthur,
1979)]. Similar patterns of uncertainty can be detected in written English in the
fifteenth century (Samuels, 1981; Smith, 1988a).

PHONOLOGY

An even more complex problem is presented by the spoken mode. Since we have
no tape recordings from the Middle Ages, we are dependent upon scholarly
reconstruction of medieval pronunciation. Although the general outlines of how
Middle English sounded are now pretty firm, details can be—and frequently
are—challenged. Medieval writers were very aware of differences in accent, and
a number express themselves forcibly on the subject—usually in amused commentary on how odd people are who speak in ways different from the writer and
his presumed audience. Trevisa's translation of Higden's *Polychronicon* includes

the following passage, ultimately derived from William of Malmesbury's *Gesta Pontificum* (1122):

> Al the longage of the Northhumbres, and specialych at York, ys so scharp, slyttyng, and frotyng, and vnschape, that we Southeron men may that longage vnnethe vndurstonde. Y trowe that that ys bycause that a buth nygh to strange men and aliens, that speketh strangelych, and also bycause that the kynges of Engelond woneth alwey fer fram that contray; for a buth more yturnd to the south contray, and yef a goth to the north contray, a goth with gret help and strengthe.
>
> [Sisam 1921:150; see also Sisam 1921:253]

Similar amused discussion can be detected in Chaucer's parody of northern dialect in the *Reeve's Tale* (see Tolkien, 1934; Elliott, 1974:390–393), and, in reverse, in the use of "mock-Southern" language in the Wakefield Master's *Second Shepherd's Play* (Cawley, 1958:131). It would seem from the character Mak's "Southren tothe" as a pretended "King's man" in this play that Southern English had some prestige as opposed to Northern English, even though Burnley points out that "this attitude is based as much on the French lexis in the speech as the southern dialectal forms" (1989:33; see also the section entitled "Lexis"). It would seem from this evidence that English dialects in late medieval times could be stigmatised on geographical rather than social grounds, and the evidence for socially stigmatised or prestigious pronunciations of Middle English is rather uncertain. [See Clark (1981) for a useful collection of various contemporary examples of "dialect awareness".]

Geographical stigmatisation continued into the sixteenth and seventeenth centuries, however, and here the evidence is more plentiful as to a possible social dimension. Edgar's "stage dialect" in Shakespeare's *King Lear* has all the ingredients for stigmatisation: Its features are found in dialects near enough to the metropolis to be comprehensible and recognisable yet far enough away to be regarded as rural and peculiar (Kökeritz, 1953:38–39). Leith (1983:148–149), following Labov (1974), has suggested that the relationship between London English and the dialects surrounding the capital may be part of the explanation for the major changes in the "long"-vowel system of Middle English at the end of the medieval period, known as the Great Vowel Shift.

In this hypothesis, the Shift can be regarded as a combination of phonetic, systemic, and sociolinguistic processes. In stage I, the phoneme /i:/—as in Chaucerian pronunciations of *time, tide,*—developed a series of "slurred" realisations with preceding "on-glides": [ɪi], [əɪ]. Such allophones of close front vowels are well attested in modern English (Wells, 1982:140). Similar "on-glides" developed with the long close back vowel, /u:/: [ʊu], [əu]. In stage II, the mid-close vowels /e:/ and /o:/ were raised to /i:/ and /u:/, respectively. The [ɪi]- and [ʊu]-type allophones were now phonemicised. (It is important for our later argument to note that this did not take place in the back vowels in Scotland and the north of England, where Middle English /o:/ became /ö:/ and then /ü/, spelt *u* [e.g., *gude* ("good")]. As a result, [ʊu]-type realisations stayed as allophones of /u:/, and regional pronunciations remain until this day [e.g., Scots [hu:s] ("house")]). In turn, Middle English /ɛ:/ and /ɔ:/ were now raised to /e:/ and /o:/, and Middle English /a:/ was raised to /ɛ:/ (Wells, 1982:184–186).

What happened seems clear enough. Why it happened is another matter. The key factor seems to be the action of the mid-vowels. Where the mid-vowels moved elsewhere in the system (e.g., Middle English /o:/ to /ö:/ in the north), the Shift failed. [For a straightforward account of the "rule," see Lass (1984:126–129, and references there cited).] There would seem, then, to be a definite causal link between these processes.

It is therefore necessary when examining the south of England, where the Shift took place fully, to investigate the situation with regard to the long mid-vowels; and there is good evidence in the dialects around London, notably those of Kent and East Anglia, that there existed a Middle English tendency to select long mid-close vowels in words where long mid-open vowels would be expected in London Middle English (i.e., /e:/ and /o:/ instead of /ɛ:/ and /ɔ:/) (Dobson, 1968:606–618, 674–678). As we have seen, these dialects surrounding the metropolis were stigmatised varieties that no aspiring social climber would wish to be associated with. In addition, because one mark of "nonstigmatisation" was to distinguish between "Middle English /e:-words" and "Middle English /ɛ:/-words," even higher vowels in the "Middle English /e:/-words" would be adopted as an affectation to maintain social difference (Samuels 1972:103–104). [The tendency to raise further, rather than lower, the original mid-vowels probably owes something to the correlation between forcefulness (natural enough when differences are being emphasised) and raised variants (Samuels, 1972:41–42).] Eventually, a redistribution of words with long vowels would take place in the system—and the Shift would have begun. Subsequently, Middle English /a:/ would move to /ɛ:/ through a "drag-chain" mechanism (i.e., more "forceful"-style variants would have room to move in the system) (Bynon, 1977:82–88). Subsequent sound changes have obscured the distinction, but it is still marked in our spelling system. Words pronounced in London with "Middle English /e:/" are frequently spelt with *ee*, whereas London "Middle English /ɛ:/-words" are often spelt with *ea*.*

SYNTAX AND MORPHOLOGY

A similar interplay of systemic and sociolinguistic factors in language change can be detected when we turn to the history of Middle English syntax and morphology. Here three examples will be chosen to demonstrate the different directions in which language change can operate: the development of the third-person pronoun system in Middle English, some interesting changes in the verb system, and the use of relative-clause markers in Middle Scots.

*Leith (1983) explains the process a little differently. He sees the Shift as beginning with a "push-chain" mechanism, arising from raised variants of Middle English /a:/ in words like *mate*. However, the evidence for such raised variants is uncertain (Dobson, 1968:597n, 606). Nor would Leith's explanation serve for the back-vowels, where a back "equivalent" to /a:/, presumably /ɑ:/, did not emerge until the seventeenth century.

The development of the third-person pronoun system in Middle English is an excellent example of "remedial" linguistic change. The classical Old English paradigm of *he* ("he"), *heo* ("she"), and *hie* ("they"), and so on, was already breaking down at the end of the Anglo-Saxon period, and reduced-stress variants of these words merged on *he*. This led to obvious functional problems, and Scandinavian, or Scandinavian-influenced, forms of these words were gradually adopted to give Middle English *scho, sche* (<*[hjo]), and *they* (cf. Old Icelandic *þeir*). [See Samuels (1965) for a conclusive demonstration of the development of Modern English *she*.] It is of some interest that mainly functional mechanisms seem to be engaged here. As we saw earlier, Scandinavian forms had no special prestige in the Middle English period. It would appear that the development of the English pronouns was essentially an unconscious piece of systemic regulation; we can see forms from a despised vernacular make their way into the "standard" language. Plainly, these pronouns were not sociolinguistically "foregrounded" items.

More interesting to the sociolinguist, perhaps, is the situation with regard to the phrasal verb. Phrasal verbs are characteristic English formations that develop during the Middle English period; they consist of a verb–particle combination of the model *give up, sit down,* and so on. In origin, these verbs derive from Old English verbs like *bistandan,* modern English *stand by.* [For a useful account, see Bennett and Smithers (1974:xxxii–xxxiv).] The pattern is highly productive and has had an effect on the formation of related nouns (cf. *stander-by* beside *bystander*).

Strang (1970:276), however, notes that there is a stylistic restriction on the use of phrasal verbs even now: "The verb-particle combinations seem always to have had the air of colloquiality that still often clings to them." In this context, it is interesting to note that a large number of phrasal verbs have semantically parallel nonphrasal verbs of greater formality, and these latter are derived from French or Latin (e.g., *come across* beside *discover, take off* beside *mimic, burn down* beside *consume, butt in* beside *interject, stand by* beside *support, look after* beside *superintend, see to* beside *address, bring up* beside *nurture, keep down* beside *suppress, give up* beside *surrender, talk into* beside *persuade, drag into* beside *entice, look forward to* beside *anticipate, break through* beside *penetrate, branch off* beside *diverge, cross off* beside *delete, pass around* beside *circulate*). [Examples of phrasal verbs are drawn from the section "Phrasal Verbs" in the *Collins Cobuild* dictionary (1987).] It is interesting that twelve of these seventeen examples are first recorded in the OED from the Middle English period. It is clear that there is a correlation with the respective social status of English and French/Latin discussed earlier. Both patterns remain today, but it is sociolinguistically interesting that they still seem to retain distinct stylistic functions.

The best-known study so far of the sociolinguistics of historical syntax is Romaine (1982). Her findings, based upon Middle Scots material, provide fascinating confirmation of the role of sociolinguistics in examining varieties of medieval English. She reports three main kinds of relative clause in Middle Scots: (1) those introduced by *(the) quhilk(is);* (2) those introduced by *that;* and (3) those where no subordinating element is used ("deletion"). Romaine discovered that these structures were used in varying ways in Lindsay's early-sixteenth-century play *Ane Satyre of the Thrie Estaitis;* she also showed that these differences correlated with the social class register of the characters. Thus, serious characters of a "high" social class in Lindsay's play use *quh*-type pronouns (type 1), whereas "low," comic characters practise "deletion" (type 3). *That* (type 2) seems to be neutral, used by both classes (Romaine 1982:166–167). [For a text of *Ane Satyre,* see Lyall (1989).]

Romaine went on to find similar patterns in contemporary Scottish letters, to make the point that there does seem to have been social differentiation with regard to syntax in Middle Scots. It was especially significant that Romaine could gather useful information by subjecting her materials to the kind of analysis developed by sociolinguists for the study of modern data (e.g., implicational scales and variable rules) (Romaine 1982:170–174, and Chapter 7). Plainly, comparable linguistic behaviour is taking place in both Middle Scots and modern English.*

These three examples demonstrate how language change is essentially multifarious, a "problem-solving" communicative heuristic that can draw on any materials available. The development of the pronoun system shows the steady adoption of dialectal forms, which cannot have had any social prestige, in order to solve a functional difficulty. The stylistic differentiation of relative clauses in Middle Scots goes back to a variety of Old English usages that do not seem to have had any social differentiation there (Mitchell, 1985, Vol.II:85–223). These social distinctions seem to have become merely stylistic (Quirk, 1957). The persistent distinction between the phrasal verbs and their French- or Latin-derived counterparts is now essentially a matter of style rather than of sociolinguistics. However, it does remain as a difference of register, unlike the other examples, and the reason for this seems plain: the distinction between *butt in* and *interject* is a matter of vocabulary, not of grammar. As Smithers puts it, "It is the vocabulary that lies nearest the surface, and is therefore most easily touched by an alien tongue" (Bennett and Smithers, 1974:1). Vocabulary, in other words, is the level of language that is affected most consciously, and given that the "imitation of prestige dialects . . . is largely a conscious process" (Samuels, 1972:103), we should expect Middle English lexis to manifest a high degree of sociolinguistic differentiation.†

LEXIS

This section deals largely with the influence of French on the structure of English vocabulary, but it would be wrong to see this influence as consisting simply of the steady, socially motivated transfer of French words into the English lexicon.

---

*Since the above was written, further work has been done on the sociolinguistics of Middle Scots; see Devitt, 1989.

†It may be significant that of the phrases recorded by Prins (1952) as showing the influence of French on English phrasing, only about 15 percent do not contain French vocabulary, and many of these are late or dubious examples. It is interesting in this context that French written in England (e.g., the Rolls of Parliament) seems to take on English patterns of syntax as the Middle Ages progress (Burnley, 1983:236–237, note 10).

As Strang (1970:251) has rightly pointed out, "there is probably nothing so widely misunderstood in the history of English as the true meaning of the influx of French words."

The general direction of the influence of French on English vocabulary is fairly clear. Up to the thirteenth century, borrowings from French reflected in English texts are comparatively few and are generally restricted to certain registers; even these do not appear regularly until after the middle of the twelfth century (Campbell, 1959:221). A useful list of these early loans is given by Serjeantson (1935:105–120). The domains of language covered are indicated by the following examples (the forms given are generally the modern ones): *arblast* (a kind of large catapult used in sieges); *service; prison; abbot* (possibly from Latin); *cancelere* ("chancellor"), *capelein* ("chaplain"), and *carite* ("charity") [the original loans came from Norman French, later replaced by central French variants with initial [č]; however, some Norman-type forms remain (e.g., Modern English *carpenter* beside French *charpentier, cauldron* beside French *chaudron*)]; *countess; duke; rent; tenserie* ("protection-money"); *justice* (the word has changed its meaning since the Middle Ages; in Anglo-Norman it meant "punishment"); *mercy; standard; war; mastery; gentelerie* ("gentility"); *crown; obedience.*

From the beginning of the thirteenth century to the end of the Middle English period, however, large numbers of French words enter the English language. These loans are commonly from Central French, not Anglo-Norman; as contact with Normandy is lost, Central French becomes the prestigious variety (see earlier, "The Eclipse of English" and "The Triumph of English"; also Rothwell, 1985). The range of domains covered by these words is vast; Serjeantson (1935:121–156) has a full and useful list. It is evident that this surge correlates with the higher social classes shifting their mother tongue from French to English (see earlier, under "The Triumph of English"), and this may at first seem paradoxical. But it is, of course, fully explicable in sociolinguistic terms, for given the status of French already discussed, the use of French expressions is an obvious way of signalling social position even if a general use of French had fallen into disuse by this time.

The influence of French is not just a matter of loan words; it also affected patterns of English word formation. Old English generally formed words through compounding, rather like Modern German [cf. *Fernsprecher* ("far-talker") beside English *telephone*] (see Mitchell and Robinson, 1986, Chapter 4 for a useful account). Old English was especially fond of using prefixes to extend or develop meaning [e.g., *brecan* ("break"), *abrecan* ("destroy"); *bærnan* ("burn"), *forbærnan* ("consume," "burn up")]. It is sociolinguistically interesting that these extended forms are frequently replaced by French-derived words, as in these examples. It has been suggested that such replacements helped obscure the traditional methods of word formation and encouraged further simple borrowing (Samuels, 1972:163–164).

French also affected English word formation in another way, although not really until the fourteenth and fifteenth centuries. As Strang (1970:189) puts it, this "illustrates . . . how considerable is the time-lag before [the] patterning properties [of formative functions] are isolated and exploited." English borrowed such words as *agreeable, profitable,* and *reasonable* from French, in which *-able* is an adjectival suffix. This suffix could easily be transferred to English words, and eventually was. Thus, we find blends, such as *believable, knowable, speakable,* all of which are recorded in the written medium by 1500 [see Strang, (1970:188–189) for these and other examples].

However, as has been pointed out by a number of scholars, simply counting the number of French-derived words in a given English text is not sufficient for distinguishing social register. The use of these words has to be investigated in each circumstance, because, given the social fluidity of the period indicated earlier, the connotations of English lexis must have been constantly changing.

The extent of the problem is indicated if we look at what is perhaps the most interesting recent work done in this area, Burnley's work on Chaucer (1983, 1989). Burnley points out (1983:155) that

> Chaucer's vocabulary . . . must not be considered to be monolithic, nor even divided into two or three etymologically differentiated blocs. It is better considered as a texture, an "architecture" of associations, wrought by the social values its users and his audience perceived in it, and by their recognition of proprieties to verbal contexts, technical discourse, literary genres, or familiar situations.
>
> [see also Davis, 1974]

Chaucer's borrowings from French fall into two groups: words that were still felt to be "non-English" and words that had been fully integrated into everyday discourse. Two examples of the latter are directly attested for by Chaucer. In the *Parson's Tale* (line 869), we are told that the English word for Latin *fructus* is *fruyt,* and in the prologue to the *Second Nun's Tale* (line 106), we are told that for Greek *leos* "'peple' in Englissh is to seye" (cited by Burnley 1983:135). As Burnley points out, both *fruyt* and *peple* are borrowed originally from French, but by Chaucer's time they had evidently lost any connotation of status they might have had earlier in the Middle English period (the equivalent Old English words are *wæstm* and *folc*). On the other hand, when Chaucer uses a word like *amphibologies* ("ambiguous discourse": OED), he is using an evident exotic, probably borrowed from Latin via French, and his intention is "to add dignity and ceremony to literary composition" (Burnley, 1983:136). This was a habit that continued with the "aureate" diction of fifteenth-century poets like John Lydgate and William Dunbar, and culminated in the "inkhorn" controversy of the late sixteenth century (Zettersten, 1979; Matthews, 1964).

Such exotic usage does not provide substantial evidence for contemporary socially differentiated registers, and it is generally hard to use Chaucer's French vocabulary as firm evidence for sociolinguistic patterns in the London English of his time. The nearest we can get to something like the true picture is indicated by, for instance, a comparison of the language of Emily in the *Knight's Tale* with that of Alisoun, the mock-courtly heroine of the *Miller's Tale.* Both women use words derived from French, but some are used by Alisoun only when imitating the language appropriate to "noble" ladies (e.g., *curteisie*), although there are others (e.g., *blame*) that she will use in less courtly settings (here when threatening to drive the amorous Absolon away with the casting of a stone) (Donaldson, 1970).

It is hard, therefore, to use Chaucer's French-derived vocabulary as firm evidence for contemporary sociolinguistic differentiation. A more certain source of information, however, is his use of Scandinavian words. As with his French vocabulary, we can distinguish two classes of words: integrated forms, and exotic forms. Burnley (1983:146–147) again gives a useful list of Norse-derived words commonly employed by Chaucer and widely found throughout the country [e.g., *casten* ("throw"), *callen, felawe, lawe, wing, wyndowe, dwellen*]. None of these words can have been socially stigmatised in Chaucer's time.

However, there is some evidence that certain words had social stigmas associated with them. This was not, of course, because of their etymology; the influence of Scandinavian on English had taken place many hundreds of years before, and these words had become fully naturalised. Rather, they were stigmatised because they originated from distant parts of the country that, coincidentally, had been exposed to an exceptionally high degree of contact with Norse speakers. Burnley (1983:147–148, 150–151) draws attention to (among others) two such words: *hope* and *carl*. Old English *hopian* meant "hope" or "expect," but Old Norse *hopa* meant something different, "think" or "believe." As Burnley indicates (1983:148), Chaucer is probably using wordplay for humorous effect when he makes the northern student John in the *Reeve's Tale* say "Oure maunciple I hope he wol be deed" (line 4029).

This, of course, could be simply a joke at the expense of provincials (see p. 58). A more certain example is *carl*, but here the interest lies in to whom the word is applied rather than in the person who uses it. The English cognate of this word is *churl* (Old English *ceorl*), which is also used abusively by Chaucer, but *carl*, derived from Old Norse *karl*, seems to have been restricted by the poet to the most socially depressed of his characters: "The Millere was a stout carl for the nones" (*General Prologue* to the *Canterbury Tales*, line 545). This usage is also, according to Burnley (1983:149), found in contemporary London documents.

It will be evident from this that Chaucer's usage is highly socially aware, but also extremely subtle, and not open to straightforward sociolinguistic interpretation. He is plainly fascinated by the interplay of registers and the way in which "appropriate" language becomes "inappropriate" (and thus ironic or humorous) when shifted across social classes. There remains a great deal of work to be done on the sociolinguistic significance of Chaucer's lexis. Burnley's use of contemporary documents as a "control" with which to compare the poet's practice suggests one way forward.*

*The possibilities for the sociohistorical study of lexis will be greatly enhanced with the completion of the *Middle English Dictionary*, and when the *Historical Thesaurus of English* is published in the near future. This latter work is a notional classification of English lexis on historical principles, making possible the study of structural changes in the meanings of English words from Anglo-Saxon times up to the present. Correlation of these structural changes in vocabulary with usage in individual texts will be of immense value. For details see Samuels (1972:180–181 and reference there cited). A pilot *Old English Thesaurus* should have appeared by the time this essay is published (Kay and Roberts, 1991).

CONCLUSION

It will be clear from the preceding that we are at the very beginning of sociolinguistic research into Middle English; however, it will also be clear that there are
great opportunities, even if they vary between levels of language. Phonology, the
traditional first object of attention for the investigator of modern English
sociolects, is perhaps the least interesting here. Rhyme evidence, a traditional
source of information for Middle English, is always difficult to interpret, and
medievalists do not have the orthoepistical evidence available for the Early Modern English period. [For the limitations of the rhyme evidence, see Stanley
(1988).] It may be possible that some more extrapolation from the later evidence
may prove illuminating, however, and Wakelin (1982) has suggested some useful new approaches (even though his article does not have a specifically sociolinguistic orientation). More coordination of rhyme evidence already established
by individual editors of Middle English texts would be valuable. [Jordan and
Crook (1974) could certainly be extended and revised.]

However, with the other levels of language there is much more hope of new
findings. The study of Middle English orthography has been revolutionised with
the recent publication of the *Linguistic Atlas of Late Medieval English* (McIntosh, Samuels, and Benskin, 1986), whose impact is still being absorbed by the
academic community; work on an *Atlas of Early Middle English* has just begun.
Smith's articles (1988a, b), deriving their orientation from the *Linguistic Atlas,*
demonstrate (amongst other things) how orthographic evidence can be interpreted sociolinguistically. Romaine's approach to Middle Scots syntax (1982)
could be fairly easily extended to cover the much larger and more varied Middle
English corpus. Above all, the complete lexicon of Middle English will need to
be reinvestigated in the light of the completed *Middle English Dictionary* and
Historical Thesaurus of English.

The key fact established, however, is that we now have a new, exciting, and
above all fruitful approach to the study of Middle English. If this essay has
encouraged anyone to look further into this subject, then it will have succeeded
in its aim.*

WORKS CITED

Aitken, A. J., and T. McArthur, eds. 1979. *The Languages of Scotland.* Edinburgh: Cham-
bers.
Bennett, J.A.W., and G. V. Smithers, eds. 1974. *Early Middle English Verse and Prose,*
2nd ed. Oxford: Clarendon.
Benskin, Michael, and M. Laing. 1981. "Translations and Mischsprachen in Middle
English Manuscripts." In Benskin and Samuels, eds. Pp. 55–106.
Benskin, Michael, and M. L. Samuels, eds. 1981. *So Meny People Longages and Tonges:
Philological Essays in Scots and Medieval English Presented to Angus McIntosh.*
Edinburgh: Middle English Dialect Project.

*I am grateful to David Burnley for comments on an earlier draft of this paper. All errors, how-
ever, are my own responsibility.

Burnley, J. D. 1983. *A Guide to Chaucer's Language.* London: Macmillan.

———. 1989. "Sources of Standardisation in Later Middle English." In J. B. Trahern, ed., *Standardizing English.* Knoxville: University of Tennessee Press. Pp. 23–41.

Bynon, Theodora. 1977. *Historical Linguistics.* Cambridge, England: Cambridge University Press.

Cameron, K. 1975. *Place-Name Evidence for the Anglo-Saxon Invasion and Scandinavian Settlements.* Nottingham.

Campbell, A. 1959. *Old English Grammar.* Oxford, England: Clarendon.

Cawley, A. C., ed. 1958. *The Wakefield Pageants in the Towneley Cycle.* Manchester, England: Manchester University Press.

Clanchy, M. T. 1979. *From Memory to Written Record.* London: Arnold.

Clark, Cecily. 1970. *The Peterborough Chronicle 1070–1154,* 2nd ed. Oxford, England: Clarendon.

———. 1981. "Another Late-Fourteenth-Century Case of Dialect Awareness." *English Studies* 62:504–505.

Collins Cobuild English Language Dictionary. 1987. London: Collins.

Crowley, T. 1989. *The Politics of Discourse.* London: Macmillan.

Dahood, R. 1988. "The Use of Coloured Initials and Other Division Markers in Early Versions of the *Ancrene Riwle*." In Kennedy, Waldron, and Wittig, eds. Pp. 79–97.

d'Ardenne, S.R.T.O., ed. 1961. *The Liflade ant te Passiun of Seinte Iuliene.* Early English Text Society o.s. 248. Oxford, England: Oxford University Press [1936].

Davis, Norman. 1954. "The Language of the Pastons." *Proceedings of the British Academy* 40:119–144. Reprinted in J. A. Burrow, ed., *Middle English Literature: British Academy Gollancz Lectures.* Oxford, England: British Academy. 1989. Pp. 45–70.

———. 1974. "Chaucer and Fourteenth-Century English." In D. S. Brewer, ed., *Geoffrey Chaucer.* London: Bell. Pp. 71–78.

———, ed. 1971, 1976. *Paston Letters and Papers of the Fifteenth Century,* Vols. I and II. Oxford, England: Clarendon.

———. 1983. "The Language of Two Brothers in the Fifteenth Century." In E. G. Stanley and Douglas Gray, eds., *Five Hundred Years of Words and Sounds: A Festschrift for Eric Dobson.* Cambridge, England: Brewer. Pp. 23–28.

Day, Mabel, ed. 1952. *The English Text of the Ancrene Riwle.* Early English Text Society o.s. 232. London: Oxford University Press.

Devitt, Amy. 1989. *Standardizing Written English: Diffusion in the Case of Scotland.* Cambridge, England: Cambridge University Press.

Dobson, E. J. 1968. *English Pronunciation 1500–1700,* 2nd ed. Oxford, England: Clarendon.

———, ed. 1972. *The English Text of the Ancrene Riwle.* Early English Text Society o.s. 267. London: Oxford University Press.

Donaldson, E. Talbot. 1970. "The Language of Popular Poetry in the *Miller's Tale*." *Speaking of Chaucer.* London: Athlone. Pp. 13–29.

Elliott, Ralph W. V. 1974. *Chaucer's English.* London: Deutsch.

Ellis, Alexander John. 1869–89. *Early English Pronunciation.* Early English Text Society e.s. 2, 7, 14, 23, 56. London: Trübner.

Fisher, John Hurt. 1977. "Chancery and the Emergence of Standard Written English in the Fifteenth Century." *Speculum* 52:870–899.

———. 1979. "Chancery Standard and Modern Written English." *Journal of the Society of Archivists* 6:136–144.

Greenway D., and J. Sayers, trans. 1989. *Jocelin of Brakelond: Chronicle of the Abbey of Bury St. Edmunds.* Oxford, England: Oxford University Press.

Hampson, N. 1968. *The Enlightenment.* Harmondsworth, England: Penguin.

Hudson, R. A. 1980. *Sociolinguistics.* Cambridge, England: Cambridge University Press.

Jordan, Richard. E. J. Crook, trans. 1974. *Handbook of Middle English Grammar: Phonology.* The Hague: Mouton.

Kay, C., and J. Roberts. 1991. *An Old English Thesaurus.* Aberdeen: Aberdeen University Press.

Kennedy, Edward D., Ronald Waldron, and Joseph S. Wittig, eds. 1988. *Medieval English Studies Presented to George Kane.* Cambridge, England: Brewer.

Kokeritz, Helge. 1953. *Shakespeare's Pronunciation.* New Haven: Yale University Press.

Labov, William. 1974. "On the Use of the Present to Explain the Past." Reprinted in Philip Baldi and Ronald N. Werth, eds., *Readings in Historical Phonology: Chapters in the Theory of Sound Change.* University Park: Pennsylvania State University Press. 1978. Pp. 275–312.

Lass, Roger, ed. 1969. *Approaches to English Historical Linguistics.* New York: Holt, Rinehart & Winston.

———. 1984. *Phonology: An Introduction to Basic Concepts.* Cambridge, England: Cambridge University Press.

Leech, Geoffrey N. 1983. *Principles of Pragmatics.* London: Longman.

Legge, M. D. 1963. *Anglo-Norman Literature and Its Background.* Oxford, England: Clarendon Press.

Leith, Dick. 1983. *A Social History of English.* London: Routledge Kegan Paul.

Lyall, R., ed. 1989. *Sir David Lindsay of the Mount: Ane Satyre of the Thrie Estaitis.* Edinburgh: Canongate.

McIntosh, Angus. 1956. "The Analysis of Written Middle English." *Transactions of the Philological Society* 26–55. Reprinted in Lass, ed. Pp. 35–57.

———, M. L. Samuels, and Michael Benskin. 1985. *A Linguistic Atlas of Late Medieval English.* Aberdeen: Aberdeen University Press.

———, M. L. Samuels, and M. Laing, eds. 1989. *Middle English Dialectology.* Aberdeen: Aberdeen University Press.

Matthews, W. 1964. "Language in *Love's Labour's Lost.*" *Essays and Studies* 1–11. Reprinted in Vivian Salmon and Edwina Burgess, eds., 1987 *Reader in the Language of Shakespearean Drama.* Amsterdam: Benjamins. Pp. 499–509.

Middle English Dictionary. 1953. Ann Arbor: University of Michigan Press.

Mitchell, Bruce. 1985. *Old English Syntax.* Oxford, England: Clarendon.

———, and Fred C. Robinson. *A Guide to Old English,* 4th ed. Oxford, England: Blackwell.

Myers, Alec Reginald. 1971. *England in the Late Middle Ages,* 8th ed. Harmondsworth, England: Penguin.

Parkes, M. B. 1973. "The Literacy of the Laity." In David Daiches and Anthony Thorlby, eds., *Literature and Western Civilisation: The Medieval World.* London: Aldus. Pp. 555–577.

———. 1979. *English Cursive Book Hands 1250–1500.* 2nd ed. London: Scolar Press.

Poole, Austin Lane. 1951. *From Domesday Book to Magna Carta 1087–1216.* Oxford, England: Clarendon.

Prins, Anton Adriaan. 1952. *French Influence in English Phrasing.* Leiden, The Netherlands: Universitaire Pers Leiden.

Quirk, Randolph. 1957. "Relative Clauses in Educated Spoken English." *English Studies* 38:97–109.

Romaine, S. 1982. *Sociohistorical Linguistics.* Cambridge, England: Cambridge University Press.

Rothwell, W. 1985. "Stratford atte Bowe and Paris." *Modern Language Review* 80:39–54.

Samuels, M. L. 1963. "Some Applications of Middle English Dialectology." *English Studies* 44:81–94.

———. 1965. "The Role of Functional Selection in the History of English." *Transactions of the Philological Society* 15–40. Reprinted in Lass, ed.

———. 1972. *Linguistic Evolution.* Cambridge, England: Cambridge University Press.

———. 1981. "Spelling and Dialect in the Late and Post-Middle English Periods." In Benskin and Samuels, eds. Pp. 43–54. Reprinted in Samuels and Smith.

———. 1983. "Chaucer's Spelling." In D. Gray and E. G. Stanley, eds. *Middle English Studies Presented to Norman Davis.* Oxford: Clarendon Press. Pp. 17–37. Reprinted in Samuels and Smith, eds. Pp. 23–37.

———. 1985. "The Great Scandinavian Belt." In R. Eaton, ed., *Papers from the 4th International Conference on English Historical Linguistics.* Amsterdam: Benjamins. Pp. 269–281. Reprinted in McIntosh et al., eds. Pp. 269–281.

———, and J. J. Smith, eds. 1988. *The English of Chaucer.* Aberdeen: Aberdeen University Press.

Sandved, A. O. 1981. "Prolegomena to a Renewed Study of the Rise of Standard English." In Benskin and Samuels, eds. Pp. 31–42.

Scragg, D. G. 1974. *A History of English Spelling.* Manchester, England: Manchester University Press.

Serjeantson, Mary S. 1935. *A History of Foreign Words in English.* London: Paul, Trench, Trubner.

Sisam, K., ed. 1921. *Fourteenth-Century Verse and Prose.* Oxford, England: Clarendon.

Smith, J. J. 1988a. "The Trinty Gower D-Scribe and His Work on Two Early *Canterbury Tales* Manuscripts." In Samuels and Smith, eds. Pp. 51–69.

———. 1988b. "Spelling and Tradition in Fifteenth-Century Copies of Gower's *Confessio Amantis.*" In Samuels and Smith, eds. Pp. 96–113.

Stanley, E. G. 1988. "Rhymes in English Medieval Verse: From Old English to Middle English." In Kennedy et al., eds. Pp. 19–54.

Stenton, F. M. 1971. *Anglo-Saxon England,* 3rd ed. Oxford, England: Clarendon.

Strang, Barbara M. H. 1970. *A History of English.* London: Methuen.

Tolkien, J.R.R. 1929. "*Ancrene Wisse* and *Hali Meidhad.*" *Essays and Studies* 104–126.

———. 1934. "Chaucer as Philologist." *Transactions of the Philological Society* 1–70.

Vleeskruyer, Rudolph, ed. 1953. *The Life of St. Chad.* Amsterdam: North-Holland.

Wakelin, M. 1982. "Evidence for Spoken Regional English in the Sixteenth Century." *Revista Canaria de Estudios Ingleses* 5:1–25.

Wells, John Christopher. 1982. *Accents of English.* Cambridge, England: Cambridge University Press.

Whitelock, Dorothy. 1952. *The Beginnings of English Society.* Harmondsworth, England: Penguin.

Wilson, David M. 1981. *The Anglo-Saxons,* 3rd ed. Harmondsworth, England: Penguin.

Zettersten, A. 1979. "On the Aureate Diction of William Dunbar." In M. Chestnutt et al., eds., *Essays Presented to Knud Schibsbye.* Copenhagen: Akademisk Forlag. Pp. 51–68.

3

"O! When Degree is Shak'd": Sixteenth-Century Anticipations of Some Modern Attitudes Toward Usage

JOSEPH M. WILLIAMS

INTRODUCTION: A HISTORY OF OUR ATTITUDES TOWARD LANGUAGE

Just as our forms of language have a history, so do our attitudes toward them. And just as understanding earlier forms helps us understand modern ones, so does understanding those earlier attitudes help us understand our own, including this immoderate but familiar sort of claim: "[Some people] are so uneducated, so deaf to what others are saying, so unable to learn the obvious that they are bound to be a major source of verbal pollution, linguistic corruption, cultural erosion" (Simon, 1980:31).

The transgression? *between you and I,* "an *unsurpassable* [his emphasis] grossness," a usage that he believed was new and should be stopped before it "multipl[ies] and proliferate[s] until all is error and confusion. . . . It will lead us to every kind of deleterious misunderstanding" (Simon, 1980:21). Had Mr. Simon known more about the history of English usage, he would have known that *I* in a conjunctive phrase after a preposition was common in polite eighteenth-century conversation, and probably well before (Campbell, 1767:67). Regardless of how we judge its acceptability today, if *between you and I* has been in widespread use for 250 years, without corrupting our understanding, we can scarcely argue that it threatens the integrity of English tomorrow.

In fact, a question more interesting than merely what we should count as good usage is why minor deviations from it inspire such immoderate passion. What is it about small points of grammar that excite otherwise reasonable people toward visions of linguistic corruption and social decay? Are such attitudes

69

recent, or have critics always believed that the health of our society depends on avoiding certain sequences of nouns, verbs, adjectives, and adverbs? These are not idle questions. As telling indicators of social origin and social class, the ways people speak and write affect their education, their careers, their entire lives. However we define standard English and whatever we do when we observe its transgressions, we should also understand not only how that standard was set, but why its violation seems to arouse such anxieties about social order.

The received views on this matter usually identify the last half of the eighteenth century as the period when linguistic prescriptivism emerged as part of our cultural heritage: "Present-day notions of 'correctness' are to a large extent based on the notion, prominent in the eighteenth century, that language is of divine origin and hence was perfect in its beginnings but is constantly in danger of corruption and decay . . ." (Pyles and Algeo, 1982:208). Not until then did grammarians such as Bishop Lowth and lexicographers such as Dr. Johnson assemble and publish under one cover the many points of usage now listed in our handbooks.

But there was, of course, social variation in language long before this. As early as approximately A.D. 700, The Venerable Bede (672?–735) wrote about Imma, a Northumbrian thane who, defeated in battle with the Mercians, tried to pass himself off as a simple foot soldier but was caught out as a princeling, because he could not mask his well-born behavior (Baedae, 1896:249–251). If we infer that his behavior included his speech, then we might suspect that speakers of Mercian were able to recognize prestigious speech in the dialect of a Northumbrian. Such recognition implies a nonprestigious speech, but we do not know whether any of the Anglo-Saxons explicitly abused that putative nonprestigious speech or whether they tacitly accepted it as an unremarked reflection of natural social distinctions, in the same way that we observe but do not ordinarily feel compelled to comment on lower-class taste in clothes, TV programs, or interior decoration.

After 1066, when the Normans replaced English with written Latin and spoken French, it would take English more than 500 years before it again would be the language of choice for almost all social, bureaucratic, and scholarly occasions. But during this period of institutional subordination, Englishmen at all social levels went on speaking English, making social judgments about one another's use of it the whole time.

In fact, during the first five centuries after the Conquest, speakers of English developed three sociolinguistic distinctions in particular, the last of which is central to the development of the way we make distinctions today. The first was between dialects of the north and those of the south: William of Malmesbury (c. 1095–1143) commented (c.1140) that the English of the northern counties was so rude that southerners could not understand it, an observation made by others through the next four centuries. (The existence of derogatory comments almost exclusively about northern English should not be surprising: Most of the writing in English was done in the south. Consequently, more southern than northern texts have been preserved.) By the fifteenth century there had developed a second distinction, one that distinguished, regardless of national geography, the polite English of the better towns from the barbarous speech of the country-side.

These distinctions, however, usually expressed only disdain toward the speech of the north or of the "uplandishman." Critics asserted only that northern or rural speech was barbarous and difficult to understand, not that it threatened the social order. In contrast, when language critics condemn forms of speech today (e.g., *between you and I*), they do so not because those forms are incomprehensible, but because their use is socially dangerous. When Webster's *Third International Dictionary* appeared in 1961, its uncritical acceptance of what many thought were vulgarisms and slang elicited reviews that associated the book with corruption and revolution: "Wherever men believe that what is, is right; wherever they discard discipline for an easy short-cut, there is bolshevism. It is a spirit that corrupts everything it touches. This column believes that . . . the greatest of all American dictionaries has been corrupted at center" (quoted in Sledd and Ebbitt, 1962:36).

This kind of severe *moral* distinction among forms of language is common in eighteenth-century linguistic criticism. But in fact it developed and flourished much earlier. It occurs infrequently before the middle of the sixteenth century, but increasingly often during the reign of Elizabeth I (1558–1603) and thereafter. The development of such attitudes laid the foundation for those eighteenth-century prescriptive judgments that we more commonly associate with Bishop Lowth and Dr. Johnson. Eighteenth-century prescriptivists were the first to specify in detail those items of usage whose violation would count as threatening. But the idea that sociolinguistic behavior could be threatening *at all* had been established in public discourse two centuries earlier.

This distinction among class-based speech became common in discourse about language at about the same time that sixteenth-century social structure was experiencing the strains of sudden demographic change and an increasingly disordered economy and that social critics were expressing anxieties about loosened social controls and about public behavior that seemed inappropriate and threatening. Their anxieties were not new. What was new was their appearing in a growing discourse that linked disordered language and social disorder. During this period, in fact, there first appeared observations about the socially proper use of any particular item of English usage, an item that happened to be unusually sensitive to social change: the ways Elizabethans used terms of address such as *sir, Mr., goodman, you,* and *thou.*

These late- sixteenth- and early-seventeenth-century discussions anticipated not only the moralizing tone of those who are anxious about linguistic corruption and social ills today, but even the choice of terms they use to abuse that corruption ("corruption" being, in fact, one of them). No less interesting, perhaps, is a similarity between our social structure and that of the Elizabethans, one that implies that our linguistic situation may share with them more than we might suspect. Once we understand the evolution of these sociolinguistic judgments in their social and economic context, we might better understand our own situation and perhaps why we now make linguistic judgments as we do. (Whether we will moderate our judgments, much less make different ones, is another matter.)

THE ENGLISH LANGUAGE IN THE
ELIZABETHAN PERIOD

The late sixteenth-century was the most inventive period in the history of English. After 500 years of assuming that English was inferior to Latin, French, and Italian, Englishmen were coming to believe that their language not only equalled but exceeded all others (Jones, 1953:168–213). Poets, playwrights, and prose writers began to explore new styles, new ways to express complex ideas and to capture in writing the rhythms of English speech. Some never got beyond the stage of play and experimentation—the literary archaism of Edmund Spenser, for example, or the euphuism of John Lyly. On the other hand, the prose style of the English-speaking world will probably always reflect the influence of Shakespeare and of the King James Bible.

This linguistic exuberance was preceded by a century of growing consciousness about language itself. About 1476 William Caxton introduced printing into England, an event that made English visible in the lives of most Englishmen. Soon after this, one of the central theological principles of Protestantism, the need for every Christian to be able to read the Bible in his own vernacular, was asserted. Thus, when Henry VIII split from Rome in the 1530s, literacy in English became a question not just for a few seeking a humanistic education or vocational advancement, but for anyone concerned with spiritual salvation.

Another force that made English an object of attention was the translation of hundreds of Greek and Latin texts, an activity that simultaneously confirmed the competence of English to express complex thoughts but revealed its occasional lexical shortcomings. As one fifteenth-century translator put it, "There ys many wordes in Latyn that we have no propre Englysh accordynge thereto" (Blunt, 1873:7), and so English translators had to "English" thousands of words from Latin and Greek. Some writers were so taken by these new words that they larded their prose with them (e.g., *reclinatory, fecundius, deruncinate,* and *suppeditate*). Those who condemned this style called it "Inkhorn" writing: "everie mechanicall mate [an artificer, or skilled craftsman] abhorres the english he was borne too, and plucks with a solemne periphrasis his *ut vales* from the inkhorne" (Nashe, 1880:5).

Interest in English expressed itself many other ways. The first rhetorics of English appeared in the early sixteenth century; the first spellers, in the middle third of that century; the first grammars, in the last third of the century. The first English-to-English dictionary appeared at the beginning of the seventeenth century. The late sixteenth and early seventeenth centuries constituted a period of linguistic playfulness, invention, and change that climaxed during and just after the reign of Elizabeth.

THE EVOLUTION OF JUDGMENTS ABOUT THE
BEST ENGLISH

If from the earliest times Englishmen were making linguistic distinctions among themselves, few were as neutral as one reported in 1426: A judge considering the legal status of two spellings, *Banester* and *Benester,* ruled that spelling was irrelevant, claiming that since the words were pronounced differently in different parts of England, one spelling was as good as another (cited in Fisher, 1977: 895n). More typical was the kind of judgment reported by John Hart, a sixteenth-century orthoepist. For most people, he said,

> no spech [is] so good as that they use. So that yf they heare their neyghbour borne of their next Citie, or d[w]elling not past one or two dais [j]orney from theim, speaking some other word then is (in that place) emongest theim used, yt so litell contenteth their eare, that (more then folishli) they seem the stranger were therfore worthie to be derided, and skorned. Who is the cause thereof? that blind tirant ignorance.
>
> [Hart, 1551:14]

As noted before, through the fourteenth century, these first distinctions applied largely to northern and southern English. But before the end of the fifteenth century, there had appeared that second distinction, one more narrowly drawn between the language of the rural person, regardless of county origin, and the language of those in the more refined cities. Even the speech of educated men was found wanting, if they were from the countryside. In 1540, John Palsgrave observed of some university students,

> because of the rude language used in their native countries [counties] where they were born and first learned their grammar rules, and partly because that, coming straight from thence unto one of your grace's universities, since they have not had occasions to be conversant in such places of your realm where the purest English is spoken, they be not able to express their conceit in their vulgar tongue. . . .
>
> [Palsgrave, 1937:3]

By the sixteenth century, most critics denigrated rural speech: "I know not what can easily deceive you in writing unless it be by imitating the barbarous speech of your countrie people" (Coote, 1968:30–31). Hart devised a phonetic alphabet so that "the rude countrie English man [could] read English as the best sort use to speake it" (Hart, 1969:173). In Shakespeare's *As You Like It,* Rosalind (like Imma) tries to pass herself off as a humble country person, but, like the Mercian king, Orlando perceives in her speech something more: "Your accent is something finer than you could purchase in so removed a dwelling" (III,ii, 359–360).

Those who criticized country speech most severely called it "rude," "broad," "vulgar," "barbarous," "boorish." More socially polished speech was "civil," "polite," and "smooth," not surprisingly, the same vocabulary used by those who denigrated English in comparison to Greek, Latin, French, and Italian (Jones, 1953:68–141).

But from the earlier sixteenth century, critics began to characterize kinds of English in the third way, one that anticipates modern judgments: They began to characterize language spoken by those that were not the "better sort" as not merely barbarous but morally degenerate. Language that they condemned they characterized as "corrupt," "false," or "foul"; language that they condoned, they described as "true," "lawful," "pure," and "natural." One of the earliest instances of this new vocabulary of abuse appeared in 1531, when Thomas Elyot urged that the children of noblemen be taught to speak "none englisshe but that which is cleane polite, perfectly and articulately pronounced, omittinge no lettre or sillable, as folisshe women often times do of a wantonnesse, whereby divers noble men and gentilmennes chyldren (as I do at this daye knowe) have attained corrupte and foule pronunciation" (Elyot, 1970:fol. 20). This next is from 1582:

> those honest men, which allow of custom in matters of life, complain verie much of corruption in manners, and naughtie behavior: and the learned men, which allow of custom in matterrs of speche and pen, do complain verie much of error in writing, and corruption in speche: and both the two, accuse the most peple as the leaders to error, and the common abuse, as the frute of a multitude.
>
> [Mulcaster, 1925:95]

In 1592, Thomas Nashe described how the common person in London aspired toward a speech uncorrupted by coarse language (my emphasis): "The poets of our time . . . have *cleansed* our language from barbarisme, and made the vulgar sort, here in London . . . to aspire to a richer *puritie* of speach than is communicated with the Comminality of any Nation under heaven" (Nashe, 1958:193; see also Hart, 1969:7, 12a; Bullokar, 1977:20; Baret, 1573:s.v. *E*; Puttenham, 1968:129, 218–221).

This kind of quasi-moralistic judgment is inappropriate to distinguishing between polished urban behavior and that which was merely rural. When a country person spat in the fireplace (a habit regularly deplored in the etiquette books of the time), he was not corrupting pure manners, but just behaving as rural folk were wont to do. On the other hand, to call language "corrupt" or "false" is to evaluate it not by standards of polite fashion, but by a measure of transcendent "goodness" and to imply that any departure from that standard must weaken the language.

Some critics did distinguish "corruption" from geographical variation: In an early dialogue on teaching, Edmund Coote has a student ask whether one might use in writing "country termes." Through the student's Master, Coote responds, "Yes: if they be peculiar termes, and not *corrupting* [my emphasis] of words: As the Northern man writing to his privat neighbour may say: My *lathe* standeth neere the *kirke garth,* for My *barne* standeth neer the *Churchyard.* But if he shuld write publikely, it is fittest to use the most knowne words" (Coote, 1968:31). The object of such criticism is the language of those who speak and write in ways that are defined not geographically, but socially.

The fullest statement of this new social distinction appeared in 1589:

> [The language of the poet should be] naturall, pure, and the most usuall of all his countrey: and for the same purpose rather that which is spoken in the kings Court, or in the good townes and Cities within the land, then in the marches and frontiers, or in port townes. . . . neither shall he follow the speach of a craftes man or carter, or other of the inferiour sort, though he be inhabitant or bred in the best towne and Citie in this realme, for such persons doe abuse good speaches by strange accents or ill shapen soundes, and false ortographie. But he shall follow generally the better brought up sort, such as the Greekes call *charientes* men civill and graciously behavoured and bred. . . . ye shall therfore take the usuall speach of the Court, and that of London and the shires lying about London within Ix. [60] myles, and not much

above. I say not this but that in every shyre of England there be gentlemen and others
that speake but specially write as good Southerne as we of Middlesex or Surrey do,
but not the common people of every shire, to whom the gentlemen, and also their
learned clarkes do for the most part condescend.

[Puttenham, 1968:120–21]

By the early seventeenth century, this new standard was appearing in more
comments that reflected a growing consciousness of social linguistic differences.
But this consciousness typically began to focus not just on the need for "pure"
speech, but also on the need for a congruence between a person's language and
his social status.

Your qualitie being above the common, I wish that your speech were also not popular . . . [it should be] plaine and perspicuous . . . not Pedantike or ful of inkehorne
termes. . . . For it is a pitty when a Noble man is better distinguished from a Clowne
by his golden laces, then by his good language.

[Cleland, 1607:186]

[once a person decides to become a servant to a gentleman] having thus altered his
vocation, he must alter his habite, countenance, conditions, qualities, cogitations:
. . . he must as well as he can make satisfaction for the Queenes currant English before
by him clipped, he must now make it full wayght, good and currant lawful English.

[*A Health,* 1931:3]

Againe, while you are intent to forraine Authors and Languages, forget not to speak
and write your owne properly and eloquently: . . . I have knowne even excellent
Schollers so defective this way, that when they had been beating their braines twenty
or foure and twenty yeeres about Greeke Etymologies, or the Hebrew Roots and Rab-
bines, could neither write true English, nor true Orthography: and to have heard
them discourse in publike, or privately at a Table, you would have thought you had
heard Loy talking to his Pigges, or John de Indagine declaiming in the praise of wilde-
geese.

[Peacham, 1634:52–53]

This sense of violated decorum applied as well to the socially inferior when they
sought to speak like their betters.

Citizens [commoners] are never so out of countenance, as in the imitation of Gentlemen: for eyther they must alter habite, manner of life, conversation, and even the
phrase of speech: which will be but a wrested compulsion; or intermingle their manners and attire in part garish, & in other part comelie, which can be but a foppish
mockery.

[Gainsford, 1616:28]

I have observed in some, a kind of carelessnesse in their forme of speaking; which,
though it gaine approbation in men of *eminent ranke,* it would seme harsh and con-
temptible in men of *inferiour condition.*

[Brathwaite, 1631:87]

By the early seventeenth century, then, critics were expressing the idea that
the language of the "better sort" was not just better, but natural to their class. It
was an attitude that applied to social behavior in general. Speaking of those who

incorrectly appealed to popular custom to determine correctness, Richard Mulcaster observed of them that "theie neither mark that the ignorant multitude is not held for mistresse, of that right and reasonable custom, which is the *naturall* custom, and which theie of the contrarie side do follow, as the best gide in right writing" [my emphasis] (Mulcaster, 1925:96).

At the same time, critics were commenting on a logical consequence of this expected decorum—attempts by speakers of nonprestigious dialects to imitate the language of their betters, inspiring, as Gainsford put it, that "foppish mockery" of those whose aspirations exceeded their social degree. One of the earliest observations was also by Elyot in 1531. He refers here to a kind of voguish swearing: "The Mass . . . is made by custom so simple an oath that it is now almost neglected, and little regarded of the nobility, and is only used among husbandmen and artificers, unless some tailor or barber, as well in his oaths as in the excess of his apparel, will counterfeit and be like a gentleman" (Elyot, 1970:fol. 193–94).

Not only did Elyot distinguish between what we might anachronistically be tempted to call upper- and lower-middle-class speakers, but he was one of the first to identify particular groups of speakers—apparently typified by tailors and barbers—who tried to behave like their betters. Shakespeare plays on this same theme in *I Henry IV* when Hotspur teases his wife about her middle-class language:

> You swear like a comfit-maker's wife!
>   . . .
> Swear me, Kate, like a lady as thou art,
> A good mouth-filling oath, and leave 'in sooth,'
> And such protest of pepper-gingerbread,
> To velvet-guards and Sunday-citizens.
>   [3.1.250, 257–260]

Only infrequently was imitation noted without disapproval. From 1618:

> I must confesse our honest Country toyling villager to expresse his meaning to his like neighbour, will many times lett slip some strang different sounding tearmes, no wayes intelligible to any of civill education. . . . Butt this being only of the ruder sort, the artificer of the good townes, scorneth to follow them when he naturally prideth in the counterfitt imitation of the best sort of language, and therefore noe cause to observe any therein.
>   [Reyce, 1902:54–55]

This general suspicion of social imitation was not limited to language, of course. It was part of a wider concern about decorum in the behavior of those at different levels of society. When writing about ornament in poetry, for example, Puttenham thought it relevant to make observations about social imitation in general. In discussing the behavior of courtiers, he thought it appropriate for them to imitate the virtuous behavior of princes, but it was not "comely to counterfet their voice, or looke, or any other gestures that be not ordinary and naturall in every common person" (Puttenham, 1968:296).

In the latter half of the sixteenth century, then, critics were for the first time explicitly commenting on the need not just for "good" English, but for a linguistic decorum that reflected social divisions. It may be that earlier critics did not condemn gentlemen who spoke like artificers or artificers who tried to sound like gentlemen, because there were few of either class who did so; perhaps their sociolinguistic differences were less pronounced; perhaps social variations mattered less. Or perhaps the occasions to engage in this kind of discourse did not exist until the volume of printing had reached a point where something like a conversation on the matter could find a forum and where the volume of commentary on language became large enough to create a common topic for that conversation. Probably all these elements conspired to discourage any extensive discourse about the social uses of language before the middle of the sixteenth century. (As we shall also see, what language critics said during this period in fact lagged substantially behind linguistic reality.)

But even if this was the case, why did this new discourse about linguistic decorum take on its moralistic tone at just the time it did? Why not a century later? To think about that, we have to understand in some detail how Elizabethan society was organized, how economic forces were changing it, why those changes were causing many to express deep anxieties about the social order, and how those anxieties were translated into a concern with controlling behavior, including language.

THE SOCIAL STRUCTURE OF ELIZABETHAN ENGLAND

As a matter of social and theological dogma, the more conservative Elizabethan observers believed that every Englishman was divinely assigned to a social "degree" or "estate," a position determined by his birth, achievement, or wealth (ideally, by all three). It was a social order expressing God's plan that some men were born to govern and that those they governed were born to work and to obey. In 1510, Edmund Dudley likened England to a tree whose branches consisted of those who ruled and whose trunk had to be

> rooted in the Comynalitie of [the] realm, for there resteth the greate nomber; therein be all ye merchants, Craftes men and artificers, laborers, franklins, grasiers, farmers, tyllers, and other generallie the people of this realme. Theise folkes maie not murmur nor grudge to live in labo^r and . . . the mo[s]t parte of their tyme wth the sweat of theire face.
>
> [Dudley, 1948:45–46]

By the Elizabethan period, there had developed a standard version of this divinely inspired hierarchy. This is from 1577: "We in England divide our people commonly into four sorts, as gentlemen, citizens or burgesses, yeomen, and artificers or laborers" (Harrison, 1968:94); from 1590: "Gentilmen, Citizens, Yeomen, Artificers and Labourers" (Segar, 1590:5.4). (This often repeated description had evolved out of a medieval view that divided people into three estates: nobles who governed and fought, clerics who prayed, and everyone else.)

The gentility consisted of two segments. One was a titled set ranging from the sovereign through his or her barons. In a population of 4 to 5.5 million at the end of the sixteenth century (estimates vary), they numbered no more than 80 or so plus their families. The other part of the gentility were mere "Gentlemen." At the end of the fifteenth century, they numbered no more than about 5000–6000; a century later, perhaps 7000–8000 (Stone, 1966:3).

We must understand that an Elizabethan "Gentleman" was not just a well-mannered adult male, but a distinct social group specifically defined by their possessing—or at least qualifying for—a coat of arms. The most prestigious gentlemen were born into families that had possessed coats of arms for generations, putative evidence that an ancestor had fought on horseback for his king. One could also become a gentleman by service to the crown or by gaining a university education and serving in a profession—as a cleric or lawyer.

In reality, the most common way an Elizabethan became a gentleman was by accumulating enough money to retire from business and buy a coat of arms from the College of Heralds, an institution that screened those aspiring to gentility. As one late sixteenth-century social observer put it, a gentleman de facto was anyone who could live "without manual labor, and thereto is able and will bear the port, charge, and countenance of a gentleman, he shall for money have a coat and arms bestowed upon him by [the College of] heralds (who in the charter of the same do custom pretend antiquity and service, and many gay things)" (Harrison, 1968:114).

This gentry with their families and servants constituted perhaps 2–3 percent of the population, but they controlled 50 percent of the land; the nobility, a miniscule fraction of the population, another 15 percent (Wrightson, 1982:24). Since the right to govern depended on owning land, this minority governed the other 95+ percent of the Elizabethan population.

Citizens constituted a second group, one not much larger than the gentry: "Citizens and burgesses have next place to gentlemen, who be those that are free within the cities and are of some likely substance to bear office in the same. . . . In this place also are our merchants to be installed, as amongst the citizens (although they often change estate with gentlemen, as gentlemen do with them, by a mutual conversion of the one into the other), whose number is so increased in these our days" (Harrison, 1968:115). The more successful merchants did not keep shop, but engaged in commerce until they—stereotypically—could buy their way into gentility. At the upper end of the scale, their political and economic influence exceeded that of lesser gentlemen; at the lower end, they were only a little removed from the more successful artificer–shopkeeper. They regularly participated in local government by serving in a municipal office.

The yeoman was defined by his legal status (a freeman, someone not obligated by historical contract to work for a particular lord); by occupation (farming); and by income: "Yeomen are those, which by our law are called *Legales homines,* free men borne English, and may dispend of their own free land in yearly revenue, to the sum of forty shillings sterling" (Harrison, 1968:117). They probably did not exceed 5 percent of the rural population (Stone, 1966:51–52). All told, gentlemen, citizen–merchants, and yeomen probably numbered fewer than half a million, no more than 10 percent of the population.

The last, lowest, and by far largest of the four estates included all the "day laborers, poor husbandmen, and some retailers (which have no free land), copy holders, and all artificers, such as tailors, shoemakers, carpenters, brickmakers, masons, &c" (Harrison, 1968:118). They were the other 90+ percent of the population—perhaps 3.5-5 million, all those with no land, no status, and no role in governance.

ECONOMIC TURMOIL AND SOCIAL CHANGE

However clearly defined these four social estates may have been in the minds of some critics and however resistant they wished those levels were to social change, many Englishmen were moving up and down a rung on this social ladder. Some were able to work their way up, a mobility particularly evident during the later sixteenth century—a period of unprecedentedly high inflation and rapid population growth. From 1500 to 1600, the population may have doubled from about 2.5 to 5 million (Chambers, 1972:18; Wrigley and Schofield, 1981:15). Prospering gentlemen and merchants created a building boom in the later sixteenth century by raising new houses on their country estates and by living the ostentatious social life in London. All this activity most benefited those artificers who were most skilled at cobbling shoes, fashioning clothes, making furniture, hammering gold, and decorating the houses built by the wealthy (Clarkson, 1971:223-228; Stone, 1948:5-8). Elizabethan England also needed a growing bureaucracy to manage the new Church of England and an increasingly complex commercial life, so the universities recruited large numbers of intelligent sons of commoners, who, once graduated, would become gentlemen by achievement. By 1580, in many of the colleges at Oxford and Cambridge, commoners numbered more than half the students, a ratio unmatched until this century (Stone, 1964:60). As a consequence of this social movement, many Englishmen were translated from merchant to gentlemen, from skilled artificer to prosperous merchant. It is no accident that at about this time the story of Dick Whittington—the legendary fifteenth century apprentice who supposedly worked his way up to member of Parliament and Lord Mayor of London—became popular.

But the lives of most Englishmen were deteriorating because they were caught in an economic and demographic vise. In the last half of the sixteenth century, inflation soared because the population and the money supply were growing faster than the food supply. As real wages fell among laborers, the numbers of unemployed increased, a development that pauperized vast numbers of unskilled workers (Outhwaite, 1969:9-15).

As one consequence of this turmoil, social boundaries became more permeable. As some tradesmen and merchants accumulated wealth and influence, distinctions blurred between them and the gentility. But elsewhere social lines were not just blurring between estates; the standard account of four levels of social structure itself was changing. Recall that in 1577, Harrison observed that England was made up of "gentlemen, citizens or burgesses, yeomen, and artificers or laborers," and that in 1590, Segar observed that England was made up of

"Gentilmen, Citizens, Yeomen, Artificers and Labourers." In his 1587 edition, Harrison amended that description to "gentlemen, citizens or burgesses, yeomen which are artificers, or laborers" [though one editor thinks this is a typographical error (Harrison, 1877:105)]. And in 1602, Segar revised his description to read "we in England doe divide our men into *five* [my emphasis] sorts: Gentlemen, Citizens, Yeomen, Artificers, and Labourers" (Segar, 1602:51).

Both seem to be trying to accommodate the increasing social visibility of goldsmiths, chandlers, textile workers, dyers, fullers, weavers, tailors, printers, vintners, carpenters, cutlers, wheelwrights, shoemakers, metal workers, and so on—all those artificers who had been prospering from the conspicuous consumption of merchants and gentlemen. Harrison and Segar solved the problem in opposite ways: Harrison apparently folded yeomen and artisans together. Segar, with a comma, made the artisans a fifth social group. [Thomas Smith, from whom both Harrison and Segar probably borrowed, seemed to split the difference, dividing English into "gentlemen, citizens or burgesses, yeomen artificers, and laborers" (Smith, 1982:65).]

In fact, artificers had always been a group that felt themselves to be a cut above other manual workers. They were more literate (see later); many had a social status derived from their professional guilds; and many were used to dealing with those born into gentle families: Artisans regularly took on as apprentices the younger sons of gentlemen, because those younger sons, excluded from inheritance by laws of primogeniture, were apprenticed out to learn a craft and make a living. Between 1570 and 1646, sons of gentlemen accounted for almost 13 percent of more than 8000 London apprentices (Wrightson, 1982:28). A good deal of Elizabethan fiction and drama was based on stories about sons of gentlemen who had been apprenticed to a craft (Dick Whittington was supposedly the son of a knight) but who made their fortune through hard work and unwavering faith. This self-confidence and sense of identity among the artificer class is nicely captured by a low-born comic character in a play (c. 1590). Mistaken for a peasant, he haughtily replies, "No sir, ye are deceived, I am no peasant, I am Bunch the Botcher [a botcher was a kind of cobbler/tailor/repair person—barely an artificer]: Peasants be plowmen, I am an Artificial" (Hart, 1912:ll. 1220–21).

In fact, some artisans were held in quite high regard. Segar, a widely read critic on honor and its traditions, wrote of artisans that "some deserve preferment for excellencie in the Art they professe, and some because they are employed in Arts more necessary and commendable, as Architectors, and such Artificers as are entertained by Princes, for they are dignified by their places" (Segar, 1975:250).

But not all artificers prospered equally. Those who made consumer goods (the goldsmiths, vintners, chandlers, drapers, tailors) earned more than did those in rougher trades (masons, thatchers, carters, and so on) (Pound, 1966:56), an economic disparity reflected by their different rates of literacy. Those whom we might call skilled domestic artificers were the most literate. According to one study, of the haberdashers, only 9 percent were illiterate; of bakers, 27 percent; of leatherworkers, 31 percent; maltsters 36 percent. In contrast, of the bricklayers 88 percent were illiterate; of thatchers, 97 percent. As a group, the more skilled artisans were not as literate as gentlemen, but they were well above average in a population in which fewer than one in three or four men could read and perhaps one in ten women (Cressy, 1976, 1977, 1980).

In short, there were developing among the artificers themselves social distinctions that at least enhanced the social status of the more successful and thereby blurred the line between them and the next urban class up, the citizen–merchant. A more extreme view suggests that they were emerging as a distinct social category (something perhaps similar to our own lower middle class). This description of Exeter suggests that artificers could be compared to merchants: "The City itself is very populous . . . now it is chiefly inhabited with Merchants, Kersey-Clothiers, and all Sorts of Artificers, among whom the Merchants are the chief and wealthiest" (Hooker, 1765:15).

In fact, well before the end of the sixteenth century, some artificers were seeking to imitate the habits of the gentility. In 1562, one critic complained that "an artifycer, such one as is no gentleman, shall give to his buriall eighte blacke gowenes with hoods, and al they shalbe moorners. And an earle by law & order of armes, may have no moe" (Legh, 1591:fol. 112, P6). This next passage is from 1586. One person is debating another about what counts as honor and gentility:

> You included [artificers] all amongest dishonourable thinges, for the base and illiberal practice of the same. If this be so, how then I pray you cometh it to passe, that so many craftes men, so many Mercers, & shopkeepers, retaylors, Cooks, victaylours, and Taverne-holders, Millioners [milliners] and suche lyke, should been suffered to cloath themselves, with the coates [of arms] of Gentlenes [?]
>
> [Ferne, 1586:68]

As social distinctions blurred between the more successful artificers and merchants, some of those artificers apparently began to emulate the behavior of their betters. Passages cited earlier (p. 75), however, testify to a growing belief that although the better sort were expected to observe a linguistic standard fit for them, those of the "meaner" sort—traditionally including the artificers—should avoid the "foppish mockery" of the speech of their betters. In fact, that emulation of speech was only a small part of a more general tendency among the artisan class toward what we today call "upwardly mobile behavior." This kind of generally disapproved of behavior made those who governed uneasy about the state of their society.

INCREASED AFFLUENCE AND A CONFUSED SOCIAL ORDER

These changes disturbed critics because the increasing wealth among some of the "meaner" sort and their visible consumption of it seemed to confuse a social order that, as we have seen, should reflect God's desire for a well-ordered society. Critics condemned not only the ambition to rise above one's station, but also public behavior that even *appeared* to be socially overreaching. And the behavior most often condemned among social climbers was the way they dressed. In his 1510 account of English social order, Dudley added that none of the lower classes should "presume or counterfet the state of his better . . . nor let them in anie wise exceede in theire apparell or dyet" (Dudley, 1948:46).

For more than two centuries, in fact, critics had been leveling this same criticism at social upstarts in an almost formulaic way: "every man weareth at this daye, as hee listeth, not so much as the Taylour and shomaker, but will be as gentleman like, as the gentleman himselfe" (Legh, 1591:fol.112, P6). From a book on language instruction, 1587: "Go the people well apparelled [in England]? Very well, and with great pomp. A handycraftsman will be a merchant, a merchant will be a gentleman, a gentleman will be a Lord, a Lord a Duke, a Duke a King; so that every one seeks to overcome another in pride" (Florio, 1578:17a).

In his manual on poetics, Puttenham thought it appropriate to comment on apparel: "Every estate and vocation should be knowen by the differences of their habit: a clark from a lay man: a gentleman from a yeoman: a souldier from a citizen, and the chiefe of every degree from their inferiours, because in confusion and disorder there is no manner of decencie" (Puttenham, 1968:237). Another, as late as 1628, wrote:

> our apparell must be made according to our office; that is, such as may be fit and convenient for us, in respect of our calling; . . . it must bee answerable to our estate and dignity, for distinction of order and degree in the societies of men. This use of attire stands by the very ordinance of God; who, as he hath not sorted all men to all places, so he will have men to fit themselves and their attire, to the quality of their proper places, to put a difference betweene themselves and others. . . . but the Artificer commonly goes clad like the Yeoman: the Yeoman like the Gentleman: the Gentleman as the Nobleman: the Nobleman as the Prince: which bringeth great confusion, and utterly overturneth the order, which God hath set in the states and conditions of men.
>
> [Perkins, 1628:333–334]

Some attacks took the form of a jeremiad:

> But now there is such a confuse mingle mangle of apparell in *Ailgna* [England], and such preposterous excesse therof, as every one is permitted to flaunt it out in what apparell he lust himselfe, or can get by anie kind of meanes So that it is verie hard to knowe who is noble, who is worshipfull, who is a gentleman, who is not: for you shall have those which are neither of the nobylitie, gentilitie, nor yeomanry; no, nor yet anie Magistrat, or Officer in the common welth [i.e., the only class left—the artisans], go daylie in silkes, velvets, satens, damasks, taffeties, and such like, notwithstanding that they be both base by byrthe, mean by estate, & servyle by calling. This is a great confusion, & a general disorder. God be mercyfull unto us!
>
> [Stubbs, 1877–1882:34]

But well before this time, many Englishmen, regardless of class, already had too high an opinion of themselves to think themselves inferior to others. In a dialogue from 1565, Cap asks Head why he doffs his hat to those who do not by their class deserve that mark of respect; Head replies, "Nowe I seeing the Ambition of men nowe a dayes to be such that even the worst thincke well of themselves, and looke for reverence, and knowing that I can doe them no greater pleasure, putte thee [his cap] of to them . . . I seeke to live according to the time" (*Pleasaunt Dialogue,* 1565:B5aᵛ).

In fact for almost three centuries, those in the governing class were so persuaded that those of different social degrees should distinguish themselves by different apparel that they tried to control public dress through a series of sumptuary laws and royal proclamations. The earliest laws were passed in 1337; the last was repealed in 1604. They had two economic objectives—to keep people from pauperizing themselves and to reduce a trade deficit that resulted partly from importing European fabrics (Baldwin; Harte).

But Elizabeth's proclamations repeatedly sounded a third note: a concern that public signs of social distinction were leading to social disorder and confusion, particularly among the "meaner" or "inferior sort." In 1562, proclamation 494 complained of "the monstrous abuse of apparel in all estates, but principally in the meaner sort" (Hughes and Larkin, 1964–1969:vol II); in 1566, proclamation 542 complained of the "disorder and confusion of the degrees of all estates" (Hughes and Larkin, 1964–1969:vol. II); in 1588, proclamation 697 complained of "the confusion of degrees of all estates, amongst whom diversity of apparel hath been always and special and laudable work" (Hughes and Larkin, 1964–1969:vol. III); in 1597, proclamation 786 spoke of "the confusion also of degrees in all places being great where the meanest are as richly appareled as their betters" (Hughes and Larkin, 1964–1969:vol. III). These proclamations, however, were generally ignored both by those who should have observed them and by those who should have enforced them.

It may be worth noting that identical language was used in perhaps the most important contemporaneous work on English pronunciation. Of the inconsistencies of English spelling, John Hart complained that "in the moderne & present maner of writing . . . there is such confusion and disorder" (Hart, 1969:2), and in an explicit comparison between the state of the language and the state of the state, he claimed that "abused and vicious writing bringeth confusion and uncertaintie in the reading, and therefore is justly to be refused, and the vicious parts therof cut away, as are the ydle or offensive members, in a politike common wealth" (Hart, 1969:12b). We must not make too much of such verbal parallels between the state of the language and of the body politic; they do, however, suggest a point of view toward stability and disorder shared by both social and linguistic critics.

But we need not rely on verbal parallels to connect opinions about the state of the language and the state of society. There was a discourse about language and social class that explicitly tied together the issues of dress, language, and appropriate social behavior.

LANGUAGE AND SIGNALS OF SOCIAL CLASS—1: TITLES OF ADDRESS

Social critics were concerned over appropriate apparel because they thought it helped maintain the social hierarchy, but they were also concerned because it indirectly affected another public signal of that hierarchy and thus a device for

control over it—the titles of address that people should use with one another.
From 1576:

> if wee meete with a man, we never sawe before: with whome, uppon some occasion,
> it behoves us to talke: without cramming wel his worthines, most commonly, that
> wee may not offend in to litle, we give him to much, and call him Gentleman, and
> other while Sir, althoughe he be but some Souter [shoemaker] or Barbar [recall
> Elyot's comment on swearing (p. 76)], or other suche stuffe: and all bycause he is
> appareled neate, somewhat gentleman lyke.
>
> [Casa, 1928:43]

Earlier some standard accounts of Elizabethan social hierarchy were cited that
define the economic and social criteria that determined membership in different
estates (p. 78); these accounts also described the traditional titles of address that
members of those different estates should use with one another. According to
Smith (c. 1565), a person who can live like a gentleman should be called "Master, for that is the title that men give to esqueirs and other gentlemen and shall
be taken for a gentleman" (Smith, 1982:27). Yeomen were to be addressed differently: "[Yeomen] be not called masters, for that (as I saide) pertaineth to gentlemen onely: But to their surnames, men adde goodman: as if the surname be
Luter, Finch, White, Browne, they are called, goodman Luter, goodman White,
goodman Finch, goodman Browne, amongest their neighbours" (Smith,
1982:37).

These observers did not stipulate how to address citizens or the "others." But
if a gentleman was called *Master* or *Mr.* and a yeoman was to be called *goodman,*
then the better citizen would be entitled to a *Master* or *Mr.* The rest—artificers
and below—were to be called by their bare name—*John* or *Dick,* or *goodman.*
Name and estate, then, traditionally correlated as follows:

Gentlemen:	Mr./Master + last name.
Citizen/Merchants:	Mr./Master + last name.
Yeomen:	Goodman + last name.
The rest:	John, Hob, Luke.

Address and dress among the meaner classes that violated this linguistic decorum became a common object of satire and abuse in the sixteenth century. In
this next passage, the satirist mocks the flattering use of the term *your worship*
because it was supposed to be used only for certain dignitaries and others above
a certain degree:

> Whyle my apparrell was not fine, but plaine,
> At [assizes]* but this stile [of address], could I obtaine.
> "God morrowe Sir; How doe ye sir to daye?"
> But when in my apparrell I grew gaie,
> Why then "God morrowe to your Worshipp sir,"
> Then's tongue without a worshipp ne're would stir.
> [Goddard, 1599:75]

---

*Assizes were county meetings to try civil and criminal cases.

Another late sixteenth-century example:

> but my younge masters the sonnes of such [yeomen], not contented with the states of their fathers to be counted yeoman and called John or Robert (such an one), but must skipp into his velvett breches and silken dublett and, getting to be admitted into some Inn or Court or Chancery, must ever thinke skorne to be called any other than gentleman.
>
> [Wilson, 1936:19]

These last citations clearly link concern over apparel to yet one more sign of destabilized social behavior: a degeneration in forms of address appropriate to different social classes. Social upstarts, some critics claimed, not only were dressing above their station; but were expecting to be addressed above it, as well. In fact, the first instance of sustained condemnation of any specific point of English usage concerned not word choice, pronunciation, or grammar, but how Elizabethans used titles of address such as *Master, sir,* and, *goodman.* It was the first topic in our social history through which critics alleged that a specific item of usage threatened the social order.

As we might infer from all this late-sixteenth-century criticism, people had not been using forms of address in traditional ways for quite a while. This complaint appeared in 1555:

> most men desire the title of worship, but few do worke the dedes that unto worship do apparteigne: yea the marchantman thinketh not himselfe well used unles he be called one of the worshipful sort of marchants, of whom the handicraftman [artificer] hath taked example, & loketh to be called maister, whose father and grandfather were wont to be called good men. Thus through the title of maistershippe most men covet to climbe the steppes of worshippe which title, had wont to appartaine to gentlemen onely, and men of office & estimacion. . . . These men ought to be called worshypful unworthie, for that they have crepte into the degree of worshippe wythoute worthiness, neyther broughte therunto by valiencye ne vertue. Theyr fathers was contented to bee called goodmen, John or Thomas and now they at every assise are clepid worshipfull Esquiers.
>
> [Grimald, 1568:Prol. blb]

To those who saw God's plan in the traditional social order, inappropriate greetings were as threatening to that order as inappropriate apparel. Stubbs again:

> And thei see the world is such, that he who hath moni enough shalbe *rabbied* [i.e., called a rabbi] & maistered at every word, and withal saluted with the vaine title of "worshipfull," and "right worshipfull," though notwithstanding he be a dunghill Gentleman, or a Gentleman of the first head, as they use to terme them. And to such outrage is it growne, that now adayes every Butcher, Shooemaker, Tailer, Cobler, Husband-man, and other; yea, every Tinker, pedler, and swinherd, every Artificer and other, *gregarii ordinis,* of the vilest sorte of Men that be, must be called by the vain name of "Maisters" at every word.
>
> [Stubbs, 1877–1882:122]

In a 1592 satire, Cloth-breeches (a solid countryman) says that the courtier Velvet-Breeches has by his conspicuous consumption made his tailor rich and elevated the way people address him: "Velvet-Breeches hath advanced [his tai-lor]: for, whereas in my time, he was counted but Goodman Tailor; now he is grown, since Velvet-Breeches came in, to be called a Marchant or Gentleman-Marchant-Taylor" (Greene, 1808–11:404). Well before the end of the sixteenth century, then, *Master* had generalized not only to the better artificers, but to those below them. In his 1611 dictionary, Randle Cotgrave defines the French word *Maistre* as "a title of honour (such as it is) belonging to all Artificers and Tradesmen; whence Maistre Pierre, Maistre Jehan, &c. which we give not so generally, but qualifie the meaner sort to them (especially in country towns) with the title of Goodman (too good for many)" (Cotgrave, 1968). He clearly suggests two levels of artificers—those that deserve the title of master and those that do not even deserve the title of goodman.

Just as *Master* had generalized, so did *sir,* a word also once reserved for Gen-tlemen:

> in farewelles and writings you must salute and take leave not as reason, but as custom will have you: and not as men wont in times past or should doe: but as men use at this day: for it is a chorlishe maner to say: What greate Gentleman is he I pray you, that I must Master Him: . . . for he that is wont to be (Sird) and likewise (Sirreth) other: may thinke you disdaine him, and use some outrage unto him, when you call him to his face, by his bare name, and give him no addition [i.e., no additional title of honor].
>
> [Casa, 1892:47].

From 1609: "If thou be ignorant of the titles or dignities of each estate, know that Lordes are honorable, Knights and chiefe Gentlemen, worshipfull: and use to any man which *seemeth* [my emphasis] to be of any good account this Title, Sir &c." (Phiston, 1609:Biii).

We do not have space for copious examples of how these forms of address were used on the stage and in fiction. An example of this wider use of *sir* and *Master* appears as early as *The Second Shepherd's Play* (c. 1420), where a boy uses *sir* and *Master* to other shepherds: "hear my truth, *Master* [my emphasis]: for the fare that ye make/ I shall do hereafter—work as I take;/ I shall do a little, *sir*" (Child, 1910:35).

By the sixteenth century, dramatists and prose writers were using conflicts over forms of address as literary devices to dramatize social conflicts. In a 1568 comedy, a collier addresses Nicholas Newfangle (a name reflecting his charac-ter): "And how doest nowadays, good Nichol?" Newfangle retorts, "And noth-ing else but even *plain* [my emphasis] Nichol?" (Fulwell, 1966:16). A few lines later, Newfangle, playing the judge in a mock trial, is again addressed as plain Nichol. He replies, "And am I *plain* [my emphasis] Nichol? and yet it is in my arbitrement/ To judge which of you two is the verier knave./ I am *Master* Nichol Newfangle" (Fulwell, 1966:16).

In a 1600 play, a character elevated to wealth upon his father's death wonders aloud about the change in the way people speak to him: "The ignorant people that before calde mee Will nowe call mee William, and you of the finere sorte call me Goodman Percevall." Another responds, "Well, good man Percevall, you speake like a wise yonge man. Why if death shoulde repente him, and give youre father his life againe, then were youe but plaine Will" (Macray, 1886:47–48).

In a 1592 play, one character says of another character whose degree is suddenly elevated, "What should I call him? Troth, he's monstrously translated suddenly! At first, when we were schoolfellows then I called him Sirrah [a peremptory and mildly insulting form of address], but since he became my Master I pared away the Ah and served him the Sir" (Rossiter, 1946:I.ii. 78ff).

In another drama, a gentleman's son has fallen to the position of servant. One of his fellows says, "no more young Master but fellow-servant; no more Master Philip, but Phil" (Heywood, 1899:30).

In *Eastward Ho!.* someone calls to Quicksilver, the son of a gentleman, now reduced to an apprentice: "Quicksilver! [no response] Master Francis Quicksilver! [still no response]; Master Quicksilver! [Quicksilver enters] So, sir; nothing but flat Master Quicksilver [without any familiar addition] will fetch you" (Chapman et al., 1926:15).

In Thomas Deloney's novel *The Gentle Craft* (1597), the employees of a successful shoemaker say of him, "And now seeing that Simon the Shoemaker is become a Merchant, we will temper our tongue to give him that title which his customers were wont to do [i.e., before he became a Merchant], and from henceforth call him Master Eyre" (Deloney, 1961:149).

And in a passage (c. 1623) that recalls the old ways of addressing each other, Thorney addresses Carter, an old Yeoman: "You offer, Master Carter, like a gentleman." Carter replies, "No gentleman I, Master Thorney; spare the Mastership. Call me by my name, John Carter. Master is a title my father, nor his before him, were acquainted with. Honest Hertfordshire yeomen; such a one am I" (Dekker, 1958:498).

There were also appropriate titles for women, and they underwent the same widening. In Dekker's *Shoemaker's Holiday* (c. 1599), Roger speaks to the wife of his Master, Margaret, whose husband is soon to become mayor of London: "Ay, forsooth dame (mistress I should say) but the old terme so stickes to the roof of my mouth I can hardly lick it off." She responds, "Even what thou wilt good Roger, dame is a faire name for any honest christian" (Dekker, 1953:50). In a 1604 play by George Chapman, a page says of a lady "I will presume to undertake the defense of that absent and honorable lady, whose sworn knight I am, and in her of all that name (for lady is grown a common name to the whole sex)" (Chapman, 1907:50).

By 1640, these conventions were the subject of detailed analysis in letter writing manuals:

> It behoves in writing to have *his* or *your Worship,* by the end along, so often as his speech hath relation to the baronets of Knights person. From a peasant, *your good Worship* will not do amisse. But from a Gentleman, ridiculous; as arguing little breeding. One Gentleman or Esquire writing to another, usually attribute onely the title of *sir,* specialy if strangers or less intimate: if better acquainted, many times some other addition, of *Noble, Worthy, Courteous, Generous, Kinde,* and the like, according to their intimacie, affection, and difference of eminency and fortunes. Sometime, if very intimate, more familiar termes, which they ordinarily use in discourse. But from one of a meaner sort, or not a Gentleman, would be thought a sawcinesse, or

ENGLISH IN ITS SOCIAL CONTEXTS

arrogancy at least, to do so; . . . To lesse eminent, or of meane fortunes, or younger
houses, sir, will suffice. The like ought to be observed in farmers, and countrey-peo-
ple, of meaner rank. . . . [when writing to a yeoman of the more substantial sort] it
will not be amisse to hang on their noses, as spectacles, at first entrance, *M*ʳ such, or
such an one, &c. writing to any kind of *Scoggin,* or hanger on, or the like, then nothing but *Dick, Thom.* &c. . . . To an ordinary yeoman or tradesman, *goodman* &c. is
a good beginning.

[Daines, 1967:90–91]

But although citations of this kind indicate that the matter of address and
social status may have been active in the Elizabethan mind, do they reflect any
measurable social reality? There may be some social and economic reflections
of these seventeenth-century linguistic conventions in a manuscript listing London renters of several parishes in 1638 (Dale, 1931). Those who compiled most
of the lists either used no title for everyone in a particular parish, entering the
renter as a bare *John Smith,* or used *Mr.* for all: "Mr. John Smith." But two of
the parishes did distinguish rent payers by titles. In the parish of St. Martins in
the Vintrey, thirty-seven of the men have *Mr.* in front of their names; eighteen
have no title. The mean rent for those with *Mr.* was £15; for those with no title,
£5 (Dale, 1931:32), suggesting that those who compiled the lists were conscious
of higher and lower social status (assuming, of course, that higher and lower rents
reflected social status).

More detailed records were kept in the parish of Trinity the Less. Whoever
compiled that list recorded name, annual rent, and for most of the names, occupation. Fifty-five of the seventy-five names are preceded by either *Mr.* (forty-five)
or *Goodman* (ten); the other twenty have no title. Here is what three of the entries
look like (representing the highest rent, the lowest, and the mean rent in pounds
for the entire group) (Dale, 1931:184–185).

Mr. Tissicke, Vintener	50
Burdon, hotpresser	10
Goodman Winne, clothworker	3

On the basis of these limited data, of course, we cannot assume that these rents
precisely reflected the social status of the renters or that this parish is typical of
all London, but neither can we ignore a significant correlation between rent and
title:

Title	Number	Mean rent (in £)	Average rent (in £)
Mr.	45	10	13.2
No title	20	7	7.9
Goodman	10	4	5.7

When the rents are rank-ordered, we find a similar correlation:

Rents (in £)	Number	% Mr.	% No title	% Goodman
20–50	12	91.7	8.3	0
12–16	9	66.7	33.3	0
10	15	66.7	26.7	6.6

Rents (in £)	Number	% Mr.	% No title	% Goodman
8	15	66.7	13.3	20.0
6–7	12	58.3	41.7	0
3–4	12	8.3	41.7	50.0

Although most of these renters, 60 percent, were listed as Mr., that title was most common among those who paid the highest rents and was least common among those who paid the lowest; on the other hand, those who paid the lowest rents were most likely to be listed with no title or with the title of goodman. Since forty-two of the forty-five Mr.'s also had their occupations listed, we may assume that they were, at least by traditional standards, not gentlemen.

This distribution of titles and rents among the various occupations seems to reflect levels of skills and literacy we described earlier. The highest rents were paid by literate tradesmen and skilled artisans: vintner, merchant, draper, calender (a cloth presser), and printer; the lowest, by a waterbearer, a cloth worker, and a porter.

There is also in these data a statistically small but interesting anomaly. Among the group of twenty-four paying the lowest rents of £3–7 there were only eight Mr.'s. But of those eight Mr.'s, six were tailors. In fact, as a group, tailors accounted for fourteen of the seventy-five rent payers, the largest single occupational category. But only one tailor paid as much as £12, and three paid £8; the remaining ten paid £7 or less.

We might recall, but must not place too much evidentiary weight on, those references to tailors as overreaching upstarts (pp. 76, 82, 85). Did these perhaps humbler tailors dress themselves well enough to style themselves as Mr. and to encourage others to call them that? We will never know, of course. But what we do see in these data is evidence that occupation and title no longer reflected a strict social order in which birth or occupation determined who would be called what. They suggest a social order in which people were addressed in ways that reflected their economic status. These data also suggest that the prestige of *goodman* may have fallen below no form of address at all. If *Mr.* was becoming the default form of address for any reasonably respectable person, then *goodman* may have been marked as affirmatively demeaning. Compare the offensive associations with the modern "My good man, ..."

If Elizabethan and Jacobean society had been as well ordered as conservative critics wished, the meaner sort would have accepted their divinely assigned station in life along with its outward signs. When the meaner sort dressed in ways appropriate to their station, they visibly supported the social order and simultaneously enabled others to use a second kind of social signal that reinforced that social order—a form of address appropriate to a person's apparent social degree. But when the meaner sort dropped their visible distinctions of dress, some feared that the social order was threatened both by the lack of sartorial distinctions and by the consequent inability to know how to address a stranger. The increasing absence of signs of the social order seemed to threaten the order itself.

The most frequent object of criticism for both his overreaching dress and language was not the humblest laborer, who could scarcely afford to clothe himself, nor, if we can believe Harrison, the most successful merchants: "Certes of all estates our merchants do least alter their attire and therefore are most to be commended, for albeit that which they wear be very fine and costly, yet in form and color it representeth a great piece of the ancient gravity appertaining to citizens and burgesses" (Harrison, 1968:148).

Rather, the predictable objects of abuse were the newly minted gentleman, but more often the up-and-coming artificer-*cum*-tradesman, the same character who became the hero in the middle-class literature developing at this time—not the gentleman or the thatcher and bricklayer, but the shoemaker, the tailor, and the goldsmith. As we shall see at the end of this discussion, this social group—skilled workers—plays a role in twentieth-century linguistic behavior that is surprisingly similar.

The problematic issue remains, which has been touched on only briefly: The kind of behavior these critics addressed had been current before any discourse about it flourished. We can only speculate about the reason for the lag. One reason may be that social conditions were changing around 1570–1620 more rapidly than earlier and the topic of dress and address provided a useful vehicle with which conservative critics could express their anxieties. As suggested earlier, it may also be that not until the second half of the sixteenth century did the community of readers and writers both reach a critical mass of interest and have sufficient opportunity to publish their views on the topic. But that is a question for another essay.

LANGUAGE AND SIGNALS OF SOCIAL CLASS—2: THE SECOND-PERSON PRONOUN

Reflecting many of these same changes was a second sociolinguistic marker, one preserved today in most modern European languages, but lost in English: the distinction between a second-person-singular pronoun that was originally singular and a second-person-singular pronoun that was originally plural but changed to singular: in German, *du* and *Sie;* in French, *tu* and *vous;* in Russian, *ty* and *vy;* and so on. In English it was the difference between the now archaic singular *thou* and the originally plural *you.* This distinction may have originated in the fourth century A.D., when the Roman Empire had two emperors, one in Rome, the other in Constantinople. By custom, anyone addressing one of them addressed both; the plural second-person pronoun was then used to address any eminent person.

Traditionally, *you* expressed deference to authority or to social superiority; *thou,* intimacy or contemptuous superiority. Thus, among family or between friends a *thou* might signal affection; but to a stranger it conveyed contempt. Equals not on close terms used *you;* underlings used *you* to superiors. In the past, a *thou* from a superior back to an underling was not uncommon. In these more democratic days, however, in languages that maintain the *you–thou* distinction, superiors predictably address their subordinates with the more courteous equivalent of *you.*

Once the deferential *you* appeared around 1250, the *you–thou* distinction flourished in English through the end of the fifteenth century. *You* then began to lose its special sense of deference for the same reasons that *Master* and *sir* began to apply more widely. The increasingly widespread use of *you* drove *thou* out in most standard usage, probably by the beginning of the eighteenth century. *Thou* continued to appear in eighteenth-century drama, but more as a convention than as a reflection of actual speech. Some Quakers today use *thee* among themselves, and within the last 50 years, *thou–thee* has been found in the speech of older speakers in northern and western rural England (Orton et al., 1963–1968; see Part 3, each of vols. I–IV). Its rise and disappearance provide another insight into the tendencies toward social leveling among the middling ranks of English society.

During the fourteenth century, *you* and *thou* were used as in most European languages today, but by the end of the fifteenth century, the respectful *you* had become so customary in public discourse that to *thou* anyone was insulting, no matter how socially subordinate that person might be. In an early play (c. 1540), a lowlife who had just been thoued responds "Avaunt caitiff, dost thou thou me!/ I am come of good kin, I tell thee" (Lancashire, 1980:215). In fact, he did not come from good kin, but the fact that he so loudly objected to *thou* suggests that even the lowest expected *you* as a sign of verbal respect. Contrast that line with this one from around 1538: "Hold your peace, ye whore!" (Bale, 1969:73). Bale seems to have felt that it was not inappropriate for a character to use *ye* even while insulting another, suggesting that well before the middle of the sixteenth century, *you* had begun to generalize to all contexts of usage, even abusive (more about this later).

Numerous episodes involving the insulting sense of *thou* appear in drama and in historical anecdotes. Perhaps the best known is from Shakespeare's *Twelfth Night,* when Sir Toby goads Sir Andrew into a duel, telling him that when he meets his opponent, "if thou thou'st him some thrice, it shall not be amiss" (3.2.50–51). In the trial of Sir Walter Raleigh in 1603, the prosecutor sought to insult Raleigh with, "I thou thee thou traitor!" (quoted in Finkenstaedt, 1963:48). From a play around 1638, a master berates an apprentice: "How dare you thou a gentleman!" (Rowley, 1910:218). In the middle of the seventeenth century, Quakers were physically abused when, for religious reasons, they insisted on thouing everyone. Clearly, *you* went through the same history as titles of respect: originally reserved for the social superiors, *you* had by the middle of the sixteenth century become so widely used in public discourse that it was demanded by all, regardless of social class.

But however common *you* was, its correct use was still a topic for courtesy books. An early (1568) bit of advice:

> If we speak to our inferiour, we must use a certayne kynde of modest and civill authoritie, in giving them playnely to understand our intent and purpose. A Marchant having many servantes, to his chiefest may speake or wryte by thys terme, you: but to them whome he less esteemeth, and are more subject to correction, he maye use this term, thou, or otherwise at his discretion.
>
> [Fulwood, 1582:40]

In 1578, the same advice:

> And many times it chaunceth, y^t men come to daggers drawing, even for this occasion alone, that one man hath not done the other, that worship and honour appon the way, that he ought. For to saye a trueth The power of custome is great & of much force (as I said) and would be taken for a lawe, in these cases. And that is the cause we say: You: to *every one, that is not a man of very base calling* [my emphasis], and in suche kinde of speach wee yealde such a one, no maner of courtesie of our owne. But if wee say: Thou: to such a one, then wee disgrace him and offer him outrage and wronge: and by such speach, seeme to make no better reconing of him, then of a knave and a clowne.

[Casa, 1892:45]

And by 1620: "To persons of lesser rank, one saith, you, without thou-ing anybody" (Hawkins, 1651–1652:16). By the early seventeenth century, then, one used *you* with everyone, regardless of rank, but the fact that it was necessary to keep saying so suggests that the use of *thou* was still a lively issue.

Social pressures alone would probably have been enough to drive *thou* out of the language, but its disappearance may have been facilitated by a linguistic mechanism with paradoxical effect. Before the *you–thou* distinction became lively (c. 1300), a speaker who addressed a single person as *Master* or *sir* would not use *you* to that person, because the grammatically correct form would have been *thou*. And in a situation that called for a plain first name (e.g., *Hob*), the speaker would of course have used the same *thou*. But by the end of the fourteenth century, when speakers felt this new social distinction between *you* and *thou,* a speaker who addressed someone with a respectful *Master* or *sir* would also probably feel compelled to choose the respectful *you*. The use of a first name, on the other hand, would at first regularly co-occur with a *thou,* because a first name and a *thou* are both signs of intimacy. But over time, *thou* would appear less frequently because it was being driven out of common usage by *you*.

Thus, as *sir* and *Master* were increasingly used to address speakers at all social levels, so would the use of the respectful *you* increase, particularly because respectful titles eventually "conditioned" the form of the pronoun. That is, by the early sixteenth century, the connection between *sir* and *you* was so strong that if in a context previously colored by *thou* there appeared a *sir,* that *sir* momentarily elicited a following *you,* but once past that *sir,* the text would then return to *thou*. There are a multitude of examples of this in the drama. From *Everyman* (my emphasis) (c. 1509):

Death:	Everyman, stande styll! whyder arte *thou* goyng
	Thus gayly? Hast *thou thy* Maker forgete?
Everyman:	Why askest *thou?*
	Woldest *thou* wete [know]?
Death:	Ye, *syr,* I wyll shewe *you:*
	In grete hast I am sende to *the*
	Fro God . . .[Cawley, 1961:3]

Even the more peremptory *sirrah* regularly elicited a momentary *you*. From a 1600 play (my emphasis): "Well, *sirrah,* for *your* truth and honesty/ I pardon *thee,* though I detest *thy* lord" (Heywood, 1825:461). (Shakespeare uses the respectful *you* with *sirrah* sixty times in the same line and the seemingly more appropriate *thou* only fifteen times.)

But before *thou* finally disappeared, there occurred a fourth stage, one in which speakers seem to have generalized the *sir/Master* + *you* principle to [*any-form-of-address*] + *you.* Only that would explain why speakers paradoxically used *you* with intensely insulting forms of address, but switched to *thou* when they stopped (my emphasis throughout): "Why *you* base slave, are *you* faint hearted, a little thing would make me strike *thee,* I promise *thee*" (Greg, 1929:ll. 1299–1300). From a comedy: "*You* sir knave, follow me closer. If *thou* losest my dogge, *thou* shalt die a dogs death" (Jonson, 1931:498). From another:

> *You* whoorsen cowardly scabbe,
> It is but the part of a clapperdudgeon,
> To strike a man in the streete.
> But darest *thou* walke to the townes end with me?
> [Clark, 1911]

In Shakespeare's *I Henry IV,* Falstaff berates Prince Hal with *you,* switches to *thee* to take a breath, then switches back to *you* when he resumes insulting him:

> Sblood, *you* starveling, *you* eel-skin, *you* dried neat's tongue, *you* bull's pizzle, *you* stockfish! O for breath to utter what is like *thee! you* tailor's yard, *you* sheath, *you* bowcase, *you* vile standing tuck!
> [2.4.247–278]

Once *you* became tied to respectful address, the connection seems to have generalized to any form of address, even the most abusive.

Titles and pronouns thus invested every sixteenth-century social exchange with potential social signification and power: The Elizabethan social world was reflected in an exchange as brief as "'How dost thou, Luke?' 'Fine, Mr. Jones. And you sir?'" Except for pronouns, many of the same principles apply today (Brown and Ford, 1961). If such usage had been the rule in the sixteenth century, then before every social exchange, participants would have had to gauge their relative social standing and adapt their behavior to the perceived relationship. Strangers were able to gauge initial standing only by how each dressed. But as critics widely deplored, apparel was increasingly often failing to indicate who deserved a *Mr.,* who a *goodman,* and who nothing but first name or *fellow.*

And so for the first time in our social history, socially determined forms of English became a matter not just of social denigration, but of social anxiety. Not until the later sixteenth and early seventeenth centuries are we likely to find many anecdotes such as this: "[A] Noble man, which came into the Painters shoppe, drew by his outward presence all due observance, & respect, even fro[m] the Maister; but when he began to speake, the boyes brake forth in laughter at his weakenesse" (Tuvill, 1614:3). Or this "For a mechanicke to affect comple-ment, would as ill seme him, as for a rough-hewen Satyre to play the Orator" (Brathwaite, 1630:74).

In one of the earliest treatises on the English language (1580), William Bullokar connected language and the social order in a way that strikingly represented the relationship between Elizabethan linguistic and social philosophy. In the opening of his *Boke at Large,* he prayed that "we continue still,/ In one household (of divers sorts) ech one in his degree,/ without grudge, in the lower sorts, without disdaine in high" (Bullokar, 1977:c.iii). And at the end, after discussing well-ordered spelling, inflections, and pronunciation, he felt it appropriate to close with this bit of verse celebrating a well-ordered social world based on a divine plan:

> . . . each part [of society] hath his proper gift, and several working:
> and [ea]ch on other doo depend, without any sev[e]ring.
>> So let us al contented be, without grudg or disdaine:
>> for no estat of God is mad[e], as thogh it w[e]r[e] in vain.
> And let us al of that estat, soever that we be:
> set helping hand, and willing stey, t'uphold his godly tre [of state and language].
>>>> [Bullokar, 1977:53]

Those who rebelled against their social place rebelled against God. Since language was a gift from God to all (Bullokar, 1977:40), but particularly to the better sort, critics who observed upstarts using language not appropriate to their degree would find such behavior not just offensive, but threatening. And those who heard a gentlemen use language appropriate to the socially inferior would see in that behavior a gentleman's failure to meet the social and moral obligations of those born to govern.

This same theme of social decorum is central to Shakespeare's *I Henry IV.* Prince Hal behaves in ways that profoundly contradict what his class expects of him. He consorts with drunkards and thieves; he even brags that he has learned their language:

> They call drinking deep, dyeing scarlet; and when you breathe in your watering, they cry 'hem!' and bid you play it off. To conclude, I am so good a proficient in one quarter of an hour, that I can drink with any tinker in his own language during my life.
>>>> [2.4.10–12]

To his father, King Henry, on the other hand, his socially inappropriate behavior seems to be God's punishment for some unknown transgression. How else, he asks,

> Could such inordinate and low desires,
> Such poor, such bare, such lewd, and such mean attempts,
> Such barren pleasures, rude society,
> As thou art match'd withal and grafted to,
> Accompany the greatness of thy blood
> And hold their level with thy princely heart?
>>> [3.2.12–17]

To the conservative Elizabethan, the world depended on order in all its parts. As his social world began to change in the sixteenth century, the matter of language became one more element subject to disorder. Its inappropriate use simply compounded the anxiety resulting from what seemed to many to be an increasingly disordered society.

MODERN TIMES

It is always a mistake to treat historical parallels as causal explanations, and so we may not uncritically assume that these Elizabethan attitudes are the "source" of our modern ones. Today we do not phrase the debate over usage in terms so explicitly theological. Nor do most of us believe that our social hierarchies are quite so divinely inspired. So we cannot assert that these Elizabethan attitudes are the source of our own, without a detailed narrative of how those attitudes toward social dialects were maintained, transformed, and transmitted from the early seventeenth century to the late eighteenth century and then through the nineteenth and twentieth centuries.

But in the best-known attack against what many perceived as a new and dangerous linguistic permissiveness in *Webster's Third New International Dictionary* (1961), Dwight Macdonald, the arch-conservative of twentieth-century pop-grammarians, resorted to Shakespeare to find a language sufficient to express his twentieth-century anxieties about a linguistic order that he believed was threatened by *WIII's* linguistic populism. He quotes Ulysses' speech on degree in *Troilus and Cressida:*

> The heavens themselves, the planets, and this centre
> Observe degree, priority and place,
> Insisture, course, proportion, season, form,
> Office, and custom, in all line of order . . .
> Take but degree away, untune that string,
> And hark, what discord follows! Each thing meets
> In mere oppougnancy. The bounded waters
> Should lift their bosoms higher than the shores
> And make a sop of all this solid globe.
> Strength should be lord of imbecility
> And the rude son should strike his father dead.
> Force should be right, or rather right and wrong
> (Between whose endless jar justice resides)
> Should lose their names, and so should justice too.
> Then every thing includes itself in power,
> Power into will, will into appetite,
> And appetite, a universal wolf,
> So doubly seconded with will and power,
> Must make perforce a universal prey,
> And, last, eat up himself. . . .

[I.iii.85—88, 109–124, quoted in Macdonald, 1962:160]

Disorder in language is linked to brute will and power, to social chaos. But Macdonald omitted some lines that are perhaps just as telling, because they suggest the social implications of untuning the string: the confusion of authority, power, and obedience. The first two lines appear just before the ones he quoted, the others in the middle of it:

> . . . Degree being vizarded,
> The unworthiest shows as fairly in the mask.
>
>   . . .

> . . . O! when degree is shak'd,
> Which is the ladder to all high designs,
> The enterprise is sick. How could communities,
> Degrees in schools, and brotherhoods in cities,
> Peaceful commerce from dividable shores,
> The primogenitive and due of birth,
> Prerogative of age, crowns, sceptres, laurels,
> But by degree, stand in authentic place?
>   [1.3.83–84, 101–108]

Macdonald omitted those lines that imply the need for a hierarchical social order in which everyone has a place and stays in it.

Macdonald and John Simon invoke the same principles of social degree assumed by those sixteenth-century critics most anxious over social confusion and linguistic disorder. When John Simon claims that "Language . . . does not belong to the illiterate" (Simon, 1980:26), and when Macdonald suggests that one tenth the population should determine how the other nine tenths should speak (Macdonald, 1962:159), they express sentiments that would have been congenial to those few Elizabethans who believed they had a divine duty to govern the other 95 percent.

There is another parallel hinting at another social continuity between the Elizabethans and ourselves. In a study of the speech of New Yorkers, the sociolinguist William Labov contrasted the speech of the upper middle class, the lower middle class, and the working class. He found that as speakers feel their speech situations become more formal, they more frequently pronounce words in ways that they perceive to be more "correct." In casual circumstances, for example, many New Yorkers tend to pronounce the word *bad* with a vowel closer to the [ɛ] in *bed* than to [æ]. But as circumstances become more formal, they more often pronounce the vowel in *bad* closer to the seemingly "correct" [æ].

He also found that speakers reveal their social class by how often they use this [ɛ] or [æ] vowel. In all contexts, upper-middle-class speakers use both the "incorrect" [ɛ] and the "correct" [æ], but in casual contexts, they use the correct [æ] more often than do the classes below them. In the same way, in casual contexts, lower-middle-class speakers use the [æ] vowel in *bad* less frequently than do the upper-middle-class speakers above them but more frequently than do working-class speakers below them.

For our purposes, Labov's third finding is the most interesting. In casual circumstances, these lower-middle-class speakers predictably use [æ] less often than do upper-middle-class speakers and more often than do working-class speakers. But in more formal, self-conscious situations, those lower-middle-class speakers behave differently. Like the other groups, when circumstances become more formal, the lower-middle-class speakers pronounce the vowel in *bad* as [æ] more frequently. But in very self-conscious situations, they use this [æ] sound *even more frequently than do the upper-middle-class speakers.* That is, the lower-middle-class speakers overcompensate; they sound more like upper-middle-class speakers than the upper-middle-class speakers themselves. Labov concludes that this "hypercorrection" is a central function in linguistic change, that, in modern times at least, it is the lower-middle-class speaker who drives much linguistic change.

Labov believes this pattern reflects linguistic insecurity, "an inevitable accompaniment of social mobility and the development of upward social aspirations in terms of the socio-economic hierarchy" (Labov, 1966:475). Elyot noticed the same thing in 1531 when he observed that in the oaths of the corresponding class, "tailor[s and] barber[s] . . . counterfeit and be like a gentlemen." Gainsford noticed it in 1618, when the equivalent of our lower-middle-class speakers, his Citizen-Artisans, "alter . . . the phrase of speech: which will be but a wrested compulsion: or intermingle their manners . . . in part garish, & in other part comelie, which can be but a foppish mockery" (Gainsford, 1616:28). Reyce noticed it in 1618: "the artificer of the good townes scorneth to follow [the country person] when he naturally prideth in the counterfitt imitation of the best sort of language . . ." (Reyce, 1902:55).

Particularly interesting for our purposes, though, is how Labov defines his lower-middle-class speaker: "Education: High School graduate, frequently with specialized training thereafter. Occupation: Semi-professionals, petty businessmen, white collar foremen, and craftsmen. Income characteristics: Enough to save for children's college education" (Labov, 1966:217).

It would be a methodological error to apply twentieth-century class structures to Elizabethan England. [For the problem of defining the lower middle class, in particular, see Mayer (1975).] But we commit no historical anachronism when we merely point out that "high school graduate . . . with specialized training" seems to parallel the artisan's grammar school education and apprentice training, and that our "foremen and craftsmen" are the functional equivalent of Elizabethan artificers, particularly artificers who supervised others. And as for the twentieth-century lower-middle-class concern with education, there is Thomas Fuller's observation about the English artisan; writing at the middle of the seventeenth century, he characterizes the artisan as someone who "seldom attaineth to any very great estate. . . . His chief wealth consisteth in enough, and that he can live comfortably, and leave his children the inheritance of their education" (Fuller, 1938:111).

In short, Labov has identified in a linguistically crucial sociolinguistic class today many of the same overcompensating social impulses as those characterizing the group that in the sixteenth century was most often accused of overdressing, of imitating the language of their betters, of illegitimately wanting to be sirred and mastered—the upwardly mobile artificers, apparently the social analogue of our twentieth-century lower middle class. After 400 years, parallel social groups seem still to behave in parallel ways.

CONCLUSION

For many historians, the sixteenth century divides Late Middle from Early Modern English. By 1600, speakers of English had developed most of the syntactic and lexical patterns that characterize Modern English. This period was also crucial in the development of modern attitudes toward usage. But it was at about this time that the vocabulary of corruption and degeneration first became standard in discussions about the differences among social dialects. It was in the sixteenth century that there was first asserted an explicit relationship between social forms of English and the English social order. And it appears to have been then that the social group clearly emerged whose counterpart today most contributes to change in our own linguistic environment, the liminal group that bridges the working class and the upper middle class: the lower middle class. John Simon explained the source of *between you and I* like this:

> [B]y a kind of dreadful linguistic social climbing, [those who say *between you and I*] decide that *I* is always a finer, classier, more educated word than *me* and attests invariably to refinement, learnedness, breeding; whereupon *between you and me, for you and me,* and all the rest get *I*'s sprinkled all over them like cheap perfume. What ignorance began, snobbery finished off.
>
> [Simon, 1980:20]

He may be right: the source of *between you and I* may be linguistic insecurity. But the point is more than to be right about a cause. The point is to understand where and how such an abusive attitude about *between you and I* originated, to understand such judgments in their larger historical and social context, and to reflect on how one's own attitudes are part of a set of larger cultural attitudes. Then if we still wish to express those attitudes toward alleged violations of usage in immoderate ways, we do so knowing that we are participating in a 400-year conversation about language and class that seems always to have reflected social anxieties about maintaining control over one's social inferiors. Once we understand that discussion and our place in it, we may want to consider carefully not just the kinds of social judgments we make about social usage, but the social and political values that may motivate them.

WORKS CITED

Baedae, Venerabilis. 1896. *Historiam Ecclesiasticam Gentis Anglorum.* Carolus Plummer, ed. London: Oxford University Press.

Baldwin Francis E. 1926. *Sumptuary Legislation and Personal Legislation in England.* Baltimore: Johns Hopkins University Press.

Bale, John. 1969. *King Johann.* 1969. Barry B. Adams, ed. San Marino, CA: Huntington Library Publications.

Baret, John. 1573. *An Alvearie or Triple Dictionary.* London: Denham.

Blunt, John H., ed. 1873. *The Myroure of Oure Ladye.* London: Trübner.

Brathwaite, Richard. 1630. *The English Gentleman.* London: Haviland.

———. 1631. *The English Gentlewoman.* London: Alsop and Fawcet.

Brown, Roger W., and Marguerite Ford. 1961. "Address in American English." *Journal of Abnormal and Social Psychology* 62:375–385.

Bullokar, William. 1977. *Boke at Large and Bref Grammar for English.* Delmar, NY: Scholars' Facsimiles & Reprints.

Campbell, Archibald. 1767. *Lexiphanes: A Dialogue,* 2nd ed. London: Knox.

Casa, John Della. 1892. *Galateo.* Robert Peterson, trans., Herbert J. Reid, ed., privately printed.

Cawley, A. C., ed. 1961. *Everyman.* Manchester: Manchester University Press.

Chambers, J. D. 1972. *Population, Economy, and Society in Pre-Industrial England.* W. A. Armstrong, ed. Oxford: Oxford University Press.

Chapman, George. 1907. *All Fools.* Thomas M Parrott, ed. Boston: Heath.

_____, Ben Johnson, and John Marston. 1926. *Eastward, Ho!* Julia H. Harris, ed. New Haven: Yale University Press.

Child, Clarence Griffin, ed. 1910. *The Second Shepherd's Play.* Boston: Houghton Mifflin.

Clark, F. W. ed. 1911. *A Pleasaunt Conceyted Comedie of George a Green, Pinner of Wakefield.* Oxford: Oxford University Press.

Clarkson, L.A. 1971. *The Pre-Industrial Economy in England 1500-1750.* London: Batsford.

Cleland, James. 1607. *Hropaideia, or the Institution of a Noble Man.* Oxford: Barnes.

Coote, Edmund. 1968. *English schoole-maister.* R. C. Alston, ed. Menston, England: Scolar Press.

Cotgrave, Randle. 1968. *A dictionairie of the French and English tongues.* Menston, England: Scolar Press.

Cressy, David. 1976. "Describing the Social Order of Elizabethan England." *Literature & History* 3:29–44.

_____. 1977. "Levels of Illiteracy in England, 1530–1730." *The Historical Journal* 20(1):1–23.

_____. 1977. "Literacy in Seventeenth-Century England: More Evidence." *Journal of Interdisciplinary History* 8(1):141–150.

_____. 1980. *Literacy and the Social Order: Reading and Writing in Tudor and Stuart England.* Cambridge, England: Cambridge University Press.

Daines, Simon. 1967. *Orthoepia, or, the Art of Right Speaking.* Menston, England: Scolar Press.

Dale, T. C., ed. 1931. *The Inhabitants of London in 1638.* London: Society of Genealogists.

Dekker, Thomas. 1953. *The Shoemaker's Holiday* in *The Dramatic Works of Thomas Dekker,* Vol. 1. Fredson Bowers, ed. Cambridge, England: Cambridge University Press.

_____. 1958. *The Witch of Edmonton.* Vol. 3. Fredson Bowers, ed. Cambridge, England: Cambridge University Press.

Deloney, Thomas. 1961. *The Gentle Craft* in *The Novels of Thomas Deloney.* Lawlis Merrit, ed. Bloomington: Indiana University Press.

Dudley, Edmund. 1948. *The Tree of Common Wealth.* D.M. Brodie, ed. Cambridge, England: Cambridge University Press.

Elyot, Sir Thomas. 1970. *The Boke Named the Governour.* Menston, England: Scolar Press.

Ferne, John. 1586. *The Blazon of Gentry.* London: Windet.

Finkenstaedt, Thomas. 1963. *You und Thou: Studien zur Anrede im Englischen.* Berlin: de Gruyter.

Fisher, John H. 1977. "Chancery and the Emergence of Standard Written English in the Fifteenth Century." *Speculum* 52:870–899.

Florio, John. 1578 *Florio His First Fruites.* [London]: Dawson.

Fuller, Thomas. 1938 *Holy and Profane State.* Maximilian Graff Walten, ed. New York: Columbia University Press.

Fulwell, Ulpian. 1966. *Like Will to Like.* In John S. Farmer, ed., *Dramatic Writings.* New York: Barnes and Noble.

Fulwood, William. 1582. *The Enimie of Idelness.* [1568]. London: Middleton.

Gainsford, Thomas. 1616. *The Rich Cabinet.* London: Bedee.

Goddard, William. 1599. *A Mastif Whelp.* Dort., England: G. Waters.

Greene, Robert. 1808–11. *A Quip for an Upstart Courtier.* In *The Harleian Miscellany,* Vol. 5. London: Robert Dutton.

Greg, W. W., ed. 1929. *The True Tragedy of Richard the Third.* London: The Malone Society.

Grimald, Nicholas. 1568. *Institucion of a Gentleman* [1555]. London: Marshe.

Harrison, William. 1877. *Description of England, Part I. The Second Book.* Frederick J. Furnivall, ed. London: Trübner.

———. 1968. *The Description of England.* George Edelen, ed. Ithaca, NY: Cornell University Press.

Hart, Horace, ed. 1912. *The Weakest Goeth to the Wall.* Oxford, England: Oxford University Press.

Hart, John. 1551. *The Opening of the Unreasonable Writing of Our Inglish Toung.* MS British Museum Royal 17. C. VII. London.

———. 1969. *An Orthographie.* Menston, England: Scolar Press.

Harte, N.B. 1976. "State Control of Dress and Social Change in Pre-Industrial England." In D. C. Colemand and A. H. John, eds. *Trade, Government and Economy in Pre-Industrial England: Essays Presented to F. J. Fisher.* London: Weidenfeld and Nicolson.

Hawkins, Francis. 1651–52. *Youth's Behaviour.,* 5th ed. London: Wilson.

A Health to the Gentlemanly Profession of Servingmen. 1931 Oxford, England: Milford.

Heywood, Thomas. 1825–27. *The Four Prentices of London.* In Robert Dodsley, ed. *A Select Collection of Old Plays.* London: Septimus Prowett.

——— and William Rowley. 1899. *Fortune by Land and by Sea.* Janet E. Walker, ed. Boston: Clarke.

Hooker [Vowell], John. 1765. *The Antique Description and Account of the City of Exeter* [c. 1575]. Exeter, England: A. Brice.

Hughes, Paul L., and James F. Larkin, eds. 1964–69. *Tudor Royal Proclamations,* 3 vols. New Haven: Yale University Press.

Jones, Richard Foster. 1953. *The Triumph of the English Language.* Stanford, CA: Stanford University Press.

Jonson, Ben. 1931. *Everyman Out of His Humour.* C. H. Herford and Percy Simpson, eds. Oxford, England: Oxford University Press.

Labov, William. 1966. *The Social Stratification of English in New York City.* Washington, DC: Center for Applied Linguistics.

Lancashire, Ian, ed. 1980. *Hickscorner.* In *Two Tudor Interludes: The Interlude of Youth, Hick Scorner.* Manchester, England: Manchester University Press.

Legh, Gerard. 1591. *The Accedence of Armorie.* London: Richard Tottell.

Macdonald, Dwight. 1962. "The String Untuned," *The New Yorker* March 10:130–134, 137–140, 143–150, 153–160.

Macray, W.D., ed. 1886. *The Pilgrimage to Parnassus, with the Two Parts of the Return from Parnassus.* London: Clarendon.

Mayer, Arno J. 1975. "The Lower Middle Class as Historical Problem." *Journal of Modern History* 47:409–436.

Mulcaster, Richard. 1925. *The First Part of the Elementarie.* E. T. Campagnac, ed. London: Oxford University Press.

Nashe, Thomas. 1958. *Pierce Pennilesse His Supplication to the Divell* in *The Works of Thomas Nashe.* Ronald B. McKerrow, ed. Oxford: Blackwell.

———. 1880. "Preface," in Robert Green, *Menaphon.* Edward Arber, ed. Birmingham, England: English Scholars Library.

Orton, Harold and Eugen Dieth. 1962. *Survey of English Dialects,* 4 vols. Leeds: Arnold.

Outhwaite, R. B. 1969. *Inflation in Tudor and Early Stuart England.* London: Macmillan.

Palsgrave, John. 1937. *The Comedy of Acolastus: Translated from the Latin of Fullonius.* P. L. Carver, ed. London: Early English Text Society.

Peacham, Henry. 1634. *The Compleat Gentleman.* London: Francis Constable.

Perkins, William. 1628. *The Whole Treatise of the Cases of Conscience.* London: Legatt.

Phiston, William. 1609. *The Schoole of Good Manners.* London: White.

Pleasaunt Dialogue of Disputation Betwene the Cap and the Head. 1565. London: Denham.

Pound, J. F. 1966. "The Social and Trade Structure of Norwich 1525–1575." *Past and Present* 34:49–69.

Puttenham, George. 1968. *The Arte of English Poesie.* R. C. Alston, ed. Menston, England: Scolar Press.

Pyles, Thomas, and John Algeo. 1982. *The Origins and Development of the English Language,* 3rd ed. New York: Harcourt Brace Jovanovich.

Reyce, Robert. 1902. *The Breviary of Suffolk.* Francis Hervey, ed. London: Murray.

Rossiter, A. P., ed. 1946. *Woodstock.* London: Chatto & Windus.

Rowley, William. 1910. *A Shoe Maker, A Gentleman.* C. W. Stork, ed. Philadelphia: Winston.

Segar, William. 1975. *The Book of Honor and Arms (1590) and Honor Military and Civil (1602).* C. W. Stork, ed. Delmar, NY: Scholars' Facsimiles & Reprints.

Simon, John. 1980. *Paradigms Lost.* New York: Potter.

Sledd, James, and Wilma Ebitt. eds. 1962. *Dictionaries and THAT Dictionary.* Glenview, IL: Scott, Foresman.

Smith, Thomas. 1982. *De Republica Anglorum.* Mary Dewar, ed. New York: Cambridge University Press.

Stone, Lawrence. 1948. "The Anatomy of the Elizabethan Artisan." *Economic Historical Review* 18(1–2):1–53.

———. 1964. "The Educational Revolution in England 1560–1640." *Past and Present* 28:41–80.

———. 1965. *The Crisis of the Aristocracy, 1558–1641.* Oxford, England: Oxford University Press.

———. 1966. "Social Mobility in England 1500–1700." *Past and Present* 33:56–73.

Stubbs, Philip. 1877–82. *The Anatomie of Abuses.* F. J. Furnivall, ed. London: Trübner.

Tuvill, Daniel. 1614. *The Dove and the Serpent.* London: T. Creede.

Wilson, Thomas. 1936. *The State of England, Anno Dom. 1600.* F. J. Fisher, ed. London: Royal Historical Society Publications.

Wrightson, Keith. 1982. *English Society 1580–1680.* New Brunswick, NJ: Rutgers University Press.

Wrigley, E. A., and R. S. Schofield. 1981. *The Population History of England 1541–1871.* Cambridge, MA: Harvard University Press.

4

Style and Standardization in England: 1700–1900

EDWARD FINEGAN

By most reckonings, the English spoken and written in England in the period between 1700 and 1900 changed relatively little when compared to other periods. Indeed, the English language remained far more stable then than contemporary English social and economic life. Whereas the language of 1900 is similar to the language used two centuries earlier, a great gulf separates the people of 1900 from those of 1700. In 1700, England and Scotland were still ruled by separate monarchs. In 1707 they were united under a single monarchy, as they are united in one island. In 1700 England was an insular nation, with a nascent empire in North America. By 1900 the American colonies had long since become independent, and the industrial revolution had transformed both Britain and its former colony into great world powers. Moreover, by 1900, the power of the British monarchy, long since weakened, had faded to the largely ceremonial and symbolic functions it retains today.

In considering the English language in the period between 1700 and 1900, it is useful to remember that there is nothing particularly natural or enlightening in dividing history into century-long chunks. If we were interested in political history, the dates of particular events might serve better, such as the Restoration of Charles II to the throne of England in 1660 or the death of the Hanover line of British rulers in 1798. Were we interested in linguistic history, still other dates would be serviceable, but the same dates might not serve equally well for tracing syntax, phonology, and inflections. Depending on one's purpose, period names such as *Restoration* or *Victorian* might prove apt or, if we were to rely on themes rather than on rulers, we might use such terms as *Augustan, Neo-classic,* or *Romantic.* Centuries may be useful for their tidiness, but human activities, including linguistic and sociolinguistic ones, are not so tidy.

SOCIAL BACKGROUND

The eighteenth and nineteenth centuries were not calm periods in English history. Britain lost the thirteen American colonies in the War of Independence and fought several wars with France. Repercussions from the social and political changes spawned by the French Revolution were felt in England. Besides upheavals in social and political life, revolutionary changes affecting the climate of production were in the air. Working in England in 1783, the same year that the War of Independence ended in America, James Watt invented the steam engine, thereby launching the nineteenth-century industrial revolution that changed the face of the English countryside and of much of the world. The industrial revolution helped strengthen a rising middle class and contributed to the extraordinary growth of urban centers so characteristic of modern Britain. In 1700, little more than 5 million people lived in England; by 1800 the population had grown to about 8.5 million; then, between 1800 and 1871, it increased by an additional 13 million souls to more than 21 million. In the meanwhile, hundreds of thousands of Britons had emigrated elsewhere: to North America and parts of South America; to Australia and New Zealand; to India and parts of Africa. If in some respects life in England was better in 1900 than in 1700, it was not so in all respects. If wife selling and slave trading had ended, poverty and disease had not, and life in the factories was exceedingly tough for many. Life expectancy in England increased only from thirty-seven years in 1700 to about forty-one years in 1872, and in a polluted industrial city such as Manchester the average age of death in the mid-nineteenth century was under twenty, so treacherous were the living conditions.

Just as significant as the changes in England from 1700 to 1900 was the social and economic diversity within Britain at any one time. Certainly the chasm between rich and poor, between rural and urban, between men and women was great at the beginning of the period. And at the end, although some gaps had narrowed, as in the case of men and women, others had widened, as with rural and urban, or merely been filled in by people occupying intermediate states, as with a middle class between rich and poor, and the distance between the extremes was as great as ever. To be sure, the eighteenth century was the age in which Wedgewood porcelain, Chippendale cabinets, and other exceptionally fine manufactured goods got their start. But alongside the expense and quality that such grand names suggest, and alongside the stately portraits of aristocratic England painted by Sir Joshua Reynolds and Thomas Gainsborough in the last half of the century, one must place the sharply contrasting world of such ordinary people as those William Hogarth depicted in some of his prints. Hogarth's "Gin Lane" is a disheartening view of Londoners, women with children as well as men, sprawled about in the streets drunk with gin to ease the pain of daily life. If the eighteenth century (and part of the nineteenth) was an age in which some men got rich in the African slave trade, as Joseph M. W. Turner's painting "Slave Ships" (1840) reminds us, it was equally an age when debtors' prison overflowed and when a husband could arrange to sell his English wife if he found her unsatisfactory.

THE ENGLISH LANGUAGE

When we shift our focus from the social landscape to the principal language being spoken in Britain, we are in the period of Late Modern English, which comprises the eighteenth, nineteenth, and twentieth centuries. As the British Empire grew and the industrial revolution altered the landscape of everyday living for millions, the experiences of Britons at home and abroad swelled the vocabulary of English with new words brought home by the new challenges and new experiences.

Despite dramatic shifts in the social and economic fabric of Britain, the grammatical characteristics of the English language remained comparatively stable between 1700 and 1900, a fact that challenges the working assumption of historians that language change increases its pace in periods of social upheaval. Surprisingly, then, the changes that affected social life in eighteenth- and nineteenth-century Britain find only a faint linguistic echo outside the vocabulary. But that is far from saying that there was no linguistic impact.

In fact, the eighteenth century is characterized by flux in linguistic attitudes, especially in notions of good English and grammatical correctness. Moreover, English was emerging then from a period of great expansion of communicative function and of the linguistic forms needed to carry out those new functions. As a consequence, prose style and judgments about what constituted good style were also in flux. If the linguistic resources provided by the grammar of English remained relatively stable in the eighteenth and nineteenth centuries, significant change did occur elsewhere, notably in the ways in which writers viewed that grammar and deployed its resources in their expressive and communicative activities.

LITERACY AND STYLE

One significant social development of the period was the expansion of the reading public, which grew larger and more varied during the eighteenth century than ever before. Whereas literacy had earlier been a privilege of the professional classes and the wealthy—and therefore principally of men—in the late seventeenth and early eighteenth centuries, middle-class men and both middle- and upper-class women swelled the ranks of the reading public, and a significant middle-class readership existed in Britain. Writers from the middle classes (e.g., Defoe, the son of a butcher, and Richardson, himself a printer) were writing about middle-class concerns for middle-class readers. In the midst of this expansion of readers and writers in the early eighteenth century, certain influential periodicals got their start, including the *Spectator* and the *Tatler. Gentlemen's Magazine,* the first general English-language magazine, was founded in 1731, and other magazines cropped up throughout the century in England and Scotland both. The broadened stripe of readers encouraged everyday subject matter, and in many instances a plain, even home-spun, writing style. Despite the significant democratization of writers and readers, however, some writers remained distinctly elitist in subject matter and intended audience. As a result, alongside the home-spun linguistic ideals of some, highly literate matters and manners were championed by others, including Jonathan Swift, Alexander Pope, and Samuel Johnson. Figure 4.1 charts the drop in illiteracy from about 60 percent

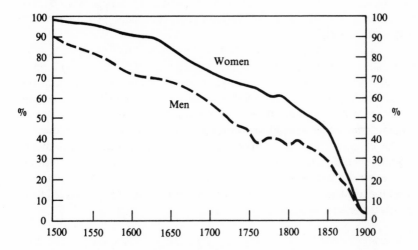

Figure 4.1. Estimated illiteracy of men and women in England, 1500–1900 (after Cressy, 1980:177).

for men and more than 70 percent for women in 1700 to almost zero for both groups by 1900.

LANGUAGE ATTITUDES

By 1700, after two centuries of effort to remedy the perceived inadequacies of English in meeting its expanded range of functions, Britons by and large expressed satisfaction with its capabilities. In fact, as the seventeenth century drew to a close, philosophical concern about features that English shared with other languages dominated thinking rather than the earlier utilitarian concerns for improvement of the language (see Aarsleff, 1983). But the philosophical concerns did not last long and quickly yielded to arguments about what kind of English should be recorded in dictionaries and grammars, about which groups would be privileged by having their variety recorded, and about the relationship between oral and literate prose styles.

The eighteenth century in Britain was a period of considerable linguistic self-consciousness, when grammatical and rhetorical treatises multiplied and the first general dictionaries of English appeared. With the increase in literacy, many readers developed an interest in literary and linguistic criticism. Journalists, philosophers, scientists, and clerics, among others, offered verbal criticism, as it was called, finding outlets in the essays of the *Tatler, Idler,* and *Rambler,* as well as in the more orthodox instruments of language codification and standardization, namely, dictionaries and grammars. The genteel concern with politeness and refinement so characteristic of the eighteenth century linked learning and moralizing, and that link prompted some writers to confound grammatical analysis and verbal criticism, indeed to confound moral and grammatical rectitude. For many, grammar and criticism could be kept distinct in theory; for no one were they divorced in practice.

At least since the eighteenth century, then, thinking and writing on the English language has been a mixture of description and prescription, a combination of analysis and advocacy. Dictionaries and grammars of necessity recorded the ways in which English speakers used their language, but they also promoted the particular views of their authors as to what shape English usage ought to take. Throughout the history of English grammar, an inclination to settle and refine the language, to eradicate variation and halt change has infused the work of dictionary makers and grammarians, amateur and professional alike. As grammarians and lexicographers came largely from the middle classes rather than the lower or upper classes, the dictionaries and grammars they wrote reflected their middle-class norms and values.

PROSE STYLE IN THE EIGHTEENTH AND NINETEENTH CENTURIES

Historians of English, like historians of other languages, tend to focus on the development of grammatical features in their accounts. The grammar of every language changes continually, and there certainly were syntactic, phonological, and lexical developments in the eighteenth and nineteenth centuries. Among them can be counted the development of the present passive progressive form of the verb *(The house was being painted)* and the virtual evaporation of the second-person-singular pronouns *thou* and *thee* other than in prayer. Still, the grammar of English remained relatively stable. Even the most prominent sound changes were relatively isolated. For example, following a vowel in words like *star* and *bird, r* disappeared from speech in much of England and that *r*-less form of talk traveled by ship to American communities along the Atlantic coast, where it can still be heard around New York City and in parts of New England and the coastal South. But, like its grammar, the sound system of English endured no drastic changes between 1700 and 1900. As to vocabulary, many words were borrowed, largely the result of commerce with Europeans, particularly the French, and of contact with the colonized peoples of the far-flung British Empire in North America, India, Africa, and Australia. [Baugh and Cable (1978) offer valuable treatment of lexical borrowing in Modern English.]

More socially significant than these grammatical and lexical changes were developments of a different kind. In a time of great social, political, and intellectual change, new types of writing arose, along with a need for vernacular discourse on topics and in situations that previously found expression in Latin. Among the most notable of these are the periodical essay and the novel, but biography, autobiography, and literary criticism developed, and physicians, lawyers, scientists, and other professionals wrote increasingly in English, greatly expanding the range of situations in which the vernacular found service. Likewise, philosophers, historians, political analysts, and other intellectuals shaped the essay to their needs and expanded its range of utility. These new and expanded genres tested the ability of English to carry out a wide range of communicative tasks in a curious and intellectually robust age.

When one thinks of English literature during the Renaissance, it is drama that comes to mind, especially the plays of Shakespeare. In the seventeenth century, despite important prose by such figures as Bacon, Hobbes, Locke, and Pepys, the poetry of Donne, Marvell, and Milton suggests itself. But when one thinks of the eighteenth century, prose comes to mind: one thinks of Addison and Steele among the essayists, of Boswell's biography and Burke's political writing, of Hume's philosophy and Gibbon's history. Gifted novelists also come to mind, among them Defoe *(Robinson Crusoe)*, Fielding *(Tom Jones)*, Sterne *(Tristram Shandy)*, and Richardson *(Pamela)*. The eighteenth century gave pride of place to prose.

English prose had a considerable history prior to 1700, and the seventeenth century gave a boost to accessible prose style as scientists and humanists adapted English to new purposes. The Royal Society of London ("for the Improving of Natural Knowledge") was founded in 1662 and energetically advanced the utility and accessibility of English prose. Some members were especially keen to simplify style while keeping it sufficiently versatile to accomplish the functions previously carried out by Latin. In the period following the restoration of the monarchy in 1660, many writers consciously strove for plain and simple prose; they aimed for a conversational style that would ensure wide accessibility to the findings of the new science, the new philosophy—to Enlightenment thought in general.

An early example of simple, lucid prose can be found in John Dryden's "Essay of Dramatic Poesy" (1668). (The capitalization of prepositions and passive voice verbs has been added for our later analysis; it does not appear in the original.)

Dryden Passage

To begin, then, WITH Shakespeare. He was the man who OF all modern, and perhaps ancient poets, had the largest and most comprehensive soul. All the images OF Nature were still present TO him, and he drew them, not laboriously, but luckily; when he describes anything, you more than see it, you feel it too. . . . I cannot say he is everywhere alike. . . . He is many times flat, insipid; his comic wit degenerating INTO clenches, his serious swelling INTO bombast. But he is always great when some great occasion *IS PRESENTED* TO him; no man can say he ever had a fit subject FOR his wit and did not then raise himself as high ABOVE the rest OF poets.
                                                                                [Monk, 1971:55–56]

The use of first- and second-person pronouns suggests a face-to-face conversational tone, as does the use of the "private verb" *feel* and the frequent use of *be* as a main verb (three occurrences of *he is* and one each of *was* and *were*). Other features suggestive of speech more than writing include the omission of the complementizer *that*, as in "no man can say Ø he ever had . . . ," and lots of present-tense verbs *(describes, see, feel, is,* and so on). Naturally, the passage has some characteristics of writing, but for a written passage it is strikingly speechlike.

Influenced by the Royal Society, English prose style in seventeenth-century scientific and philosophical writing, as well as literature, seems relatively close to speech: It is relatively colloquial, or "oral." This oral ideal continued into the eighteenth century, bolstered by the fact that writers, now typically lacking the patronage of the wealthy that earlier writers enjoyed, could best earn a livelihood if they could attract and hold an audience. With an increasingly literate middle class, a potentially large readership could be cultivated.

Following in the path of such oral prose as Dryden's is the early-eighteenth-century prose of writers like Daniel Defoe and Joseph Addison, whose middle-class concerns appealed to a middle-class audience. In the 1711 essay from the *Spectator* that follows, Addison illustrates the continuing influence of oral norms on written prose.

Addison Passage (colloquial)

There is no place in the town which I so much love to frequent as the Royal Exchange. It gives me a secret satisfaction, and, in some measure, gratifies my vanity, as I am an Englishman, to see so rich an assembly of countrymen and foreigners consulting together upon the private business of mankind, and making this metropolis a kind of emporium for the whole earth. . . . Factors in the trading world are what ambassadors are in the politic world; they negotiate affairs, conclude treaties, and maintain a good correspondence between those wealthy societies of men that are divided from one another by seas and oceans, or live on the different extremities of a continent. I have often been pleased to hear disputes adjusted between an inhabitant of Japan and an alderman of London, or to see a subject of the Great Mogul entering into a league with one of the Czar of Muscovy. I am infinitely delighted in mixing with these several ministers of commerce, as they are distinguished by their different walks and different languages; sometimes I am justled among a body of Armenians; sometimes I am lost in a crowd of Jews; and sometimes make one in a group of Dutchmen. I am a Dane, Swede, or Frenchman at different times; or rather fancy myself like the old philosopher, who upon being asked what countryman he was, replied, that he was a citizen of the world.

[Bond, 1965. 1:292–294]

Addison's discussion of the Royal Exchange abounds in colloquial features: *be* as a main verb (seven times); first-person pronouns (nine times); hedges (*"a kind of* emporium"); private verbs *(love, see, hear, delight, fancy, please);* and emphatics *(so much, so rich).* But Addison did not limit himself to such oral prose. Like the writers of the eighteenth century taken together, his style ranged widely, from the colloquial to the highly literate. The following discussion of the material world from a 1712 issue of the *Spectator* exemplifies his more literate prose.

Addison Passage (literate)

Though there is a great deal of pleasure in contemplating the material worlds, by which I mean that system of bodies into which nature has so curiously wrought the mass of dead matter, with the several relations which those bodies bear to one another, there is still, methinks, something more wonderful and surprising in contemplations on the world of life, by which I mean all those animals with which every part of the universe is furnished. . . . If we consider those parts of the material world which lie the nearest to us and are, therefore, subject to our observations and inquiries, it is amazing to consider the infinity of animals with which it is stocked. . . . Existence is a blessing to those beings only which are endowed with perception and is, in a manner, thrown away upon dead matter any further than as it is subservient to beings which are conscious of their existence. . . . Infinite Goodness is of so communicative a nature that it seems to delight in the conferring of existence upon every degree of perceptive being.

[Bond, 1965. 4:345–347]

Among the literate features of this passage are its frequent nominalizations and relative clauses. Nominalizations are nouns formed from verbs or adjectives by adding *-tion (relations, contemplations, observations, perception)*, *-ence (existence* three times), *-ing (contemplating, blessing, beings* and *being, conferring)*, and *-ity* and *-ness (infinity* and *Goodness)*. Relative clauses are introduced by relative pronouns, in this instance the nine *which*'s of the passage, including *by which*'s, *with which*'s, and an *into which*.

Thus, alongside the oral norm there was a competing norm, fueled by the neoclassical ideals of influential writers like Swift, Johnson, and Pope. (These neoclassical ideals honored the great writers and writing styles of antiquity.) Quite elitist, these influential figures advocated that written English be divorced from the common idiom and evolve a character of its own. They urged a more elaborate and sophisticated prose, more carefully wrought than conversation could normally be. Thus, two trends are discernible in eighteenth-century prose: one oral and egalitarian, the other literate and aristocratic, removed from the idiom of ordinary speech.

Many eighteenth-century writers honored literate norms and disdained the colloquial. Consider how far from speech is Johnson's discussion of the representation of virtue in fiction in a 1750 issue of the *Rambler*. (Again, ignore the added capitalization and italics for the moment.)

Johnson Passage

That the highest degree of reverence should *BE PAID* TO youth, and that nothing indecent should *BE SUFFERED* to approach their eyes or ears, are precepts extorted BY sense and virtue FROM an ancient writer BY no means eminent FOR chastity OF thought. The same kind, though not the same degree, OF caution, *IS REQUIRED* IN everything which *IS LAID* BEFORE them, to secure them FROM unjust prejudices, perverse opinions, and incongruous combinations OF images. . . .

IN narratives where historical veracity has no place, I cannot discover why there should not *BE EXHIBITED* the most perfect idea OF virtue, OF virtue not angelical, nor ABOVE probability (for what we cannot credit, we shall never imitate), but the highest and purest that humanity can reach, which, exercised IN such trials as the various revolutions OF things shall bring UPON it, may, BY conquering some calamities and enduring others, teach us what we may hope, and what we can perform. Vice (for vice is necessary to *BE SHOWN*) should always disgust; nor should the graces OF gaiety, nor the dignity OF courage, *BE* so *UNITED* WITH it as to reconcile it TO the mind. Wherever it appears, it should raise hatred BY the malignity OF its practices, and contempt BY the meanness OF its strategems: for while it *IS SUPPORTED* BY either parts or spirit, it will *BE* seldom heartily *ABHORRED*.

[Johnson, 1969. 3:21–24]

The complicated syntax of this passage differs from the syntax of speech. As an illustration, note that the first sentence has a compound subject consisting of a pair of clauses that serve as noun phrases: *(that) the highest degree of reverence should be paid to youth* and *(that) nothing indecent should be suffered to approach their eyes or ears.* Note too the frequent passive voice verbs (nine of them) and nominalizations (*reverence, chastity, combinations, probability,* and at least that many again). Further characteristic not of speech but of writing, the first sentence of the second paragraph *(In narratives . . .)* continues for eighty-two words and contains no fewer than ten clauses. That would be a mouthful (as reading it aloud will demonstrate), but it exists for the eyes to read, not for the tongue to utter. It exemplifies a literate style par excellence and was as removed from the everyday acquaintance of most English speakers in Johnson's time as it is today.

Thus, some writers honored the egalitarian ideal of orality and simplicity that had been endorsed in the seventeenth century, whereas others promoted more literate standards (and some did both). These competing ideals produced a wide range of prose styles in the eighteenth century, with Dryden and Johnson writing at opposite extremes. To gauge the differences between them, we can compare the use of four linguistic features in the passages by Dryden and Johnson; capitalization and italics highlight the features. Because the passages differ in length (the one by Dryden on page 107 has 118 words; the one by Johnson on page 109 has 228 words), comparing raw counts of features would be misleading; instead, our frequencies represent the number of instances per 100 words. We examine two features characteristic of oral styles and two characteristic of literate styles (see Table 4.1).

Of course, all four features occur in both passages (they are the tools of expression provided by the grammar of English), but Johnson favors the literate features while Dryden favors the oral features. Johnson has nearly five times as many passive voice verbs as Dryden and one and a half times as many prepositions, whereas Dryden has ten times as many instances of *be* as a main verb and somewhat more first- and second-person pronouns. It is Johnson's frequent use of such literate features that gives his prose a somewhat stiff and unfamiliar feel, whereas Dryden's prose seems more fluid and familiar, more oral and therefore more accessible.

Functionalism and Dimensions of Variation

Among the possible aims of writers and speakers, discourse can be relatively informational, or it can focus more on interaction and personal involvement, and the linguistic features of a text will reflect those differing purposes. Likewise,

Table 4.1. Frequency (per Hundred Words) of Four
Linguistic Features in Prose Passages by Dryden and
Johnson

	Dryden	Johnson
Literate Styles		
Passive verbs	0.8	3.9
Prepositions	8.5	12.7
Oral Styles		
1st/2nd pronouns	2.5	1.8
Be as a main verb	4.2	0.4

some discourse (notably face-to-face conversation) can afford to rely heavily on its immediate context for interpretation, whereas other discourse (particularly certain written varieties) must use elaborate referencing strategies to aid interpretation, and the linguistic features of the discourse will reflect those strategies. Thus, written language varieties and spoken language varieties typically differ from one another in their utilization of linguistic features. The reason is simple enough: Linguistic features serve particular communicative functions. A pronoun, for example, is an efficient way to refer to someone or something only if interlocutors can readily determine who or what it refers to. Unlike the noun phrases *William Shakespeare* and *the author of "Romeo and Juliet,"* both of which can readily be interpreted outside a context of utterance, the pronoun *he* has an untold number of possible references (from Adam to Zeus, so to speak). In the first line of the preceding Dryden passage, readers can understand that *he* refers to Shakespeare only because the noun *Shakespeare* is mentioned just before and no one else has been introduced who could be referenced by the pronoun *he.* Once a referent has been identified by a noun phrase, the pronouns *he, him,* and *himself* (and the determiner *his*) can function efficiently to refer to Shakespeare without repeating his name; so efficient are these pronouns that they occur thirteen times in the Dryden passage. When a pronoun would not be adequate to identify a referent, writers must use more elaborate noun phrase expressions, sometimes including relative clauses ("those wealthy societies of men *that are divided from one another by seas and oceans*"—Addison).

One way to characterize discourse and texts is by their use of features associated with particular contextual dimensions. Of the several situational factors that influence the choice of linguistic features in discourse, we focus on two that are associated with orality and literacy because of the social and linguistic importance of that contrast in the eighteenth and nineteenth centuries. One factor has to do with purpose (whether the discourse is more informational or more personally involved), and the other has to do with strategies of making reference (whether noun phrases are linguistically elaborated and relatively context independent or relatively compressed and therefore reliant on the context of utterance for interpretation). [These situational factors and several others are thoroughly discussed in Biber (1988).]

Because individual linguistic features serve particular functions and because different kinds of discourse have different purposes, functionally related linguistic features tend to co-occur in particular kinds of texts. For example, face-to-face conversation and personal letters typically use high frequencies of features that express personal involvement, whereas scholarly articles have an informational focus and exhibit few features of involvement. The features associated with involvement tend to be more common in oral language; the informational features tend to be more typical of written discourse.

Thus, each situational factor has an associated set of linguistic features. Discourse that is involved (such as personal letters and face-to-face conversation) typically shows frequent use of private verbs *(think, believe), do* and *be* as main verbs, present tense verbs, contractions *(won't, it's),* first- and second-person pronouns, demonstrative pronouns *(this, those),* indefinite pronouns *(any, some),* hedges *(kind of* tall, *sort of* scared), emphatics *(really* tall), and amplifiers *(absolutely* dazzling, *totally* mad), as well as wh-questions (those beginning with *where, when, who,* and *how).* Texts with lots of involved features typically have relatively few instances of the features associated with informational content: nouns, prepositions, attributive adjectives ("an *ancient* writer"), long words, and varied vocabulary.

Reference features are also of two kinds: those marking elaborated reference (typically associated with literate situations) and those marking situated (or situation-dependent) reference (associated with oral situations). Situated texts use lots of linguistic features that rely on the context for interpretation: adverbials of time, such as *now* and *yesterday,* and adverbials of place, such as *here* and *above.* Such features require knowledge of the situation of utterance—of its time and place—for interpretation. On the other hand, a text whose interpretation stands independent of its immediate context achieves that independence by using elaborated referencing strategies. (Contrast *yesterday* with *Tuesday, December 21, 1988; here* with *at the top of the world World Trade Center in New York City; he* with *the Israeli cook in the Chinese restaurant that Prince Charles ate at on New Year's Eve in 1987.)* One important linguistic feature used for making explicit reference is relative clauses, which help specify the referent of a noun and aid in its identification: "narratives *where historical veracity has no place."*[1]

Historical Development of Three English Genres

Figure 4.2 reports the average values for the choice between elaborated and situated kinds of reference for fiction, essays, and letters in the eighteenth and nineteenth centuries, as well as for the periods immediately preceding and following. Figure 4.3 reports the average values for the choice between features reflecting informational and involved purposes.[2] The figures (taken from Biber and Finegan, 1989) represent the average value for a selection of texts in each genre in the seventeenth century, eighteenth century, nineteenth century (to 1865), and modern period (1865 to about 1950). For each factor (i.e., for purpose and for reference), the numerical value assigned to a text is determined by tallying the number of instances of the defining features at one pole (the features listed above the dotted line in Table 4.2) and subtracting the number of instances of the fea-

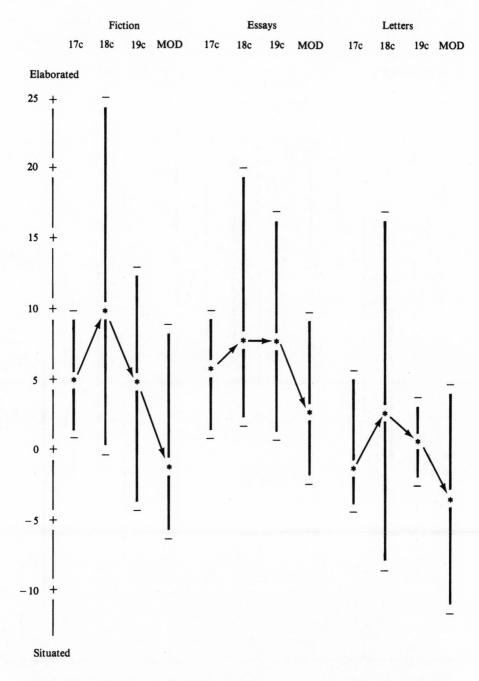

Figure 4.2. Historical development of discourse along the reference dimension for fiction, essays, and letters; an asterisk (∗) marks the average score for each genre (after Biber and Finegan, 1989:508).

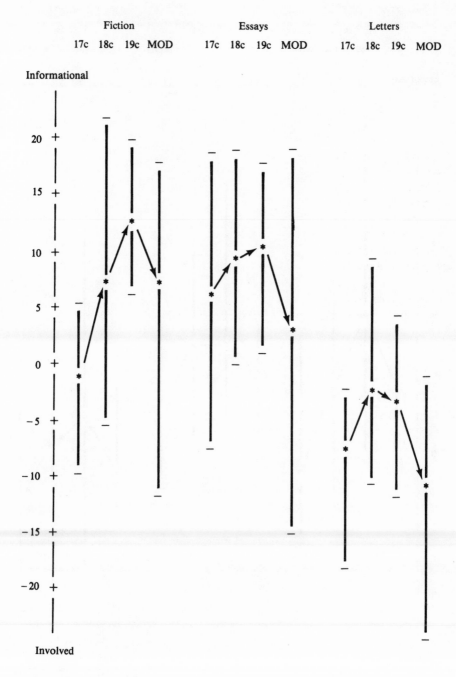

Figure 4.3. Historical development of discourse along the purpose dimension for fiction, essays, and letters; an asterisk (∗) marks the average score for each genre (after Biber and Finegan, 1989:510).

Table 4.2. Linguistic Features Defining Two Situational Dimensions

Purpose Dimension	Reference Dimension
Informational Features	*Elaborated Features*
Nouns	Wh-relative clauses
Word length	Pied-piping constructions
Prepositions	Phrasal coordination
Lexical variety	Nominalizations
Attributive adjectives	
Involved Features	*Situated Features*
Private verbs	Time adverbials
Do, be as main verbs	Place adverbials
Possibility modals	Other adverbs
Present-tense verbs	
That-deletion	
Contractions	
1st, 2nd person pronouns	
Pronoun *it*	
Indefinite pronouns	
Demonstrative pronouns	
Emphatics, hedges, amplifiers	
Sentence relatives	
Wh-questions, wh-clauses	
Nonphrasal coordination	
Sentence-final prepositions	

After Biber (1988).

tures at the other end of the pole (features below the line in Table 4.2). Thus, a text with frequent informational features and few involved features would rank relatively high (toward the informational end) on the purpose dimension; a text with a negative value would be involved and not very informational.[3]

We can trace the historical development of three genres (fiction, essays, and letters) by comparing their average values for each period and the range of variation of texts of each genre within the period. The average value is marked on Figures 4.2 and 4.3 by an asterisk, and the range of values is indicated by the length of the vertical lines. For example, on the reference dimension (see Fig. 4.2), eighteenth-century fiction has an average value of +10 (fairly elaborated), but one text ranks as high as +24.9 (not surprisingly, it is by Samuel Johnson), whereas another ranks as low as 0.4 (it is by Jonathan Swift).

Reference Dimension

Figure 4.2 shows that eighteenth-century fiction uses elaborated kinds of reference more frequently than seventeenth-century fiction and that nineteenth-century and seventeenth-century fiction use situated kinds of reference to about the same degree. Modern fiction is the least elaborated (i.e., the most context dependent). A similar pattern characterizes essays and letters historically. For all three genres, seventeenth-century texts use fewer elaborated reference features than those of the eighteenth century, whereas the nineteenth century and modern periods become progressively more situated. The eighteenth century has the widest range of texts along the reference dimension for all three genres, a range that reflects the competing norms for prose style discussed earlier.

Purpose Dimension

As Figure 4.3 reveals, the overall pattern of historical development is similar along the purpose dimension, except that the nineteenth century and the eighteenth century lean toward more informational purposes in fiction and letters. On this dimension, the modern period shows the greatest range of texts. The essays, for example, range from a high of + 18.9 (a text by Hart Crane) to a low of -14.6 (a text by D. H. Lawrence). Even the American Mark Twain's fiction (which, at − 10.8, is the most involved fiction of any in the four centuries) is not as involved as Lawrence's essay.

At least for these three genres, then, English has been shifting to increasingly oral styles over the past few centuries, as the reading public has grown.[4] But eighteenth-century writing clearly bucks the trend. During that century, under the literate norms advocated by the neo-classical philosophy, fiction, essays, and letters all became more literate than they had been in the preceding century.

With the Romantic movement at the end of the eighteenth century and the early decades of the nineteenth, the norm of orality gained the upper hand again. Emphasizing closeness to nature, writers of the Romantic period endorsed literary norms that were likewise natural, and in the case of language that meant speech. As Wordsworth put it in the 1802 preface to *Lyrical Ballads* (1974:123–125):

> The principal object . . . in these poems was to choose incidents and situations from common life, and to relate or describe them, throughout, as far as was possible, in a selection of language really used by men. . . . Low and rustic life was generally chosen, because in that condition, the essential passions of the heart . . . speak a plainer and more emphatic language. . . . The language . . . of these men is adopted . . . because such men hourly communicate with the best objects from which the best part of language is originally derived; and because . . . they convey their feelings and notions in simple and unelaborated expressions.

In keeping with this Romantic spirit, nineteenth-century literary language hugged the ground; it took form in "simple and unelaborated expression." We can illustrate the "familiar" prose of this period with passages from Hazlitt and Lamb. Here is Hazlitt writing on gusto in a style that is relatively involved but (as is not surprising in writing) moderately elaborated.

Hazlitt Passage

There is a gusto in the coloring of Titian. Not only do his heads seem to think—his bodies seem to feel. This is what the Italians mean by the *morbidezza* of his flesh color. It seems sensitive and alive all over; not merely to have the look and texture of flesh, but the feeling in itself. For example, the limbs of his female figures have a luxurious softness and delicacy, which appears conscious of the pleasure of the beholder.

[1817; cited from Abrams, 1986:440]

Note the use of *be* as a main verb, the use of *it* and *this* as subjects, the present-tense verbs, the predicate adjectives *(sensitive, alive),* and other features characteristic of involvement. With respect to reference, note that there are quite a few examples of the elaborated reference features: one relative clause *(which appears . . .),* several nominalizations *(coloring, feeling, softness, delicacy).*

As another example of the "familiar" style that characterized many nineteenth-century essays, we cite Lamb writing on old china:

Lamb Passage

I have an almost feminine partiality for old china. When I go to see any great house, I inquire for the china closet, and next for the picture gallery. I cannot defend the order of preference, but by saying that we have all some taste or other, of too ancient a date to admit of our remembering distinctly that it was an acquired one. I can call to mind the first play, and the first exhibition, that I was taken to; but I am not conscious of a time when china jars and saucers were introduced into my imagination.

[1823; cited from Abrams, 1986:433]

Very striking in this passage is Lamb's frequent use of first-person pronouns and present-tense verbs, which both reflect and create its involved character. The passage is largely devoid of features marking situated reference and exhibits only a few features of elaboration.

In the historical patterns we have examined, Victorian prose is included with the Modern period (whose texts date from 1865 in this study). It is clear from Figures 4.2 and 4.3 that Victorian and modern prose has increasingly honored oral norms. The trends advocated by members of the Royal Society in the late seventeenth century have continued strong into the twentieth century, renewed by the oral ideals of the Romantic movement. Only the explicitly literate norms espoused by certain elitist writers of the eighteenth century gave the development of oral prose styles any pause at all, but the drive toward an accessible, familiar, colloquial, egalitarian style of written prose has proven strong. As the middle classes continued to grow and become more literate, the size of the potential reading audience increased, and writers wanting to make their work widely available aimed for an accessible style. Of course, in arenas where little motivation existed for accessibility, writing remained distinctly literate. One striking example is modern legalese. The arcane and inaccessible character of the prose used by the legal profession is often impossible for the uninitiated to grasp; it is as far from oral norms as prose can be.

STANDARDIZATION AND LANGUAGE ATTITUDES

In the preceding section, we noted a wide range of colloquial and literate prose styles, although all our passages are written in the English that is recorded in dictionaries and grammars, that is, the English that is called "standard." Thus, even in formal writing there are many styles of Standard English. Standard English is not invariant; it differs from situation to situation.

If some people today seem inclined to believe that standard languages have sprung full-blown from a garden of Eden and that nonstandard varieties are flawed spin-offs from them, the facts are otherwise—for English and for every other standard language. Generally, the standard variety of a language is only a regional variety (typically of the capital or other commercial or cultural center) that has been made suitable for the range of functions that a standard language has to carry out. Whereas local varieties serve local needs, particularly in speech, a standard variety must serve supra-local needs, particularly in writing. Technological, scientific, medical, and legal matters (to mention just a few) must be conducted and recorded in a variety that can be used and understood across local boundaries; such a variety requires reference tools such as dictionaries to define vocabulary and grammars to describe sentence patterns.

Three aspects that have been identified in the process of standardizing a language concern us here: (1) selection of a variety to be standardized; (2) elaboration of its functions and features; (3) codification (Haugen, 1966). The process of standardization can take centuries and never really ceases for a living language. In the case of English, the dialect used in and around London and the university towns of Oxford and Cambridge emerged around 1500 as the variety that would be standardized. Its selection was less a conscious choice than a historical accident. The royal court and the printing presses were in London, and the great centers of learning were not far away. As is typical for a young standard, the dialect of London needed to be developed and elaborated. For one thing, it lacked sufficient vocabulary for all the arenas of discourse that a standard language must serve. To remedy this weakness, English vocabulary expanded greatly in the sixteenth and seventeenth centuries as the vernacular replaced Latin for use in learned and technical fields from medicine to mathematics and from physics to philosophy. Simply by adapting familiar Latin words to English contexts over the course of the sixteenth and seventeenth centuries, writers added something in the neighborhood of 12,000 Latin words to English (Baugh and Cable, 1978).

Of course, the workaday English of daily interactions was always adequate, and the literary language had been vital at least since the time of Chaucer (who died in 1400). But in the course of the sixteenth and seventeenth centuries English came gradually to be used in nearly all learned and professional arenas where Latin had been used previously. As late as the early eighteenth century, Isaac Newton, a prolific writer on subjects as diverse as cosmology, astronomy, theology, and celestial mechanics, still wrote sometimes in Latin. The famed *Principia Mathematica* of 1687 and the *Arithmetica Universalis* of 1707 are in the classical language, though his *Opticks* of 1704 is written in English. Even English grammar books, of which there were not yet many in the seventeenth century, were sometimes written in Latin: John Wallis published one in 1653, and Christopher Cooper published another in 1685, both under the title *Grammatica Linguae Anglicanae.* At Oxford some instructors lectured in Latin, and elsewhere dissertations continued to be written in Latin for more than a century after that. (Some university seals and diplomas are still written partly in Latin.)

With its extensive expansion, Standard English had become robust and vigorous, so much so that early in the eighteenth century a reaction set in. Under the spell of neo-classical ideals, many in eighteenth-century England judged their own language to be unregulated and unrefined, in comparison not only with the classical tongues but also with certain languages of Europe that had academies to regulate them. Dryden described English as "extremely imperfect," and Johnson found it "copious without order" and "energetick without rules"; it needed to be settled and given stability. There was genuine fear that if the language continued to change at the fast pace of the preceding centuries, subsequent generations of English speakers would be unable to read materials composed in the eighteenth century. Writers fretted over dialect variation, abbreviations, contractions, words borrowed from foreign tongues, and inconsistent use of many structures, such as *shall* and *will, who* and *whom,* sentence-final prepositions, and double negatives.

Striking variation in local pronunciation could certainly be found throughout Britain. The complex history of settlement and limited mobility had established an abundance of local dialects. To gauge the extent to which dialect differences troubled some prominent figures, consider Daniel Defoe's report of a visit to Somerset (about 150 miles southwest of London) in the first quarter of the eighteenth century.

> When we are come this Length from London, the Dialect of the English Tongue, or the Country-way of expressing themselves, is not easily understood. It is the same in many Parts of England besides, but in none in so gross a Degree as in this Part. As this Way of boorish Speech is in Ireland called, *"The Brogue upon the Tongue,"* so here it is named *Jouring.* It is not possible to explain this fully by Writing, because the Difference is not so much in the Orthography, as in the Tone and Accent; their abridging the Speech, *Cham,* for *I am; Chil,* for *I will; Don,* for *do on,* or *put on;* and *Doff,* for *do off,* or *put off;* and the like. [Continuing, Defoe tells of a pupil reading aloud from the Bible.] I sat down by the Master, till the Boy had read it out, and observed the Boy read a little oddly in the tone of the Country, which made me the more attentive; because, on Inquiry, I found that the Words were the same, and the Orthography the same, as in all our Bibles. I observed also the Boy read it out with his Eyes still on the Book, and his Head, like a mere Boy, moving from Side to Side, as the Lines reached cross the Columns of the book: His Lesson was in the *Canticles of Solomon;* the Words these;
>
> 'I have put off my Coat; how shall I put it on? I have washed my Feet; how shall I defile them?' The Boy read thus, with his Eyes, as I say, full on the Text: 'Chav a doffed my Coot; how shall I don't? Chav a washed my Feet; how shall I moil 'em?'
>
> How the dexterous Dunce could form his Mouth to express so readily the Words (which stood right printed in the Book) in his Country Jargon, I could not but admire.
> [1724–1727; cited from Tucker, 1961:61–62]

Defoe was astonished (as "admiration" implies here) that the boy read aloud in "country jargon" that might be written differently from the standard spelling of the Bible. He seems not to have understood that spellings must be relatively independent of local pronunciations if they are to function as a standard across different dialects. If, on the other hand, spelling *and* pronunciation are to be uniform, either people of different regions must bring their pronunciation into harmony with standardized spellings or spelling must vary from place to place to reflect local pronunciations. The latter clearly will not work because different spellings would prevent the uniformity that motivates a standard orthography in the first place. (Even if a dictionary noted different spellings, which region's spelling would be alphabetized as the entry? And which spellings would be used in newspapers, and for laws, tax records, and information on how to use medicines? If each region had a dictionary of its own, there would be as many standard varieties as regions, and that is the same as no standard at all.[5])

Besides dialect variation, writers in the eighteenth century were exercised by clipped and shortened forms of words, including spoken contractions like *'tis* and orthographic contractions like *wou'd* and *compos'd*. Swift, for one, was also distressed at the use of such "manglings and abbreviations" as *incog* (for *incognito*), *rep (reputation), pozz (possible), bam (bamboozle), plenipo (plenipotentiary)*, and *mob*. Only *mob* survives, and few know that it is an abbreviation of *mobile vulgus*.

Still another sore spot was the importation of foreign words. Though they were quite the fashion and English speakers had been using them for centuries, many in the eighteenth and nineteenth centuries regarded foreign borrowings as "barbarous." Given the widespread knowledge of French among the upper classes, the number of French words used in eighteenth-century Britain was considerable, and many found them irksome. Dryden disapproved of those "who corrupt our English idiom by mixing it too much with French" (cited in Baugh and Cable, 1978:287), and Addison suggested an academy to guard against foreign words when he wrote in the *Spectator* (1711):

> I have often wished, that . . . certain Men might be set apart, as Superintendants of our Language, to hinder any Words of a Foreign Coin from passing among us; and in particular to prohibit any *French* Phrases from becoming Current in this Kingdom, when those of our own Stamp are altogether as valuable.
>
> [Bond, 1965. 2:149]

Even Sam Johnson, though personally opposed to an academy, conceded that one useful task would be "to stop the license of translatours, whose idleness and ignorance, if it be suffered to proceed, will reduce us to babble a dialect of France" ("Preface" to the *Dictionary*, 1755).

Academies and Codifiers

In 1700, English still lacked substantial codification, as Britons recognized when they called for an academy to regulate their language, as the academies of France and Italy regulated their tongues. The *Dictionnaire de l'Académie française* had been published in 1694, and some of the learned in Britain believed that English needed equal care. In 1697, Defoe proposed a society whose work "shou'd be to encourage Polite Learning, to polish and refine the *English* Tongue, and advance the so much neglected Faculty of Correct Language, to establish Purity and Propriety of Stile, and to purge it from all the Irregular Additions that Ignorance and Affectation have introduc'd." Fifteen years later, Swift called for an academy in his *Proposal for Correcting, Improving and Ascertaining the English Tongue,* addressed to the Lord High Treasurer of Great Britain (1712):

> My LORD; I do here, in the Name of all the Learned and Polite Persons of the Nation, complain to Your LORDSHIP as *First Minister,* that our Language is extremely imperfect; that its daily Improvements are by no means in proportion to its daily Corruptions; that the Pretenders to polish and refine it, have chiefly multiplied Abuses and Absurdities; and, that in many Instances, it offends against every Part of Grammar. . . . BUT what I have most at Heart is, that some Method should be thought on for *ascertaining* and *fixing* our Language for ever, after such Alterations are made in it as shall be thought requisite. For I am of Opinion, that it is better a Language should not be wholly perfect, than that it should be perpetually changing. . . .
>
> [Bolton, 1966:108–117]

Despite such calls, Britain never established a language academy, and the codification of the language fell to entrepreneurs. They undertook to codify the language in dictionaries and grammars as best they could, given their own information and predilections. Most notable among the codifiers was Samuel Johnson, whose *Dictionary of the English Language* appeared in 1755 (nearly seventy-five years before Noah Webster's big American dictionary of 1828—the one Americans ultimately refer to when they say "Look it up in Webster's!"). The British recognized that in Johnson they had better than an academy, for his dictionary was perceived from the first as superior to the one published by the French academy. Seven years after the British got their dictionary, they found the grammar they wanted in Robert Lowth's *Short Introduction to English Grammar.*

Thus, although most eighteenth-century observers agreed that the English language needed settling, or "ascertaining," it was left to individuals to accomplish it—to decide among competing usages which was right and to codify those preferences in reference books. In a frequently quoted passage from the preface to his dictionary, Dr. Johnson reflects the sense of many eighteenth-century grammarians:

> When I took the first survey of my undertaking, I found our speech copious without order, and energetick without rules: wherever I turned my view, there was perplexity to be disentangled, and confusion to be regulated; choice was to be made out of boundless variety, without any established principle of selection; adulterations were to be detected, without a settled test of purity; and modes of expression to be rejected or received, without the suffrages of any writers of classical reputation or acknowledged authority.

In the circumstances, the tasks of disentangling perplexity and regulating confusion fell to amateurs, gifted ones in some instances, and these middle-class men (they were largely middle class and almost exclusively male[6]) aimed to teach a nation and its colonies how English should be used. They first had to settle questions of divided usage, to sort out confusion, and to prescribe the forms of English they thought should prevail. "Adulterations were to be detected," Johnson said, and "modes of expression . . . rejected or received." The task was made difficult, as he noted, by the absence of an accepted canon of work by "writers of classical reputation or acknowledged authority." During the two centuries in which the codification of English was substantially completed, knowledge increased about language in general and English in particular. Linguistic science was born at the end of the eighteenth century with recognition that most languages of Europe and India had descended from a common ancestor, and it matured in the nineteenth century as our knowledge of linguistic change developed.

Among the most gifted codifiers was Samuel Johnson, who in 1747 announced his intention to compile a dictionary and about eight years later published the completed work in two large volumes. The earliest dictionaries had been short lists of hard words, among which Robert Cawdrey's *Table Alphabeticall of Hard Words* (1604) glosses unfamiliar Latin words being used in English. In 1721 Nathaniel Bailey made an attempt to list all the words of the language in his *Universal Etymological English Dictionary.* Johnson, as an exponent of conservative neo-classical values, had originally hoped his dictionary could impede linguistic change, but the experienced dictionary maker of 1755 knew better, as he acknowledges in his preface:

> When we see men grow old and die at a certain time one after another, from century to century, we laugh at the elixir that promises to prolong life to a thousand years; and with equal justice may the lexicographer be derided, who being able to produce no example of a nation that has preserved their words and phrases from mutability, shall imagine that his dictionary can embalm his language, and secure it from corruption and decay, that it is in his power to change sublunary nature, or clear the world at once from folly, vanity, and affectation.

Although the dictionary is well known for a few idiosyncratic definitions (Oats: "A grain, which in England is generally given to horses, but in Scotland supports the people"; Lexicographer: "A writer of dictionaries; a harmless drudge"), Johnson's reputation as a lexicographer rests upon the bulk of his definitions, which are serious and sophisticated. He defined a *span* as "the space from the end of the thumb to the end of the little finger extended"; a *sot* as a "blockhead; a dull ignorant stupid fellow; a dolt" and as "a wretch stupified by drinking"; a *zealot,* he wrote, is "one passionately ardent in any cause." As one recent commentator summed it up: "By the force of his reason, his wide reading and the excellent memory with which he put it to use, and his masterly command of the art of lucid expression, Johnson fashioned a work that engendered such respect that for well over a century it was without peer as the most authoritative dictionary in English" (Landau, 1989:56). A reference in the *London Chronicle* demonstrates that Johnson provided Britain a substitute academy: "he hath supplied the Want of an Academy of Belles Lettres, and performed Wonders towards fixing our Grammar, and ascertaining the determinate Meaning of Words, which are known to be in their own Nature of a very unstable and fluctuating Quality. To his Labours it may hereafter be owing that our Drydens, our Addisons, and our Popes shall not become as obsolete and unintelligible as Chaucer" (1757; cited from Sledd and Kolb, 1955:150).

In 1857, little more than a century after Johnson's dictionary appeared, the Philological Society in London appointed a committee to prepare a dictionary of words not treated elsewhere. The committee reported that a completely new dictionary was needed, thus launching the *Oxford English Dictionary*. Following Johnson's lead in citing the actual usages of writers for definitions, the first installment of the letter *A* was published in 1884, and the letter *Z* appeared in 1928. Published in ten large volumes, the "OED" is based on more than 5 million excerpts from English literature, and the dictionary itself contains about 1.8 million of these quotations in illustration of meaning and usage. Hundreds of volunteers read thousands of books to determine which words to include and what their definitions were (the list of books runs to eighty-nine pages of three columns each). But whereas Johnson had started and finished his dictionary almost single-handedly in about nine years, the *OED* took nearly seventy-five years from conception to completion, sticking to its plan of recording every word used in English literature since the year 1000 and of providing a historical treatment of each word. This was an undertaking of mammoth proportions, and it is not surprising that the time required to complete the work was consistently underestimated.

The product of the best contemporary linguistic scholarship, the *OED* is also a reflection of the social mores of its times. For example, middle-class Victorians commonly used euphemisms to refer to certain body parts and undergarments: even pants were called *pantaloons* because the word *pants* was thought too risqué. The *OED* defines *pants* as "a vulgar abbreviation of *Pantaloons* (chiefly U.S.)" and as "colloquial and 'shoppy' for 'drawers'." To press the negative point home, the first quotation is from an American, the distinguished jurist Oliver Wendell Holmes: "The thing named 'pants' in certain documents, A thing not made for gentlemen but 'gents'."

The *OED* was dedicated to Queen Victoria (who reigned from 1832 to 1901), and it is unmistakably a product of Victorian Britain. For example, it omits all the four-letter "Anglo-Saxon" words (although they had been listed in some eighteenth-century dictionaries[7]). The extent to which this great lexicographical achievement suffered the confines of Victorian mores is further illustrated by its failure to record not only words but even senses of words that its editors thought tainted. For example, the entry for *to die* runs to many columns, but readers will be unable to learn from the *OED* that Shakespeare sometimes used the verb in the sense of "to have an orgasm." For that (and for the citations), readers must turn to Eric Partridge's *Shakespeare's Bawdy* or other specialized works. Despite such characteristic shortcomings, the *OED* is the single most important landmark in the codification and standardization of English. [For more on Victorian linguistic practices, see Phillipps (1984).]

Grammar

What Johnson's dictionary did for the codification of vocabulary and orthography in the eighteenth century, Robert Lowth's *Short Introduction to English*

Grammar (1762) did for sentence structure and the parts of speech. Like many of his contemporaries, Lowth regarded English as inadequately regulated. Taking up Swift's claim that "in many instances [English] offends against every part of grammar," he asked: "Does it mean, that the *English* language as it is spoken by the politest part of the nation, and as it stands in the writings of our most approved authors, oftentimes offends against every part of Grammar?" Yes, he replied: "the charge is true." But English is not "in its nature irregular and capricious. . . . It is not the Language, but the practice, that is in fault. The truth is, Grammar is very much neglected among us" (1762:ii–vi). To write and speak well, Lowth believed that the systematic study of grammar was necessary. "Much practice in the polite world, and a general acquaintance with the best authors, are good helps, but alone will hardly be sufficient. . . . our best Authors for want of some rudiments of grammar have sometimes fallen into mistakes, and been guilty of palpable errors in point of Grammar." Defining grammar as "the Art of rightly expressing our thoughts by Words," Lowth offers sections on letters, syllables, words, and sentences, building from the smaller units of (written) language to the larger ones. The purpose of a grammar, then, is "to teach us to express ourselves with propriety . . ., and to be able to judge of every phrase and form of construction, whether it be right or not. The plain way of doing this, is to lay down rules, and to illustrate them by examples. But besides shewing what is right, the matter may be further explained by pointing out what is wrong" (1762:x).

In his discussion of what modern grammarians call "pied-piping" ("the keys *with which* she opened the door"), which is the alternative to ending a sentence with a preposition, Lowth points out that the preposition is sometimes separated from the relative pronoun as in "Horace is an author, *whom* I am much delighted *with.*" He says:

> This is an Idiom which our language is strongly inclined to; it prevails in common conversation, and suits very well with the familiar style in writing; but the placing of the Preposition before the Relative is more graceful, as well as more perspicuous; and agrees much better with the solemn and elevated style.

If Lowth is sensitive to what suits the conversational style and recognizes that written language can differ from spoken language, he nevertheless discounts the colloquial style, finding the pied-piping "graceful" in itself and more suitable to the "solemn and elevated style." Recall that the Addison passage (on pages 108–109) had an abundance of these "graceful" and "perspicuous" *with which*'s and *by which*'s. The influence of Johnson and of the other proponents of a distinct literate style is discernible in Lowth, as in most grammarians of the eighteenth and nineteenth centuries. In his analysis Lowth privileges a style of writing that is distinct from speech, and in his work we can see the roots of a preference for aristocratic rather than egalitarian standards in English grammars. (We should also note that Lowth's own writing style does not follow his own recommendations; in the very sentence in which he says, "This is an idiom *which* our language is strongly inclined *to,*" he uses the colloquial idiom himself, not the pied-piping he is recommending in the passage.)

Lowth's views of language were admittedly influenced by conservative writers like Swift and Johnson. Indeed, the shape of grammatical discussion during the next two centuries reflected the popular discussions of the early and mid-eighteenth century, especially as they were incorporated into grammar books like Lowth's. His was the most important grammar of the period, casting a shadow over virtually every British and American school grammar in its wake. Thanks to the currency its imitators achieved, English speakers today remain concerned about the use of *shall* and *will*,[8] *lie* and *lay, who* and *whom,* and double negatives. Lowth laid down careful rules for such competing forms and prohibited the use of double negatives (see Finegan, 1980; Leonard, 1962; McIntosh, 1986). More important than these particular points of usage is the fact that Lowth's discussion incorporates notions that have become part of the fabric of discussion of grammatical analysis and criticism today (see Crowley, 1989; Leith, 1983). Notions like "false grammar," "right" and "wrong," "mistakes," and "errors" permeated the discourse of English grammar in the eighteenth century and structured the terms of that discussion in ways that have lasted to the present day. Even in the twentieth century it has been impossible for linguists to alter the terms of the discussion from absolutes (*right* or *wrong*) and morality *(guilty)* and refinement (*propriety* and *the polite world*) to relative terms such as *appropriate* and *suitable.*

Lowth's views were popularized most by an American named Lindley Murray, who retired from his Philadelphia law practice and moved to England. There, at the invitation of the head of a local girls' school, he wrote an enormously popular grammar that reached 300 editions on both sides of the Atlantic and sold more than 2 million copies. Not an original thinker, Murray did little more than compile what he read in other grammars, but so much had been accomplished in codification by 1795 that he could say, "little can be expected from a new compilation, besides a careful selection of the most useful matter, and some degree of improvement in the mode of adapting it to the understanding, and the gradual progress of learners" (1795:iii).

Murray's grammar discusses orthography (on letters and spelling), etymology (on the parts of speech), syntax (on the structure of phrases and sentences), prosody (including pronunciation), punctuation, and "rules and observations for promoting perspicuity and accuracy in writing." Much can be imagined of the contents of the book from the opening line, which defines English grammar as "the art of speaking and writing the English language with propriety." For eighteenth-century grammarians, propriety included what was proper and correct, "conformity with good manners, or polite usage; correctness of behavior and morals," according to the *OED.*

One striking feature of many eighteenth- and nineteenth-century grammars is the connection their authors made between grammatical correctness and moral rectitude. For many of them, it is clear, grammatical correctness (not cleanliness, as the proverb would have it) stood next to godliness. In a concluding word addressed to pupils, Murray reveals that as author he was influenced "by a desire to facilitate your progress in learning, and . . . to impress on your minds principles of piety and virtue. He wished also to assist, in some degree, the labours of those who are cultivating your understandings; and providing for you a fund of rational and useful employment, in place of those frivolous pursuits, and that love of ease and sensual pleasure, which enfeeble and corrupt the minds of many inconsiderate youth, and render them useless to society" (1805:327).

At the beginning of the third quarter of the eighteenth century, George Campbell, the most distinguished rhetorician of his age, drew a distinction between grammarians and "verbal critics." He proposed that grammarians should no more comment on desired improvements in the language than the writer of a legal digest could incorporate desired alterations to the law. Only the verbal critic could suggest improvements on any basis, and Campbell provided nine maxims for criticizing language. He rebuked Swift, Johnson, and Lowth for mixing verbal criticism and grammatical analysis, especially for offering criticism in the guise of description. Thus, Campbell was a supporter, in principle, of "the tribunal of use" as arbiter of correctness. "It is not the business of grammar, as some critics seem preposterously to imagine, to give law to the fashions which regulate our speech"; rather, "use, or the custom of speaking, is the sole original standard of conversation . . . and the custom of writing is the sole standard of style. . . . to the tribunal of use, as to the supreme authority . . . we are entitled to appeal from the laws and the decisions of grammarians" (1963:139,141).

Only one eighteenth-century grammarian came close to meeting the ideal set out by Campbell. Joseph Priestley, known today as the discoverer of oxygen, published a grammar that succeeded remarkably well in describing contemporary English. He supported the descriptivist position that grammars should codify what speakers and writers say and write rather than prescribing what they should speak and write. He thought it "absurd" in living languages "to pretend to set up the compositions of any persons whatsoever as the standard of writing, or their conversation as the invariable rule of speaking."

His *Rudiments of English Grammar* (1761) was "a collection of observations" and "a system of rules for the proper use" of English, as he put it. If the prescriptive spirit shows through in the term *proper use,* the descriptive spirit is highlighted in the word *observations.* Priestley recognized the inherent variability of language and observed that "were the language of men as uniform as the works of nature, the *grammar of language* would be as indisputable in its principles as the *grammar of nature.*" Like the verbal critics, he had his favorite expressions ("I have seldom scrupled to say which . . . I prefer") but, he said, "this is to be understood as nothing more than a conjecture, which time must confirm or refute." Thus, besides being a descriptive codifier, Priestley indicated in some instances the direction he wished the refinement of the language to take. His view that the "best forms of speech will, in time, establish themselves by their own superior excellence" was not characteristic of the period and did not prevail, partly because a month after the *Rudiments* appeared, it was overshadowed by Lowth's *Short Introduction,* whose blend of description and prescription proved more appealing to the linguistically insecure readership of its own time and the two centuries afterward.

Dialect Suppression and Language Death

In discussing the standardization of English, I have mentioned both positive and negative consequences. We saw that a standard variety would be capable of use in many situations and that it could be used in writing by people throughout the English-speaking world regardless of local dialects. On the other hand, we saw that some codifiers ignorantly or perversely linked English usage with morality and that the norms imposed through codification were sometimes the arbitrary preferences of individual codifiers and were generally the preferences of members of a single social class determined to homogenize the language.

A further cluster of negative consequences ought to be mentioned, for great harm befell other dialects of English and other languages of Britain as a result of the successful program of standardization. Partly as a result of the expansion of the standard variety into the mass media, as well as in the professional discourse of law, medicine, and science, the Celtic languages of Britain grew weaker, and two of them died out completely. Cornish, which had been spoken in Cornwall, in the southwest of England, died toward the end of the eighteenth century with the death, as tradition has it, of Dolly Pentreath in 1777 (Thomas, 1984:278). Manx, which was spoken on the Isle of Man, can be said to have died on 27 December 1974 with the death of its last native speaker (Thomson, 1984:257). Though there are groups today speaking Manx and Cornish as second languages and attempting to revive them, their future is uncertain. In addition, the vitality of the other Celtic tongues spoken in the British Isles since before English was introduced is precarious, though there are sizable numbers of Irish speakers [perhaps three quarters of a million, according to Thomson (1984:257), of whom only 30,000 to 35,000 are native speakers], Scots Gaelic speakers [almost 80,000 in 1981, according to Clement (1984:318)], and Welsh speakers [almost half a million in 1971, according to Thomson (1984:257)]. The territories of the Celtic tongues are shrinking, and the number of monolingual speakers is small; most speakers are bilingual in a Celtic tongue and English. Welsh, Irish, and Scots Gaelic have been yielding ground to English. Of course, local newspapers and even local radio broadcasting can be maintained in local dialects or regional languages, but it is an uphill battle against the encroachments of a financially and socially powerful standardized language, which has sole control in so many domains of discourse.

Not only are other languages threatened by the standardization and spread of one variety throughout a country, but local dialects of the same language are also diminished—sometimes by simple neglect and sometimes by active disdain or hostility, as in the case of Defoe's visit to Somersetshire. Indeed, there seems to be an unfounded tendency to regard dialects that have not been standardized as being inherently faulty. It is important, especially for speakers of standard varieties, to recognize that the accidents of birth have given them a certain social and economic advantage over other speakers, who must learn the standard variety in addition to their own. A parallel advantage falls to those whose socioeconomic status puts their speech closest to the standard variety. In particular, since the codifiers of English were members of the middle class, middle-class forms naturally predominate. As students arrive at school speaking particular social-class varieties, those who fortuitously speak a variety close to the one written in school texts and spoken by teachers enjoy an immense advantage over students of the working class and other less privileged groups.

To the extent that it is used in writing in the schools and throughout the life of a nation, at least a "passive" knowledge of the standard variety is necessary to achieve literacy. Still, the disadvantage that students of lower socioeconomic status suffer because they do not speak the standard variety could be minimized by encouraging respect for local dialects in schools and by allowing their use in speech on a par with standard dialects. It is no less indecent today to disparage local dialects than it was for Defoe to disparage the native tongue of the Somerset boy, and it is worth noting that to read as that boy read was to demonstrate that he understood the meaning of what he read and could pronounce it as his own. More generally, the emphasis in schools should be on written language, where a standard is especially useful.

NOTES

1. Abstractness is a third situational factor associated with orality and literacy, but it will not be discussed here because of lack of space. Passive-voice verbs and certain other features that we have identified as characteristic of literate style mark abstractness.

2. The texts are both British and American, but the overall patterns for British texts alone are not likely to differ significantly.

3. The frequency numbers are standardized such that a value of zero would indicate that a text has precisely average values for mid-twentieth-century texts in its exploitation of the defining features of that situation factor; see Biber (1988) for details.

4. The same patterns characterize fictional and dramatic dialogue. On average, these speech-based genres are more situated than the three written genres we have examined, and the ranges of variation are narrower. Likewise, these kinds of dialogue move from slightly to highly involved over time, except that dramatic dialogue is more informational in the eighteenth century than in the seventeenth or nineteenth centuries.

5. Although orthography sometimes influences speech (as in the spelling pronunciations of *palm* with *l* and *often* with *t*), spelling cannot fix pronunciation, because speech is inherently variable. Fast speech does not sound like slow speech, and formal speech differs from informal speech. (Compare *Did you eat yet?* with "J'eat yet?" or *swimming* with "swimmin'"). Further, the same lexical item often has different pronunciations in different words. Consider *music* in *musical* ("muzakal") and *musician* ("muzishan"); contrast *senator* ("senader") and *senatorial* ("senatorial") or *restore* ("reestor") and *restoration* ("resderayshan"). Only with a very few words whose singular pronunciation ends in *f* does spelling change to reflect such variation, as in *life/lives.* But for the great bulk of English lexical items, there is a uniform spelling, and it facilitates reading.

An interesting comparison with English exists in Chinese, some of whose spoken dialects are mutually unintelligible. Still, the nearly total independence of the meaning and pronunciation of written characters makes it possible to read and understand the same Chinese-language newspaper no matter which dialect the readers speak.

6. Though published anonymously, at least one eighteenth-century grammar was written by a woman. According to R. C. Alston, in his facsimile reprint of her *A New Grammar*

(1750), Ann Fisher produced a number of elementary books for teaching English. At least thirty-five editions of the *New Grammar* appeared by the year 1800. Alston indicates that Fisher's grammar, though generally conventional, is responsible for introducing a practice that was subsequently followed in many grammars, namely, providing examples of "Bad English," as Latin grammars commonly provided examples of "false syntax."

7. Landau (1989:47) reports that Nathaniel Bailey had entered *shite* in his 1721 dictionary, giving as its definition "to ease Nature, to discharge the Belly"; he also listed *fuck*, though he defined it only in Latin: "Foeminam subagitare."

8. "*Will* in the first Person singular and plural promises or threatens; in the second and third Persons only foretells: *shall* on the contrary, in the first Person simply foretells; in the second and third Persons commands or threatens" (Lowth, 1762:58–59).

ACKNOWLEDGMENT

I am grateful for comments by Dwight Atkinson and Douglas Biber.

WORKS CITED

Aarsleff, Hans. 1983. *The Study of Language in England, 1780–1860.* Minneapolis: University of Minnesota Press [1967].

Abrams, M. H., ed. 1986. *The Norton Anthology of English Literature,* 5th ed., Vol. 2. New York: Norton.

Biber, Douglas. 1988. *Variation Across Speech and Writing.* Cambridge, England: Cambridge University Press.

_____, and Edward Finegan. 1989. "Drift and the Evolution of English Style: A History of Three Genres." *Language* 65:487–517.

Baugh, Albert C., and Thomas Cable. 1978. *A History of the English Language,* 3rd ed. Englewood Cliffs, NJ: Prentice-Hall.

Bolton, W. F., ed. 1966. *The English Language: Essays by English and American Men of Letters 1490–1839.* Cambridge, England: Cambridge University Press.

Bond, Donald F. 1965. *The Spectator.* 5 vols. Oxford: Clarendon.

Campbell, George. 1963. *The Philosophy of Rhetoric.* Ed. Lloyd F. Bitzer. Carbondale: Southern Illinois Press [1776].

Clement, R. D. 1984. "Gaelic." In Peter Trudgill, ed., *Language in the British Isles.* Cambridge, England: Cambridge University Press. Pp. 318–342.

Cressy, David. 1980. *Literacy and the Social Order: Reading and Writing in Tudor and Stuart England.* Cambridge, England: Cambridge University Press.

Crowley, Tony. 1989. *Standard English and the Politics of Language.* Urbana: University of Illinois Press.

Finegan, Edward. 1980. *Attitudes Toward English Usage: The History of a War of Words.* New York: Teachers College Press, Columbia University.

Fisher, Ann. 1750. *A New Grammar.* Ed. R. C. Alston. Menston, England: Scolar. 1968.

Haugen, Einar. 1966. "Dialect, Language, Nation." *American Anthropologist* 68:922–935. Reprinted in Pride and Holmes.

Johnson, Samuel. 1747. *The Plan of a Dictionary of the English Language; Addressed to the Right Honourable Philip Dormer, Earl of Chesterfield.* London. Reprint. Menston, England: Scolar Press, 1970.

_____. 1755. *A Dictionary of the English Language.* 2 vols. London.

_____. 1969. *The Rambler.* In W. J. Bate and Albrecht B. Streuse, eds., *The Yale Edition of the Works of Samuel Johnson.* New Haven: Yale University Press.

Landau, Sidney I. 1989. *Dictionaries: The Art and Craft of Lexicography.* Cambridge, England: Cambridge University Press. [1984].

Leith, Dick, 1983. *A Social History of English.* London: Routledge & Kegan Paul.

Leonard, Sterling Andrus. 1962. *The Doctrine of Correctness in English Usage 1700–1800.* New York: Russell & Russell. [1929].

Lowth, Robert. 1762. *A Short Introduction to English Grammar.* London.

McIntosh, Carey, 1986. *Common and Courtly Language: The Stylistics of Social Class in 18th-Century British Literature.* Philadelphia: University of Pennsylvania Press.

Monk, Samuel Holt, et al., eds. 1971. *The Works of John Dryden.* Vol. 17. Berkeley: University of California Press.

Murray, Lindley. 1795. *English Grammar.* Reprint. Menston, England: Scolar Press, 1968.

———. 1805. *English Grammar, Adapted to the Different Classes of Learners,* 12th ed. York.

Partridge, Eric. 1969. *Shakespeare's Bawdy,* rev. ed. New York: Dutton.

Phillipps, K. C. 1984. *Language and Class in Victorian England.* Oxford, England: Basil Blackwell.

Pride, J. B. and Janet Holmes, eds. 1972. *Sociolinguistics: Selected Readings.* Harmondsworth, England: Penguin.

Sledd, James H., and Gwin J. Kolb. 1955. *Dr. Johnson's Dictionary: Essays in the Biography of a Book.* Chicago: University of Chicago Press.

Thomas, Alan R. 1984. "Cornish." In Peter Trudgill, ed., *Language in the British Isles.* Cambridge, England: Cambridge University Press. Pp. 278–288.

Thomson, R. L. 1984. "The History of the Celtic Languages in the British Isles." In Peter Trudgill, ed., *Language in the British Isles.* Cambridge, England: Cambridge University Press. Pp. 241–258.

Tucker, Susie I. 1961. *English Examined.* Cambridge, England: Cambridge University Press.

Wordsworth, William. 1974. *The Prose Works of William Wordsworth.* Ed. W.J.B. Owen and Jane Worthington Smyser. Vol. 1. Oxford: Clarendon.

5

The Mayflower to the Model-T: The Development of American English

CRAIG M. CARVER

THE MOTHER TONGUE

When the English brought their language to their first permanent colony in the New World—Jamestown, Virginia (1607)—Shakespeare had only recently completed "Macbeth." John Donne was preaching with poetic eloquence at St. Paul's when the *Mayflower* pilgrims were harvesting their first crop at Plymouth. These first colonists had grown up in Elizabethan England and learned the language of Shakespeare, Bacon, Marlowe, and Donne. It was a time of great change and new worlds, the beginning of the British Empire and of English as a world language.

English itself was undergoing important changes. For example, the colonists and Londoners did not always pronounce such words as *meat, sea,* and *lean* with the same vowel. Sometimes they used the old pronunciation [e], rhyming these words with *mate, say,* and *lane.* At other times they used the vowel [i], pronouncing these words as we do today. It was not until about 1700 that the conservative pronunciation [e] faded from hearing. Similarly, the pronunciation of the vowels in such words as *food, good,* and *flood* were in flux and the vowel in *cut* was a recent innovation. Words like *clerk* were sometimes rhymed with *jerk* and sometimes with *dark.* There were other important phonological changes in progress during the colonial period (see Kökeritz, 1953; Pilch, 1980), several of which had important consequences for American English and its dialects.

Seventeenth-century English also preserved the double forms of the second-person pronouns: formal *you, ye,* and *your,* used to address lords and ladies, and informal *thou, thee,* and *thy,* reserved for everyone else. The Quakers of the Pennsylvania colony eschewed this pronominal distinction as negating the inherent equality of all persons and advocated the use of *thou* in all situations. Their protest had little effect on American English. It was only a matter of time (c. 1750) before the *thou* forms were dropped altogether and *you* and *your* were used without regard to status or social occasion, ironically fulfilling the Quakers' egalitarian program.

Seventeenth-century American writing to us seems quaint with its Elizabethan features. For example, William Bradford, governor and early historian of
Plymouth, describing a dramatic incident that took place in the colony in 1638,
uses language (c. 1650) not too distant from Raleigh's and Shakespeare's:

> *Amongst* other *enormities* that fell out amongst them, this year 3. men were (after
> due triall) executed for robery & murder which they had committed. Arthur Peach
> was the cheefe of them, and the ring leader of all the rest. He was a *lustie* and a des-
> perate yonge man, and had been one of the souldiers in the Pequente warr, and had
> done as good servise as the most ther, and one of the forwardest in any attempte. And
> being now out of means, and *loath* to worke, and falling to idle *courses* & company,
> he intended to goe to the Dutch plantation; and had alured these 3., being other mens
> servants and apprentices, to goe with him. But another cause ther was allso of his
> secret going away in this maner; he was not only rune into debte, but he *had gott* a
> maid with child . . . The other 3. *complotting* with him, rane away from their maisters
> in the night, and shaped such a course as they thought to avoyd the pursute of any.
> But falling into the way that *lyeth* betweene the Bay of Massachusetts and the Nar-
> rigansets, and being disposed to rest them selves, *struck fire,* and took tobaco, a litle
> out of the way, by the way side. At length ther came a Narigansett Indean by, who
> had been in the Bay *a trading,* and had both cloth & beads *aboute* him. . . . Peach
> tould the others he would kill him, and take what he had from him. But they were
> *some thing* afraid. . . . So they let him alone to doe as he would; and when he saw his
> time, he [Peach] tooke a rapier and rane him [the Indian] through the body once or
> twise, and tooke from him 5. *fathume* of *wampum,* and 3. coats of cloath, and wente
> their way, leaving him for dead. But he [the Indian] scrabbled away, when they were
> gone, and *made shift* to gett home (but dyed within a few days after,) by which means
> they were discovered; and by subtilty the Indeans tooke them. For they desiring a
> canow [canoe] to *sett them* over a water, (not thinking their *facte* had been known,)
> by the *sachems* comand they were carried to Aquidnett Iland, & ther accused of the
> murder.

[Bradford, 1901:432–433; italics added]

Aside from the odd spellings that were not yet uniformly established by printers,
editors, or schools, one of the first things we notice about the passage is the number of words that are obsolete or archaic. *Amongst* ("among"), *loath* ("disin-
clined"), and *make shift* are little heard today. Bradford uses *enormity* in its old
sense, "a breach of law or morality," whereas today, influenced by *enormous,* we
reserve it for more monstrous crimes. *Courses* ("personal behavior"), *complot-
ting* ("plotting" or "conspiring"), and *fact* ("crime") are all essentially obsolete,
though we might still hear the last in *after the fact.* Bradford's *lustie* may mean
"healthy or vigorous," which the *Oxford English Dictionary* (*OED*) labels
"somewhat archaic," or he may be referring to Mr. Peach's arrogance and inso-
lent self-confidence, in which case Bradford would be using it in an outright
obsolete sense.

Fathom (a unit of length, about 5 feet) is still used, but exclusively in sounding
or measuring water depths in navigation. Bradford uses it as a measurement of
wampum strings. *Strike fire* is obsolete because fires today are rarely started by
striking flint on steel. The awkward locution *make shift to get home* is marked
"obsolete" by the *OED,* as is the equally ungainly expression "a canow *to sett*

them over a water." The preposition, *a*, prefixed to a present participle in *a trad-ing* survives today only in folk speech and dialect, as does the adverbial use of *something* in *something afraid.*

Bradford's use of *lyeth* is also a sign that he is writing in essentially Elizabethan English, which had two inflectional endings for the third-person singular, the earlier *-eth,* which was on its way out, and *-s,* the modern form.

Though Bradford's language is essentially standard British English from the Elizabethan era, it shows elements of nascent American English. This miniature drama also reveals the close association the colonists had with the Indians, who more than once saved the naive Englishmen from starvation and taught them some of the techniques for surviving in the wild new land. The association is also evident in Bradford's un-self-conscious use of the Indian loanwords *wampum* ("shell beads used as a medium of exchange") and *sachem* ("an Indian chief").

EVOLUTION OF ENGLISH IN AMERICA INTO AMERICAN ENGLISH

American English, or as Samuel Johnson derisively called it, the "American dia-lect," was not generally recognized as distinct from British English until well into the eighteenth century. But the seeds of American English were planted before the first colonists set foot on New World soil. Even when immigrants were rel-atively homogeneous, were more or less from the same cultural region, and spoke the same dialect in England, their experiences coming to America, such as contact with other languages, including sailor's jargon and pidgins (see Dil-lard, 1985:27–49), doubtless had an impact on their original speech patterns.

The *Mayflower* pilgrims, for example, were primarily from a single congre-gation from Nottinghamshire and spoke a variety of Elizabethan English rela-tively unmixed with other English dialects. Leaving England to escape religious persecution, they first went to Amsterdam in 1607 and in 1609 moved to Ley-den. In the next decade or so, constant contact with the Dutch meant greater and greater assimilation. Soon their children were marrying among the Dutch and seeking their fortunes wherever Dutch ships sailed, coming into contact with maritime varieties of speech. Fearing among other things that they would lose their language, as well as their identity as a religious sect, the 102 Pilgrims set sail in the *Mayflower* for the New World in 1620, thirteen years after leaving England. It is likely that the linguistic complications they encountered before arriving at Plymouth modified in subtle ways their relatively homogeneous dia-lect.

Most of the groups emigrating to the New World were more mixed than the Plymouth Rock pilgrims. The language they brought with them not only was subtly altered by the crossing, but was mixed with varieties of English, although the dominant speech was of southeastern England. American English was incho-ate in this melting pot of English dialects and maritime varieties.

The greatest changes in the process of distinguishing American from British English, of course, happened in the New World itself and in ways that can be more easily documented. The colonists encountered a strange landscape and unfamiliar forms of wildlife for which they had no English names. When, for example, they came upon a furry, cat-sized creature with a masklike marking, they were at a loss as to what to call it. They naturally adopted the Indian name, which for Europeans was difficult to pronounce. Captain John Smith spelled it *rahaugcum* and *raugroughcum* in his account (1608) of the Virginia colony. He was trying to write the Algonquian word *ārā`kun* from *ārā`kunem,* literally, "he scratches with his hands," which probably alludes to the raccoon's habit of scrabbling for crabs and other tidbits on stream bottoms. The name was also used in the New England colonies and was spelled *rackoone* or *rockoon.* By 1672 the current spelling was established and the Indian word was fully assimilated into colonial English.

Some American Indian terms had already found their way into Elizabethan English, usually by way of Spanish and Portuguese borrowings from Nahuatl, the tongue of the Aztecs, and from various Indian dialects of the West Indies and Central and South America. Some of these words are *potato, tomato, chocolate, cocoa, canoe, cannibal, barbecue, maize,* and *savannah.*

Although numerous Indian languages were spoken on the North American continent, only one language group, the Algonquian, is the nearly exclusive source of the Indian words borrowed by the colonists. This huge group of tribes included the Arapaho, Blackfoot, Cheyenne, Cree, Delaware, Fox, Micmac, Ojibwa or Chippewa, and Penobscot, each speaking a different Algonquian dialect.

About half of all the 300 or so American Indian loanwords current today entered the language in the seventeenth century, including *caribou, hickory, hominy, moccasin, moose, possum, papoose, persimmon, pone, powwow, skunk, squash, squaw, terrapin, tomahawk, totem, wigwam,* and *woodchuck.* Some, like William Bradford's *wampum* and *sachem,* dealt primarily with the Indian culture and today are not used much, even though *sachem* was extended to mean "a political leader or government head" ("The home-office sachems have more time for reflection, but they are in danger of becoming elder statesmen, nodding over dispatches from the battlefield," *Saturday Evening Post,* 1949). Others, like *pecan, caucus, chipmunk, toboggan, succotash, mackinaw,* and *mugwump,* were borrowed later.

A colonial Indian would probably not recognize any of these words because they were radically changed in the course of being adopted into American speech. Algonquian has many sounds and sound combinations that were completely foreign to English speakers, making them difficult to pronounce. Often the words were abbreviated or clipped (*hominy* from *rockahominy, squash* from *asquutasquash, hickory* from *pawcohiccora*). Sometimes the Indian word was changed by folk etymology, an attempt to make sense of a new and unusual-sounding word by analyzing it (incorrectly) in terms of known words. For example, the Indian word *muskwessu* or *muscassus* became *muskrat,* a musky-smelling rodent; *otchek* or *odjik* became *woodchuck;* and *achitam* became *chipmunk.*

The influence of the Indian culture was not negligible when we take into account the numerous combinations in which these loanwords occur (e.g., *skunk*-cabbage, *skunk* bear, *skunk* weed), not to mention the couple hundred combinations with *Indian* (e.g., *Indian pony, Indian mallow*). In addition, there are many expressions derived from features of Indian life: *on the warpath, peace pipe, to bury the hatchet, to hold a powwow, Indian summer, pale face, brave* (noun), *firewater, Indian file, Indian giver, happy hunting grounds, Great Spirit, medicine man, war paint, war dance, to scalp,* and *a ticket scalper.*

In the larger picture, however, given that the American Indians were reduced to a conquered people, it is not surprising that their languages had a relatively slight influence on American English, aside from the large number of place names that are of Indian origin (over half of American state names, for example, are Indian loanwords). Moreover, all the American Indian loanwords are nouns, which indicates a casual rather than a true mingling of the two cultures.

American English also borrowed many words from non-English Europeans as well as from Africans brought in with the slave trade. These loanwords tend to be regionalized to wherever a given immigrant group settled—African in the South, French in Louisiana, Spanish in the Southwest, German in Pennsylvania, Dutch in New York—and have greater importance in the development of American regional dialects, which will be dealt with later.

The English spoken by the colonists almost immediately began drifting away from the mother tongue. Many words and pronunciations died out in England over two or three centuries but survived in America, such as *copious, fox-fire, flap-jack, jeans, molasses, home-spun, andiron, bay-window, cesspool, clodhopper, cross-purposes, greenhorn, loophole, ragamuffin, trash, stock* ("cattle"), *din, underpinning, adze, offal.* Sometimes it was one of the senses of a word that died out in England but survived in America, such as *fall* ("autumn"), *raise* ("to breed, rear, grow") *clod, quit,* and *cabin.*

Among the older English pronunciations surviving in America but not in England are the two vowel sounds in (1) *fast, bath, aunt* and (2) *four, earth.* In England the vowel of the first group of words [æ] (the vowel sound in *cat*) shifted to [ɑ] (as in *father*) during the the late sixteenth and seventeenth centuries. The colonists of New England and Virginia, who looked to England for their standards of fashion in speech and culture, imitated the British pronunciation. This pronunciation still survives in New England and parts of Virginia today, whereas the rest of the country uses the older [æ] pronunciation. The same thing happened during this period with so-called postvocalic [r], which became the unstressed vowel [ə] or was dropped altogether. In England, as well as in New England and the lower South, the latter group of words are pronounced approximately [foə] and [ɜθ], whereas in the rest of America the [r] is pronounced, [for] and [ɜrθ].

Often English dialect terms became standard American words. This is the case for *cordwood, shoat, deck, cater-cornered, drool, squirt, pond, wilt,* and many others.

A word used in England with a particular sense frequently developed new meanings after being transplanted to America. This happened with *creek, squat* ("to settle on land"), *bug, tariff, sick, apartment, baggage, fraternity, barn, team, store, shop, lumber, pie, dry-goods, cracker, rock, to haul, to notify,* and many more. For example, *lumber* in eighteenth-century English meant "disused goods," the sense that survives in England today, as in *lumber room.* But the American colonists used it to designate cut timber. *To haul* in England meant, and still means, "to move by force or violence" ("They were pushing and hawling [sic] every body about." *Sporting Magazine,* 1810). In America since colonial times it has meant "to transport in a vehicle."

THE UNIFORMITY OF COLONIAL AMERICAN ENGLISH

Much has been made of eighteenth-century British accounts of the so-called uniformity of American speech. One often quoted example is from a letter of 1770 written by a certain William Eddis:

> In England, almost every county is distinguished by a peculiar dialect; even different habits, and different modes of thinking, evidently discriminate inhabitants, whose local situation is not far remote: but in Maryland, and throughout adjacent provinces, it is worthy of observation, that a striking similarity of speech universally prevails; and it is strictly true, that the pronunciation of the generality of the people has an accuracy and elegance, that cannot fail of gratifying the most judicious ear.
>
> The colonists are composed of adventurers, not only from every district of Great Britain and Ireland, but from almost every other European government, where the princples of liberty and commerce have operated with spirit and efficacy. Is it not, therefore, reasonable to suppose, that the English language must be greatly corrupted by such a strange intermixture of various nations? The reverse is, however, true. The language of the immediate descendants of such a promiscuous ancestry is perfectly uniform, and unadulterated; nor has it borrowed any provincial, or national accent, from its British or foreign parentage.
>
> For my part, I confess myself totally at a loss to account for the apparent difference, between the colonists and persons under equal circumstances of education and fortune, resident in the mother country. This uniformity of language prevails not only on the coast, where Europeans form a considerable mass of the people, but likewise in the interior parts, where population has made but slow advances; and where opportunities seldom occur to derive any great advantages from an intercourse with intelligent strangers.
>
> [quoted in Read, 1933:323]

Eddis is observing how, despite the diverse mix of dialects from Britain and Ireland in the colonies, Americans speak with generally the same pronunciation or "accent." One might expect an Irish descendant in America to sound like his foreparents, a descendant of Yorkshire to speak with that accent, a descendant of Cornwall to have that brogue, and so on. Instead, the differences in the varieties of British English taken to America tended to be leveled out over a period of 150 years or so. We must be careful, however, about drawing conclusions concerning colonial speech based on contemporary impressionistic observations. At least one recent scholar (Dillard, 1985:59) claims this is evidence of the linguistic process known as *leveling,* which he believes occurred in the speech of all the colonies from about 1720 to 1785. Leveling is the obliteration of a linguistic distinction. For example, the vowel [ɛ] in *kettle* was variously pronounced in colonial English [ɪ] and [ɛ]: *kittle* and *kettle*. Eventually it was leveled to *kettle*, the variant *kittle* almost completely dying out except in folk speech.

To be sure, some leveling did occur on a "national" basis, but the extent is difficult to ascertain. One of the few studies to investigate this phenomenon found that, at least for certain features, no leveling took place during the colonial period. Based on pronunciations reconstructed from orthography and rhyme, Sen (1974) shows that in colonial America the phoneme /ɛ/ (the sound in modern *breath*) had the three variations [ɪ], [æ], and [e], which "were commonplace throughout the early American colonies" (Sen, 1974:45). *Keg*, for example, was sometimes pronounced with [æ] (as in *hat*), sometimes with [e] (as in *pain*), and sometimes with [ɛ] (as in *shed*); *devil* was sometimes *divil*; and *head* was often *haid*. These variations were used in both urban and rural areas and by speakers of all social classes. A few centuries later they were restricted socially and regionally, but in the colonial period they were not yet leveled to a single pronunciation in general speech.

On the other hand, there is evidence that colonial pronunciation, at least for certain other features, tended to level out in the direction of standard British English, the speech of eighteenth-century southeastern England, notably the language of Londoners. Colonial America, especially the coastal towns and seaports, maintained close ties with England. The leading colonial families, who spoke the prestige dialect, followed English fashions of speech and culture and were the model for the majority of uneducated settlers. Noah Webster disapprovingly observed this situation:

> In many parts of America, people at present attempt to copy the English phrases and pronunciation—an attempt that is favored by their habits, their prepossessions and the intercourse between the two countries. This attempt has, within the period of a few years, produced a multitude of changes in these particulars, especially among the leading classes of people.
>
> [Webster, 1789:23–24]

When standard British English began dropping [r] after vowels, most colonial English speakers adopted this pronunciation, except in Pennsylvania, or the middle colony.

In a novel approach Allen Walker Read (1938) used the indirect evidence of colonial newspaper advertisements for runaway white indentured servants to show that new British immigrants were under pressure to assimilate their dialects into the general colonial vernacular. The ads he looked at frequently described runaways as having "a thick Northern" accent or as speaking a "broad" or "flat" English, implying that English dialects were a notable deviation from general American speech. Often two principal dialects were distinguished in the ads, that of western and northern England. Moreover, no mention was ever made of runaways from the southeastern counties of England, because the dialect of that region, where most early settlers originated, closely resembled colonial American speech. Read concludes, "Thus in the colonial period American English had a consistency of its own, most closely approximating the type of the region around London" (Read, 1938:79).

The leveling process probably began soon after settlement and continued until the regional dialects became well established, probably around the mid-eighteenth century. Leveling at the national level, however, has never really stopped, though it has gone through phases. It was probably at its weakest point during the late eighteenth and nineteenth centuries, when American regional cultures and regional pride were asserting themselves. In the twentieth century, with the urbanization of America and the advent of a powerful national media, leveling again gained strength.

Whatever the degree of leveling, the main effect during the colonial period was to unify American English, in contrast to British English. Lexically, American English was also becoming more unified. The Indian borrowings discussed earlier, for example, were current in all the colonies and formed a shared lexicon. *Creek, freshet,* and *nor'easter,* which survive in the Atlantic states, the area of the original colonies, are remnants of a colonial lexicon. When the colonists encountered the numerous saltwater inlets along the coast, they naturally called them *creeks,* using the word in its oldest and standard English sense. In time *creek* was extended to refer to any small freshwater stream, which today is the most widely used sense in American English (see the *Dictionary of American Regional English* for the precise distribution of this word). The original sense, however, was preserved along the entire Atlantic coast at least into the 1930s, when the data were collected for the Linguistic Atlas of the United States (see Kurath, 1949: Fig. 92).

A *freshet* ("a small freshwater stream") was extended during colonial times to refer to incidental streams or rivulets caused from flooding or heavy rains. This sense only survives in the original thirteen colonies. In the same region a wind blowing from the northeast has been called a *northeaster* or *nor'easter* since the eighteenth century (see Carver, 1987: map 5.3).

The issue of a unified language in America was an important one to post-Revolutionary Americans. Noah Webster was especially vocal about it. In his *Dissertations on the English Language* (1789), he declared linguistic independence:

> As an independent nation, our honor requires us to have a system of our own, in language as well as government. Great Britain, whose children we are, and whose language we speak, should no longer be *our* standard; for the taste of her writers is already corrupted, and her language on the decline.
>
> [Webster, 1789:20]

To Webster "our political harmony" was "concerned in a uniformity of language." If the provincial dialects were allowed to grow and flourish, disunity would follow. A standard of American English was necessary: "Nothing but the establishment of schools and some uniformity in the use of books, can annihilate differences in speaking and preserve the purity of the American tongue" (Webster, 1789:19).

Conveniently, Webster would supply such books, one of the most influential being his *American Spelling Book,* first published in 1788 "containing an easy

Standard of Pronunciation." It was one of the best sellers of all time, having sold, by one reasonable estimate, some 100 million copies. Many of the differences between American and British spelling, such as *honor* and *favor* instead of *honour* and *favour,* are the result of Webster's "blue-back speller." It also influenced American pronunciation, such as its distinct articulation and tendency to give syllables their full value, the effects of using spelling as a guide to pronunciation.

Perhaps more influential was Webster's *American Dictionary of the English Language* (1828). Not only was it a reference standard specifically for American usage, but it initiated an important tradition of lexicography in America that culminated in the ground-breaking, nonprescriptive Merriam-Webster's *Third New International Dictionary* (1961).

VARIETIES OF AMERICAN ENGLISH

Just as English in America began distinguishing itself from the English of Britain almost from the first day of colonial life, so the varieties of English spoken in each colonial region began the process of differentiating themselves from every other.

Newcomers to the colonies speaking the dialects of the English homeland had an incentive to blend in, to assimilate, and to adopt quickly the speech patterns of the established colonists. They would have felt the same sort of peer pressure that children feel about not speaking like their friends. But the speech patterns they heard and tried to conform to were the local or regional ones that were becoming more and more distinctive. Much of the linguistic leveling really took place regionally rather than for the colonies as a whole.

Note that William Eddis, in the quote given earlier refers to "Maryland" and "adjacent provinces" in making his observations. It is likely that the uniformity he heard was for a specific region, namely, the Chesapeake Bay area. Another British observer at the time (1777) remarked on the uniformity of American speech but in the same sentence contradicted himself by observing that New England speech was distinctive: "No County or Colonial dialect is to be distinguished here, except it be the New Englanders, who have a sort of whining cadence that I cannot describe" (quoted in Read, 1933:323).

More often than not, British observers noted the regional diversity of American English rather than its overall uniformity. A British traveler, one J.F.D. Smyth, who had spent several years in the Southern colonies, made this observation in 1784 while touring Connecticut: "The whole face of nature as well as the manners and dialect of the people here are widely different from that of the southern provinces, and," he added in a bit of regional chauvinism, "greatly to the disadvantage of New England" (quoted in Read, 1933:326).

The cultural and economic forces that created the American dialects were operative almost from the very beginning. For example, many regionalisms—words and phrases used chiefly in a particular region of the country—can be traced back to the colonial period. A casual reading of the first two volumes of the *Dictionary of American Regional English* reveals the following words that were current in colonial Massachusetts, Connecticut, or New Hampshire and that are still used today primarily in New England or its northern settlement areas (the dates are of the earliest citation): *alewife* ("a fish of the herring family," 1633), *banker* ("fisherman," "fishing vessel," 1704), *barvel* ("fisherman's apron," 1629), *basket-fish* ("brittle star," 1670), *beaver meadow* ("an open, grassy area," 1644), *black ash* ("American ash," 1673), *bonnyclabber* ("solidified sour milk," 1731), *buttery* ("pantry," 1654), *caboose* ("a cook's galley on a ship," 1747), *case* ("general health," 1634), *chamber* ("an upper room or floor," 1639), *clapboard* ("wooden siding," 1632), *creek stuff* (or *thatch*) ("cordgrass," 1669), *cusk* ("a saltwater fish," 1677), *deacon seat* ("front-row seat in church," 1667), *dish kettle* ("a heavy pot for cooking," 1747), *drag* ("harrow," 1655), *dresser* ("sideboard," "cupboard," 1651), *election sermon* (1644), *ex* ("axle," 1648), *fare* (a catch of fish, 1707), *flake* ("a rack for drying fish," 1635), *flitch* ("salt pork," 1632), *general* ("bill of expenses," 1763), *green corn* ("sweet corn," 1645), and *hire* ("to borrow money," 1782).

The same reading produced these Southern regionalisms that were current in the Virginia or Carolina colonies: *ambeer* ("tobacco spit," 1763), *baldface* ("a white face," 1709), *bamboo (briar)* ("greenbrier," 1709), *bat* ("nighthawk," 1709), *black gum* ("tupelo," 1709), *blade* ("leaf of corn plant," 1688), *brake* ("thicket," 1657), *branch* ("stream," 1663), *case* ("a condition of tobacco leaves," 1640), *cat* ("catfish," 1705), *chicken snake* ("rat snake," 1709), *chinquapin* ("chestnut," 1612), *fanner* ("winnowing basket," 1797), *fever and ague* ("malaria," 1671), *Frenchman* ("a spindly tobacco plant," 1688), *fresh* ("stream," 1608), *gallbush* ("inkberry," 1728) *ground worm* ("cutworm," 1708), *ground pea* ("peanut," 1770), *groundnut* ("peanut," 1770), *(hog) crawl* ("enclosure for hogs," 1733), and *honey tree* ("honey locust," 1705).

Social status was not very well defined in colonial America, nor, consequently, were the social dialects (i.e., the varieties of English spoken by particular social and ethnic groups). Language variation correlated more closely with the cultural geography of the speakers than with their social class. As Read pointed out (1938:70), although indentured servants might be considered the lowest social class, once they had finished their period of service, they generally set up a business for themselves, often on the frontier, and hence social stratification did not take place. In this new world of fiercely won democratic ideals, class distinctions were at best loose. Regional dialects, then, were more important in the early history of English in America than dialects that characterized specific classes. Toward the end of the nineteenth century, however, with increasing urbanization and corresponding social stratification, such variables as class, economic status, education, and gender become more prominent in describing American English.

Because language is one of the most important characterizing features of a culture, the geography of language variation, or *linguistic geography,* is necessarily a branch of cultural geography. The guiding principle in this approach is that settlement patterns have shaped and defined the geography of American life and language. To understand the character of a given cultural region, its features and boundaries, we must begin by examining the cultures that the settlers brought to it. Immigrants or American-born settlers carried their culture with them westward, first from England, then from the colonies into the frontier, shaping the evolution of the cultural landscape.

On a macroscopic level the British settlement of the Atlantic coast of North America defined the boundaries within which American English established itself. The individual colonies along the coast then became the focal points or "hearths" out of which developed the various regional cultures and their dialects. There are five seminal hearths corresponding to the earliest colonies: eastern Virginia or the Chesapeake Bay area [Jamestown, Virginia (1607)]; New England [Plymouth, Massachusetts (1620); Hartford, Connecticut (1635)]; coastal South Carolina [Charleston (1670)]; Philadelphia (1681); and New Orleans (1717).

New England and the North

The first colonists established two dominant centers from which sprang New England's regional characteristics: the Massachusetts Bay area and the Lower Connecticut River Valley. The arriving immigrants were generally groups of families, often from the same congregation led by an elected minister, and settling as neighbors in the same areas. They came primarily from eastern and southern England, bringing with them their local dialects, along with the farming, fishing, and shipping expressions that have given the New England lexicon its unique flavor.

Beginning with the landing of the 102 *Mayflower* pilgrims and ending with the last of the 4000 or so families of the "Great Migration" some twenty years later, the Massachusetts Bay Colony was established and with it the basic cultural features that persisted relatively unaltered by newcomers. By 1675 civilization extended along the entire coast from Cape Cod to the Penobscot Bay in Maine and inland along the rivers and saltwater creeks.

The second dominant center began in the Hartford, Connecticut, area with the arrival overland in 1635 of several groups of families from the Bay Colony. As so often happened in the story of the westward expansion, these settlers left small parcels of exhausted land to seek a better fortune. In the following four decades the fertile valley of the lower Connecticut River received many other settlers primarily from southeastern England. By the time of the war with the Indians known as King Philip's War (1674–1676), settlement extended up the river valley well past Springfield, Massachusetts. At this date there were about 120,000 residents of English origin.

To the seventeenth-century colonists, waterways were vital to trade and communication and were an integrative force to the region as a whole. Consequently, the New England towns settled to about 1675 were all accessible by water, along either the coast or the rivers. It is not surprising, then, that many of the words and phrases that characterize the regional dialect today have to do with the sea. Of the more or less random sample of colonial New England words cited earlier, almost half deal with the sea: *alewife, barvel, basket-fish, fare, flake, banker, caboose, cusk, general, creek stuff* (or *thatch*).

The Connecticut Colony had no true nucleus, being spread out along the river and coast. By contrast, the Boston Bay area was the distinct cultural and economic center of the Massachusetts Colony and has remained so to this day. The two colonies formed the cultural and linguistic core for the two major regions in New England, eastern and western New England, divided by a line that runs close to the Connecticut River. East along this river was a sparsely settled area that impeded communication between the two halves of New England. The division was further reinforced when each region developed its own more or less autonomous transportation system, notably railroads, that radiated from the old centers outward to the peripheral settlements. These separate systems helped consolidate the two regions economically, socially, and ultimately linguistically.

Eastern New England speech is one of the most conservative of American regional dialects and is rooted in the colonial period. Many of its expressions date from before the Revolution, such as *notch* ("mountain pass"), *hatchway* or *bulkhead* ("sloping cellar doors"), *buttry* ("pantry"), *swale* ("a marshy depression in level land"), *bannock* ("a thin corn cake") and *hasty pudding,* also known as *Indian pudding* ("cornmeal mush with milk and molasses"). It borrowed words from the Indians, including *mummichog* ("a saltwater minnow or killifish"), *guahog* ("a thick-shelled edible clam") and *pogy* and *scup* ("menhaden"), more reminders of this culture's close connection with the sea. Like many conservative dialects, it tends to be euphemistic and avoids slang. Primarily in folk or rural speech *sire,* for example, is used instead of *bull* and *meadow* or *top dressing* instead of *manure. Gone by* is a euphemism for *died* and a funeral wake is also known as *calling hours.* Two recent New Englandisms are *rotary* ("traffic circle") and *parkway* ("a divided highway with extensive greenery").

The history of the North, particularly the Upper North, is the story of the westward expansion of primarily western New England, first into New York, and then, along with New Yorkers, into the Great Lakes states.

New Englanders first entered New York when it was still known as New Netherland, establishing Southold and Southhampton on Long Island in 1640. A hundred years later the area between the Connecticut and Hudson rivers was brimming with New England settlements. After the defeat of the French and their expulsion from North America in 1763, Yankees from Vermont and western Massachusetts pushed into the northern and western sections of New York, culminating in the 1790s with "Genesee fever," when New Englanders poured into the Genesee Valley in far western New York. Vocabulary remnants of this settlement pattern include *a-yuh* ("yes"), *adder* ("snake"), *cow corn* ("field corn"), *go cross-lots* ("to take a short-cut"), *hatchway (doors)* ("sloping cellar doors"), *matterate* ("suppurate"), *snap-the-whip* ("a game played on ice"), and *titman* ("the runt of a litter").

By the time of the Revolution three broad cultural regions were established in New York: cosmopolitan New York City; the Yankee region, which included most of Long Island and western and northern New York; and the Dutch area of the Hudson Valley.

The Dutch had been the first to colonize New York, though with little of the vigor that the English brought to the New World. In 1664 at the end of Dutch rule, New Amsterdam, as New York City was called, had barely 1500 residents. Even so, the Dutch culture and language persisted tenaciously well into the eighteenth century, when Albany, for example, was still completely Dutch in character. German families also settled in the Hudson and Mohawk valleys, strengthening the non-English character of the region and diverting New Englanders to the north and west.

Inevitably, the English spoken in the Hudson Valley became a regional variety marked by Dutch borrowings, including *hay barrack* ("a roofed structure for covering haystacks," from *hooiberg*), *olicook* ("doughnut," from *oliekoek*, "oil cake"), *rolliche* ("roulade," from *rolletje*, "little roll"), *pot cheese* ("cottage cheese," from *potkaas*), *suppawn* ("cornmeal mush," borrowed by the Dutch from the Indians), *cruller* ("a doughnut or sweet cake") and *teeter-totter* ("seesaw"). These are all obsolete or dying out rapidly, except for the last two, which are also used in the northern and most of the western United States. One of the few Hudson Valley terms not borrowed from Dutch is *skimmilton* ("shivaree"), which derives from English dialect.

Many Dutch borrowings did not stay confined to the Hudson Valley or New York but are in general use in American English, including *cole slaw, cookie, dope, dingus, saw buck, snoop, stoop* ("porch"), *caboose, sleigh, waffle, spook, logy, boss, boodle, dumb* ("stupid"), *poppycock, Santa Claus,* and probably *Yankee.*

Late in eighteenth-century New England, overcrowding, high land prices, steep taxes, and religious and social restrictiveness drove settlers west beyond New York to the Ohio frontier. Numerous "improved" roads constructed after the Revolution made travel relatively easy, especially just before the spring thaw, when sleds heaped with household goods could glide over the rugged terrain.

Travel by boat was a favored mode. Flatboats, which were broken up at the end of the trip and used to construct cabins, plied the Ohio River, a water highway into the wilderness. The Great Lakes, especially after the opening of the Erie Canal in 1825, became an easy and inexpensive route, transporting the new surge of migration in the 1830s from New York and New England into northern Ohio and Michigan. After 1833 thousands of settlers arrived by regular steamer service in Detroit's bustling lake port. From there they fanned north and west into the fertile Michigan countryside or down the Chicago Road to northern Illinois. The Erie Canal also made the bounty of western grain and wool cheaply available to the east, undermining the New England farms, whose exhausted rocky land could not compete, and hastening the spread of New England settlement westward.

In the 1840s steamboats landed thousands of passengers at Chicago, increasing that city's population sevenfold in that decade. Most arrivals, however, moved into northern Illinois and southern Wisconsin. In the 1850s the flood of New Englanders increased the population of Wisconsin tenfold.

Western New England expansion gave the Upper North its basic substratum of cultural and linguistic features. Though much of the upper North regional lexicon can be traced to New England, some colonial New England terms transplanted westward died out in the parent region but survived in the rest of the

North. Among these are *wheatcake* ("pancake"), *friedcake* ("doughnut"), *stone fence* ("a mortarless wall made from field stones"), and *crick* ("a small stream").

Upper Northern regionalisms, however, tend to be relatively recent innovations and coinages, most coming into use in the nineteenth century, and many not appearing until the twentieth. Unlike conservative eastern New England, there are relatively few relics or archaisms, and there are few loanwords, despite the flood of northern Europeans to the region in the nineteenth century. Slang is characteristic of its regional lexicon and includes *canuck* ("Canadian"), *strapped* ("to be without money"), *ass-end-to* ("backward," "reversed"), *squealer* ("informer"), *milquetoast* ("a weak, timid person"), *coffin nail* ("cigarette"), *beanery* ("cheap restaurant"), *duck soup* ("something that is easily accomplished"; "cinch"), *yap* ("mouth"), and *schnozz* ("nose"). Reflecting its industrial and urban character, especially in contrast to the South, it has relatively fewer ruralisms than any other major U.S. dialect region.

Pennsylvania, the last of the Atlantic cultural hearths, was not colonized until the 1680s, when William Penn established a Quaker community in what is now Philadelphia. Because Penn's colony had rich farmland and was liberal and open to any religion, it attracted large numbers of immigrants, including English and Welsh colonists, who tended to stay in the urban Philadelphia area, and Germans and Scotch-Irish settlers, who moved immediately into the back country and later moved southward. Western Pennsylvania was not settled until after the 1760s.

Immigrants from Pennsylvania were an important element in the settlement of the Lower North, which includes the central and southern portions of Ohio, Indiana, Illinois, southern Iowa, and northern Missouri, especially after the construction of the National Road running through the middle of these states almost to the Mississippi River. *Dornick* ("a small stone"), *piece* ("snack") and *redd (up)* ("to clean up") are Scots-Irish remnants of the Pennsylvania settlement in this region, as *smearcase* ("cottage cheese"), *spatzie* ("sparrow") and *hot potato salad* are German remnants.

Southerners from Virginia, Kentucky, and Tennessee pushed northward across the Ohio River, giving the lower portions of these states a Southern character and making this one of the most mixed dialect areas of the country. Because it is the region where the North and the South meet it is a transitional zone between these two dominant American cultures.

The South

The South's physical features are more varied than any other section of the country, ranging from the Blue Ridge Mountains, the highest east of the Rockies, to the swampy lowlands of the Florida everglades and the Louisiana bayous. This topography was a major influence on the development of the South's human regions. The shape of this variform land channeled or impeded the flow of settlement, and its soil and climate attracted specific types of economic activities. Although the Southern United States contains a complex patchwork of dialects, it is divided first into two major regions corresponding to its two physiographic and cultural provinces: the Highland, or Upper South, and the Lowland, or Lower South.

The highlands dominate the physiography of the Upper South. They consist of the Appalachian and Ozark mountain systems separated by a plateau in central and western Kentucky and Tennessee and include most of the piedmont of the Atlantic South. A series of parallel ridges and valleys running through the Appalachians, sometimes called the Great Valley, acted like a conduit to pioneer migration into the inland South.

Upper South settlement sprang essentially from the Virginia and Pennsylvania hearths. The early Virginia colonists discovered that the soil and heavy rainfall in warm temperatures were ideal for growing the new cash crop, tobacco, the economic base on which Jamestown (1607) and St. Mary's (1634) flourished. By 1670 the two tobacco colonies had spread throughout the Chesapeake Bay area, forming a fountainhead of future Southern settlement. The importance of tobacco to the colonial South is hinted at in the regional vocabulary. Of the more or less random sample of colonial Southern terms cited earlier, three have to do with tobacco: *ambeer, case,* and *Frenchman.*

Soil exhaustion and the increasing price of land drove the tidewater colonists inland into the Old West, the hilly, forested piedmont region. In the 1730s the Germans from southeastern Pennsylvania moved into the Shenandoah Valley, followed by the Scots-Irish, who pressed into the Great Valley of Virginia and North Carolina, overflowing into the Carolina piedmont. These hard-working frontier yeomen were relatively isolated from the tidewater aristocracy of eastern Virginia and the Carolinas. This, along with their distinctive background, established a strong cultural and linguistic boundary through the Atlantic South at the edge of their original settlements near the fall line, where the piedmont meets the coastal plain.

These two groups, especially the Scots-Irish, adapted quickly to wilderness America, making extensive use of Indian crops and forest lore, and gave Upper Southern culture some of its characteristic features, such as the loghouse and single-family farm, in contrast to the plantations worked by slaves and hired hands of the Lower South. They also made their mark on American English, for example, giving it its "r-fulness" pronunciation, as well as many words and phrases. A partial list would include *poor* ("scrawny," "weak"), *nicker* ("the sound that a horse makes"), *blate* ("the sound of a sheep"), *hippin* ("baby's diaper"), *back* ("to address an envelope") and *to pet a child to death* ("to overindulge or spoil a child"), which are used in the South as a whole. Representative Scots-Irish words confined primarily to the Upper South include *brickle* ("brittle"), *fornent* or *ferninst* ("near to," "opposite"), *scoot* ("to move or slide something"), and *muley* ("hornless cow").

By 1760 the Appalachian valleys and the piedmont were filled and migration began pushing through the Cumberland Gap into Tennessee and the Kentucky Valley. After the War of 1812, Missouri and Arkansas were also swiftly settled, primarily by immigrants from Illinois, Kentucky, and Tennessee. By 1821 Missouri had enough population, primarily along the Mississippi and Missouri rivers, to become a state. By 1836 Arkansas had achieved statehood.

Except for the cultural islands of the Kentucky Bluegrass region, the Nashville Basin, and the alluvial lands along the Mississippi, the Upper South was not a plantation culture. Its very small black population, perhaps more than any other feature, sets it in contrast to the Lower South. Its relatively poor land, especially in the mountainous areas, could not support farms much larger than 25 or 50 acres, which reinforced the isolation of the region. In addition, roads were difficult to build. Prior to 1930 there was still no network of paved roads into the back country.

The effects of this isolation on the Upper South were long range and profound. With markets distant and commerce virtually nonexistent, there was little urban growth. Few new immigrants were willing to settle this economically depressed region. Without new blood added to the cultural pool, the area's ethnic background remained that of the early Scots-Irish, English, and German settlers, strongly conservative and thoroughly Protestant.

The language of the Upper South region, whch harbors many old-fashioned and relic expressions, reflects this isolation and conservativism. Some scholars have even claimed that Ozark and southern Appalachian speech is a form of Elizabethan English (e.g., Combs, 1916), a claim that is probably more poetic than true. The old-fashioned folk flavor of the Upper South is heard in expressions like *hidy* ("hello"), *smothering spell* ("momentary feeling of weakness"), *cuss fight* ("argument"), *carrion crow* ("vulture"), and *cur dog* ("mongrel").

The coastal plain, extending from Maryland to Texas and varying in width from a mile to over 500 miles, is the dominant physiographic feature of the Lower South. Its numerous rivers facilitated settlement and trade, and its warm, moist climate fostered an agrarian culture. This is the natural province of the Old South, of cotton plantations and genteel manners. Just as the history of the Upper North is the story of New England's expansion, so the Lower South, which covers the coastal plain from Virginia to east Texas, is the historical extension of Charleston and to a lesser extent tidewater Virginia.

As the Virginia and Maryland colonies flourished, the Lower South's second cultural hearth was just taking form in 1670 at Charles Town on the South Carolina coast. The first colonists from England had to endure a difficult trip by way of Barbados, where they stayed for a time regrouping before continuing on. This foreshadowed the close tie that later developed between the Carolina colony and the West Indies.

Tobacco did poorly in this climate, but the colonists soon discovered that rice thrived in the low, semitropical tidewater. By the 1690s the crop was bringing in tremendous wealth. But because large amounts of capital for land and labor were needed to grow rice, only the richest families could afford to share in the huge profits. This fostered the plantation and slave system and made South Carolina from the beginning the largest mainland importer of African slaves. By 1708 there were as many slaves as there were white freemen, and by 1724 there were three times as many slaves.

Plantation agriculture shifted from rice to indigo to cotton and spread inland, bringing thousands of new acres into Charleston's economic and cultural sphere, expanding along the coast and westward into Georgia as the Indians were systematically dispossessed. By 1830 plantation settlement had crept to the Chattahoochee River in Georgia, which was the political borderline between the Indians and the white settlers and where for a time settlement halted, postponing white migration into Alabama. As a result, the Chattahoochee became the western dialect boundary for the Atlantic South region. Centered on the Charleston hearth, it covers all of Georgia, South Carolina, most of Florida, and the coastal plains of North Carolina, forming a cultural and linguistic subregion of the Lower South.

In this region one can hear such expressions as *cracker* ("a poor white person"), *frog skin* ("dollar bill"), *lightwood* ("dried pine used for kindling"), and *ground peas* ("peanuts"). The Atlantic South also shares a number of expressions with eastern New England, which, like the loss of postvocalic [r], are fossil evidence of a shared and relatively unified colonial lexicon. These include *piazza* ("porch," "veranda"), *bush hook* ("a hand tool for cutting underbrush"), *belly girt* ("harness band"), *adder* ("snake"), and *hog's head cheese,* these last two also occurring in the Lower South, the settlement region of the Atlantic South. This pattern of words distributed in New England and the Atlantic South is fading. Many expressions that were formerly shared, such as *haslet* ("edible organs of a hog"), *whicker* ("neigh"), and *lulling down* ("a subsiding of the wind"), are viable today only in the linguistically more conservative Atlantic South.

The Gulf States were settled from the Atlantic South after 1815 with the construction of national highways, such as the Great Valley Road through Knoxville into northern Alabama and central Mississippi and the roads through the Carolinas and Georgia into the Gulf plains. The plantation culture and economy spread throughout the Gulf states. Maps of cotton production for virtually any year until about 1950 show the "cotton belt" to coincide essentially with the Lower South's cultural and dialect area. Moreover, the distribution of slaves conformed closely to the limits of the cotton culture. As late as the 1930 census the black population density still showed the early settlement pattern.

Though this picture has changed considerably since World War II, with the migration of Southern blacks to the urban North, the early Afro-American subculture—the product of social isolation and an almost fogotten African heritage—has left a lasting influence on the religious, artistic, and linguistic aspects of Lower Southern culture. Many expressions unique to its lexicon are African in origin, such as *cooter* ("turtle"), *goober* ("peanut"), *gumbo* ("a dish made with okra"), *juke* ("immoral," "disorderly"), *juju* ("amulet," "fetish"), *okra* ("edible pods of a tall annual plant"), *pinder* ("peanut"), *poor joe* ("great blue heron"), and *tote* ("carry"). Many African words brought to the South by the slaves have spread through the United States, such as *banjo, bogus, boogie-woogie, chigger, hep* or *hip, jazz, jitter, jive, mumbo-jumbo, phoney, voodoo, yam,* and *zombie.* Black speech has had a creative influence on American English, but today, instead of being confined to the South, it is national and primarily urban.

The settlement of New Orleans in 1717 created the third hearth of the Lower South, but, unlike Tidewater Virginia and Charleston, its influence was restricted, barely extending beyond southern Louisiana. New Orleans began as a French colony, but few Frenchmen were eager to settle in the subtropical locale infested with malaria-bearing mosquitoes. By 1744 there were only about 5800 inhabitants, including some 2000 slaves from Africa and the West Indies, indicative of the impoverished and slow growth of the colony under French rule. When Spain took over the colony in 1766 there were still only about 7500 persons to be governed.

Oddly enough, very few Spaniards settled in New Orleans. Except for the Acadian French who arrived in 1765 from Nova Scotia, the American colonies supplied the largest group of immigrants. After the Americans took over the colony in 1803 with the Louisiana Purchase, Louisiana continued to be New World French. This is reflected in the regional lexicon, which includes *banquette* ("sidewalk"), *get down* ("to get off," for example, a bus, translated from French *descendre*), *armoire* ("wardrobe"), *poule d'eau* ("mudhen"), *gaspergou* ("a freshwater drum"), *boudin* ("sausage"), *jambalaya* ("a rice dish"), *marais* ("swamp"), *gallery* ("veranda"), and *praline* ("a pecan candy"). Other words used in this subregion, the Delta South, which covers all of Louisiana and southwestern Mississippi, include the Indian loanwords *lagniappe* ("gift," "bonus"), *bayou* ("a slow-moving stream"), and *pirogue* ("a crude canoe or open boat") and the contemporary expressions *neutral ground* ("median strip in a highway"), *cream cheese* ("cottage cheese"), and *coon-ass* ("Cajun").

The Upper and Lower South, though distinct in many cultural details, form a more or less unified region, the South. Aspects of the South's cultural personality can be seen in its distinctive vocabulary. Its famous cuisine provides a whole lexicon by itself. Bread, for example, has many dialect terms, particularly when made with the South's preferred basic ingredient, the New World grain, *corn* (itself an Americanism). *Corn cake, corn pone, corn dodger, pone bread, fritters, hush puppies, awendaw, spoon bread, ash cake, hoe cake, egg bread,* and just *bread* are all versions of Southern cornmeal bread. Wheat or white bread is *light bread, biscuit bread, baker's bread, bought bread,* and *loaf bread*. Pork is also a favored culinary ingredient and has numerous Southern forms, including *cracklins, souse, hasslet, breakfast bacon, middlins, middling meat,* and *chitlins*.

Folk speech is generally characterized by euphemism and inversion, but in America it is a particularly common feature in the South, especially among poorly educated and working-class speakers. Among the euphemisms are *male cow* for "bull," *woods colt* for "bastard," *bad place* for "hell," and *big* or *she swallowed a pumpkin seed* for "pregnant." Among the inversions, two classic examples are *peckerwood* for "woodpecker" and *hoppergrass* for "grasshopper." Redundancy is also characteristic of Southern folk speech, such as *boar-hog, brogan-shoe, granny woman, hound-dog, might maybe, neighbor people,* and *preacher man*.

The Linguistic Continental Divide

The South and the North form the primary cultural and linguistic division in the United States. The boundary between the two begins somewhere in central Delaware, extends westward along the old Mason–Dixon Line, and continues approximately along the Ohio River, through central Missouri, then south through central Oklahoma and eastern Texas. U.S. political history during the nineteenth century leading up to the Civil War was dominated by the differences between these two great regions. The nation's politics were preoccupied with the struggle between the North and the South over, among other things, tariffs, slavery, and control of the emerging West. The historical, social, and economic forces that divided the nation and led to the "Confederate War" (as it is still called in the South) are the same forces that created the cultural and linguistic Mason–Dixon Line.

The 1850s saw a large influx of northern Europeans, with their hatred for slavery, into the Old Northwest, especially Michigan, Wisconsin, and Minnesota, helping politically and culturally to ally this area with the Northeast. At the same time the rapid development of railroads in the North altered the South's connection to the Old Northwest via the Mississippi River trade route to New Orleans. With this railroad system, agricultural surpluses could easily be transported over the Appalachian barrier to the rich seaboard markets, economically allying the Northwest with the Northeast, in contrast to the South. As the South became increasingly isolated, both economically, with its base in agriculture, and culturally, with virtually no foreign immigration, the North continued to feel the pressure of languages and cultures in contact as Europeans flooded its thriving industrial region well into the twentieth century.

The West

It can be argued that it was not until the nineteenth century that a genuinely home-grown American consciousness began to make itself felt. Most of the country east of the Mississippi was well settled, and America's eyes turned to the Far West. A self-confident, uncouth, daring spirit asserted itself, epitomized in folk heroes like Andrew Jackson, Daniel Boone, and Davy Crockett, pioneers of the frontier par excellence. Backwoods "tall talk" was its favorite mode of expression, the aggressive speech of rough men who bragged they could "lick their weight in wildcats and chaw off the ear of a grizzly."

Tall talk fostered an exuberant linguistic creativity represented by outlandish coinages like *absquatulate* ("to depart stealthily"), *clamjamfry* ("nonsense," "rubbish"), *dedodgment* ("exit"), *helliferocious* ("very ferocious"), *obflisticate* ("obliterate"), *ripsniptiously* ("in a lively manner"), *slang-whanger* ("orator"), and *teetotaciously* ("completely"). Some "tall" words survive today, such as *rambunctious* ("wild"), *hornswoggle* ("to deceive"), *in cahoots* ("in league with"), *cavort* ("to prance about"), *go the whole hog* ("to go all out"), *kick the bucket* ("to die"), and *pick a crow with someone* ("to find fault with someone"). This tradition of linguistic inflation is alive in America today as seen in occupational titles like *sanitary engineer* ("garbage collector") and *mortician,* and in bureaucratic and professional jargon, such as *underprivileged* for "poor" and *character disorder* for "insane."

Though the mainstream of language flowed east to west with the tide of settlement, there was also a countercurrent from the edges of the frontier eastward. Gambling and card playing, for example, a favorite pastime of the Wild West, has given American English a sizable body of expressions, such as *ace in the hole, blue-chip* (stock), *bluff, break even, cash in one's chips, deal (someone) in* (or *out*), *follow suit, hit the jackpot, in hock, load the dice, pass the buck, renege, stack the deck,* and *when the chips are down.*

With this brash frontier self-confidence in charge, the nineteenth century was perhaps the most fertile period for the coining of Americanisms. A small sampling of the thousands recorded in the *Dictionary of Americanisms* is like a cross section of American culture: *anesthesia* (1846), *apartment* (1876), *automobile* (1895), *baby-talk* (1838), *ballpark* (1899), *basketball* (1892), *billion* (1834), *blizzard* (1859), *bootleg* (a. 1889), *brainstorm* (1894), *burglarize* (1871), *bushwhacker* (1809), *casket* (1863), *chewing gum* (1850), *cocktail* (1806), *confidence man* (1849), *crackerjack* (1896), *downtown* (1851), *drugstore* (1819), *electric chair* (1890), *firecracker* (1829), *grammar school* (1823), *grubstake* (1863), *homestretch* (1841), *ice box* (1846), *mail order* (1867), *panhandle* (1856), *prom* (1894), *pussyfoot* (a. 1893), *referendum* (1870), *rowdy* (1823), *tenderloin* (1828), *tenement house* (1859), and *underdog* (1879).

The new West, the vast territory west of the Mississippi River, sometimes called the "American desert" in the nineteenth century, is barely 100 years old, excluding the early Spanish settlement of the Old Southwest. Its language has barely gone through two or three generations, not enough time to distinguish itself clearly as a separate dialect. In effect, the settlement of the West is still in progress and Western speech is still undergoing the modifications and leveling processes of a region in social flux. But this in itself is a contrast with the rest of the nation.

Immigration to the West was disproportionately from the Northern states, whch has given its speech a strong Northern base. Most Northern regionalisms are shared with the West, whereas only a handful of Southern features have this pattern. Southern features, however, play a role, especially in the Southwest, by extending the North–South linguistic divide into the West.

Whereas settlement in the East was more or less continuous and comprehensive, spreading in even waves from the coastal colonies, settlement in the West was insular, leapfrogging across wide, empty areas. The Mormons, for example, moved from Illinois to the Great Salt Lake Valley; Lower Northerners moved to Washington and Oregon; and New Yorkers and Missourians settled in California, all without leaving intervening settlements. Pockets of settlement created distinct cultural areas, notably the Northwest, northern and southern California, the Rocky Mountain West, and the Southwest, each having a small body of characteristic linguistic features.

The most distinctive of these subregions is the Southwest, the dry, mountainous area extending over 1000 miles from west Texas to southern California. The Spanish established some of the oldest settlements in North America in New Mexico and southern California. From this region come most of the Spanish loanwords, both in American English at large and in the regional speech of the Southwest. Not surprisingly, a large number of these loanwords in American English have a strong Western flavor, such as *ranch, canyon, bonanza, bronco, rodeo, corral, fiesta, gringo, mesa, mustang, patio, pancho, stampede,* and *vigi-*

lante. Similarly, the loanwords unique to Southwestern speech usually have to do with the stark physiography, the ranching economy, or ethnic food: *arroyo* ("gorge," "gully"), *barranca* ("ravine"), *bosque* ("clump of trees"), *remuda* ("a spare horse"), and *frijoles* ("beans").

The development of American English began the moment the English colonists set sail for a New World that would demand that their language have the same vigorous, democratic, and self-confident qualities that they themselves would need to flourish in the wilderness. This first involved a gradual but clear break from the mother language, the Elizabethan tongue of Shakespeare and company. After one or two generations, the direction of American English was set and all subsequent settlers had to assimilate to it. By the early eighteenth century, observers were noting the differences between British and American speech, differences that became clearer over time, until in the late nineteenth century Oscar Wilde could quip in his inimitable way that the British "have really everything in common with America nowadays, except, of course, language."

But as American English became distinctive, so did its regional dialects (and much later, its social varieties), so much so that one is hard pressed to find any such entity as "American English." Except perhaps in writing, there is no national or standard form of American speech. Southerners speak just as pure a version of American English as their Yankee cousins. The history of American English, then, is also the story of its regional settlement and the emergence of its cultures and dialects.

WORKS CITED

Allen, Harold B. 1973–76. *The Linguistic Atlas of the Upper Midwest.* 3 vols. Minneapolis: University of Minnesota Press.

_____, and Gary Underwood, eds. 1971. *Readings in American Dialectology.* New York: Appleton-Century-Crofts.

_____, and Michael Linn, eds. 1986. *Dialect and Language Variation.* Orlando, FL.: Academic Press.

Babcock, C. Merton, ed. 1949. "The Social Significance of the Language of the American Frontier." *American Speech* 24:256–263.

_____. 1961. *The Ordeal of American English.* Boston: Houghton Mifflin.

Billington, Ray Allen. 1960. *Westward Expansion: A History of the American Frontier.* New York: Macmillan.

Bradford, William. 1901. *Bradford's History "Of Plimoth Plantation".* a. 1656. Boston: Wright and Potter.

Bronstein, Arthur J. 1960. *The Pronunciation of American English: An Introduction to Phonetics.* New York: Appleton-Century-Crofts.

Brooks, Cleanth. 1935. *The Relation of the Alabama–Georgia Dialect to the Provincial Dialects of Great Britain.* Baton Rouge: LSU Press.

_____. 1937. "The English Language of the South." Reprinted in Williamson and Burke, eds. Pp. 136–142.

Brown, Ralph H. 1948. *Historical Geography of the United States.* New York: Harcourt Brace Jovanovich.

Carver, Craig M. 1986. "The Influence of the Mississippi River on Northern Dialect Boundaries." *American Speech* 61:245–261.

———. 1987. *American Regional Dialects: A Word Geography.* Ann Arbor: University of Michigan Press.

Cassidy, Frederic G. 1963. "Language on the American Frontier." In Kerr and Aderman, eds. Pp. 85–110.

———, ed. 1985. *Dictionary of American Regional English.* Cambridge, MA: Harvard University Press.

Combs, Josiah H. 1916. "Old, Early, and Elizabethan English in the Southern Mountains." *Dialect Notes* 4:283–297.

Craigie, Sir William, and James R. Hulbert, eds. 1938. *A Dictionary of American English on Historical Principles,* 4 vols. Chicago: University of Chicago Press.

Crozier, Alan. 1984. "The Scotch–Irish Influence on American English." *American Speech* 59:310–331.

Dillard, J. L. 1975. *All-American English: A History of the English Language in America.* New York: Random House.

———. 1976. *American Talk: Where Our Words Came From.* New York: Random House.

———, ed. 1980. *Perspectives on American English.* The Hague: Mouton.

———. 1985. *Toward a Social History of American English.* New York, Berlin, Amsterdam: Mouton.

Dohan, Mary Helen. 1976. *Our Own Words.* New York: Knopf.

Ellis, Stanley, ed. 1968. *Studies in Honor of Harold Orton.* Leeds.

Ferguson, Charles, and Shirley Brice Heath, eds. 1981. *Language in the USA.* Cambridge: Cambridge University Press.

Forgue, Guy Jean. 1986. "American English at the Time of the Revolution." In Allen and Linn, eds. Pp. 511–523.

Francis, W. Nelson. 1959. "Some Dialect Isoglosses in England." *American Speech* 34:243–257. Reprinted in Allen and Underwood, eds. Pp. 245–254.

———. 1961. "Some Dialectal Verb Forms in England." *Orbis* 10:1–14. Reprinted in Allen and Underwood, eds. Pp. 255–264.

Gastil, Raymond D. 1975. *Cultural Regions of the United States.* Seattle: University of Washington.

Gibson, James R., ed. 1978. *European Settlement and Development in North America.* Toronto: University of Toronto Press.

Hansen, Marcus Lee. 1940. *The Atlantic Migration 1607–1860: A History of the Continuing Settlement of the United States.* Cambridge, MA: Harvard University Press.

Hill, Archibald A. 1940. "Early Loss of [r] before Dentals." *PMLA* 55:308–321. Reprinted in Williamson and Burke, eds. Pp. 87–100.

Kökeritz, H. 1953. *Shakespeare's Pronunciation.* New Haven: Yale University Press.

Kerr, Elizabeth M., and Ralph M. Aderman, eds. 1963. *Aspects of American English.* New York: Harcourt Brace Jovanovich.

Krapp, George Philip. 1925. *The English Language in America,* 2 vols. New York: Modern Language Association of America.

Kurath, Hans. 1928. "The Origin of Dialectal Differences in Spoken American English." *Modern Philology* 25:385–395. Reprinted in Williamson and Burke, eds. Pp. 12–21.

_____. 1939–43. *Linguistic Atlas of New England.* 3 vols. Providence, RI: Brown University Press.

_____. 1949. *A Word Geography of the Eastern United States.* Ann Arbor: University of Michigan Press.

_____. 1964. "British Sources of Selected Features of American Pronunciation: Problems and Methods." Reprinted in Allen and Underwood, eds. Pp. 265–272.

_____. 1965. "Some Aspects of Atlantic Seaboard English Considered in Connection with British English." *Communications et Rapports* 3:236–240. Reprinted in Williamson and Burke, eds. Pp. 101–107.

_____. 1968. "Contributions of British Folk Speech to American Pronunciation." In Ellis. Pp. 129–134.

_____. 1970. "English Sources of Some American Regional Words and Verb Forms." *American Speech* 45:60–68.

_____. 1972. *Studies in Area Linguistics.* Bloomington: Indiana University Press.

_____, and Raven I. McDavid. 1961. *The Pronunciation of English in the Atlantic States.* Ann Arbor: University of Michigan Press.

Laird, Charlton, 1970. *Language in America.* Englewood Cliffs, NJ: Prentice-Hall.

Lederer, Richard M. 1985. *Colonial American English.* Essex, CT: Verbatim.

Leonard, Sterling Andrus. 1929. *The Doctrine of Correctness in English Usage, 1700–1800.* University of Wisconsin Studies in Language and Literature, No. 25. Madison.

Marckwardt, Albert H. 1958. *American English.* New York: Oxford University Press.

Mathews, Louis Kimball. 1909. *The Expansion of New England: The Spread of New England Settlement and Institutions to the Mississippi River 1620–1865.* Boston: Houghton Mifflin.

Mathews, Mitford McLeod. 1931 (1963). *The Beginnings of American English.* Chicago: University of Chicago Press.

_____, ed. 1951. *A Dictionary of Americanisms on Historical Principles.* Chicago: University of Chicago Press.

McDavid, Raven I. 1966. "Sense and Nonsense about American Dialects." *PMLA* 81:7–17.

_____. 1967. "Historical, Regional, and Social Variation." *Journal of English Linguistics* 1:24–40.

McKnight, George H. 1925. "Conservatism in American Speech." *American Speech* 1:1–17.

Mencken, H. L. 1947. *The American Language: An Inquiry into the Development of English in the United States,* 4th ed. 2 supplements. New York: Knopf.

Michaels, Leonard, and Christopher Ricks, eds. 1980. *The State of the Language.* Berkeley: University of California Press.

Newmeyer, Frederick J., ed. 1989. *Language: The Socio-Cultural Context.* New York: Cambridge University Press.

Orbeck, Anders. 1927. *Early New England Pronunciation as Reflected in Some Seventeenth Century Town Records of Eastern Massachusetts.* Ann Arbor: George Wahr.

Pilch, Herbert. 1980. "The Rise of the American English Vowel Pattern." In Dillard, ed. Pp. 37–70.

Poulsen, Richard C. 1985. *The Mountain Man Vernacular: Its Historical Roots, Its Linguistic Nature, and Its Literary Uses.* New York: Peter Lang.

Pyles, Thomas. 1952. *Words and Ways of American English.* New York: Random House.

Read, Allen Walker. 1933. "British Recognition of American Speech in the Eighteenth-Century." *Dialect Notes* 6:313–334.

_____. 1934. "Words Indicating Social Status in America in the Eighteenth Century." *American Speech* 9:204–208.

_____. 1936. "American Projects for an Academy to Regulate Speech." *PMLA* 51:1141–1179.

_____. 1937. "Bilingualism in the Middle Colonies." *American Speech* 12:93–99.

_____. 1938. "The Assimilation of the Speech of British Immigrants in Colonial America." *Journal of English and Germanic Philology* 37:70–79.

Rollins, Richard M. 1976. "Words as Social Control: Noah Webster and the Creation of the American Dictionary." *American Quarterly* 28:415–430.

Rooney, John F., Wilbur Zelinsky, and Dean R. Louder, eds. 1982. *This Remarkable Continent: An Atlas of United States and Canadian Society and Cultures.* College Station: Texas A&M University Press.

Rowse, A. L. 1959. *The Elizabethans and America.* London: Macmillan.

Sen, Ann Louise Frisinger. 1974. "Dialect Variation in Early American English." *Journal of English Linguistics* 8:41–47.

Simpson, David. 1986. *The Politics of American English: 1776–1850.* New York: Oxford University Press.

Southard, Bruce. 1979. "Noah Webster: America's Forgotten Linguist." *American Speech* 54:12–22.

Stewart, George R. 1945. *Names on the Land: A Historical Account of Place-Naming in the United States.* New York: Random House.

Tucker, Gilbert M. 1921. *American English.* New York: Knopf.

Webster, Noah. 1785. *Sketches of American Policy.* Hartford, CT.

_____. 1789. *Dissertations on the English Language, with an Essay on a Reformed Mode of Spelling.* Boston. (Menston, England: The Scolar Press Ltd., 1967, facsimile).

Williamson, Juanita V., and Virginia M. Burke, eds. 1971. *A Various Language: Perspectives on American Dialects.* New York: Holt, Rinehart and Winston.

Wolfram, Walt, and Ralph W. Fasold. 1974. *The Study of Social Dialects in American English.* Englewood Cliffs, NJ: Prentice-Hall.

Wright, Louis B. 1957. *The Cultural Life of the American Colonies, 1607–1763.* New York: Harper.

Zelinsky, Wilbur. 1973. *The Cultural Geography of the United States.* Englewood Cliffs, NJ: Prentice-Hall.

6

Sociolinguistic Attitudes and Issues in Contemporary Britain

JOHN ALGEO

Language varies socially in the United Kingdom today in some ways that are similar to those in the United States but in others that are characteristic of British English. The main dimensions of contemporary sociolinguistic variation within the United Kingdom are the relationships between the following:

English and other languages
England English and the English of other parts
    of the United Kingdom
British and American English
Standard and nonstandard varieties
Dialect and accent
Regional and social varieties
Urban and rural varieties
Ethnic varieties and the standard
Varieties and the schools

ENGLISH AND OTHER LANGUAGES

As in the United States, English is only one of the languages spoken in the nation, although in the number of its speakers and its role in society, it is the dominant language, with no significant competition. In the United Kingdom, English interacts with the Celtic languages, Welsh and Scots Gaelic particularly. Other Celtic tongues, such as Cornish and Manx, are no longer the first speech of a community, and Irish Gaelic is more usual in the Irish Republic than in Northern Ireland. Other languages with long-standing use in the British Isles are the French of the Channel Islands, Orkney and Shetland Norn, Romani and Anglo-romani, and two argots, Shelta and Polari, that may be the remnants of full languages. A number of more recent immigrant languages are also represented.

The relationship between English and certain non-English languages in the United Kingdom is strikingly different from the relationship between English and other languages in the United States because Welsh and Scots Gaelic, in particular, are spoken in and identified with subnations within the United Kingdom. Before the fifth-century invasion of the Anglo-Saxons, which introduced English into Britain, Celtic languages were spoken over the islands. Their present-day fringe status is the consequence of that invasion and subsequent "internal colonialism." Welsh in particular remains an object of considerable local interest and the focus of intense nationalistic aspirations.

Welsh is now spoken by about one fifth of the population of Wales, chiefly rural in the north and west. The percentage of Welsh speakers has declined through the twentieth century; in 1901 approximately 50 percent spoke Welsh. During the past generation, however, efforts have been made to secure the future of Welsh and extend its use. Bilingual education has been encouraged; Welsh has legal standing in the courts; Welsh-language television and radio programs are broadcast; and in 1988 a Welsh Language Board was established by the government to advise it on questions pertaining to language. Whether these measures will be sufficient to stem the erosion in the use of Welsh is doubtful. By the early nineteenth century, Cornish, closely related to Welsh and Breton on the Continent, had died out as a mother tongue, though antiquarian efforts have been made to revive it.

Scots Gaelic has a much smaller base, being spoken by about 1.5 percent of the population of Scotland, mainly in the northwest and the islands.

Irish Gaelic, although favored by national policy in the Republic, is not prominent in Northern Ireland, where about two thirds of the population are descended from seventeenth-century Scots or English settlers.

Manx, closely related to Gaelic, was spoken on the Isle of Man through the first half of the twentieth century. A few Manx speakers remained until a generation ago, but the language is not now learned as a first language, although it is taught in the schools.

Other non-English languages with a long history in the British Isles have even fewer speakers than the Celtic tongues. On the Channel Islands of Guernsey, Jersey, and Sark, a variety of Norman French is spoken that has been little influenced by standard French, but much by English. The status of the islands is unusual. They are not part of the United Kingdom but, as part of the old Duchy of Normandy, have been dependencies of the English sovereign since the Norman Conquest. They are largely self-governing in local matters but depend upon the British government for foreign relations and ultimately for general oversight. Use of the Channel Islands French patois has declined sharply since World War II, so the language will probably soon disappear.

A variety of Scandinavian called Norn was spoken in northern Scotland until the eighteenth century by descendants of the Vikings. Today it survives only as a substratum in the English of the Orkney and Shetland islands.

Romani, the language of the Gypsies, is spoken by a handful of people, mainly in north central Wales. A creolized version, Angloromani, is spoken by a much larger number (estimated at up to 80,000). Gypsies have been in Britain since the late Middle Ages.

Two argots, Shelta and Polari, may once have been more fully developed linguistic systems than they are today. Both show heavy non-English influence but are of uncertain history. Shelta (also called Gammon, Tarri, or the Cant) is basically English with heavy influence on its vocabulary from Irish Gaelic and some grammatical features unlike either English or Irish. It involves deliberately disguised words and may have developed from a secret trade argot. Polari survives in only about 100 words, the remnant of what was probably once a fuller criminal argot derived in part from Lingua Franca, a Mediterranean pidgin. It is a vocabulary, rather than a full language, used by vagabonds and homosexuals in the theater and navy.

Immigration during the latter twentieth century has introduced a good many newer foreign languages to the United Kingdom. Important among them are a number of languages from the Indian subcontinent—Bengali, Gujarati, Panjabi, and Hindi—and Urdu from Pakistan. Other non-English languages with significant numbers of speakers are Greek, Turkish, Italian, Spanish, Portuguese, French, French-based creoles, Jamaican Creole, Chinese (particularly Cantonese), Yoruba, Arabic, Pashto, Ukrainian, Polish, and German. To the extent that they maintain their linguistic and cultural identity, speakers of these languages form ethnic enclaves primarily in the cities of the United Kingdom.

ENGLAND ENGLISH AND THE ENGLISH OF OTHER PARTS OF THE UNITED KINGDOM

The cultural and political structure of the United Kingdom differs from that of the United States, among other ways, in being divided into four lands or countries: England, Wales, Scotland, and Northern Ireland. England is the dominant member of the partnership in area, population, gross national product, political power, cultural dominance, and therefore language. Yet the four lands have some degree of autonomy, and two of them—Wales and Scotland—have groups actively pushing for devolution of authority and, at the most extreme, for independence, whereas Northern Ireland is riven between an Irish, Catholic minority that wants to unite with the Republic of Ireland and the Scots-English, Protestant majority that seeks close ties with the United Kingdom. In Wales and Scotland especially, language differences assume intense symbolic value.

Scottish English

Scottish English, spoken especially in the lowlands (the south and east) and therefore known as Lallans or simply Scots, has a distinguished history as a literary and official variety of English (McClure, 1983, 1988). Originally a development of the Northumbrian dialect of Old English, it became the national language of Scotland until the accession of the Stuarts to the throne of England in 1603 and the removal of the seat of government out of Scotland by the Act of Union in 1707. Although Gaelic is spoken in the north, Scots for the most part fills the role of "national language" in Scotland that is occupied by Welsh in Wales.

For over 200 years the imminent demise of Scots has been forecast. In one form or another, however, it has gone on being used, although not for the high and official purposes it had before the crowns of Scotland and England were united. During the last third of the twentieth century several organizations were founded to preserve and further the use of Scots, including the Scots Language Society and the Association for Scottish Literary Studies. Scots is actively promoted by Scottish patriots as the medium for literature, government, and private communication.

Scottish English exists in a continuum ranging from vernacular Scots (the "broadest" in pronunciation, vocabulary, and syntax) to educated standard Scottish English (standard England English spoken with a Scots accent). In the north and west, Highland and Hebridean English are variants of standard Scottish English.

The "Scots Renaissance" is a cultural expression of Scottish nationalism. It involves the promotion of Scots for a wide range of uses now served by the English of England and the increased differentiation of Scots from the latter. Efforts to revive Scots for literary and official use in place of the standard English of England have created a variety dubbed "New Scots" by analogy with the "Nynorsk" of Norway, an artificial revival of Norwegian dialect forms to replace Danish. Of this "New Scots," Caroline Macafee says (Görlach, 1985:11):

> The literary variety, or register, so created was known at first as "synthetic Scots," and also from the 1940s as "Lallans." The terms "aggrandised Scots" and "literary Scots" are also used. This literary variety has been deliberately created to fill the role of a Standard Scots, and to a large extent the status of Scots as a language independent of St[andard] E[nglish] hinges on the successful propagation of this variety.

Scotticisms (the characteristic features of Scottish English of any variety) have been distinguished as "covert" or "overt." The former are features typically used without a speaker's awareness that they mark him or her as Scots. They include features such as *I'll better* for *I'd better* and *outwith* for *outside*. Overt Scotticisms are expressions deliberately chosen to advertise the speaker's Scottish identity, for example, *dinna* for *don't*.

Wales, Northern Ireland, and the Isle of Man also have their characteristic varieties of English, but they lack the richness of historical use for official and literary purposes that characterizes Scots.

Welsh English

Welsh English has three main varieties: a southeastern one that is increasingly accommodating itself to the model of standard England English; a southwestern one (many of whose speakers are bilingual) with more influence from Welsh; and a northern one that is very heavily influenced by Welsh. Influences on Welsh English come not only from England English and Welsh, but also from the regional dialects of western England bordering Wales.

Language questions are so sensitive in Wales that the discussion of Welsh English, or even the acknowledgment of its existence, has been criticized as a political act (Coupland, 1990:2). That is, to describe Welsh English is to treat Wales and Welsh ethnicity as subordinate to and dependent on England.

Many nonstandard grammatical features used in Wales are widely distributed in the English-speaking world. Others, more characteristic of Welsh English, are the following (Alan R. Thomas in Viereck, 1985:213–221), some of which doubtless reflect the influence of the Welsh language on English:

1. Use of unstressed and uninflected *do* or past tense *did* to mark the habitual aspect of the verb: "He do/did go to the cinema every week."
2. Fronting a stressed element to focus it: "*Coal* they're getting out, mostly." "*Singing* they were."
3. Use of *there's* before adjectives in exclamatory sentences, where standard English has *how:* "There's tall you are!"
4. Use of an existential clause structure to show possession: "There's no luck with the rich" for "The rich have no luck."

Ulster English

The seventeenth-century Plantation of Ulster settled many Scots, mainly from the southwest of Scotland, and a smaller number of English persons, mainly from the west of England, in the northern counties of Ireland. Today Northern Ireland has several varieties of English, spoken generally from north to south: Ulster Scots (also called Scotch-Irish), very close to the Scots of southwestern Scotland; Ulster English, in several subvarieties; and Hiberno-English, close to the English of the Republic of Ireland.

Manx English

Traditional Manx English was closer to standard English than to the nearest English regional dialects; however, it is following Manx Gaelic on the road to extinction. The English used on the Isle of Man today is said to be increasingly under the influence of Liverpool.

BRITISH AND AMERICAN ENGLISH

Although every English-speaking nation has, or is in the process of developing, its own national variety of English, there are two main branches of World English: British and American. Since the American branch has nearly three times as many speakers as the British, with most of them concentrated in one nation, it is inevitable that it should be influential. One British writer (Honey, 1989:98) has observed that

> the greatest single influence on the grammar, vocabulary, and idiom of English as spoken and written in Britain is American English. This is because of the substantial number of American-made films and serials shown on Britain's four TV channels, and because of the influence, especially on writers and journalists, of books, maga-

zines, and other written material originating in the USA. American idiomatic usages
. . . have invaded British English, and I have watched the development in my own
TV-addicted children of US grammatical forms such as the simple past rather than
the perfect tense with the adverbs *yet, just,* or *already,* expressing time ("I already did
it" for "I have already done it").

The reasons given for the influence of American English on British may not be
fully adequate to account for it, but the fact of that influence is clear, as is the
distaste many Britons feel for it. That distaste appears covertly in the foregoing
comment by the choice of diction in "invaded" and "addicted." It is far more
overt in the following (Hudson, 1983:31–32):

> Nearly all Americans are distinguished or handicapped, according to one's point of
> view, by a remarkably coarse ear, which is probably the result of a levelling process
> brought about by the mixture of races which has gone to make up the American
> nation. Out of this speech-cauldron came a form of language which concentrated on
> basic communication between members of a population which was socially and geo-
> graphically extremely mobile. The subtleties of speech which had characterised the
> much more stable British society for generations had little place or point in America.
> They were undemocratic, as the Americans understood the term, and there was no
> time for them.
>   As Donald Davie pointed out in a brilliantly perceptive article on the subject, in
> American you have to make "the context of your speech do everything that in Britain
> might be managed merely by the tone of it." The American voice and the American
> ear, he goes on to say, is remarkably insensitive—"the ear's not hearing finely stops
> the voice from speaking finely, or vice-versa."
>   There is perhaps a little exaggeration here—some Americans must have a finer ear
> than others—but, in general, Donald Davie's argument is well founded and reason-
> able.

The foregoing excerpt from a much longer comment on the linguistic deficien-
cies of Americans is from a jeremiad on British teenage talk, which the author
would like to blame on the influence of American pop culture. It expresses very
nicely, however, the self-satisfaction that many Britons feel when they compare
themselves with Americans.

Anti-Americanism is an old and enduring tradition in England. Fred Vanderschmidt (1948:2), who at the time was chief London correspondent for *Newsweek* magazine, estimated that "in the year 1947, one out of three Englishmen
were more or less antagonistic to anything that came from America, from Buicks
to businessmen." Of course there is also staunch pro-American sentiment in the
United Kingdom, but very little of it extends to American English. Prejudice
against American culture (which many English people dismiss as a contradiction
in terms) and the American variety of English is endemic.

The British attitude, popular and sometimes academic as well, is that England
holds the copyright on English, which is only lent to others, who should not feel
free to do with it as they like. Sidney Greenbaum (1990:15), in a perceptive essay
on the subject, cites a 1988 speech by Enoch Powell, a former Member of Parliament: "Others may speak and read English—more or less—but it is our language not theirs. It was made in England by the English and it remains our dis-

tinctive property, however widely it is learnt or used." That attitude is perhaps more than merely Colonel Blimpism. As a double-barreled article in the *Times* (Binyon, 1989; Greaves, 1989) notes, teaching English is big, lucrative business, so keeping English British is an investment with dividends.

STANDARD AND NONSTANDARD VARIETIES

The ideal of the standard variety of a language has been said to be "maximal variation in function, and minimal variation in form" (Leith, 1983:32). British English has a standard written variety of the language used throughout the country for institutionalized purposes—publishing, education, government, commerical correspondence, and so on. It is codified by dictionaries and grammar books and is not different in its essentials from the standard English used in other nations where English is the dominant first language. Complications arise, however, in spoken English in both pronunciation and general colloquial usage. In those realms, social class is marked, in pronunciation by RP (received pronunciation) and in colloquial use by U (upper-class) vocabulary. To be an RP and U speaker is to be top-drawer linguistically, although not necessarily in other respects.

It is sometimes said that Americans are more concerned about correctness in language than Britons. However, it is worth remembering that what James and Lesley Milroy (1985) call "the complaint tradition" had its roots in England and that the archetypal usage maven is H. W. Fowler. On the whole, concern with correctness seems fully as intense in the United Kingdom as it is in the United States. The impression that it is not may be based at least partly on the fact that British attention to correctness is often focused on accent, whereas Americans are seldom greatly exercised about matters of pronunciation.

RP is a class pronunciation without local associations. Although basically Southern English, RP was inculcated through the public schools (i.e., prestigious private boarding schools) and accepted as the correct pronunciation for upper-class English men and women. It was selected for use in broadcasting, and so is also known as BBC English.

The technical term *received pronunciation* and its abbreviation *RP* were both used by A. J. Ellis, a nineteenth-century phonetician, in 1869 and 1889, respectively. They were popularized by another phonetician, Daniel Jones, whose *English Pronouncing Dictionary* (first published in 1917) became an authoritative record of which pronunciations were in fact "received." Jones characterized RP as "very usually heard in everyday speech in the families of Southern English people who have been educated at the public schools" (*EPD,* 11th ed., xv). It was once also called *PSP* for *public school pronunciation.*

Although pronunciation and correctness have been concerns of English writers since the days of the sixteenth- and seventeenth-century orthoepists, who wrote books about spellings and the sounds they represented, the particular style of pronunciation called RP may not be greatly older than the term. What is fashionable in language, including pronunciation, is constantly changing. RP itself has changed notably over the past century, and today some variations in RP reflect change in progress. So, a conservative, older-generation type of RP has a triphthong [taiə] in *tyre* (American spelling, *tire*) and pronounces *paw, pore,* and *poor* as three different sounds: [pɔː], [pɔə], [puə]; a more general type of RP has a diphthong [taə] for *tyre* and pronounces both *paw* and *pore* as [pɔː], but *poor* as [puə]; and an innovative, younger-generation type of RP has a monophthong [tɑː] for *tyre* and pronounces *paw, pore,* and *poor* all alike as [pɔː].

John Wells (1982:279–301) speaks of several varieties of RP. "Mainstream RP" is the most usual type, with a good deal of variation in it. "U-RP" or "upper-crust RP" is a particularly "plummy" type, associated with the upper class, narrowly defined. "Adoptive RP" is that learned by someone as an adult rather than as a child, and hence imperfect in details. Presumably it is what Mrs. Thatcher speaks, as described later. "Quasi-RP" is a particularly divergent form of adoptive RP, the result of unrealistic elocution training. "Near RP" is an accent without strong regional identity that would generally be regarded as educated, middle-class, and "well-spoken" but that would not be regarded as RP by RP speakers.

Though the status of RP today is no longer what it once was, it is still the power accent of the United Kingdom. It has been estimated that only about 3 percent of the population of England speaks RP (Trudgill, 1986:3), yet many treat it as the norm for pronunciation, and Britons are sensitive to its implications (Hudson, 1983:5–6):

> In England, one of the most significant clues to the sub-culture to which one belongs is the way one speaks, especially one's accent and intonation. To appreciate the difference between Mrs Thatcher, Mr Heath and Mr Whitelaw in this respect demands a good ear and a long experience of the subtleties and idiocies of English society. It is something not easily sensed by a foreigner. One might express the difference by saying that Mr Whitelaw's English is pure white and that of Mrs Thatcher and Mr Heath off-white. Mr Whitelaw speaks the English of the atmosphere in which he was reared as a child, with the unmistakable tune and accent of the British upper class. Mrs Thatcher and Mr Heath, on the other hand, do not speak the English of their childhood; consciously or unconsciously, they have changed their sounds since they became adult. The change has probably been gradual, but in neither case has it reached perfection. It is nearly right, but not quite. To anyone who understands England, it announces as clearly and unmistakably as a biography could that neither Prime Minister was born to the purple. They are, so to speak, self-made.

A more detailed and sympathetic history of Mrs. Thatcher's accent is given by John Honey (1989:136–137):

> Margaret Thatcher is a classic example of an individual's rise from humble origins through merit, determination, and effort. Her parents both came from working-class backgrounds: by sheer hard work and sound business sense—qualities her supporters would claim she has inherited—they achieved success in running a modest grocer's shop in Grantham, Lincolnshire. . . . It has been said that after winning a scholarship at the age of ten, which took her from the local state school to the town's grammar school for girls, Margaret took elocution lessons. . . . Even so, biographers stress that

after she won her way to Oxford to study for a degree in chemistry, she arrived there
"an unsophisticated lower-middle-class Lincolnshire girl.". . .

It may have been at Oxford, therefore, that she adapted her accent to the rather
posh, marked RP variety which was detectable when she was first an MP (from 1959)
and then a Cabinet minister (1970). After she replaced Edward Heath as leader of the
Conservative party in 1975 . . . she went to some trouble to modify her hairstyle, and,
even more, the pitch of her voice, replacing its hint of stridency with a more soothing,
persuasive quality. It may be that her accent's hyperlectal features also became less
obvious. . . .

A year before Mrs Thatcher became Prime Minister, the historian and socialist
writer A.J.P. Taylor, after watching her on television, reassured his wife that the
leader of the Conservative party was in no danger of achieving power "as she has such
an awful voice."

If the accounts are to be believed, Margaret Thatcher has been continually
modifying her accent and style of speech to achieve the right mixture of upper-
class authority and appealing persuasiveness. And other recent politicians have
also exploited the value of accents, though of different kinds: Harold Wilson's
touch of the northern counties, Neil Kinnock's hint of Welsh lilt, Roy Jenkins's
hyperlectal RP (i.e., a variety of pronunciation regarded as superior to any
other), and so on. Those who modify their speech may be sniffed at, but those
who do not must face harsh judgment (Honey, 1989:145):

> The claim of the Conservative party to be the party of the people—in striking con-
> trast to its upper-class image of earlier generations—can only be strengthened by
> such a range of accents, though old-fashioned journalists from Labour party back-
> grounds may find them hard to accept. Thus Alan Watkins in the *Observer* on the
> Newcastle-under-Lyme by-election in 1982, in which the conservatives fielded a can-
> didate born in Wolverhampton: "He talks in an unaffected Midlands accent. He is
> clearly a perfectly nice man. But he is equally clearly just not up to it. His difficulties
> with the English language are not so great as those experienced by the new Conser-
> vative Member for West Derbyshire, but they are getting on that way."

To succeed in British politics, or at least with political commentators, it is necessary to mind not just your Ps and Qs, but all your consonants and vowels. John
Kennedy, Lyndon Johnson, and Jimmy Carter were all the butt of jokes concerning their accents; but Massachusetts, Texas, and Georgia English were not
widely regarded as disqualifications for public office.

RP is primarily a class accent—geography and education are secondary features in it. Before World War II, those who wished to make their way in the
world—whether in business, government, the military, the church, or society—
had to speak RP. Any other accent marked the speaker as not suitable for admis-
sion to the inner circles that provided security and the opportunity for advancement. In addition, speakers of RP have been perceived as pleasant-sounding,
high in status, comfortable to be with, and intelligent, whereas speakers of an
urban dialect such as that of Birmingham are perceived in the opposite way
(Wakelin, 1972:167; Trudgill, 1986:7). It is the function of RP to evoke such
responses, for an upper-class accent is most effective when the voice of authority
is admired and respected.

G. B. Shaw's play *Pygmalion* (as well as the musical *My Fair Lady,* based on it) takes the sociolinguistic fact of RP as the basis for a joke. In the play, a teacher of phonetics named Henry Higgins (modeled on an actual philologist, Henry Sweet) undertakes to teach a Cockney flower girl how to pronounce English like a duchess. The joke is that it makes no difference what sort of grammar the girl uses, or how vulgar her vocabulary may be, or that the subjects she discusses and her view of the world are clearly lowest class. As long as she pronounces correctly, she is received in the best social circles. Shaw's play is satire, but like all good satire, however outrageously it exaggerates, it is based in reality.

After World War II, however, the position of RP in British public life and the corridors of power began to yield somewhat. Now regional accents are commonly heard on the BBC and from leading politicians. Yet pronunciation is still a class marker in England, and those desirous of getting ahead are likely to modify their native speech styles strongly in the direction of RP. The speech of most English people, urban and working or lower middle class, is not RP, but not very different from it either—just different enough to mark their class.

The relative prestige of accents follows a pattern. Howard Giles (in Coupland, 1990:258–282) reports experiments in which participants who listened to English passages spoken with variable degrees of Welshness by the same person were asked to rate the speaker for various qualities. Speakers of Welsh English tended to rate Welsh-English speech as more socially attractive (trustworthy, kind-hearted, good-natured, humorous, talkative, etc.) than RP but as less competent (intelligent, ambitious, self-confident, determined, industrious, etc.). Similar differences have been found in other communities in the United Kingdom and the United States. It is hardly surprising that we are more comfortable with those who talk like us but attribute powerfulness to those who speak the language of power.

Children from South Wales and Somerset were similarly asked to rate various British and other accents (Giles in Coupland, 1988: 96–97). The accents ranked in prestige as follows (with average ratings in parentheses—low figures being high prestige):

general RP (2.1)
exaggerated, aristocratic RP (2.9)
North American and French (3.6)
German (4.2)
South Welsh (4.3)
Irish (4.6)
Italian (4.7)
Northern English (4.8)
Somerset (5.1)
Cockney and Indian (5.2)
Birmingham (5.3)

The ratings fall into four clear groups. The most prestigious accent was general RP. It was followed by a markedly tony type of RP, often satirized, but still prestigious. The third prestige group consists of two foreign accents: North American and French. The fourth group, in which nine accents are closely clustered, includes others that are foreign (German, Italian, and Indian), British regional (South Welsh, Irish, Northern English, Somerset), and urban (Cockney and Birmingham). The South Welsh and Somerset children showed community loyalty since each community ranked its own accent above that of the other; however, both fell into the least prestigious group of accents. The least prestigious accents were the urban ones and Indian, which is doubtless perceived as urban too because of the large Indian immigrant population in some British cities.

Not only is RP the most prestigious accent, but other accents vary in prestige as they approximate to it. That is, a regional dialect may have varying degrees of broadness, the broadest types being most local and least like RP. The less broad an accent is, the more favorably it is likely to be rated, even by persons who speak it. The prestige of RP is firmly established and pervasive.

The concept of U (for upper-class British usage, as opposed to non-U, or everything else) was introduced by Alan S. C. Ross (1954) and was taken up by Nancy Mitford (1956), becoming for a time something of a parlor game in which the participants tested themselves and everyone else for signs of U and non-U status. Despite the ludic aspects of the subject and some tendency to self-promotion and therefore inaccurate judgment, a serious point underlies the subject. Class status in Britain is signaled not only by pronunciation, but also by word choice and other aspects of language use.

Though the generalization is sound, Ross's specifics are not necessarily so. They may have been true for the circles in which he moved, but there was a joking element about them from the beginning, and the passage of time has seen a social revolution in Britain. In the following list, the first option in each pair is supposed to be U and the second non-U: *have one's bath/take a bath; false teeth/ dentures; house/home; England/Britain* (the Scots and Welsh would not equate the two, although they are both perhaps to be considered collectively non-U); *helping/portion* (of food); *jam/preserve; knave/jack* (in cards); *lavatory paper/ toilet paper; loo* or *lavatory/toilet; looking-glass/mirror; mackintosh/raincoat; pudding/sweet* (American, *dessert*); *rich/wealthy; riding/horseback riding; Royalties/Royals* (members of the royal family—the latter is still labeled "informal" in both Collins and Longman dictionaries, whereas the former has no restriction); *scent/perfume; Scotch/Scottish* (U speakers are unconcerned with what the Scots call themselves); *Sorry!/Pardon!* (as an apology for brushing against someone); *spectacles/glasses; sweat/perspire; table napkin/serviette; wireless/ radio* (*wireless* is now, however, not so much U as very old-fashioned). Individual items on such a list are disputed. Sir Iain Moncreiffe, described on the dust jacket of *U and Non-U Revisited* (Buckle, 1978) as "the world's acknowledged master snob," rejects *Scotch* as U and *mirror* as non-U, but as a Scotsman, he may not be authoritative.

Forms of address also signal class status. In the past this was clearer than it is today, although distinctions linger (Frost and Jay, 1968:29–30):

> The only people now aware of the distinction between the classes are the upper class; the rest of us are confident the whole thing has been abolished. "I don't have to call

you 'Sir' do I?" says the party worker to the Cabinet Minister, the waiter to the famous playwright, the train driver to the chairman of a nationalized industry, the gamekeeper to the scrap millionaire. "Certainly not, my good man," is the brisk reply; and any vague feeling of uncertainty it might arouse is soon assuaged. "After all," he tells himself, "I *am* a good man; good as he is any day, even if I don't play polo." Then he goes off for a nice game of darts.

A U speaker is supposed to refer to his or her spouse as "my wife [or husband]," whereas a non-U speaker says "Mrs. [or Mr.] Jones." However, U speakers talking to a clearly non-U person may refer to their spouses by social title and last name, to avoid any implication of equality with the addressee. Titles of the nobility form a complex system whose intricacies are not mastered even by all British commoners and are largely a mystery to everyone else.

DIALECT AND ACCENT

A dialect is a variety of a language with distinct pronunciation, vocabulary, and grammar, native to a subgroup of a language community. It is a variety of language associated with a group of users and so contrasts with *register,* which is a variety of language associated with a particular use (e.g., a profession or activity like law, computer hacking, church services, and so on). The term *dialect* has been used in English in two quite different though often confused ways. In one use, every such variety of language is called a dialect; in another use, however, one variety is called the "standard" and all other varieties are called "dialects."

In Britain, the term *accent* is used to refer specifically to the pronunciation, as opposed to the vocabulary and grammar, of a linguistic community. Thus, it is possible to say that a person speaks the standard language (i.e., vocabulary and grammar) with an accent (a regional or social pronunciation). The same difference in use as noted for *dialect* applies also to *accent;* that is, some persons regard an accent as a variation from RP rather than as simply a type of pronunciation:

> I have used the word *dialect* for any form of English which differs from Standard English in grammar, syntax, vocabulary, and of course in pronunciation too, though a difference in pronunciation alone is not enough to make a different dialect.... Some people speak Standard English, with an accent, and some speak it without.... This "accentless" pronunciation ... I shall refer to as RP.
>
> [D. Abercrombie, cited by Petyt, 1980:17]

Those words were written in 1951 and express an attitude frequently assumed then but less common now. Today standard English would usually—though not universally—be regarded as a dialect like any other, and RP as an accent like any other, although both have obvious functional differences from regionally limited forms of language.

The differences in attitude that underlie the two uses of *dialect* and *accent* are not trivial. In the older use, well expressed by Abercrombie, one variety of the language ("Standard English") and one pronunciation of it ("RP") are not just specialized in use, but hierarchically superior, the zenith from which all other varieties decline. That use of the terms is imperial, class-conscious, and intrinsically evaluative. The other use, by which all varieties are dialects and all pronunciations accents, even though one dialect or accent may have been institutionalized as a standard, evinces a democratic, egalitarian, and pragmatic attitude instead. In the first use, regional dialects are dialects of (or variants from) standard English and therefore imperfect versions of it. In the second use, all dialects—regional, standard, and others—are variants of English, functionally different versions of the language. The change in the use of the terms mirrors a change in progress in British society as well. Today both uses are possible for the terms, and both attitudes can be found in British society.

The distinction between *dialect* (variation according to the user) and *register* (variation according to the use) is a convenient one, but is not absolute. Dialect differences are themselves variable, more or less broad, and the same dialect speakers will use more or less broad dialect, depending on circumstances. All speakers accommodate their language to their interlocutors in various ways (Coupland, 1988:108–113).

Two speakers will converge in their usage when there is no social pressure to be different and communicative efficiency is served by their becoming more alike, when group solidarity calls for them to be alike, or when some other communicative advantage is to be gained by convergence. Conversely, a speaker may intentionally diverge from the language of an interlocutor, either to gain an advantage or to show solidarity with a group.

For example, a customer may encounter a shop assistant (*Am.*, sales clerk) who uses an accent closer to RP than the customer's normal speech is. The shop assistant's language will seem aloof and superior; the customer may therefore choose to shift into a yet higher-prestige accent in order not to be disadvantaged in the transaction. Conversely, dialect speakers talking with an RP speaker who criticizes their dialect may shift into a yet broader dialect as a statement of local pride and aggressive rejection of the criticism. In such cases of either convergence or divergence, dialect has been converted into a type of register.

REGIONAL AND SOCIAL VARIETIES

In the United Kingdom there is a correlation between regional and social varieties, especially in how greatly speakers differ among themselves. The language of those on the higher social levels differs relatively little, geographically or in other ways. It is relatively uniform. On the other hand, between groups on the lower social levels, there are striking linguistic differences, especially by region, but also by sex and other factors.

The relative uniformity of upper-class speakers is probably a consequence of their traveling about more. Their children are sent to boarding schools usually away from their home areas, where they meet other children from different regions and learn to use standard English and RP. Middle-class speakers are less mobile, and their children are likely to attend schools in their regions, whose teachers themselves may use the regional accent. Lower-class speakers are the least mobile of all, the most geographically and culturally bound to their home areas.

A few years ago, news reports told of a coal mine in the west of England that was being closed as unprofitable, with the miners reassigned to other mines a few miles distant. The miners objected strenuously to being deprived of a place of work in the immediate neighborhood of their residence on the grounds that they had worked there all their lives, as had some of their fathers. To be forced to travel 10 miles to work was regarded as an insufferable hardship. In a class among whom such notions of space are the norm, distinctive regional features of language are inevitable.

Not only are lower-class speakers more representative of their home regions and upper-class speakers less so, but on the whole, men are more regionally identified than women. Within the same social class, women tend more strongly toward standard use and RP than do men. Indeed, it appears that two contrary forces are at work. Middle-class women are especially likely to move in the direction of standard English, which has great prestige for them. Lower-class men (manual laborers), on the other hand, are likely to move in the direction of nonstandard regional forms. For the men of that class, the nonstandard forms of regional dialects carry prestige as signs of tough masculinity. In evaluating their own speech, they may even claim to use more nonstandard English than they actually do, a claim that attests its prestige (Petyt, 1980:158, 160).

The prestige among its speakers of a dialect typical of the lower class is sometimes called "covert" because those who actually value it highly, as shown by their use of it, publicly denigrate it or give higher rank to the standard upper-class dialect, which therefore has "overt" prestige. The prestige of lower-class language is frequently not covert, however. Instead its speakers may cheerfully, even aggressively, acknowledge their preference for it or assert its inherent superiority. They perceive its effectiveness and the inappropriateness of standard English within their community.

URBAN AND RURAL VARIETIES

Dialect study has traditionally focused on rural varieties of the language, but recently urban dialects have received a greater share of attention (Petyt, 1980:151–170). That attention is appropriate, since as much as 90 percent of the population of England is urban. The major population centers of the United Kingdom today are London, Bristol, Birmingham, Nottingham, Sheffield, Manchester, Liverpool, Leeds and Bradford, Newcastle upon Tyne, and Glasgow. Other significantly dense areas include Cardiff, Edinburgh, Belfast, and a number of towns in England. Some urban dialects are known by special names: Cockney (in London), Geordie (in Tyneside, including Newcastle), Scouse (in Liverpool), and Brum (in Birmingham).

A distinctive characteristic of language prestige in Britain is that rural dialects are regarded more favorably than urban ones. In many parts of the world, urban dialects, especially that of the capital city, are regarded as cosmopolitan and fashionable—urbane. In the United Kingdom, however, urban accents—such as those of London and Birmingham—are at the bottom of prestige rankings. Thus, although South Welsh English fares relatively well in prestige among regional dialects and southeastern Welsh English in particular has closely assimilated to RP, the accent of Cardiff, the largest city of Wales and located in the southeast, is highly stigmatized, along with other urban accents (Coupland, 1988:97–98). "The notorious Cardiff accent—said by some to be the worst in the world"—is accused by the press of "uniquely strangled vowels" and a "quirkiness of the voice"; and Cardiff natives label the local accent "common," "ugly," "rasping," and "dreadful."

Urban dialects typically mix regional features from the areas around them and illustrate a "structured heterogeneity"; that is, variation within an urban dialect correlates with the social characteristics of its speakers. For example, there are sharply defined language differences for the social classes, for males versus females, and for age groups.

Norwich

Local studies of nonstandard features have shown clearly the correlation between social class and approximation to standard use. In one of the best known of such studies, conducted in Norwich (Trudgill, 1974:44), it was found that an East Anglian dialect feature—the omission of the verb marker -s—was strikingly indicative of social class. The lowest group of middle-class speakers omitted the ending only 2 percent of the time in casual speech. The highest group of lower-class (or working-class) speakers omitted it 70 percent of the time, and the lowest subgroup of the lower class omitted it 97 percent of the time.

The omission of verbal -s is a diagnostic feature of lower-class speech in Norwich. Other features are also consistent (although less striking) in their correlation with social class—for example, dropping initial h in hot and hammer (6 percent of middle middle-class use, 61 percent of lower working-class use); "dropping g" in walking and eating (31 percent middle middle-class, 100 percent lower working-class); and use of a glottal stop instead of t in butter and fatter (41 percent middle middle-class, 94 percent lower working-class).

London

Cockney is a working-class variety of London speech, specifically that of the East End. Historically, cockneys were born within the sound of "Bow Bells," that is, about a quarter of a mile from the church of St. Mary-le-Bow in Cheapside near London Bridge and the Billingsgate fish market. The term originally was a compound meaning "cock's egg" and was early used for a pampered child, then for a city person, and finally for a Londoner. "Cock o' the walk" associations still cling to the term, for Cockney is seen as a strutting, show-off variety of language, admired by those who use it and the object of amused interest by others.

Present-day Cockney is the heir of centuries of London speech, seen in early forms in Beaumont and Fletcher's *Knight of the Burning Pestle* and Shakespeare's tavern scenes in *Henry IV*. In pronunciation it is characterized by such features as the shifting of many vowel sounds, as in *fancy* ("fency"), *gone* ("gawn"), and *plate* ("plite"); the substitution of an *f* or *v* sound for the *th* sounds in *worth* ("worf") or *other* ("ovver"); the loss of *h* ("'ead and 'eart"); and an abundance of glottal stops, as in *bottle* ("bo'le") and *kipper* ("ki'er"). It has a characteristic vocabulary, including words like *cack-'anded* ("left-handed"), *cock* ("buddy"), *dekko* ("look around"), *lolly* ("money"), and *moggy* ("cat"), many of which have made their way into general informal use.

Riming slang is especially associated with Cockney, although it is found elsewhere in the United Kingdom and abroad, especially in Australia. For a given word it substitutes a riming expression, such as *pen and ink* for *sink*. Preferably, the riming expression makes a sardonic comment on the rimed word, such as *trouble and strife* for *wife* and *God forbids* for *kids*. In a more advanced stage, the riming expression is clipped to its first element, omitting the rime and thus disguising the meaning, as *butcher's* from *butcher's hook* for *look*. Some instances of riming slang have entered general English use: *chew the fat* ("have a chat") *duke* (in "put up your dukes," from *Duke of York* for *fork* and hence—since fingers came first—"hand," "fist"), *loaf* (as in "use your loaf," from *loaf of bread* for *head*), *raspberry* (in "give someone the raspberry" from *raspberry tart* for "fart"), and *tiddly* from *tiddlywink* ("drink"). Cockney also uses other kinds of coded language (similar to the Pig Latin known to American children), such as back slang, which pronounces words backward, like *yob* for *boy*.

Cockney became a staple of music hall songs and comedians, being particularly associated with the "pearly kings and queens," that is, costermongers (fruit and vegetable peddlers) and their wives, who dress in garments covered with pearl buttons. Like urban dialects generally, Cockney has been the object of scorn. But it also occupies a unique slot in English life, as can be seen from the popularity of the 1980s television program *East-Enders,* about Cockneys. On the whole, the English attitude toward Cockney is ambivalent.

General Nonstandard Features

A study of the language of children ages 9–17 in Reading identified nonstandard grammatical features such as the following (Cheshire, 1982):

1. Use or nonuse of *-s* with present-tense verbs and the past of *be:* "I starts Monday." "Well, how much do he want for it?" "Wasn't we more greasers than we was skinheads?" "'Cos I were going to smash him up."
2. Past tense and participle forms: "It woked everyone up." "I've never fighted with her." "She done it, didn't she?" "I've driv that from there over here."
3. Verbs in past-time conditional sentences, either conditional forms in both clauses or a simple preterit in the conditional clause: "If she would

have drowned, she wouldn't have been a witch." "If he didn't look up, it'd have caught him in the eye."

4. *Ain't (in't, in')* for *be not* or *have not:* "How come that ain't working?" "You ain't been around there, have you?"

5. Aggressive tag questions: "—I can't bloody go. —Why not? —'Cos I'm going on fucking holiday, in' I?"

6. An invariant tag: "She makes her laugh, in' it?"

7. Negative concord: "It ain't got no pedigree or nothing."

8. *Never* for general negation: "I never went to school today."

9. *What* as a definite relative: "Are you the little bastards what hit my son over the head?"

10. Zero relative in subject function: "Tell us the one about the lady couldn't get a lift."

11. Prepositions: "She jumped *off of* the climbing frame." "I'll go and get a light *off* Al." "They chucked him *out* their house." "We was smoking *up* his nan's." "I lived one year *down* Staverton." "If you walks across this road, and *over* them bus stops. . . ." "She hit her *round* the face twice."

12. *Them* for *those:* "I've seen them students."

13. Reflexives: "Once he was scratching hisself." "One of his girls burnt their-self."

14. *Me* for *my:* "Where's me fags gone?"

15. Singular nouns of measurement: "It's only thirteen mile."

16. Comparison: "She's badder." "It's usually worser than this." "Not as worse as these two stupid idiots." "He's much more higher than me."

17. Adjective form for adverb use: "I can't read that good." "He writes really quick."

18. Double plurals: "Womens ain't allowed to look."

19. Adverbial *-s:* "And here they go nows."

None of these features are limited to the English of Reading. Some are found in nonstandard use throughout the English-speaking world. A few [*off of; off* ("from")] are in standard colloquial use, although objected to by precisionists. One (adverbial *quick*) is standard both historically and in present-day use, although usage proscribers often inveigh against it.

Similarly, many expressions cited as characteristic of a particular city in the United Kingdom may be found in widely distributed use, regionally, nationally, or even internationally. The following is a short selection from a glossary supposed to concentrate on words exclusive to Glasgow (Munro, 1985): *Arab* (as a term of abuse, generally used for a street kid since 1848, though now old-fashioned), *clatty* ("muddy," "dirty"— a seventeenth-century use in English), *shut your geggie* ("close your mouth"; "shut up"), *lucky bag* (an older British term for what is now called a *lucky dip* or in the United States a *grab bag*), *Paddy's Market* ("a messy place"—from an open-air second-hand market in Glasgow), *punter* ("bloke," "guy"—widespread in the United Kingdom), *two-up* (an obscene gesture generally known in Britain as the *V-sign* and comparable to a differently made American gesture called *the finger* or *the bird*), *yous* (a plural for *you,* also common elsewhere in Britain and in the northern United States).

What marks urban dialects is not so much a unique set of features as a combination of features, most of which are individually found elsewhere.

ETHNIC VARIETIES AND THE STANDARD

The second half of the twentieth century saw extensive immigration to Britain from various of the former colonies and Commonwealth countries. As a result, there are now ethnic enclaves in the United Kingdom in which non-English languages are spoken, as well as various types of foreign-influenced English. A number of such languages were mentioned earlier; here the Caribbean community is touched on briefly.

The settlement of blacks in Britain began in the sixteenth century. Extensive immigration from the West Indies, however, dates from after World War II and largely dried up after the early 1960s when the Commonwealth Immigration Acts stemmed the influx from the West Indies. Most British blacks today were born and reared in the United Kingdom. They have, however, two linguistic inheritances of their ancestry: British varieties of Caribbean Creoles, sometimes called "Patois" or "Jamaican," and a dialect called British Black English or Afro-Caribbean English, which combines urban English speechways with Caribbean influences. Some younger-generation blacks, however, are losing command of the Creole (Edwards, 1986:98):

> Sometimes when I speak to a Rasta guy I cannot speak Patois because I feel I'm going to slip up and feel stupid. If a chap says to me, "You a go burn fire, mi a go deal you a dis, dat" . . . I feel div [stupid] and I'm thinking, "What's he saying?"

British Black English is distinguished by prosodic features and perhaps a more conservative phonology than whites use. It has some characteristic words, such as *facety* ("impertinent") and *duppy* ("ghost"). Its syntactic features include a particle *se* borrowed from Jamaican Creole to introduce clauses after verbs of knowing, discovering, believing, and the like: "A all white jury found out se 'e was guilty."

An extreme modification of English is the result of Rastafarianism, a politicoreligious movement originating in Jamaica. Its name is derived from the pre-coronation name of Haile Selassie I, emperor of Ethiopia: Ras ("prince") Tafari. Rastafarian beliefs hold that blacks are the true Jews, exiled from Africa and under white dominance for their sins, but to be redeemed by a divine messiah, the Ethiopian emperor, who was to restore them to a paradisiacal Africa. After the failure of the expected restoration, Rastafarianism developed a militant political tendency alongside cultural separatism and African-influenced mysticism. It was brought to Britain with Jamaican immigration and has spawned a lingo called Afro-lingua, which involves the deliberate alteration of English words to convey a political message: *inity* for *unity, politricks* for *politics, shitstem* for *system,* and *downpression* for *oppression.*

VARIETIES AND THE SCHOOLS

The presence of communities of non-English speakers, such as those of Indic languages or Jamaican Creole, in England has given rise to educational questions. The desire of such communities to maintain their cultural identity has raised the question of whether their members have a right to literacy in the mother tongue of the community and, if so, who has the responsibility for creating that literacy. In turn, the question of bilingual teaching arises. These issues are essentially political ones productive of great intensity of feeling.

The question of maintaining a non-English mother language through teaching in the schools is complicated by the fact that the speech of non-English communities is modified in Britain. When those communities are well established, a new dialect grows up, for example, British Panjabi, which is what the children of the community are exposed to. What, then, should such children be taught—the Panjabi of Punjab or British Panjabi?

In opposition to those who seek to maintain non-English cultures, including languages, in the United Kingdom, are those who believe that the unity of the nation would be served by assimilating as rapidly as possible all non-English persons into the cultural community of Britain. Between those two opposing views, a compromise is hardly possible.

Educational questions comparable to those concerning foreign-language communities also arise for native regional and urban dialect groups. Several attitudes are held and argued vigorously: that cultural minorities, foreign or domestic in origin, should be assimilated; that minority cultures should guard against their assimilation and assure separate development; that bicultural skills and competence should be developed for economic security; that the government and schools have an obligation to preserve minority cultures; and so on. Two clearly defined positions have emerged with political, although not necessarily philosophical, coherence (Crowley, 1989:258–274; Honey, 1983; Quirk, 1989 a, b).

One position is associated with the political Left, radical social programs, socialism, nationalization of commerce, and antielitism. It proposes to preserve and indeed promote ethnic differences and cultural variety. It opposes the imposition or even the teaching of standard English or of a traditional literary canon (associated with the definition and transmission of standard literary English). Its position is that instead of teaching children to conform to an arbitrary linguistic standard, the schools should concentrate on teaching them tolerance and respect for variation. It views the role of the schools not as transmitting culture but as transforming attitudes.

The other position is associated with the political Right, conservative social positions, capitalism, individual initiative, and the reward of merit. It proposes to preserve and extend cultural homogeneity in opposition to social balkanization. It favors the teaching of the institutionalized standard variety of the language and a common core of knowledge in the interests of the community as a whole, as well as that of its individual members. Its position is that a complex society requires a standard language and a basic common culture and that individuals can be most effective for their own good and that of others if they master the standard language and participate in the common culture. It views the role of the schools as preserving traditional culture while fostering individual initiative within it.

Clearly, both sides in the bitter conflict have ideals and justifications. The Left regards the program of the Right as repressive and designed to preserve the existing social structure's exploitation of the masses in favor of a ruling clique. The Right regards the program of the Left as chaotic and designed to subvert social order and destroy historical continuity as well as to deprive minorities of their best opportunity to develop and succeed.

The controversy has focused on the content, method, and effectiveness of teaching English in the schools. In 1988 a government-appointed body, the Kingman Committee (fifteen persons from education, journalism, literature, linguistics, and industry, chaired by the mathematician Sir John Kingman) delivered a report that defined the duty of the schools as "to enable children to acquire Standard English, which is their right" in opposition to the view that use of the language "can and should be fostered only by exposure to varieties of the English language" (cited in Quirk, 1989a:15). The Kingman report will doubtless not settle the issue, but for the present at least it defines national policy. Whether that policy can be effectively implemented in the schools is a pragmatic question.

These issues are by no means new. In the early 1970s, the sociologist Basil Bernstein proposed that social differences in family life were responsible for differences in the use of language (Gregory and Carroll, 1978:78–85; O'Donnell and Todd, 1980:139–141). Middle-class families were said to be person centered and to promote an "elaborated code" for language use, which expresses individuality and personal values and maintains social distance. It is advantageous in the classroom and so assists academic and social success. Lower-class families were said to be "positional" and to promote only a "restricted code," which expresses commonality and public values. It is disadvantageous in the classroom and so inhibits academic and social success. Bernstein's theories were highly controversial, primarily for political reasons. They lacked empirical support, however, and so could be seen themselves as mainly political.

The educational issues can also be said to be as old as the rise of standard English in the sixteenth century. Complaints about the diversity of the language are coeval with the elaboration and institutionalization of the standard form of the language and probably must be seen as an inevitable accompaniment to it. However, to the extent that the concept of a standard and its usefulness has been challenged—in theory or practice—the controversy has been carried to a new level in recent years in the United Kingdom.

CONCLUSION

Despite challenges from non-English languages (indigenous or immigrant), from regional forms of British English (in lands of the United Kingdom or in provinces and cities within England proper), and from the rising national varieties of the language in Commonwealth countries such as Australia, British standard English is in little danger of disappearing. It will certainly change in the coming century—doubtless in ways we cannot foresee. The two great international branches of English—British and American—which are also at the present time the only two fully institutionalized varieties of the language, will continue to influence each other. Together, they are likely to form the basis for World English.

The social flux that Britain is experiencing today is likely in the long run to appear no more than a further stage in the historical flow of English-speaking peoples from earliest times. Looking back, we can see the socialization of Britain and the loss of Empire after World War II, the growth of Empire and the beginning of political reform in the nineteenth century, the growth of commerce and the victory of parliamentary government in the eighteenth, the struggle between crown and parliament in the seventeenth, the beginnings of Empire in the sixteenth, the civil strife of the War of the Roses in the fifteenth, and so on back to the migration of the Anglo-Saxons in the fifth century, before which we have only speculation and reconstruction.

Throughout its long history, English has endured, adapted, and triumphed. It will doubtless continue on that same course.

ACKNOWLEDGMENT

I am grateful for comments on this paper by Adele S. Algeo, Robert W. Burchfield, Charles Clay Doyle, Manfred Görlach, Randolph Quirk, and Suzanne Romaine.

WORKS CITED AND OTHER REFERENCES

Binyon, Michael. 1989. "Europe Takes a Tongue-lashing." *The Times of London*, October 23, p. 14.

Britain 1989: An Official Handbook. 1989. London: Her Majesty's Stationery Office.

Brook, G. L. 1965. *English Dialects*, 2nd ed. London: Andre Deutsch.

Buckle, Richard, ed. 1978. *U and Non-U Revisited*. New York: Debrett's Peerage and Viking.

Chambers, J. K., and Peter Trudgill. 1980. *Dialectology*. Cambridge, England: Cambridge University Press.

Cheshire, Jenny. 1982. *Variation in an English Dialect: A Sociolinguistic Study*. Cambridge, England: Cambridge University Press.

Coupland, Nikolas. 1988. *Dialect in Use: Sociolinguistic Variation in Cardiff English*. Cardiff: University of Wales Press.

———, in association with Alan R. Thomas, eds. 1990. *English in Wales: Diversity, Conflict and Change*. Clevedon, Avon: Multilingual Matters.

Crowley, Tony. 1989. *Standard English and the Politics of Language*. Urbana: University of Illinois Press.

Crystal, David. 1984. *Who Cares About English Usage?* Harmondsworth, Middlesex: Penguin.

Edwards, Viv. 1986. *Language in a Black Community.* San Diego, CA: College-Hill.

Frost, David, and Antony Jay. 1968. *The English.* New York: Stein and Day.

Görlach, Manfred, ed. 1985. *Focus on Scotland.* Amsterdam: Benjamins.

Greaves, William. 1989. "Selling English by the Pound." *The Times of London,* October 24, p. 14.

Greenbaum, Sidney. 1988. *Good English and the Grammarian.* London: Longman.

———. 1990. "Whose English?" In Christopher Ricks and Leonard Michaels, eds. *The State of the Language.* Berkeley: University of California Press. Pp. 15–23.

Gregory, Michael, and Susanne Carroll. 1978. *Language and Situation: Language Varieties and Their Social Contexts.* London: Routledge & Kegan Paul.

Honey, John. 1983. *The Language Trap: Race, Class and the "Standard Language" Issue in British Schools.* London: National Council for Educational Standards.

———. 1989. *Does Accent Matter? The Pygmalion Factor.* London: Faber and Faber.

Hudson, Kenneth. 1983. *The Language of the Teenage Revolution: The Dictionary Defeated.* London: Macmillan.

Hughes, Arthur, and Peter Trudgill. 1987. *English Accents and Dialects: An Introduction to Social and Regional Varieties of British English,* 2nd ed. London: Edward Arnold.

Jones-Sargent, Val. 1983. *Tyne Bytes: A Computerized Sociolinguistic Study of Tyneside.* Frankfurt am Main: Lang.

Kingman, John. 1988. *Report of the Committee of Inquiry into the Teaching of English Language.* London: Her Majesty's Stationery Office.

Leith, Dick. 1983. *A Social History of English.* London: Routledge & Kegan Paul.

McClure, J. Derrick, ed. 1983. *Scotland and the Lowland Tongue: Studies in the Language and Literature of Lowland Scotland in Honour of David D. Murison.* Aberdeen: Aberdeen University Press.

———. 1988. *Why Scots Matters.* Edinburgh: Saltire Society.

Milroy, James, and Lesley Milroy. 1985. *Authority in Language: Investigating Language Prescription and Standardization.* London: Routledge & Kegan Paul.

Mitford, Nancy, ed. 1956. *Noblesse Oblige: An Enquiry into the Identifiable Characteristics of the English Aristocrat.* London: Hamish Hamilton.

Munro, Michael. 1985. *The Patter: A Guide to Current Glasgow Usage.* Glasgow: Glasgow District Libraries.

O'Donnell, W. R., and Loreto Todd. 1980. *Variety in Contemporary English.* London: Allen & Unwin.

Petyt, K. M. 1980. *The Study of Dialect: An Introduction to Dialectology.* London: Andre Deutsch.

Price, Glanville. 1984. *The Languages of Britain.* London: Edward Arnold.

Quirk, Randolph. 1989a. "Language Varieties and Standard Language." *JALT Journal* 11:14–25.

———. 1989b. "Separated by a Common Dilemma." *Times Higher Education Supplement* February 10, pp. 15–18.

Rosen, Harold, and Tony Burgess. 1980. *Languages and Dialects of London School Children: An Investigation.* London: Ward Lock Educational.

Ross, Alan S. C. 1954. "Linguistic Class-indicators in Present-Day English." *Neuphilologische Mitteilungen* 55:20–56.

Sivertsen, Eva. 1960. *Cockney Phonology.* Oslo: Oslo University Press.

Sutcliffe, David, and Ansel Wong. 1986. *The Language of the Black Experience: Cultural*

Expression Through Word and Sound in the Caribbean and Black Britain. Oxford, England: Blackwell.

Trudgill, Peter. 1974. *The Social Differentiation of English in Norwich.* Cambridge, England: Cambridge University Press.

———, ed. 1978. *Sociolinguistic Patterns in British English.* London: Edward Arnold.

———, ed. 1984. *Language in the British Isles.* Cambridge, England: Cambridge University Press.

———. 1986. *Dialects in Contact.* Oxford, England: Blackwell.

Vanderschmidt, Fred. 1948. *What the English Think of Us.* Reprint. London: Quality Press, 1951.

Viereck, Wolfgang. 1985. *Focus on England and Wales.* Amsterdam: Benjamins.

Wakelin, Martyn F. 1972. *English Dialects: An Introduction.* London: Athlone Press of the University of London.

Wells, J. C. 1982. *Accents of English.* 3 vols. Cambridge, England: Cambridge University Press.

Wright, Peter. 1981. *Cockney Dialect and Slang.* London: Batsford.

7

A Polyphony of Voices: The Dialectics of Linguistic Diversity and Unity in the Twentieth-Century United States

JUDITH RODBY

> Backward I see in my own days where I sweated through fog with linguists and contenders.
>
> WALT WHITMAN, "Song of Myself"

In the United States in the latter half of the twentieth century, Americans are increasingly multilingual, but no one, it seems, hears sweet polyphony in this multitude of voices. No one is content with the linguistic state of affairs. In the national media, we find tales of a beleaguered "standard" English battling to preserve its status and power as the "majority" language. In this drama, "minority" languages and nonstandard dialects of English threaten to repeat the tragedy of Babel. English needs to be protected, or so the story goes.

From the "other" perspective, however, English is a megalomaniacal bully who recognizes no voice but his own. English is a kind of inverse Robin Hood, stealing mother tongues from the poor so that only the rich can use them in the confines of the foreign language class.

Ideologues of nationalism pressure for linguistic unity, while advocates of cultural pluralism and champions of ethnicity extol the value of linguistic diversity. Former President Reagan implies that bilingualism is un-American, while "pluralism and diversity" are currently badges of honor in the American academy (quoted in Hakuta, 1986:207). Both the majority and the minority are awhirl with these pressures. From the English monolingual to the Lao trilingual, all are affected; the forms and functions of each language, whether English, Spanish, or Hmong, are continuously reshaping themselves, as are the social relations these languages mediate. To describe the linguistic milieu in the United States in the latter half of the twentieth century, this essay looks closely at how these divergent pressures have come into being in the last thirty years and how the current situation contrasts with the linguistic forces of the early twentieth century.

LINGUISTICS, SOCIOLINGUISTICS, AND HISTORY

This essay critically surveys and synthesizes sociolinguistic research on language use in the United States in the twentieth century, with particular attention on the period since World War II. It is historical in its approach, documenting and analyzing changes in language use, attitude, and policy diachronically. The essay is written largely from a macrosociolinguistic perspective; the unit of analysis is not the individual's language use but that of the group, specifically the ethnic group and the nation. I attend to language use within communities—for example, how casual attitudes and offical policies and how schools, courts, and other institutions shape language use and the social relations that language mediates.[1]

I rely on Soviet language theorist M. M. Bakhtin for the central premises and terms of this argument. I have chosen Bakhtin because of his dialectical view of language, a perspective that emphasizes the continual transformation of language and its uses in response to opposing forces. This perspective, it seems to me, accurately captures the linguistic milieu of the twentieth-century United States. I also employ Bakhtin to escape the conceptual tether that American sociolinguists inherited from Ferdinand de Saussure (1857–1913) and Noam Chomsky. From Saussure, American linguists acquired the inclination to analyze the internal and structural aspects of language rather than its use in the social universe. Saussure's contemporary Meillet thought that twentieth-century linguists would develop a kind of historical analysis of language by examining language change embedded in social change: "But students of Saussure such as Martinet actively repudiated this notion" (Labov, 1972:185). The point is that the Saussurian point of view influenced even early American sociolinguists in the methods and terms they used to document and describe language in society.

Furthermore, continuing in the Saussurian tradition, American linguist Noam Chomsky thought that the appropriate goal of linguistic study was to develop a model of linguistic "competence." Competence, Chomsky maintained, is the unconscious knowledge or rules that every native speaker possesses about her language. In Chomsky's model of competence, the native speaker is hardly flesh and blood; instead she is an "ideal [ized] speaker-listener, in a completely homogenous speech-community" (Chomsky, 1965:3). Although American sociolinguists rejected Chomsky's claim that linguists should study only the linguistic competence of ideal speaker-listeners rather than the language use of real people, they implicitly accepted Chomsky's distinction between competence and performance. As a result, even such innovative sociolinguists as Dell Hymes and William Labov do their work within the limits of the terms and methods of the competence model. Hymes has focused on the competence of communication (or communicative competence) and Labov has developed rules for language variation (otherwise called variation rules). However, communicative competence and variation rules do not exhaustively explain real (thus heteroglossic) language performance.

Moreover, the notions of rules and competence are conceptual blocks to understanding linguistic diversity. These concepts suggest that language is a thing, a finished object or an organic unity. Bilingualism and other phenomena of linguistic diversity challenge the notion of language's organic unity because these phenomena make salient the ragged margins and permeable boundaries of a language. The bilingual person's utterance, for example, may be described as being part of two language systems at once (see the following discussion of code-switching). Einar Haugen remarks on the consequences of this propensity to study language as a closed system:

> As of the census of 1940, [there were] 21,996,240 white Americans whose native language had not been English. . . . Yet [bilingualism] was for many years markedly neglected in this country, and we might say that popularly and scientifically, bilingualism was in disrepute. Just as the bilingual himself was often a marginal personality, so the study of his behavior was a marginal scientific pursuit.
>
> [Haugen, 1971:59–60]

This tendency to reify or hypostasize language has prevailed not only in the study of standard English but also in the approach to nonstandard dialects.

In contrast, for Soviet language theorist M. M. Bakhtin, a "unitary language" is not a natural and material reality but rather is:

> always in essence something posited—and at every moment of its linguistic life is opposed to the realities of heteroglossia. But at the same time it makes its real presence felt as a force for overcoming this heteroglossia, imposing certain limits to it, guaranteeing a certain maximum of mutual understanding and crystalizing into a real though relative unity—the unity of the reigning conversational (everyday) and literary language, "correct language."
>
> [Bakhtin, 1981:270]

Bakhtin argues that all language is always and forever in the push–pull motion of a dialectic: Centripetal forces homogenize and centralize language use. Centrifugal forces work to diversify and decentralize language. Heteroglossia is the term that describes "the collision" of centripetal and centrifugal forces.

Bakhtin's emphasis on heteroglossia, linguistic openness, diversity, and change captures the dialectical forces in language use in the twentieth-century United States. Within the framework of mainstream American linguistics, these aspects of language are not salient because, as Bakhtin's American editor remarks, heteroglossia is "that which a systematic linguistics must always suppress"(Bakhtin, 1971:428).

An optimist would argue that centripetal forces promote unity and communication and that centrifugal forces nurture diversity and change. Dialectically, however, centripetal forces are also conservative, preservationist impulses working for linguistic unity through the careful and conscious exclusion of alien languages. In a conservative spirit, centrifugal forces lead to the cacophony of Babel.

In the late 1980s and early 1990s, centripetal forces have manifested themselves in the "English Only" movement, in the writings of language purists such as John Simon and Edwin Newman, in the jeremiads of E. D. Hirsch and Alan Bloom, and in the assimilationist tale of Richard Rodriguez. Centrifugal forces are comprised of new waves of non-English-speaking immigrants, euphemistically referred to as "changing demographics," non-standard dialects of English, and the discipline of linguistics itself.

To understand language use at the end of the century, we need to examine the dynamics of language and social relations in the first half of the century. As we know, language mediates social relations, and, dialectically, social relations influence language; centripetal and centrifugal social forces unify and diversify languages and language use.

NATIONALISM, ETHNICITY, AND MOTHER TONGUE SHIFT: 1900–1960

Between 1840 and 1924, two thirds of the 35 million new immigrants spoke a native language other than English. Even though these immigrants tried to maintain their mother tongues and pass them on to their children, within a few generations most immigrants had encouraged or at least allowed their children to acquire English as their mother tongue. In 1938, Einar Haugen, a scholar of bilingualism in the United States, described this process of language shift, which many have seen as an unquestionable good. Haugen points out the position of privilege that English held then and would continue to hold for the next forty years at least:

> America's profusion of tongues has made a modern Babel, but a Babel in reverse. City and countryside have teemed with all the accents of Europe and the rest of the world, yet America has never swerved from the Anglo-Saxon course set by her founding fathers. In the course of a century and a half the United States has absorbed her millions and taught them her language more perfectly than Rome taught the Gauls and the Iberians in centuries of dominion. . . . All of this done without political compulsion, through the social pressure of a culturally and economically dominant language.
>
> [Haugen, 1971:1–2]

For our purposes, it becomes the central question to discover what exactly were the "social pressure[s] of a culturally and economically dominant language" such that it forced immigrants to the United States to give up their native tongue for English so rapidly. What were, in other words, the centripetal or unifying forces that prevailed over the centrifugal forces of the time?

In the United States, centripetal and centrifugal forces are related to the ideologies and processes of nationalism and ethnicity, respectively. In some sociological literature, including that of many sociolinguists, the terms *ethnicity* and *nationalism* appear to be nearly synonymous. In one sense this conflation is easy to understand; the word *ethnos* is Greek for nation. Both ethnicity and nationalism promote unity within a group, a feeling of "we," of "our people." Some scholars see the difference between the two as simply a matter of scale; a nation can be seen as nothing more than a self-aware ethnic group (Connor 1978:388), an ethnic group with a wish for self-control. In the case of Ireland, for example, nationalism is highly ethnic. Nationalistic discourse emphasizes the people's desire to protect cultural authenticity in a culturally homogeneous state. In the United States, however, nationalism and ethnicity are not coterminous. They are dialectical processes; they emerge from different types of social relations, and they shape different patterns of language use.

LANGUAGE AND NATIONALISM

The idea that a particular language is somehow indelibly linked with a people and by extension with a nation is a product of late eighteenth- and early nineteenth-century German romanticism. Johann Herder was perhaps the first in a line of thinkers to maintain that a native language expresses a nationality's spirit or soul. A contemporary version of this reasoning, which connects not language and nation necessarily but language and culture, is found in what has come to be called the Sapir–Whorf hypothesis. The hypothesis is named for linguists Benjamin Whorf and Edward Sapir, who suggested that forms of language influence thought. Sapir wrote that language "actually defines experience for us by reason of its formal completeness and because of our unconscious projection of its implicit expectations into the field of experience" (Sapir, 1931:578). Gathering data from insurance claims and the Hopi language, Whorf worked to develop and substantiate Sapir's claim. He extended the argument by maintaining that when culture and language develop together, forms of language and aspects of culture are related in significant ways.

Although the notion of connections among language, culture, and nation has fascinated the American academy, the idea has never really become part of the national consciousness. In popular lore the English language has not been linked to the spirit and soul of the United States. For much of the century, Americans have paid only slight attention to English:

> The English language—as a symbol, as a cause, as a supreme good—does not figure prominently in the scheme of values, loyalties, and traditions by which Americans define themselves as "Americans." Americans do not find English particularly beautiful, divine, or indivisible from American traditions. Americans have no . . . particular concern for its purity, subtlety or correctness.
>
> [Fishman, 1966:30]

Throughout most of U.S. history, the English language has been neither a national cause nor a nationalistic force. English was not built into the Constitution. Unlike many European countries, there is no official language academy to regulate English "usage." In fact, John Adams' proposal for such an academy was judged inimical to the spirit of freedom in the United States (Heath, 1976). As exceptions to this national ethos, there were times and places, however limited, in which English was revered. In the early 1900s a nationalistic, isolationist policy in the United States led to nationwide imposition of English-only instruction policies. These policies also resulted in literacy tests as a prerequisite for voting (Gonzalez, 1975:6). During World Wars I and II, the German and Japanese languages were prohibited in certain public places. However, in none of these cases did anyone argue for the sanctity of the American connection to the English language. Rather, emphasis was on the dangers of the "other," the Spanish-speaking majority in the Southwest and the Japanese enemies of wartime.

LANGUAGE AND ETHNICITY

In the early part of the twentieth century, ethnicity was a centrifugal and diversifying linguistic force. Most immigrants lived in rural communities with others from their home countries. They spoke the language, ate the foods, played the games, sang the songs, and generally lived the life of the mother country as much as possible. This "primordial" ethnicity promoted the use of the mother tongue in each ethnic group. On a national scale, this way of life encouraged the use and maintenance of many languages. Sociolinguists Joshua Fishman and Vladimir Nahirny (1966:170) argue that the immigrants living in rural ethnic communities established a "staunch fortress of language maintenance without any ideological-symbolic commitment." People did not think much about their language, foods, and other cultural patterns setting them off from others and creating a "we-ness." They did not think ethnicity worthy of much discussion.

This pattern of social and linguistic relations did not last long, however. As more and more immigrants began to move to cities in search of work, the rural ethnic community began to disappear. In cities, ethnicity became "transmuted" (Fishman, 1966:70). It became ideologized and self-conscious. Many of the everyday ways of the mother country were lost. Yet the ethnic group persisted, through consciousness of the boundary between "us" and the other (Barth, 1969). Even though the groups lost their specific folkways, they shared an ideology that "we are not them." As part of this trend, the ethnic organization began to replace the ethnic community (Fishman and Nahirny 1966:156). This change in ethnicity was not due to the "development" in cities, but rather to the social relations that were both possible and unavoidable in cities (Lieberson, 1981).

When ethnicity became transmuted, language maintenance became ideologized. As ethnicity became increasingly ideological, use of the mother tongue became less a mediator of the "we," and language less a part of ethnicity. Immigrant groups talked about the importance of the mother tongue, but they actually spoke it less and less. Increasingly, ethnic organizations became de-ethnicized; at the card games and dinners "all [were] welcome." In reaction, older members of ethnic communities established new organizations that encouraged immigrants to speak the non-English mother tongue. Meanwhile, mother-tongue newspapers died, non-English schools closed, and churches switched to English to attract new members (Glazer, 1966:361).

Transmuted ethnicity easily evolved into a centripetal force. When ethnicity was denuded of actual folkways and languages, what remained was group consciousness, the desire to belong to a group. Practically without notice, however, this need to belong shifted from the local ethnic group to a larger, more abstract national group.

These centrifugal forces, the forces of diversity, invent their opposite, the centripetal forces. As we have seen, in the second generation, English is the mother tongue most often in cities with high mother-tongue diversity (Lieberson, 1981:168). Centripetal forces grew with universal education, institutional pressure from public schools, and laws that supported an informal policy privileging English (Lieberson, 1981:68).

Dialectically, social relations changed language use and language use changed social relations. For the second-generation immigrant living in an urban area where mother-tongue diversity was high (Lieberson 1981:168), the cohesion of the mother-tongue-speaking ethnic group broke down. The immigrant began to need English as a mother tongue to feel a part of the group—and the group that had become important was the nation.

Centrifugal forces emerged from first-generation communities speaking many languages. Centrifugal forces gave rise to a need for unity. This need, this centripetal force, produced a second generation that spoke English as the mother tongue. With the third generation, centrifugal forces again began to have some influence as these Americans became interested in their history, their roots. They spoke nostalgically of many "ethnic" things—but not of (immigrant mother-tongue) language maintenance (Fishman and Nahirny 1966:164). Instead, they were interested in folkways, in religious traditions, and perhaps in vestiges of the mother tongue in greetings and other phatic expressions.[2]

Through this dialectic of centrifugal and centripetal forces, ethnicity became transmuted ethnicity and transmuted ethnicity, in turn, became nationalism. Demographically, the end results were that: "By 1930 fewer spoke non-English mother tongues than ever before" (Fishman and Hofman, 1966:39). By 1940, 53 percent of second-generation white Americans reported English as their mother tongue, whereas only 25 percent of their parents did. Furthermore, fewer and fewer were foreign born, reaching a low in 1960 with 9,738,143—the lowest point in fifty years, a decrease of 12.35 percent since 1940. With this decrease in new immigrants and with the death of old immigrants came fewer language-maintenance institutions, ethnic organizations, mother-tongue newspapers and schools (Fishman and Hofman 1966:39). Because "national unity" is an idealization, it can never exhaustively shape the language of real people who want to speak and write to each other.

In the United States, language use—conversations, speeches, songs, letters, notes, and books—promotes national unity, but it also encourages the local, the ethnic "we." Centripetal forces are strongly ideological; they are abstractions. As a result, centrifugal forces are always inherent in centripetal forces.

THE CASE OF SPANISH: 1900–1970

In the first half of the twentieth century, use of Spanish grew while most immigrant language use waned (Fishman, 1972:146–147). This phenomenon is popularly explained as follows: Spanish speakers, especially those from Mexico, cling stubbornly to Spanish, coldly and irrationally spurning English, while Europeans make the effort to acquire English, "without bilingual education." In fact, throughout the twentieth century Spanish use has risen continually, but the increase has resulted primarily from continuing immigration rather than from parents' passing on Spanish as a mother tongue. As sociolinguist Eduardo Hernandez-Chavez notes, a number of studies have shown that within a family, Spanish use has declined sharply with each new generation (in Penalosa, 1981:156).

The continual stream of new Spanish-speaking immigrants exerted centrifugal force on English and its speakers. These new immigrants created the (albeit true) impression that more and more Spanish was being spoken in the United States. And the story about Mexican fervor for Spanish and disdain for English developed to ease native English speakers' discomfort with the centrifugal pressures of language diversity. Because of this confusion over Spanish use, I will attempt to untangle and reinterpret the story. Because Spanish speakers in the United States are overwhelmingly Mexican, my discussion will concentrate on language use in these communities.

In 1848, southwestern lands and approximately 75,000 Mexican Spanish speakers were annexed to the United States through military force (McWilliams, 1968:52). Since about 1900, and continuing throughout the twentieth century, Mexican immigration has been a continuous source of cheap labor in the United States. Spanish speakers first worked in the mines and on the railroads. After the Chinese Exclusion Act of 1882 and the 1907 Gentlemen's Agreement with Japan, Mexican immigrants were needed in agriculture too. Between 1900 and 1910 came 48,900 new immigrants; between 1910 and 1920 another 163,000. By 1920, Mexican (Spanish-speaking) immigrants were the major labor force on railroads and in agriculture (Cardenas, 1975). The years 1920 to 1930 brought an additional 487,700 new immigrants, many of whom were deported during the Depression. In wartime, however, the Mexicans were once again encouraged to labor in the United States.

Social interaction is essential for language acquisition to occur. Since most Mexican Spanish-speakers were in the United States only temporarily, working with other Spanish speakers in the fields, in the mines, and on the railroads, they had little social contact with English speakers. The Mexicans lived in company housing and migrant camps. They were supervised by bilinguals. When the work ran out, they left. When moving into cities, they found themselves in communities like East Los Angeles, where they lived among "the smoggy midst of soap factories, chemical plants, railroad switching yards, gas works, sausage factories, warehouses, stockyards and junk yards" in segregation from Anglo society (Herrera 1971:235). Because of segregation and job insecurity, these Mexicans spoke Spanish of necessity. There was nothing overtly ideological about their choice of language.

The tale that blames Mexicans for not learning English also praises other Spanish speakers for their quick acquisition of English. The differences in situations are striking, however; historically, these other Spanish speakers—Cubans,

Puerto Ricans, and Central Americans—have had more opportunities to interact with English speakers than the Mexicans have had. Beginning in the late 1950s and the early 1960s, many upper- and middle-class Cubans fled their country because of Castro's reforms. These people generally received a sympathetic welcome from Americans. Their lives in the United States were very different from those of the Mexican farm workers, and as the Cubans interacted with Americans, they learned English. Since the 1940s many Puerto Ricans have migrated to northeastern inner cities, where they have lived among English speakers, especially speakers of Black English Vernacular. As a result of this contact with black Americans, many Puerto Ricans, particularly the youth, have acquired features of Black English Vernacular (Wolfram, 1972). The Central Americans who began coming to the United States as political refugees in the late 1970s were able to interact with Americans because, at least initially, they came in relatively small numbers to live in cities. Because of their social circumstances, these groups of Spanish speakers have appeared to maintain their Spanish less fervently and acquire English more readily than the Mexicans. However, when Mexicans were able to stay in the United States, find permanent jobs, and send their children to school, they too began to interact with English speakers, and this interaction promoted language shift to English, even when the contact placed the Spanish speakers in a subordinate position (Sanchez, 1983:7).[3]

Patterns of language use change throughout time. Cultural and linguistic systems arise out of social conditions, but new uses of language may, in turn, destroy the conditions that gave rise to them. What this means is that the Mexican community did not proceed through a series of stages of social and linguistic developments beginning with separatism (a centrifugal force) and ending with assimilation (centripetal). Both centrifugal and centripetal forces were always possible and present in language use. The outcome of this dialectical opposition is balanced only temporarily. Each position pushes on the other until it becomes its opposite.

A chronological account of Spanish use in the United States yields a dizzying portrait of opposing impulses: a desire to preserve ethnicity, with maintenance of Spanish as a side effect, and a desire to belong to the national unity, with English acquisition as a side effect. For example, from the 1950s until the mid-1960s, a stance that Santillan calls cultural democracy gave rise to groups such as the Viva Kennedy and Johnson clubs and the Mexican-American Political Association (MAPA) (Sanchez, 1983:22–23). After a fairly silent thirty years (approximately 1920 to 1950), in and through these groups Mexicans began to articulate their discomfort with their position in Anglo society (Love, 1970:461). The life story of Enrique Hank Lopez, founding member of MAPA and one-time national coordinator for the Viva Kennedy clubs, illustrates the dialectic that grounded these groups. He refers to his childhood as a "cultural tug of war" in which language was the rope. He learned English "rapidly and rather well' by drilling on tongue twisters with a mouth full of pebbles. Nonetheless, he says that "the hard core of me remained stubbornly Mexican." In the midst of this dialectic, a process that "almost pulled me apart," he would at one moment "identify almost completely with the gringo world" and in another "feel so acutely

Mexican that I would stumble over the simplest English phrase" (Lopez, 1971:264–265).

The 1960s Chicano movement was also dialectically rooted. On the one hand, it was about the separatist emotions of El Plan de Aztlan (1969), El Plan de la Raza Unida (1967), and the Alianza Federal de Merceds (Federal Alliance of Land Grants), a millenarian movement attempting to "reclaim" forcefully the Kit Carson National Forest and Tierra Amarilla courthouse (Love 1970:460). On the other hand, it was about "equal opportunity"—that is, joining American society.

Chicana sociolinguist Rosaura Sanchez rightly argues that language has never been a "rallying symbol in the various labor and student protests in the Southwest throughout the century, although it has served as a vehicle for expressing community concerns." Spanish, in other words, has functioned solely to mediate ethnicity. In contrast, in 1929, in a rare instance in which language was an ideological issue, LULAC (League of United Latin American Citizens) wrote the following preamble to its Constitution:

> To develop within the members of our race, the best and purest and most perfect type of true and loyal citizen of the United States of America. The acquisition of the English language, which is the official language of our country, being necessary for the enjoyment of our rights and privileges . . . we pledge ourselves to learn and speak and teach the same to our children.
>
> [Sanchez, 1983:22]

Generally, however, Spanish use was not an ideological issue until bilingual education began to hold national attention. Spanish was part of a pattern of primordial rather than transmuted ethnicity.

BILINGUALISM AND CODE SWITCHING

In the United States, generally, first-generation immigrants have become bilingual and their children or their grandchildren have become native speakers of English. Bilingualism aids the transition, and, because it facilitates a mother-tongue shift, it is unstable (Lieberson, 1981:158; Hakuta, 1986:166). This is not true of bilingualism in all societies, but this pattern has been true of the United States throughout much of the twentieth century. I shall now briefly examine how bilingualism has acted as a centripetal force in the United States—how it has worked to promote linguisitc unity.[4]

Bilinguals choose and vary the languages they use according to the social interactions in which they are involved. Some sociolinguists argue that language choice depends on the social "domain" in which language is used; example domains are school, recreation, government, employment, and home. In some societies, specific domains are rather rigidly and more or less permanently associated with a specific language, and only one language is ever used at a time. This is not, however, the case in the United States.

Bilingualism in the United States can be characterized as a process of "lan-

guage contact of a subordinate lingual-national minority with a politically, economically and linguistically dominant majority." Rosaura Sanchez argues that
"this scenario leads first to the overlapping of functions for the languages and
eventually to a transition from the subordinate to the dominant language even
in those areas previously reserved for the minority language" (Sanchez,
1983:139). In other words, bilingualism is not stable but dynamic.

For example, take a case in which initially only Spanish is spoken in the home.
After the children go to school with English speakers, they may begin to speak
English at least occasionally with each other at home, and their attitudes toward
their family may be altered. Richard Rodriguez says that once he learned English
his relations with his famiy did indeed change: "the house I returned to each
afternoon was quiet. Intimate sounds no longer rushed to the door to greet
me. . . . Once I learned a public language, it would never again be easy for me to
hear intimate family voices" (Rodriguez, 1982:27–28). For Rodriguez, the
domains of language use were in flux because social relations were in flux.[5]

"Dynamic" bilingualism leads to massive code switching (Sanchez,
1983:139). Code switching, it is generally agreed, occurs in "situations of rapid
transition where traditional intergroup barriers are breaking down and norms of
interaction are changing" (Gumperz, 1982:64). Code switching is "the juxta-
position within the same speech exchange of passages of speech belonging to two
different grammatical systems or subsystems" (Gumperz, 1982:59). Code
switching can be distinguished from borrowing because phonological rules are
maintained. Code switching must also be distinguished from what linguists have
called "interference."

An example follows (Sanchez, 1983:143):

> *Jaime:* Es de ellos el aeroplano?
> *Father:* No, no ellos rentan. Sí.
> *Jaime:* You gotta have those. In Mexico they do that. . . .
> *Mother:* Y luego tienen una cosa para hacer agujeros.
> *Son:* About a half a million dollars, Jaime, American money, worth of farming
> equipment from the United States.

Although some analysts might argue that the switches into English are determined by the topic of the utterance (money) or the speech act of boasting in this
conversation (Sanchez, 1983:142), following John Gumperz I would argue that
speakers also choose their language based on the type of relationship they wish
to build with their interlocutors. When they want to establish the sense of an
ethnic "we," the ethnic language is used or shifted into; if they want to include
themselves and the speaker in a national English-speaking unity, they choose to
speak in English.

In the preceding conversation, Jaime switches from Spanish into English with
his second utterance. With this switch, Jaime wants to establish that he and his
addressees belong together to an English-speaking unity or nation of English
speakers. With the phrase "In Mexico they do that . . .," he removes not only
himself but also his addressees from the motherland. Here both the language
structures ("they" referring to Mexico and Mexicans) and the code-switch itself

carry information about the kind of relationship Jaime wants to construct with his addressees. He defines both his interlocutors and himself as Americans through their difference, by referring to the Mexicans as "they," "in Mexico."

When the son replies, however, he distances himself from the United States, while speaking in English. He speaks of the United States as though it were the foreign country. In the son's utterance, we find not only code switching but heteroglossia. We find the collision of centripetal and centrifugal forces, the desire for unity with and the need for difference from English speakers. We find the nationalistic and the ethnic *we.*

BILINGUAL EDUCATION

In the United States bilingual education did not begin in the late 1960s and early 1970s, as is commonly thought. Indeed, during the 1700s German was the primary language of instruction in Pennsylvania, Maryland, Virginia, and the Carolinas, whereas Spanish was used in education in California in the 1800s and in New Mexico as late as 1884 (Briere, 1979:1).

As mentioned earlier, periodically there have been attempts to forbid the use of non-English tongues in education. One of the earliest legal challenges to these policies was seen in 1923 in *Meyer* v. *Nebraska.* The Supreme Court eventually declared unconstitutional a state statute that prohibited the teaching of a foreign language below the eighth grade. The statute was a move against linguistic diversity.

In 1963, in Dade County, the first contemporary bilingual education program had explicit ideological aims—to facilitate cultural and linguistic diversity. Funded by the Ford Foundation to help the thousands of Cuban refugees who moved to Florida in the late 1950s, the program's stated goal was to make both English-speaking and Spanish-speaking students into functional bilinguals and to "[broaden] their understanding of other people." Bilingual education, it was claimed, would enable the refugees to "contribute to their bicultural community and their country" (Mackey and Beebe, 1977:81). In the next decade, while the bilingual program continued, as did the immigration of Spanish speakers, most students were placed in ESL classes. The bilingual program itself was slowly transformed until Spanish was envisioned as only a transitional tool. No longer was the goal of bilingual education to maintain diversity; instead the aim was to facilitate monolingualism and national linguistic unity.

In recent times, bilingual education has been conceived as a remedy to discrimination, not as a protection of diversity. In 1968 Congress passed the Bilingual Education Act (Title VII, an amendment to the 1965 Elementary and Secondary Education Act). This bill followed in the wake of the Civil Rights Act of 1963, when Chicano organizations were demanding "equal opportunity" and bilingual education for children failing in school (Hakuta, 1986:199). Title VII sanctioned, but did not mandate, bilingual education.

In 1974, in a case known as *Lau* v. *Nichols,* the parents of a group of Chinese students in California brought a class action suit against the San Francisco Unified School District. *Lau* was argued on the basis of the plaintiffs' constitutional rights and Title VI of the Civil Rights Act. The Supreme Court ignored the constitutional issue and used Title VI, which states that "no person in the United States shall, on the ground of race, color or national origin, be excluded from participation in, be denied benefits of, or be subjected to discrimination under any program or activity receiving Federal financial assistance" (42 U.S.C. 2000d to 2000d-4). The Supreme Court ruled that "there is no equality of treatment merely by providing students with the same facilities . . .; for students who do not understand English are effectively foreclosed from any meaningful education" (Hakuta, 1986:200). With the *Lau* decision, it became clear that in the minds of the courts and the legislatures, bilingual education was to compensate for "language deficiency." So much for cultural enrichment and linguistic diversity.

In practice, most bilingual programs promote monolingualism. Sociolinguist Eduardo Hernandez-Chavez argues that bilingual education is insidious; he claims that "if anything [bilingual education] has exacerbated and accelerated the pernicious deculturation process" (Hernandez-Chavez, 1979:52). Furthermore, he decries the "emotional damage engendered by the devaluation of language and culture." Clearly Hernandez-Chavez feels the centripetal pressures and is angered by them. In this force field, he pronounces that "a truly effective bilingual education can only be possible in a national context in which bilingualism and cultural diversity are themselves viable and dynamic ways of life and in which non-English native tongues can flourish and serve the people in all activities" (Herandez-Chavez, 1979:55). It is evident that Hernandez-Chavez believes that the United States is not such a national context.

Fear of linguistic diversity is as old and as enduring as the tale of Babel itself. Because of this fear, bilingual education causes great apprehension. And, in spite of all the evidence to the contrary, bilingual education is frequently equated with permanent rather than temporary multilingualism. Former President Reagan, for example, maintained that: "It is absolutely wrong and against American concept to have a bilingual education program that is now openly, admittedly dedicated to preserving their native language and never getting them adequate in English so they can go out into the job market" (quoted in Hakuta, 1986:207).

THE DIALECTICS OF LITERACY

In the United States, literacy, much like code switching and bilingualism, provides a window through which to view the dialectics of linguistic diversity and unity. Literacy is often described as a force of linguistic unification; sociolinguists hypothesize that as national literacy rates rise, mother tongue diversity declines. This hypothesis, however, dramatically oversimplifies the dynamics of literacy and social interaction.[6] In fact, literacy is a nexus of heteroglossia, the crash/bang of centripetal and centrifugal forces. For example, in the Chicano community, centripetal forces such as schooling, occupational mobility and urbanization have contributed to English acquisition and acted against Spanish maintenance. These same forces have also facilitated literacy acquisition and practice. Literacy has not, however, always been a force for linguistic unity. From the late 1960s on, literacy has replaced or supplemented a waning oral tradition, a tradition that was used to mediate ethnicity—to carry forth the memories that become a people's history and shape their collective soul (Mendez, 1980:88). Whether in Spanish or in English, or a combination of the two, literacy practices have served to preserve and continue ethnic traditions, ethnic history, and ethnic group consciousness. In turn, this group consciousness exerts a fracturing centrifugal force on the idea and the ideal of a monolingual United States.

The pattern described here is true not only of the Chicano community but of "ethnic" literature in general. American black writers use Standard English, Black English, and combinations of the two that make a division between the two appear entirely artificial. Using these languages in poetry and prose, black American writers continually define and affirm their identity and their community.

The picture becomes even more complex when we consider literacy practices in many Native-American tribes, particularly those of the Pueblo communities of the Southwest (Brandt, 1982). In the early 1900s, a vernacular literacy was introduced to the Navaho, and a standard orthography was developed by 1937. It has never been widely adopted; in many instances, vernacular literacy was actually opposed, whereas literacy in English was welcomed (Spolsky and Irvine, 1982:78). Literacy in the vernacular was accepted only when the functions of the literacy were congruent with uses of language that already existed in the culture. For example, after the Cherokee had accepted a vernacular literacy, they began to write down the formulas for various rituals and performed a ceremony with the books. This ceremony was the same one they would use with a tribe member who had committed the material to memory (Spolsky and Irvine, 1982:75).

On the other hand, English literacy is preferred for functions of an alien culture. The Navaho use English and not vernacular literacy to fill out all the forms for the Bureau of Indian Affairs (BIA). Law cases, the newspaper, local broadcasting scripts are all completed in English. In other words, neither English nor literacy per se exerts a painful centripetal pressure; rather the force for unification comes from alien uses of language that mediate social relations in foreign and feared ways.

With the Navaho, some elders perceive literacy in the vernacular as a threat to traditional culture. They would prefer a kind of diglossia or stable bilingualism in which English is used for literacy and the native tongue is used for speech. This move would help to keep the cultures separate and protect the integrity of the Navaho culture. However, to the Navaho nationalists "literacy in Navajo is crucial as a symbol of positive cultural identity" (Spolsky and Irvine, 1982:77–78). This latter attitude is reminiscent of the force behind the ethnic literature discussed earlier. Such divergent views well reflect the complex relationships between literacy and social interactions.

"LINGUISTS AND CONTENDERS": CENTRIFUGAL FORCES AND FOES FROM THE 1950s ON

Returning to a chronological account of language use, we find ourselves in mid-century, a time of "ideological calm." In this era of television programs entitled "Father Knows Best," the nation was not overtly worried about foreigners in its midst; as Fishman and Nahirny note, even "de-ethnicization proceeded from internal rather than external expectations" (1966:173).

Beginning in the 1920s and culminating in the 1950s and early 1960s, linguists (and English professors who were heavily influenced by linguists) worked to gain acceptance for a "doctrine of usage." This doctrine was based upon the idea that "rules of grammar and lexical entries in dictionaries [should be based] on actual language practice" (Finegan, 1980:11). In 1951 the National Council of Teachers of English (NCTE) published an influential report entitled *The English Language Arts*. This document formulated the following five maxims about language and recommended that they inform the teaching of language (Finegan, 1980:105):

1. Language changes constantly.
2. Change is normal.
3. Spoken language is the language.
4. Correctness rests upon usage.
5. All usage is relative.

This report was most heavily influenced by Charles Fries, English professor and linguist of the University of Michigan. He thought his views appropriate to a "pluralistic democracy tolerant of diversity" and he "urged teachers to extend greater tolerance to diverse grammatical and lexical usages" (Finegan, 1980:110).

Although the English Language Arts Report was influential and controversial in the education community, it was not until 1961 when the Merriam-Webster Company published *Webster's Third New International Dictionary* that the debate over standards for English became truly public. Based on, or at the very least reflecting, the "doctrine of usage," *Webster's Third* was highly criticized for its democratic spirit. Italian Professor Mario Pei accused the dictionary of obliterating distinctions between "standard, substandard, colloquial, vulgar and slang"; the *Detroit News* associated the dictionary with a "bolshevik spirit"; and English pundit A. M. Tibbetts quite tellingly condemned the dictionary with the following epithet: "as democratic and mechanical as a bean-picker" (Finegan, 1980:7). The dictionary controversy illustrated that centripetal forces may contribute not only to linguistic unity but also to social stratification. In the words of Sheridan Baker, "Good English has to do with the upper classes." Conversely, for many linguists an interest in language diversity was connected to an ideological agenda of egalitarianism. As Baker astutely noted, "Linguistic relativism has a fervently democratic base" (Finegan, 1980:124).

BLACK ENGLISH

In the twentieth century many black Americans speak varieties of English that have been called Black English, Black English Vernacular, Standard Black English, Black Dialect, and Nonstandard Negro English. Following William Labov, I will use the term *Black English* to refer to a range of forms used by black Americans. At one end of this continuum of linguistic forms is Standard Black English, which is the variety "used by educated black speakers in public and formal situations. It contains phonological variation from standard forms, but the same standard English syntax." At the other end of the spectrum is Black English Vernacular (BEV), which is the language "used by children growing up in the Black community and by adults in the most intimate in-group settings" (Labov, 1983:33). The subsequent discussion focuses primarily on the functions of BEV.

Educator and linguist Geneva Smitherman (1977:2-3) explains BEV "in a nutshell":

> Black Dialect is an Africanized form of English reflecting Black America's linguistic-cultural African heritage and the conditions of servitude, oppression and life in America. It has allowed blacks to create a culture of survival in an alien land, and as a by-product has served to enrich the language of all Americans.

In other words, Black English Vernacular mediates ethnicity; it "create[s] a culture . . . in an alien land." Acting as a centrifugal force, BEV changes the contours of the language we call English; BEV has served to "enrich the language of all Americans." The BEV lexicon is the aspect of BEV most readily and widely appropriated by speakers from other speech communities. In the North, white youth (and some white adult jazz musicians) may adopt elements of BEV syntax as well. In the Southern United States, where white children have been raised by black women and have played with their children, there are great similarities betwen black and white speech. In Mississippi, sociolinguist Walt Wolfram (1974) found whites who had acquired elements of black syntax from their contact with black Americans.

Although the main concerns of this essay have little to do with the particulars of BEV syntax, it may still be useful to illustrate briefly some of the differences between BEV and Standard American English (SAE). The syntax of BEV differs most from SAE in the structure of the verb, particularly in the ways that tense and aspect are expressed. For example, in BEV the verb *be* is used to indicate habitual action. Labov gives the following example: "They be hitting on peoples," which indicates habitual action. This habitual *be* is not normally found in SAE, and it illustrates "how BEV makes useful distinctions that aren't made as easily in classroom English" (1983:35).

The roots of contemporary BEV are found in the seventeenth-century slave trade. Historically, slave owners had organized the slaves' social universe so that it was difficult for them to communicate. The Ibo, Hausa, Yoruba, Mandingo, and Wolof tribes, for example, lived together even though they spoke languages that were only minimally mutually intelligible. These slaves who did not speak the same language and did not have the opportunity to learn English developed a pidgin language to communicate with each other and with whites. Gradually, the pidgin became creolized; it was regularized, expanded, and passed from one generation to another as a mother tongue (De Camp, 1971:15). Slave creole was based largely on the syntax of West African languages and the lexicon of English and was the historical antecedent of contemporary Black English.[7]

In the twentieth century, American blacks have had increasing institutional opportunities for contact with white Americans. Migration to the north and the civil rights movement have broken down some of the structures of strict social isolation. The resulting social contact has been a catalyst for Black English to undergo the process of decreolization; that is, BEV is becoming less like a creole such as Jamaican English and more like Standard American English (Smitherman, 1977:10–11).

Black English is characterized not only by its syntax and lexicon but also by its functions or uses. Smitherman speaks of "black Americans' long-standing historical tendency to appropriate English for themselves and their purposes" (1977:58). In contemporary black life, the words and syntax may be a variety of "English," while the functions of speech and language come from African oral traditions. Smitherman argues that these traditions and the importance of the verbal performance itself are maintained as a way of "learning about life and the world and . . . achieving group recognition." For example, "raps"—stylized, flamboyant, dramatic verbal performances—are used for acculturation into a "black value system" (1977:80). They are used in the street and in church. "Rap" also serves as evidence that BEV, in both its functions and its forms, has influenced white speech and language use. In the 1980s and 1990s, "rap" music has been widely appropriated by white teen-agers.

Smitherman describes the dialectics of social relations for American blacks as a "push–pull" syndrome in which black Americans find themselves "pushing toward White American culture while simultaneously pulling away from it" (1977:10–11). This push–pull syndrome is mediated by language: it takes place through and finds expression in the heteroglossia of SAE and BEV. The push–pull syndrome can be equated with what I have called the dialectic of centripetal and centrifugal forces. The forces of ethnicity—the desire to create and be a part of a black community—promote the use of BEV. This is the "pull."

On the other hand, black Americans are economically motivated to join a group that extends beyond the black community, however abstract that group may actually be. As one of our national myths has it, the ability to get and keep a "good" job depends on the ways one uses language. As a result, black Americans feel the "push" toward SAE. Whereas BEV exerts centrifugal pressure on SAE and its speakers, black Americans feel the sway of both centrifugal and centripetal pressures.

Sociolinguist John Baugh has written about the fluidity of BEV, about the ways in which its structures and lexicon change at an abnormally fast pace. This process of change has its historical roots in the social context of slavery and oppression. Slaves had to disguise their speech from the white man; even when it was totally banal, communication among slaves was greatly feared by whites.

Thus black speech served to enable black Americans to develop what John Ogbu (1987:164) has called "oppositional identity." Through "countless incidents of [racism and oppression], throughout their history, . . . black Americans developed their sense of peoplehood (or their social identity system) which they perceive not merely as different from white Americans' social identity but in many respects in opposition to it" (Ogbu, 1987:164). BEV mediates this disjunction, this opposition, this sense of ethnicity, and thus it must stay recognizably separate from SAE to continue its function. As pointed out earlier, BEV often has been taken up by white Americans. When BEV is appropriated by whites, it can no longer maintain ethnic boundaries. This process of appropriation creates the need for constant change, so that the BEV may continue to fulfill its oppositional centrifugal function.

In 1979, in a case popularly known as the "Ann Arbor Black English case," a federal court ruled that fifteen black children who were having trouble learning to read had not been given "equal opportunities" for education. The lawyers for the plaintiffs argued that the children's difficulties in school had something to do with language:

> The plaintiffs assert that as a class of black economically disadvantaged children living in the social isolation of a housing project they speak a vernacular of English, referred to as "Black English," which is so different from the English commonly spoken in the public schools as to constitute a language barrier which impedes their equal participation in King School's instructional programs.
>
> [In Chambers, 1983:157]

Apparently, the teachers had not known how to deal with their black students' linguistic differences and had put them in special education classes that had stigmatized them, according to their lawyer:

> In this lawsuit the plaintiffs allege that in the process of determining the eligibility of all students for special education services pursuant to M.C.L.A. 380.1701 *et seq.*, the defendants have failed to determine whether plaintiffs' learning difficulties stem from cultural, social and economic deprivation and to establish a program which would enable plaintiffs to overcome the cultural, social and economic deprivations which allegedly prevent them, in varying degrees, from making normal progress in school.
>
> [In Chambers, 1983:148]

The judge found for the plaintiffs and against the defendant, the Ann Arbor Board of Education:

> The failure of the defendant Board to provide leadership and help for its teachers in learning about the existence of "Black English" as a home and community language of many black students and to suggest to those same teachers ways and means of using that knowledge . . . in connection with reading standard English is not rational in light of existing knowledge of the subject.
>
> [In Chambers, 1983:2]

Unfortunately (but predictably, given our dread of linguistic diversity), the media led the public to think that Judge Joiner had ordered that the children be taught in BEV. In fact, the opposite was true. Joiner's was not a radical opinion;

it was profoundly conservative. In truth, the court had ordered that the children be taught to read in "the standard English of the school, the commercial world, the arts, the sciences and the professions." But the court had also recognized that BEV exists and is not error ridden or sloppy SAE. Officially, legally, BEV gained recognition as a separate, rule-governed dialect.

The public misunderstanding of the Ann Arbor case (officially *Martin Luther King Junior Elementary School Children et al.* v. *Ann Arbor School District Board,* 473 F. Supp. 1371 [1979]) occurred because of the dialectics of centrifugal and centripetal forces. In the words of Richard W. Bailey, a University of Michigan professor of English who testified on behalf of the plaintiffs, "In a broader context, the Black English case and others like it address the profound issues of national unity and of our willingness to accept the cultural and linguistic diversity that characterizes our society" (Bailey, 1983:25). Bailey suggests that Americans believe that "unity must spring from uniformity and that diversity must eventually devolve into a weak confederation of mutually distrustful communities." As evidence of this bias against linguistic diversity, Bailey provides the following ruling in a case about bilingual/bicultural education:

> Linguistic and cultural diversity within the nation-state, whatever may be its advantages from time to time, can restrict the scope of the fundamental compact. Diversity limits unity. . . . Syncretism retards and sometimes even reverses the shrinkage of the compact caused by linguistic and cultural diversity. But it would be incautious to strengthen diversity in language and culture repeatedly trusting only in syncretic processes to preserve the social compact.
>
> [*Guadelupe* v. *Tempe Elementary School,* 578 F. 2d 1022 [1978] at 1027]

Some linguists involved in the Ann Arbor case tried to show that the students' difficulties in school, particularly their reading difficulties, resulted from the differences between BEV and SAE. For example, William Labov contended that "Because the tendency to delete final /r/, /l/, /d/, /v/, and other consonants is more extreme in BEV than in other dialects, the relation between the spelling forms and the spoken language can be much harder to figure out for children learning to read and write the standard language" (Labov, 1983:43). Although Labov's contribution to our understanding of Black English is profound, this is a questionable analysis. First, he uses a model of the reading process that inappropriately inflates the role of oral language. This view of reading as a bottom-up process of decoding small bits of language that are pieced together little by little to form a whole has been repeatedly challenged since the time of the Ann Arbor case. Second, and perhaps most important, Labov places language rather than social relations in a determining role. In his analysis of the Ann Arbor situation, he seems oddly unconcerned with the dialectical relations between social relations and language form and function.

The problems that a BEV speaker may have with school are more accurately explained by John Ogbu's notion of opportunity structure and boundaries. Ogbu argues that black children fail in school because of social structures that prevent them from fully participating in school (opportunity structure) and because of their history, which has led them to develop an "oppositional cultural frame of reference." This frame serves as a psychological boundary that tells them that if they do well in school they will lose their identity and community—their selves and their homes (Ogbu, 1987:156). According to Ogbu, a third factor in the education of black children is the fact that speakers of BEV are often "from a segment of society where people have traditionally experienced unequal opportunity to use their literacy skills in a socially and economically meaningful and rewarding manner" (1987:151). In spite of the "push," the national myth which tells them that literacy will help them get and keep a good job, black youth experience an equally strong, if not stronger, "pull" when they see their parents underpaid or unemployed.

"LINGUISTS AND CONTENDERS": A REPRISE

According to its self-appointed guardians, English has been plagued by a series of roguelike villains: From the 1950s on, the NCTE and the linguists have caused continual problems, justifying linguistic sloppiness by claiming that Black English, for instance, is a separate but equal language. In the early 1960s, *Webster's Third International Dictionary* was the culprit, giving official recognition and codification to language changes brought about through diversity and "linguistic democracy." Finally, since about the mid-1970s, people themselves, the "minorities," have been blamed as a source of linguistic contagion.

Whereas earlier in the century "English" was not a part of nationalistic discourse, since the mid-1970s linguistic nationalism and language purity have been intertwined. Many Americans are prepared to defend not only the American flag, but also the need for "standard," "correct," or "good" English. The fear is not that English will become riddled with foreign words. Instead, until now the apprehension has been that English will be spoken incorrectly. Language correctness has become indelibly linked to the national good. Language watchdog Edwin Newman, for example, argues that "It is at least conceivable that our politics would be improved if our English were, and so would other parts of our national life" (1974:5).

One version of the correctness argument, one permutation of centripetal forces, is presented by columnist John Simon. It is worth discussing this version at length, because Simon so clearly reveals that his objections to language forms are tied to his feelings about social class and race. In an article from 1982, Simon writes that it is "the throng" (55) who uses the language incorrectly whereas the "disciplined" (59), "tidy" (60), "cultivated" (61), and "moral" few take pains to preserve good English. Ruthlessly mixing his metaphors, Simon equates "incorrect" English with bad manners, lack of self-discipline, and pollution, whereas good English, he maintains, gives one the satisfaction of "a cap snapping on a container perfectly" (60).

Finally, however, Simon gets down to the real problem. He suggests that it is not the rude or the slovenly of the world who are causing linguistic havoc; it is "the minorities." "How in the devil is one to accomplish [purity of speech] under the prevailing conditions: a democratic society full of minorities that have their own dialects or linguistic preferences . . . ," he opines (64); they are "ignorant" and "less educated than we" (66). He blames this sad state of linguistic democracy on (who else but) the "structural linguists," those "democratic respecters of alleged minority rights, or otherwise misguided folk." "These linguists," according to Simon, "believe in the sacrosanct privilege of any culturally underprivileged minority or majority to dictate ignorance to the rest of the world." Clearly, Simon feels the centrifugal pressures of language use in the last decades of the century. He worries about "an English improvised by slaves and other strangers to the culture" (67). Clearly, he is fearful that with linguistic democracy, he will lose his position of privilege. He is not alone.

ENGLISH ONLY

In 1981, Senator S. I. Hayakawa proposed a constitutional amendment known as S.J. Res. 72 that would have made English the official language of the United States. In addition, it would have banned bilingual ballots and maintenance forms of bilingual education. It could even have allowed for the banning of foreign-language instruction. This specific bill was not highly regarded in Congress; in fact it was not even debated (Marshall, 1986:24–25). Nonetheless, it did reopen the question of whether English should be named the official language. Since 1981 there has been a flurry of similar bills at the national and state levels. In 1986 California became the first state to declare English an official language by passing an amendment to the state constitution (Roy, 1987:40). Through legislative bills or voter initiatives, eleven other states have made English the official language. Clearly, the centripetal "push" is on.

U.S. English and English First are two organizations that have been responsible for backing, if not initiating, most of the legislative efforts. In one version of their solicitation letter, Alistair Cooke (1990) tells a bucolic tale of "a moving experience" when he went to "P.S. 45 in the Bronx" to watch an English as a second language class. So impressed was Cooke that he says he gained "a new appreciation of the foresight of the Founding Fathers in impressing on every American coin" "E Pluribus Unum—*Out of Many, One.*" Cooke agrees with Saul Bellow, whose battle cry he quotes: "A melting pot, yes. A tower of Babel, no." By the mid-1980s "English" had become an ideological problem in the United States.

The tower of Babel is the specter that haunts the social imagination of Cooke and his cohorts. U.S. English questionnaires ask their recipients: "In order to avoid the political upheavals over language that have torn apart Canada, Belgium, Sri Lanka (Ceylon), India and other nations, would you favor legislation designating English the official language of the United States?" U.S. English should be wary, however, of spurious comparisons. In Canada the apocalyptic scenario of French-speaking rebellion and secession has never materialized. Furthermore, Elliot Judd points out, "Granted there may be examples of civil wars based on linguistic differences between rival groups, such as currently occurring in Sri Lanka, but is language the source of the problem?" (Judd, 1987:123). In Sri Lanka (and India and . . .) social, economic, and religious differences create schisms among groups. Language mediates these divisions. In a country such as

Switzerland, where language differences do not accompany (and mediate) social stratification, repression, and exploitation, there is relative harmony among the many voices and many peoples. Certainly, monolingualism is no insurance against civil war. The people of Central America have killed each other by the thousands and thousands, and they have all spoken to each other in Spanish and only Spanish while doing it.

Another enemy of U.S. English is bilingual education, which is accused of perniciously helping to maintain linguistic diversity. However, as we discussed earlier, bilingual education is not destructive to national unity. There is no evidence that either transition or maintenance bilingual education slows down the process of learning English. There is enormous evidence that non-English-speaking children should continue to be taught to read, write, and compute, even if this instruction has to occur entirely in their native languages. In other words, children are damaged immeasurably when academic instruction is delayed until they have learned enough English to do academic work in English only (Cummins, 1986). English-only instruction for non-English-speaking children leads to problems of "cognitive development," according to psycholinguist Jim Cummins.

English First, a companion organization to U.S. English, has made the case that previous generations of immigrants "were proud to have learned English"; it was something they took for "granted" (Pratt, 1987:4). It is important to note once again, however, that census bureau figures show that throughout American history, most immigrants have acquired English as a mother tongue only within three generations.

The materials and arguments of the "English Only" legislation (such as U.S. English and English First) reveal a xenophobia that has an economic base. Jobs are insecure and scarce. The national budget deficit grows, and foreign workers in foreign countries are blamed. In this time of economic insecurity centripetal social forces and the ideology that constitutes them keep speakers of SAE at the top of the ladder of social privilege. In the minds of those frightened by sitting on top of shaky ladders, it is the foreigners and their foreign languages that bring centrifugal forces to threaten our social hierarchy; as in the land of Babel, "they" may fracture our "unity" and dominate "us."

CONCLUSION

Dialectical relationships are dizzying. There is no beginning or ending. Everything is becoming something else. Everything is imminently its opposite. Centrifugal and centripetal forces are both social and linguistic, the products of culture and creators of culture. Social relations and social interactions create language, and language creates social relations.

Centrifugal forces are equated with "linguistic democracy," with a sense that "English" is many many things and is constantly changing. Ethnicity, diversity, and difference are produced through centrifugal forces. Conversely, centripetal forces work toward a monoglotic ideal, a sense that "English" is a fixed unity.

They ensure a core of sameness in the many "Englishes." Centripetal forces plead for linguistic unity; they level linguistic differences, yet they enforce social stratification and hierarchies.

The champions of linguistic unity tell an appealing tale. They seem to have the solution to misunderstanding, division and dissent among people. They seem to know a route back to a simpler time, a time once upon a time when "America" was homogeneous, cohesive, and monolingual. In truth, their project is scary. In real time centripetal forces create unity through exclusion, and, sadly, in the last decade of the twentieth century we are deep in the throes of a centripetal movement.

To counteract this movement, we would do well to reconceive the American experiment and abandon the grotesque "melting pot" metaphor. We would also do well to abandon an image of ourselves as monoglots and an image of our language as an edifice.

Americans need not fear either the idea of diversity or the people who bring it to their communities. The truth is that immigrants do learn English, but they also change English and themselves in learning and using it. "They" become and change "us." Traditionally, immigrants want to assimilate—to join or create a national unity—and they also want to preserve their ethnicity. Rather than try to still this push/pull, we would be wise to understand and even "foster this dialectic of desires" (Bizzell, 1989). Perhaps then we could hear polyphony in the voices of the many.

ACKNOWLEDGMENTS

The author wishes to thank Tom Barrett, Patricia Bizzell, Marilyn Cooper, Tom Fox, and Sharon Jones for their help with the ideas in and drafts of this article. Also, the author would like to express her appreciation to Joshua Fishman for his longstanding interest in language diversity in the United States.

NOTES

1. This is not an inclusive survey, however, and the reader may find certain gaps to be odd. For example, the field of sociolinguistics is heavily indebted to William Labov's early work with the social stratification of /r/ in New York City. This study broke new methodological ground, yet the details of Labov's procedures are essentially ignored here because they are not especially pertinent to the central themes of this essay.

2. This departure from and return to ethnicity happened in more or less three generations. In other words, the three-generational curve is an average.

3. Obviously, there are many individual Mexicans who acquired English rapidly, and there are many individual Cubans or Puerto Ricans who have maintained their Spanish. But the point is twofold: first, that these communities did not have structural opportunities for language acquisition, only random and individual ones; second, whether the majority of the Mexicans speak English or not, they are still perceived by Anglo society as a centrifugal, diversifying pressure on English. On the other hand, the Puerto Ricans,

Cubans, and early arrivals from Central America exert centripetal, unifying pressures on English-language use in the United States.

4. Sociolinguists have developed an array of terms to describe the language of bilinguals in the United States. Some of these terms create the illusion that the languages of a bilingual are stable and fixed rather than in flux and changing with social relations and social formations. Compound bilinguals, for example, are individuals who have fused two meaning systems because the languages were spoken interchangeably or one language was learned through the other. Coordinate bilinguals, on the other hand, are those who have two separate meaning systems because they learned the two languages in different contexts. This terminology does not take into account the fact that in the United States bilingualism seems to be a highly mutable and temporary state of language use. At least one scholar of Chicano discourse claims that the Chicano bilingual community of the Southwest is rapidly shifting to English alone (Floyd, 1985).

5. Professor Kenji Hakuta of Yale, the author of *Mirror of Language: The Debate on Bilingualism*, maintains that the "rapidity of the language shift in the United States remains a deep mystery" (1986:174). However, it does not seem mysterious to me at all. It results from the social situation. Unfortunately, Hakuta, a psycholinguist, missed the main event(s) by concentrating on cognition.

6. Stanley Lieberson compared various populations and could find no such trend. For example, in Canada and in Turkey there has been a stable level of mother-tongue diversity as more people have become literate. In Bulgaria, Finland, and the USSR there have been downward trends in both diversity and illiteracy, but the fluctuations are unrelated. In 1897 to 1926, in the Soviet Union, diversity dropped more than in previous census periods, but the opposite was the case for illiteracy (Lieberson, 1981:31).

7. "A pidgin is a contact vernacular, normally not the native language of any of its native speakers. It is used in trading or in any situation requiring communication between persons who do not speak each other's native languages. . . . Unlike a pidgin, a creole is the native language of most of its speakers. . . . A creole is inferior to its corresponding standard language only in social status. A pidgin, however, is so limited both lexically and structurally that it is suitable only for specialized and limited communication" (De Camp, 1971:15–16).

WORKS CITED

Bailey, Richard W. 1983. "Education and the Law: The King Case in Ann Arbor." In John Chambers, Jr. ed., *Black English: Educational Equity and the Law*. Ann Arbor: Karoma. Pp. 1–28.

Bakhtin, M. M. 1981. *The Dialogic Imagination*. Michael Holquist, ed. Caryl Emerson and Michael Holquist, trans. Austin: University of Texas Press.

Barth, Fredrik, ed. 1969. *Ethnic Groups and Boundaries*. Boston: Little Brown.

Baugh, John. 1983. "Language Variation in American English Vernaculars." In John Chambers, Jr., ed. *Black English: Education Equity and the Law*. Ann Arbor: Karoma. Pp. 71–80.

Bizzell, Patricia. 1989. Letter to author. 8 December.

Bloom, Allan. 1987. *The Closing of the American Mind*. New York: Simon and Schuster.

Brandt, Elizabeth. 1982. "A Research Agenda for Native American Languages." In Florence Barkin et al., eds., *Bilingualism and Language Contact: Spanish, English, and Native American Languages*. New York: Teachers College Press, Columbia University. 26–47.

Briere, Eugene J. 1979. "Introduction." *Language Development in a Bilingual Setting.* Los Angeles: National Development and Assessment Center. Pp. 1–7.

Cardenas, Gilberto. 1975. "United States Immigration Policy Toward Mexico: A Historical Perspective." *Chicano Law Review* 2:68–69.

Chambers, John Jr., ed. 1983. *Black English: Education Equity and the Law.* Ann Arbor, MI: Karoma.

Chomsky, Noam. 1965. *Aspects of the Theory of Syntax.* Cambridge: MIT Press.

Connor, W. 1978. "A Nation Is a Nation, is a State, is an Ethnic Group, is a. . . ." *Ethnic and Racial Studies* 1:377–400.

Cooke, Alistair. 1990. Letter for "U.S. English."

Cummins, Jim. 1986. "Empowering Minority Students: A Framework for Intervention." *Harvard Educational Review* 56:18–36.

De Camp, David. 1971. "The Study of Pidgin and Creole Languages." In Dell Hymes, ed., *Pidginization and Creolization of Languages.* Cambridge, England: Cambridge University Press. Pp. 13–39.

Finegan, Edward. 1980. *Attitudes Toward English Usage: The History of a War of Words.* New York: Teachers College Press, Columbia University.

Fishman, Joshua. 1972. *Language in Sociocultural Change.* Stanford, CA: Stanford University Press.

———, et al., eds. 1966. *Language Loyalty in the United States.* The Hague: Mouton.

Fishman, Joshua, and John E. Hofman. 1966. "Mother Tongue and Nativity in the American Population." In Joshua Fishman, ed., *Language Loyalty in the United States.* The Hague: Mouton. Pp. 34–50.

Fishman, Joshua, and Vladimir C. Nahirny. 1966. "Organizational and Leadership Interest in Language Maintenance." In Fishman, ed., *Language Loyalty in the United States.* The Hague: Mouton. Pp. 156–189.

Floyd, Mary Beth. 1985. "Spanish in the Southwest: Language Maintenance or Shift?" In Lucía Elías-Olivares et al., eds., *Spanish Language Use and Public Life in the United States.* Berlin: Mouton, Pp. 13–25.

Glazer, Nathan. 1966. "The Problems and Process of Language Maintenance: An Integrative Review." In Fishman, ed., *Language Loyalty in the United States.* The Hague: Mouton. Pp. 358–368.

Gonzalez, J. 1975. "Coming of Age in Bilingual/Bicultural Education: A Historical Perspective." *Inequality in Education* 19:5–14.

Gumperz, John J. 1982. *Discourse Strategies.* Cambridge: Cambridge University Press.

Hakuta, Kenji. 1986. *Mirror of Language: The Debate on Bilingualism.* New York: Basic Books.

Haugen, Einar. 1971. *The Ecology of Language.* Stanford, CA: Stanford University Press.

Heath, Shirley Brice. 1976. "A National Language Academy: Debate in the New Nation." *International Journal of the Sociology of Language* 11:19–43.

Hernandez-Chavez, Eduardo. 1979. "Meaningful Bilingual/Bicultural Education: A Fairy Tale." *Language Development in a Bilingual Setting.* Los Angeles: National Dissemination and Assessment Center. Pp. 48–57.

Herrera, Albert. 1971. "The Mexican American in Two Cultures." In Ed Ludwig and James Sanibanez, eds., *The Chicanos: Mexican American Voices.* New York: Penguin. Pp. 249–254.

Hirsch, E. D. 1987. *Cultural Literacy.* Boston: Houghton Mifflin.

Hymes, Dell, 1974. *Foundations in Sociolinguistics.* Philadelphia: University of Pennsylvania Press.

Judd, Elliott L. 1987. "The English Language Amendment: A Case Study on Language and Politics." *TESOL Quarterly* 21:113–135.

Labov, William. 1972. *Sociolinguistic Patterns*. Philadelphia: University of Pennsylvania Press.

——— 1983. "Recognizing Black English in the Classroom." In John Chambers, Jr., ed., *Black English: Educational Equity and the Law*. Ann Arbor: Karoma. Pp. 29–55.

Lieberson, Stanley. 1981. *Language Diversity and Language Contact*. Stanford: Stanford University Press.

Lopez, Enrique Hank. 1971. "Back to Bachimba." In Ed Ludwig and James Sanibanez, eds., *The Chicanos: Mexican American Voices*. New York: Penguin. Pp. 261–270.

Love, Joseph L. 1970. "La Raza: Mexican Americans in Rebellion. In John H. Burma, ed., *Mexican Americans in the United States*. Cambridge, MA: Schenkman. Pp. 459–472.

Mackey, William F., and V. N. Beebe. 1977. *Bilingual Schools for a Bicultural Community: Miami's Adaptation to the Cuban Refugees*. Rowley, MA: Newbury House.

Marshall, D. 1986. "The Question of an Official Language: Language Rights and the English Language Amendment." *International Journal of the Sociology of Language* 60:7–75.

McWilliams, Carey. 1968. *North from Mexico*. New York: Greenwood.

Mendez, Miguel. 1980. Interview. *Chicano Authors: Inquiry by Interview*. Austin: University of Texas Press. Pp. 83–94.

Nahirny, Vladimir C., and Joshua Fishman. 1966. "Ukranian Language Maintenance Efforts in the United States." In Fishman, ed., *Language Loyalty in the United States*. The Hague: Mouton. Pp. 318–357.

Newman, Edwin. 1974. *Strictly Speaking: Will America Be the Death of English?* Indianapolis: Bobbs Merrill.

Ogbu, John. 1987. "Opportunity Structure, Cultural Boundaries and Literacy." In Judith A. Langer, ed., *Language Literacy and Culture: Issues of Society and Schooling*. Norwood, NJ: Ablex. Pp. 149–177.

Peñalosa, Fernando. 1981. *Introduction to the Sociology of Language*. Rowley, MA: Newbury House.

Pratt, Larry. 1987. "The Case for English First." *Hispanic Link Weekly Report* (20 April):4.

Rodriguez, Richard. 1982. *Hunger of Memory*. New York: Bantam.

Roy, Alice. 1987. "The English Only Movement." *The Writing Instructor* 7(1):40–47.

Sanchez, Rosaura. 1983. *Chicano Discourse: Sociohistorical Perspectives*. Rowley, MA: Newbury House.

Sapir, Edward. 1931. "Conceptual Categories of Primitive Languages." *Science* 74:578.

Simon, John. 1982. "Why Good English Is Good For You." In James C. Raymond, ed., *Literacy as a Human Problem*. University: University of Alabama Press. Pp. 55–72.

Smitherman, Geneva. 1977. *Talkin and Testifyin: The Language of Black America*. Boston: Houghton Mifflin.

Spolsky, Bernard, and Patricia Irvine. 1982. "Sociolinguistic Aspects of the Acceptance of Literacy in the Vernacular." In Florence Barkin et al., eds. *Bilingualism and Language Contact: Spanish, English and Native American Languages*. New York: Teachers College Press, Columbia University. Pp. 73–79.

Wolfram, Walt. 1972. "Overlapping Influence and Linguistic Assimilation in Second-Generation Puerto Rican English." In David Smith and Roger Shuy, eds., *Sociolinguistics in Cross-Cultural Analysis*. Washington DC: Georgetown University Press. Pp. 15–46.

———. 1974. "The Relationship of White Southern Speech to Vernacular Black English." *Language* 50:498–527.

8

Social Contexts in the History of Australian English

JOHN GUNN

Less than fifty years ago most Australians did not accept that their language was simply another variety of English and bowed to the notion that the best English for Australia should be modelled on the one spoken by people of good breeding "back home" in England. Australians were frequently described as being slangy and uncouth and using fractured vowels in the manner of street larrikins—qualities doubtlessly imputed to the harsh climate, the vegetation, or the convict ancestry. Equally misguided were those Australians who regarded their speech as part of the dynamic, pioneering spirit that gave them a "fair dinkum" character. Eric Partridge, for example, was almost in heroic vein as he depicted early arrivals "thrown together on the edge of a vast wilderness . . . the grey, bleak unknown" (Bevan, 1953:213). He proceeded to describe the emerging language as one that accepted the direct and unadorned, linguistic unconventionality and the freedom to do one's own thing without regard for the social strata of language.

There are elements of truth in all of this, and each group in the settlement—whether convict, migrant, soldier, man on the land, adventurer, or business-man—used great initiative and resourcefulness in everyday activities and in fostering a new English. Their lives and language were unusual from the beginning, and both were carried forward by a high level of undisguised scorn for pretence, pomposity, and official interference. But this background did not mean that the language became chaotic or, in time, that a standard of some kind was not thought desirable.

Various books and other media have often overstated their case in describing things Australian, feeding off one another to give a kind of authority to much exaggeration and distortion, especially in some of our fictional heroes. The usage of the folk of the bush and outback was sometimes extended to suit character, but not always unrealistically. At the same time, in town and city, newspapers have informally and un-self-consciously used terminology that was familiar to their readers and unmistakably Australian. Henry Lawson and other realist writers since the 1890s used such terminology, and fifty years before them, Alexander Harris did not hesitate to make some use of what must have been a thriving, familiar idiom. Inevitably, there were those who overdid it; in this century, C. J. Dennis was one of several who have had to provide glossaries to explain the idiom of certain characters for Australian readers.

When we consider the history of the development of Australia in its loose, undefined social structure, it is little wonder that an unpretentious, colloquial variety of English was preferred. The emergence of a popular form, regarded as disreputable by most "polite" speakers, was the result of a natural linguistic growth from humble beginnings. This form was not going to be restricted by strong traditional values or faddish notions about foreign models of accent and usage; and it demonstrated that "different" pronunciation is not necessarily peculiar or ugly and that an idiom that is colorful may also be useful, entertaining, and comprehensible. Australian is like any other kind of English, the product of social and historical forces that affect a people at a particular time and place. The intention of this essay is to discuss selected topics to illustrate some of the historical, social, and cultural forces behind the growth of Australian English, avoiding where possible "down under" word lists and descriptions that are available in other published work. I am indebted to many other researchers, whose good work goes on, and accept full responsibility for any expressions of opinion that may appear contentious.

THE ROOTS OF AUSTRALIAN ENGLISH

English was established about 1500 years ago, and each dialect was able to become regionally distinctive and preservable in a parochial, conservative way. Centuries later, "Standard English" emerged as the result of social and cultural pressure for a nationally recognised form, a prestige dialect to overlay the regional ones and become the literary language, available to those born into it or aspiring to speak and write it. The conventions, practices, and rules of this minority dialect gained broad acceptance and authority throughout Britain and in various colonial outposts, usually as modified standards, with the degree of variation depending on location and the social and cultural mix of the inhabitants. From its British base each "standard" may have had to integrate with an already settled native race, nearby colonists from other European nations (French, Dutch, Spanish, etc.), a strange environment, and the impact of fresh immigrations.

Australia might be regarded as different, perhaps still a little unstable, because of its comparatively recent settlement and greater isolation. In addition, it was settled at a time when revolutionary notions on matters linguistic had become entrenched in the motherland. Ideas about "logic," "purity," "correctness," and other right-sounding description of the best English had been taken up by strong-minded teachers, grammarians, and orthoepists who fostered, in their own occasionally inconsistent ways, what they thought "proper" for standard English. Their reasoning was usually arbitrary and not linguistically based, and they paid scant attention to levels of usage and the language spoken by the majority of the people for generations. Nonconforming writers and the popular speech of London were damned in a social climate in which language was the plaything of too many often well-meaning but uncritical "reformers." People like Savage (1833), who drew up a collection of vile utterances and vulgarisms in popular speech, would not have been impressed by the vigorous English that had been thriving "down under" for over forty years.

It was hardly fair that eighteenth- and nineteenth-century London English should have come under attack at a time when Cockney was a distinctive form within the area, and when general London English had become a useful, advanced speech as a result of commerce, education, and various regional influences. According to Joan Platt, those moving into urban areas "speedily lost touch with regional dialect and adopted the vulgar urban English spoken in the towns" (1925:541). London speech may also have been contaminated or enriched, according to one's view, by such things as thieves' cant and the jargon of costermongers and various occupational groups. Platt (1926:71–81) also observed that the so-called colloquial vulgarisms could be viewed as an advanced stage of a long process of flexibility and simplification that had been going on for over three centuries in popular London speech. Some of the vulgarisms were also used un-self-consciously by many of those who also held themselves aloof from the common herd. In addition, she noted (1925:540) that most urban speakers used a less fastidious type of speech, not to be confused with that of a low-class minority of London thieves and vagabonds who spoke a slang idiom of their own. For her, 1750 to 1825 was the period of transition to modern colloquial English, under pressure from sociological and historical forces on the one hand, and the constraints of conservative forces and respect for polite English on the other.

Matthews also saw the development of London English as part of a long, historical pattern, and stated that "it contained nothing which might not have been heard from some good speakers" (1937:241). London English was certainly on the rise during the eighteenth century, although it needed to avoid and keep ahead of the language legislators. Matthews (1937) properly observed that Cockney was a distinctive London slang, quite unlike the regional dialects, that it had taken up aspects of low London speech involved in drink, rogues and their women, and that it had spread into the colonies and elsewhere.

Transportation of large numbers of speakers familiar with popular London and thieves' slang no doubt resulted in this variety being much in evidence in Sydney town, where it was very public and unlikely to feature a large number of those secret, criminal words and phrases that went under the name of *flash*. Nonetheless, one James Hardy ("Flash Jim") Vaux, a thrice-transported convict, was persuaded (by himself, no doubt) to dedicate and present the first copy of his flash vocabulary to Thomas Skottowe, commandant at Newcastle, so that it might provide some amusement and because Skottowe might "occasionally find it useful in [his] magisterial capacity" (1819:i).

The eighteenth-century desire to rescue English from vulgarity was also directed toward irregularity and diversity of pronunciation. Writers like Walker (1791) and Nares (1784), for example, were appalled by what they heard in London. Walker desired what he called "just" pronunciation, giving it almost a legal status, and warned dialect, foreign, and London speakers to avoid gross errors, especially those exemplified by Cockney speakers. Others published collections of examples, and some composed fictitious letters, littered with deliberate mis-spellings to make their point about such illiterates as chambermaids and foot-men. Writers, before and since, have found this an easy method of identifying uneducated, low-class folk. With their rules designed to produce "pure," "organic" pronunciation, most of the orthoepists tended to ignore the fact that historical shifts of natural language emerge first in popular speech; nor did they comprehend the gradual movement of such forms across class barriers. Some were more objective. Ellis, for example, noted that the thriving, popular London pronunciation was also to be found to some extent in those professing educated speech, as is the case everywhere today. Once again one might remark that if all the reformist zeal did not prevent popular English from thriving (even if marking time) in the heartland of standard, neither was such zeal likely to succeed in the society embracing the hotch-potch citizenry being shipped to Australia.

EARLY COLONIAL SOCIETY AND ITS LANGUAGE

Events leading up to the industrial revolution left a class of labouring poor that included thieves, vagabonds, and unemployed craftsmen seeking to try their luck in large towns and cities, especially London. Transportation of lawbreakers, and emigration of those disadvantaged by progress, must have had great appeal as a solution to the compound problems of unemployment, the lack of penal accommodation, the need for an alternative to the death penalty, and the later demand for labour in New South Wales. Martin (1978) offers several other inter-pretations of the colonisation of Australia: as an eastern trading base, as a clear-ing port for flax and pines for the navy, and as a response to influential social and political pressure for settlement.

British dumping of its embarrassing social and political undesirables began with the passing of a law in 1597 prescribing banishment as a penalty for vaga-bondage and related offenses (Ribton-Turner, 1877:128–129). The law was repealed in 1713, but those uneducated, unreliable, and resentful individuals whom it had affected remained, especially in urban areas. America received many such people, but it was never a penal colony like Australia. In the eigh-teenth century, in fact, legislation was introduced by America against this forced immigration; though a noble gesture, this legislation was compromised by the fact that America already had a source of cheap labor in the slave trade. New South Wales began as a penal settlement when (Governor) Phillip's fleet sailed in 1787, accompanied by a few soldiers and government servants. With a steady and increasing number of immigrants, convicts played their part in what was to become a free, self-governing colony.

The Early Social Mix

During the first forty years or so, 150,000 convicts arrived, and, overall, they outnumbered the rest of the population by about four to one. The migrants that came had much in common with the convicts in being mainly lower class and underprivileged, and speaking a type of English that reflected this background. The education of both groups was slight (about two years of schooling on average), but their influence became significant because the rigid stratification that existed elsewhere was almost impossible to achieve in the social and linguistic environment of New South Wales. There would have been some shuffling of pronunciation and of dialect and occupational terms, but the resulting speech was heard by all, including superior-class or educated citizens. The ambition of most new arrrivals, no matter what the circumstances of their coming, was not to be taken for "new chums," an attitude that encouraged adoption of any distinctive speech of the colony, as as well as dress, and so on. Such variation from the home language happened in other colonies, each with its own character, but none was as receptive as Australia to radical speech. The reason for this reception lies in the mingling of three social groups, not including the Aborigines, who will be mentioned in another context.

The Top Social Group

At the top of the social ladder was the powerful but numerically small group of educated civic officials and military officers, later joined by their counterparts among new settlers, many of whom became large landholders. This group might have been expected to foster superior English in the manner of that used in reports, dispatches, and all official documents in which anything smacking of lower-class usage was either "translated" or marked by underline or inverted commas. Editors and printers frequently bowdlerized the work of those who recorded faithfully, and amanuenses, writing for the less literate, were usually careful in their choice of vocabularly and usage.

Not only were there few refined, well-educated arrivals, but even these were unable to cut themselves off completely from the vulgar, substandard speech in workplaces and in the town. A desire for something better than low English was felt by many citizens, but converts to the refined English model would have been very rare. To the present day, those who have attempted to impose an artificial "standard" have made little headway, and some have suffered public ridicule.

Convicts

Convict transportation lasted from 1788 until it ceased in 1841 in New South Wales, 1852 in Tasmania, and 1868 in Western Australia, where it had begun very late. South Australia was the only state that was free of convicts, but its speech differs from that of other states in only minor ways; South Australians, for example, preserve ther "pure" pronunciation of the "pool" vowel (i.e., [u]). Elsewhere the influence of the large and very public, low-class group was felt very early, and its radical mode of speech and other behaviour were available for all to adopt, reject, or modify as they saw fit. Up to 1830, as I have already noted, convicts outnumbered the free settlers by four or five to one. Their greatest influx was in the decade of the 1830s, but over 60,000 free immigrants in this period greatly outnumbered them. One must keep in mind that at this time about 40 percent of the free citizens in the colony were ex-convicts and that most of the remainder had convict connections.

About a third of the 760 convicts in the first fleet came from London or the Home Counties, and many of the others were wanderers who had shared close association with them in jails, the hulks, and transports for the nine months' journey to New South Wales. Such a gathering would be expected to adopt any unifying low dialect used by those at the top of the pecking order. Contemporary opinion of convicts varied; to some they were "a demoralised, dissolute, drunken and lazy, though perhaps not quite unenterprising set of men and women" (Ward, 1970:29ff), and to others "All in all, a disreputable lot" (Shaw, 1971:165). Shaw describes a picture of habitual crime and of people from the dregs of society, which is not a surprising picture when one considers the harsh treatment of such groups and the high probability of a life of crime for those who were born into the "family" or those who joined it as vagabonds or thieves. Five sixths of the convicts were men, the average age was about twenty-six, few were married, and the place they knew best was London, where the majority were tried and sentenced. Most of those professing a faith were Protestants, but religion, like the law, was usually regarded as part of the system used against them. Former occupations were commonly described as labourer or farm worker, and the most frequent sentence was seven years, usually for theft or burglary with previous convictions. There might have been some who stole only a pocket handkerchief or similar petty items, but habitual crime was much more common, and a proportion were hardened, more brutal criminals, even if the hangman helped many of these to avoid transportation.

With few exceptions the convicts were illiterate, and many were orphans or knew only their mother, who, in most cases, was "on the town" when they were conceived. They had to fend for themselves when very young, and the workhouse or the *flash ken* ("a public house patronised by the thieving fraternity") was the only home many had ever known. Boys were usually trained as pickpockets or burglars, and girls often became prostitutes or thieves. Although young first offenders were usually protected from transportation, they often made their initial acquaintance with the *family* (of thieves) in jail, and so they had little hope of avoiding crime in the future.

The trip to Australia was in cramped quarters below deck, but convicts were moderately well exercised and organised under a captain into messes of six for convenience in ration control. According to some, they were not much worse off than poor migrants, if bondage is ignored. Surgeons and *agents for transports* looked after their welfare and prevented ill treatment and victimization as best they could. There were bad times, but, overall, the survival rate of those in reasonable health was high. Soon after arrival and a *muster,* convicts were allocated to suitable work, frequently in one of a number of *government gangs* (*clearing-, falling-, lime burners-,* etc.). There were the *defaulters-, chain-, gaol-,* and *iron(ed)-gangs* for the more recalcitrant types, who might make the *probationary gang* with good behaviour, but who would rarely become eligible for the privileged *government indulgent gang.* Trusted and skilled prisoners quickly found a

kind of freedom in being *assigned* (hence, *assignable, assignee,* etc.) to free citizens, including ex-convicts, in farming and business activities. The women convicts were assigned as domestic servants or sent to the *female factory* at Parramatta to make the coarse woollen parramatta cloth for slop clothing in
Australia's first secondary industry.

Any convict guilty of further crime in the colony was known as a *double convict* and was usually *retransported* to such places of brutal treatment as Norfolk
Island or Moreton Bay. Punishment for "everyday" offenses not warranting
retransportation was very harsh—by the lash, the treadmill, stocks, or close con-
finement. Magistrates, being from the same class as masters, usually showed
scant mercy to lapsed assignees. There were reasonable and vicious masters, and
the brutality of the latter often turned servants into *bolters* or *runaways* or, more
euphemistically, *absentees,* who frequently became *bushrangers.* This term
soon became associated with bush banditry, a blot on Australian society for
almost a century.

In this strange settlement convicts were familiar figures, nor was it unusual to
find them serving as *overseers* or even *superintendents* of their fellows; one or
two made it to the post of magistrate. Trusted convicts were allowed to work in
the town in their spare time, a practice frequently extended to living out in lodg-
ings by holding a *ticket-of-exemption.* Anyone with a good record could obtain
a pass that entitled him special leave to visit family or settle business that concerned him. General mixing of convicts in the community was markedly
increased by the early introduction of the *ticket-of-leave* (hence, *ticket-of-leave-
branch, -holder, -man,* etc.). This permitted the well behaved to work full-time
for themselves in a specified district for the remainder of a sentence, on condition that they reported at prescribed monthly or quarterly musters. If the ticket
was held for a set period without unfavourable endorsement, one was entitled to
consideration for *conditional-emancipation,* allowed freer movement in the colony, and often described as *free on the ground* or *on his own hands.* An *absolute*
or *free pardon* unconditionally remitted the remainder of any sentence and gave
the holders a *certificate of freedom,* also called a *warrant of emancipation,* even
to leave the colony and return "home" to England if they wished. Of course, all
was not plain sailing or clear-cut, and the system was sometimes abused by the
intercession of a well-placed friend or enemy.

Ex-convicts usually remained in familiar territory where they had friends and
acquaintances who knew them favourably. Some returned to England, occasionally to old haunts and a chance to be transported again, but most remained
in Australia to "make a go of it" and in many cases to attain great prosperity.
Ex-convicts certainly fostered and spread widely a strong antipathy for the British government and its colonial administrators. McNab noted that their influence "on the attitudes and values of the whole colonial society, and especially
on those of the lower classes, was consequently very strong" (1962:296). Most
convicts cast off any fondness for the mother country, and many seized the
chance to advance their lot, like any other citizen. There is every reason to accept
their impact on the Australian language as well, not only because of their pen-

chant for colourful, slangy idiom, but also because of their reinforcement of the quite distinctive accent emerging in Australia.

Was this to mean that for one branch of the English language a horrific fate as thieves' cant, vulgarity, and an unspeakable pronunciation overwhelmed all that was pure and fine? Such a fate was accepted as most likely by Wakefield's informant (1829), who presents a society, including children, inured to bloody punishments, a law without moral force, slave-driving employers, and drunkenness gone mad. Concerning the language, he deplored that "Terms of slang and flash are used, as a matter of course, everywhere, from the gaols to the Viceroy's palace, not excepting the Bar and the Bench . . . bearing in mind that our lowest class brought with it a peculiar language, and is constantly supplied with fresh corruption, you will understand why pure English is not, and is not likely to become, the language of the colony" (1829:51). Although exaggerated and second-hand opinion, there was a great deal of truth in this view, but such speech was part of a phase and, over time, subject to considerable self-monitoring and modification.

The vocabulary of convictism was of three kinds, and two of them were of comparatively short duration. Usage associated with the bureaucracy and administration tended to die out with the system, as did most of the phrases mentioned earlier. To this may be added terms to describe convicts: *felon, canary* (from the yellowish dress of some), *towny* (usually someone from London), (Irish) *defender,* and *croppy* (someone who shaved his hair to signify sympathy with French revolutionaries). The convicts themselves would probably have preferred more jocular names of origin such as *Cork-, Dublin-* or *North-boy* or to be one of the *specials* or *gentlemen convicts* who were able to gain favour through influence or education. Many of them preferred euphemistic names such as *government-man* or *-servant,* or even *public servant,* still the name for an Australian civil servant. The public took these up and generated other terms such as *emancipist* ("one in favour of ending transportation and of equal rights for ex-convicts") and *exclusionist* ("one who wanted social distinction between those who *came free* and the *bonded*"). Some of the administrative words survived in general use and gained fresh meaning, for example, *hutkeeper, station, property,* all with specific reference to land settlement.

Another terminology associated with convictism was the *flash* ("thieves slang") that so disgusted purists like Wakefield's informant and was always confusing to untutored ears. Langker (1980) provides a good discussion of the phenomenon with sources and examples, a few of which follow:

> A convict, later shot as a bushranger was quoted, "if they should *scrag* 'hang' him he would *quiz* 'confound' them all and show them some *gig* 'fun' at the *nubbing cheat* 'gallows', before he was *turned off* 'executed.'"
>
> [1980:7]

> The *rum cove* 'head man' of this *vile* 'town' is *up to* 'good at ' *lushing* 'drinking' *max* 'gin.'
>
> [1980:27]

The refrain to the *Song of the Young Prig* goes,

Frisk ("pick") the *cly* ("pocket"), and *fork* ("take") the *rag* ("money"),
Draw the *foggles* ("handkerchiefs") *plummy* ("skillfully"),
Speak to ("steal") the *tattler* ("watch"), *bag* the *swag*,
And *finely* ("dexterously") hunt the *dummy* ("wallet").

[1980:20]

Very few of such terms would have had significant use in Australia, because
Vaux's early nineteenth-century list of about 750 entries (one of Langker's
sources) was based as much on his London life as on his experience as a trans-
portee. Langker was able to find about sixty-five examples that lasted long after
the convict period, and many are still part of the Australian vernacular. Other
varieties of English also have them, and, of course, most have always been well
embedded in popular London slang. A few that could hardly be called flash
today are: *bounce* ("impudent assertion"), hence *bouncer; cadge* ("beg"), hence
cadger, on the cadge; cove ("master of an establishment"), generalised to "fellow" (Australia also had *covesses,* and *the cove* was a station boss until recently);
crack ("break open"), hence *crack it* ("achieve") and *(safe) cracker; cross* ("dis-
honest," "illegally come by"), opposite of *square* ("honest," "genuine"); *frisk*
("search"); *gammon* ("deceit" or "humbug"); *gig* ("to ridicule," and as a noun
"fool"); *kicksies* ("trousers," later "pocket"—hence, *kick in, hit the kick* ["to
contribute" or "pay up"]); *lag* ("sentence" [verb and noun], "prisoner," e.g., *old
lag*); *mill* ("fight," thus cattle *mill* when agitated, and it is *stacks on the mill* in a
rugby scrimmage); *mob* ("gang," now widely generalised and said to be the Australian noun of multitude; I have heard, for example, "mob of sausages"); *peter*
("trunk" or "box," "cashbox"—hence, to *tickle the peter* is to pilfer it); *pig*
("policeman"); *plant* ["to hide," "hiding place"—hence, *spring the plant* ("to
reveal or discover a plant")]; *prig* ("thief," "to steal"); *push* ("crowd" or "gang,"
now also a "clique" or "group"); *queer* ("criminal" or "base," often in compounds like *queer-card* ["low person"], *-cove* ["jail-bird"], *-ken* ["prison"]); *rig*
("scheme," "dodge"); *rum* ("strong")—hence, *rum cove* ("great rogue"); *swag*
("booty," now the bundle of possessions of a *swagman* or *swaggie*); *trap*
("policeman"); *tog* ("coat"; *togs* are now one's clothes—hence, *swimming togs,
tog oneself out*).

Middle Social Groups

The middle section of colonial society was occupied by the relatively few tradesmen, free settlers, and some emancipees, who were greatly outnumbered by the
convict and ex-convict element for about forty years. This group's occasional
dialectisms and occupational terms were sometimes absorbed or extended in
Australian use, often to become Australianisms. They also played their part in
filling the naming gaps in normal linguistic ways through loanwords, semantic
and functional variation, and word-building techniques. Like fresh convicts, settlers did not wish to be obvious "new chums" and seemed more than ready to
adopt the accepted colloquial language and other modes of behaviour that they
found in the colony.

SOCIAL CONTEXTS IN THE HISTORY OF AUSTRALIAN ENGLISH   213

A most important middle group arose with the first generation of native born, the *currency* lads and lasses, as distinct from the British born or *sterling*. Almost 90 percent of them had convict ancestry, and most did not know their fathers; they were raised in a very poor social situation, especially as far as home life and education were concerned. Even their nickname *(currency)* was derived from the pound currency of the colony being worth less than sterling. Their extremely lurid language was frequently remarked on by observers: Cunningham, for example, noted of the children that "a number of slang phrases in St. Giles [a London area] Greek bid fair to become legitimized in the dictionary of this colony . . . the London mode of pronunciation has been duly ingrafted on the colloquial dialect of our Currency youths . . . [and] stamped the language of the rising generation with their unenviable peculiarity" (1827, 2:59–60). The blasphemy and filthy oaths to which they were partial also came in for comment.

In direct contrast were remarks on the moral and physical character of the currency, which led Commissioner Bigge to conclude that they were "a self-respecting, moral, law-abiding, industrious and surprisingly sober group of people" (Ward, 1962:289). Bigge went on to praise their physique and fine features, notwithstanding the fact that they were "remarkably awkward in their movements . . . irascible but not vindictive" (1962:291). Their prowess in most sports was highly praised, and challenges were constantly being issued to such foreigners as the English and Americans. Others noted few of the vices of the parents and the fact that, in spite of being raised in the most revolting conditions of drunkenness, their behaviour was very temperate. McNab suggested that their unexpected conduct was a psychological reaction against their convict taint, combined with stimulation from the socioeconomic environment—that is, the need to "start work young" to survive. Additional motivations were much better wages than were available in England and, one might cynically add, almost daily witness of the brutal punishments that were inflicted on malefactors in the colony.

Where necessary, the currency and well-motivated freed convicts would have found it in their own interests, and relatively easy, to avoid socially degrading profanity or other despised usage, without reducing the general popularity of colloquial English. For instance, the widespread and apparently acceptable London idiom, except to the fastidious minority, was too firmly embedded to be easily erased. Moreover, the low-class accent, quite un-self-consciously used by most citizens, would have been unremarkable and not under great pressure to be modified in colonial times.

The social, cultural, and historical circumstances and the absence of emotional ties with Britain also produced in the currency a strong sense of Australian identity; they asserted this by supporting causes such as that of the emancipist party. This sense of identity might have been the beginning of the celebrated Australian inferiority complex, but behind it was a strengthening sense of real nationalism, stimulating and quite different in feeling from the usual resentment by convicts suffering under the agents of a distant authority. Many emancipees and free arrivals in the urban areas were taken up by the wave of nationalistic feeling engendered by the currency. In rural districts the currency lads were the forerunners of the skilled, taciturn, proud bushmen, who, along with immigrant land settlers, had to struggle to acquire and develop their holdings, especially after the 1830s, when free land grants were discontinued.

EMERGENCE OF AUSTRALIAN PRONUNCIATION

The pronunciation of Australians, especially their accent, has always roused intense interest and argument, both at home and abroad. A comment by a visitor or a local dignitary, a leg-pull about "strine" (Australian), or a plug for teaching "standard" English is usually enough to produce a host of letters to the news-papers, and opportunity for comment by lay experts and academics, and per-haps an article or two. Most discussions get off the track, and the public lose interest for another decade or so. Nevertheless, most Australians are now real-ising that it is quite normal for one accent to be as acceptable as another, in its context, and for people to choose for themselves for occupational, social, or per-sonal reasons. At least today most Australians do not bridle or become apolo-getic on being identified overseas as a national of their own country, nor are they so anxious to emulate some other English or to change an accent for the wrong reasons.

There is no intention of describing Australian phonology in detail in this essay; I intend only to explain the accent in a very simple way. The 10 or 15 percent who speak with a "cultivated" accent that approximates good standard English might still be detected as Australians in subtle ways, such as fronting of the "cup" ([ʌ]) and "path" ([a]) vowels, raising the "sat" ([æ]) vowel, lowering and centering the "sit" [ɪ]) and "pull" [ʊ]) vowels, stressing the second syllable of the days of the week or the usually unstressed first syllable in words like *refer* and *defer*. The remaining majority of speakers range through the general and broad bands of accent, about 40 percent in each. They are detectable by the pro-nunciation of the vowels and diphthongs of the six words in the following three pairs:

mean/moon—cultivated pronunciations are the close front and back narrow diphthong that combine the "pit" and "peat" vowels in *mean* and the "pull" and "pool" vowels in *moon*. A light half-close schwa (neutral) vowel replaces the initial "pit" and "pull" vowels in the general accent of each vowel, increasing in length and strength as the speaker moves into and through the broad part of the spectrum.

main/moan—cultivated *main* is a diphthong combining the half-close front "pet" with the "pit" vowel, and *moan* combines a half-close schwa quality with the "pull" vowel. As these sounds broaden, the initial vowels centralise to a "cup" vowel quality, remaining slightly front of centre in *main* and back in *moan*. In very broad speech the initial vowels become more open and assume a "balm" vowel quality.

mouse/mice—cultivated forms of these diphthongs glide to a very close posi-tion from the central open "balm" vowel—back to the "pull" vowel in *mouse,* and forward to the "pit" vowel in *mice.* As it broadens, the initial vowel in *mouse* is fronted and raised to the half-open "cat" vowel and further raised to the "met" vowel in very broad accents; the initial vowel in *mice* is retracted and raised to the half-open "dog" vowel as it broadens and is further raised and lengthened to the "cord" vowel in very broad forms.

This is a very generalised and oversimplified statement and, without going into detailed phonetic notation, can only be approximate in specifying Australian sounds. Adjacent sounds also affect vowel quality, and speakers are usually not consistent in grade of accent over the six sounds. In addition, many Australians find it quite easy to move up and down the spectrum according to different social, occupational, or other situations, although one could say that, with growing self-confidence, there is now more stability and consistency. Investigators are noticing some tendency for a movement to the general accent down from the cultivated and up from the broad. This prompts one to suggest that if there is a standard Australian, it would approximate the upper section of the general accent.

As for the beginnings of all this, I believe that the Australian accent is not far removed from that of the early settlers, although distribution across the spectra has changed. Originally, there could well have been more conservatism than in other transported varieties of English because of the greater isolation, lack of early educational pressure, resistance to other modes (especially British), as a result of very strong nationalist feelings, and, in the first several decades, a readiness, even eagerness, in new chums to fall in with the ways of old hands, speech patterns included. Two interesting questions arise from this: first, what was the nature and source of this mode, and second, is the form now referred to as cultivated Australian a descendant of standard English used by some of the socially superior colonists or a separate development?

Some commentators are inclined to label Australian speech as Cockney in relation to its special dialect sense and a general tone of low class. I accept the point, not in reference to modern Cockney but to the more widely used and accepted, less affected, popular London form of the late eighteenth century, so well described by Matthews (1938). There is no need to be concerned here with the glottal stop, not in use before about 1800, or the Cockney rhythm, voice quality, and intonation, with all of which Australians have nothing in common. Certainly in Australia there were early colonial spellings to indicate Cockney [f] and [v] substitutions for [θ] and [ð] *(bofe, muvver, wiv)* and reciprocal use of [w] and [v] *(wery, vhy);* these did not last, probably the result of their being used in a denigrating fashion to portray the speech of uneducated literary characters. In nonstandard Australian we still hear: voicing of medial [t] and to a lesser extent [k] and [p] *(beauty, little, ticket, paper);* elision of final dentals *(kep, blin'),* g from final *-ing (runnin', fishin')* and occasionally medial [w] *(for'ard, awk'ard);* elision of initial unstressed vowels *('bove, 'way, 'stralia);* lengthening of [o] to [ɔ] before voiceless fricatives, now standard English but not Australian *(cross, froth, off);* fronting of [ʊ] to [ɪ] in some words *(just, such);* wrongly elided or intruded initial [h]; occasional intrusions (medial [r] in *drawing* and *sawing,* medial schwa ([ə]) in *athletic, film,* etc.); substitutions such as the "up" vowel [ʌ] for [ər] *(burst, first);* and [ɪŋk] for final [ɪŋ] in the four words *anything, everything, nothing, something.*

Such aberrations as these have long been regarded as uneducated in Australia and elsewhere and are at best circumstantial as a link with low-class London of the eighteenth century. Much more significant are the descriptions of the popular accent of the period by such scholars as Matthews (1938), who had little interest in Australian speech. He described an eighteenth-century London pronunciation whose features are almost identical with those put forward earlier in this section as distinctive markers of the Australian accent and substandard speech. As far as one can determine, these forms have changed little since early colonial days and are usually accepted as having emerged from an amalgamation of English dialects after the convict transports began arriving. One might also consider that the greatest users of this accent were not a widely mixed group of people thrown together for the first time in Australia. They were of a distinctive, low class, a very large number of whom had been living together in their part of London for a long time. In the immediate sense, they shared the gaol or hulk existence to which were added many months in close contact on the journey to Australia and for an indefinite time after that.

The postarrival amalgamation theory as an explanation of the uniform speech pattern is a safe one, but there is also the view that this pattern could have been well in evidence, as a social dialect, before they left England and reinforced after arrival. In the "family" of thieves and vagabonds the situation was ideal for a common, unifying form determined by a dominating, popular mode. What better than colloquial London with a strong flavour of low-class, "advanced" pronunciation, larded with a little criminal cant of the day? Such speakers were the largest group of Australia's very early arrivals, and we know that many of the rest, especially successive newcomers, felt obliged to adopt their "prestige" form. If the amalgamation had not yet taken place, why was there little linguistic indication of western, northern, or Irish immigrants in the "amalgamated" pronunciation?

Barbara Strang, a language historian, noted that the urban dialect of London in the eighteenth century was difficult to identify with any regional variety and that it had most affinity with what we know now as Australian. Her main interest was elsewhere, but she did ask a pertinent question—did the Australian pattern include respect or any positive attitude toward standard English that might have acted as a controlling influence on the popular speech? The most likely, negative answer suggests wide Australian acceptance of a radical, substandard form, emerging from what the grammarian Buchanan called "that vicious, drawling uncouth pronunciation among the generality of [London] people" (1762:vii). In a very short period, what we call the Australian accent could well have become established and been used un-self-consciously at all levels of society.

A cultivated accent either remained or emerged in a minority of speakers, but not necessarily one identical with English standard or "received" pronunciation (RP). One might question whether even the very few RP English speakers could have maintained such a form in the physically and, to an increasing extent, socially unstratified society of early New South Wales and later of the general Australian community. Distance alone would have prevented such maintenance, so it is probable that cultivated Australian has not developed from an imported model, but is the result of a pronunciation shift from general, or even broad, Australian, no doubt influenced by the distant RP (see Bernard, 1969).

One might ask what happened to the late-eighteenth-century, popular, non-criminal form (the Australian prototype?) left back in London. Though this form did advance in status, such advancement would have been extremely slow against nineteenth-century respect for standard and a social system that would easily denigrate the speech of a lower class. In the present century, especially since World War II, Britain has witnessed great educational reform, more exposure to the mass media, a social climate favouring more acceptance of popular speech, and some blurring of class boundaries, particularly among the young. The phonetician Gimson and scholars of language history like Barber and Potter have noted contemporary, generally accepted "variations" in popular English pronunciation. The interesting point is that the features of this pronunciation are very similar to those in the earlier description of the Australian accent that has been around for almost 200 years. Implications from this are very well summarised by George Cochrane, who suggests that "at the level of segmental phonology" there is "almost total system congruence between London English and Australian English. Vowel for vowel and consonant for consonant they match with only an occasional marginal difference. . . . At the level of realisation there is a most striking congruence of Australian and London English in socially relevant variation" (1989:178–189).

There is, of course, no question of the English adopting an Australian pronunciation. In simple terms, popular London English, with some contamination, became acceptable almost immediately in unprotected Australia, whereas "back home" it had to battle with traditional conservative and social pressures for 150 years or so. This striking parallel also suggests that had the original settlers not been convicts, but a socially depressed group from the same general area, there would have been negligible difference in the type of English that developed in Australia.

SOME CONTACT LANGUAGES

After a long period of steady immigration, Australia has become one of the most multicultural countries in the world. There has been little conflict, and any Australian fears about threats to jobs, lower living standards, and so on, have usually been groundless. Most newcomers, as elsewhere, have felt some sense of isolation from the Australian community, to a great extent caused, or at least exacerbated, by language difficulties in a strongly monolingual country. Fortunately, most government policymakers, forward-looking Australians, and migrant leaders are aware of the social and cultural problems and have been vigorously promoting "multiculturalism" in its proper sense of a blending of peoples, rather than of a separation into discrete groups that are identifiable by race or language.

During Australia's history some migrant people have successfully "gone it alone" in the face of resistance to foreigners. Chinese, most of them gold prospectors, constituted about half of the non-British citizens of Australia in the mid-nineteenth century, though they remained aloof, preserving their own ways, language, culture, and religion. Those who remained in Australia either were assimilated into the community at large or remained in city Chinatowns. Italians also formed close groups in several areas such as north Queensland and the Riverina of New South Wales, and Greek communities did the same, usually in the larger cities. For over a century German immigrants established a virtual colony in South Australia with its own schools, press, church, and agricultural development, especially in viniculture. Such close settlements would not have contributed very much to the acquisition of English or easy integration with Australian society. With the passing of time, awareness of educational opportunities for the coming generation, and less social pressure in both directions, immigrants' successors have tended to spread more widely in the general Australian community. More recently, they have tended to favour certain city suburbs, mainly for economic reasons. Most have made their mark in professions, industry, trades, and rural work, but they have also contributed to the cultural and social development of their adopted country. However, their impact on Australian English has been slight; some foreign terms are listed in various publications, usually in relation to foods and other items that have improved our way of life, but much of these were introduced via American usage.

Only modest research was done on the acquisition of English by foreign immigrants before Michael Clyne began his work on the vocabulary and construction of German–English colloquial dialects. Most researches have substantiated the general opinions that informal use of mixed language yields an interim imperfect English more frequently than continued improvement toward standard and that the native tongue usually suffers as well. In a different vein, Andreoni described an interesting pidgin and properly saw this "Australitalian" as having a necessary function as a quasi-dialect for Italians talking to other Italians, not necessarily with Australians. He quoted and "translated" a letter from a cane-cutter to show how a new environment leads to a certain kind of creativity: *ringo barrcare* (ringbark), *arvesto* (harvest), *landa, cana, moneta, killare il tempo, un bel bissenisse.* He noted in his conclusion that "after the beginnings of this process of linguistic invention a habit of Anglicization has been formed which perpetuates the process beyond its real needs" (1967:119). Such a "good enough to get by" mixture becomes a social barrier even if it has historical value as a critical stage in language learning by people in a hurry to "get on" in a new land. A few useful, intact, foreign terms might be expected to move into general use, and Barbara Horvath in fact found some evidence of such movement in her study of sociolects in Sydney.

All migrant groups do not respond in a consistent way in acquiring a new language, nor could many speakers be expected to attain uniformity with Australian English. Most learners would be somewhere on a continuum between the native tongue and Australian, depending on how much personal and social motivation there was to work from barely comprehensible or just satisfactory performance to something better. Attainment of an optimal performance is now being helped much more than previously by a change in Australian attitudes: some understanding of the social barriers to bilingualism, a less dictatorial attitude about the prestige of good Australian (whatever that is), and much more sympathy and cooperation with the new citizens. Australians are even becoming aware again of the value of a second language for its own sake, instead of simply regarding it as "handy" for social or economic reasons, and consequently are not ostracising second-language speakers whose English is imperfect to some degree. Unfortunately, corrupted forms of English are not always recognised by those users who persist with them, and satisfactory performance should not be the point at which new language learning stops.

Some host countries also tend to forget that migrants cannot be lumped together as one group; they are diverse in culture, education, and other aspects of background that might have a positive or negative impact on the degree of new language acquisition or maintenance. Adjustment to the learning continuum in vocabulary, usage, syntax, and pronunciation might be affected by such background factors as one's work, previous life-style, experience with other tongues, age at migration, sex, and the structure of the home language. This impact is different from what is called "ethnolinguistic vitality" (Ball et al., 1989:95), which is a strong capacity to remain distinct, or a culturally based preservation of the native language, usually in pockets of dense and lasting foreign settlement of the kind already discussed. In this situation, the sheer weight of non-English speech, especially if its speakers were held in high enough esteem, could well lead to accepted transfers of phonology or terminology into the English of the district in what Collins calls "stabilised transference" (1989:8).

That migrants must not be regarded simply as a homogeneous group and that language and culture are of vital importance in the success of assimilation are illustrated in Ruth Johnston's work on language usage in the homes of Polish immigrants. The Poles in her study strongly believed that language survival means cultural survival, and she concluded that both assimilated and nonassimilated parents spoke more Polish than English in the home and insisted that their children do the same. Not unexpectedly, considerable conflict resulted; more boys than girls spoke English at home, but tension with parents, even those well assimilated, became very strong irrespective of the sex or ages of the children. Additional comparative studies are needed to determine the strength and impact not only of different cultures but also of those other sociolinguistic factors mentioned earlier.

Just how much such research would improve the rate and quality of English acquisition, and presumably assimilation, is open to question. Migrants will always have cultural and societal hurdles to jump, but in Australia they seem to manage very well. Perhaps Australians are becoming more tolerant and are abandoning unfair stereotyping of migrants; Collins (1989:8–9) cites the use of "matched guise" techniques to detect prejudice, however, and these show continuing discrimination against migrant English. Similar experiments have also shown idiosyncratic reasons for preferring female voices, French over Italian, and German over all other migrant tongues, presumably because German immigrants have a reputation for rapid assimilation and often hold occupations with greater social prestige.

Australian tolerance may have to be improved still more, if only in appreciating the linguistic difficulties our language presents to foreigners. One could also suggest that migrants might be encouraged to persevere longer on the continuum toward better English rather than to be satisfied with an in-between, imperfect, sometimes socially damaging form. In any case, migrant families, along with native Australians, live in every area and at all social levels. They attend all types of schools and tertiary institutions; they are found in all professions, industries, and trades; they marry Australians; and they are numbered among millionaires as well as sharing a place (perhaps out of proportion for a time) with the Aussie "battlers." Migrants also play a prominent part in this country's sporting and cultural achievements. In the broader view, the old and new Australians have not managed too badly together, the old at embracing a great variety of social and cultural innovations, and the new in adjusting to a fresh life-style and, with more difficulty, a strange language.

The largest immigrations have always been English speaking and set the original pattern. I have already offered some selective discussion of the development of the English that was established in Australia to be preserved, adapted, and modified (as in other colonies) to suit special needs and purposes. A unique society was able to give great vitality to British dialectisms that were fading or very localised at home, to vary meaning, and to make fresh formations, especially compounds, in many areas of necessary new naming. Creation of new words was rare, occurring almost by accident as a proper name or some other form seemed appropriate at the time. As in most varieties of English, a kind of creativity rose from the strong Australian desire for colloquial idiomatic phrases, shortenings, frequently with an -*ie* or -*o* suffix, or a dash of rhyming slang just to confuse or entertain outsiders.

Other Englishes

Some readers may feel that New Zealand and Australia should have been considered together in this essay, as a wider study of Australasian or Antipodean English. The two Englishes do appear to have much in common: they were established as British colonies at about the same time in the same isolated area of the world; their vocabularies, especially for flora and fauna, have benefited from contact with their native peoples; and there has been constant free movement between them by seasonal workers, tourists, and migrants. In 1988, indeed, only British settlers outnumbered the New Zealand ones in Australia. Although emanating mainly from Australia, much of the colloquial vocabulary is shared, and the accents seem very similar.

But much of this is oversimplified; the society in each colony was very different, as was the manner of settling the land, the nature of the country, and the attitudes and culture of the native inhabitants. An important distinguishing feature was the emergence of nationalism, strong and early in Australia, whereas New Zealand maintained firm, long-lasting ties, both emotional and linguistic, with the mother country. There are also different, sometimes subtle variations in phonology, lexis, and possibly rhythm. To combine New Zealand English with Australian, or attach it to an essay of this kind, would not be giving it a "fair go." New Zealand English would be either swallowed up by Australian matter or end up hanging to Australian coat tails, since the source material for Australian is currently so much greater. But present resurgence of interest in thorough research in New Zealand should make possible future cooperative work on Antipodean English, perhaps including New Guinea and the Pacific Islands.

American influence on the language of Australia and other countries has been different because it has had little to do with migration. Apparently, American English enjoys enough of the prestige that has to be established before any foreign tongue is likely to be regarded as a significant source of fresh vocabulary or usage. By comparison, in an address to the 48th ANZAAS Congress (1977, Sidney University), Brian Taylor illustrated the prestige German had in the United States by citing it as a probable source not only of much vocabulary but also of such usage as combinations with *-ful* and *-wise* (*insightful, timewise, healthwise*, etc.), idioms like *no way* (emphatic negative), and *hopefully* as a modal or sentence adverb.

In colonial times American contacts with Australia were spasmodic and sometimes hostile. Sealers, whalers, and various speculators in grog and other trade called in (although they were ineffectively barred from entry as early as 1804), but the first real impact came with the reciprocal emigration to the other's goldfields. In the 1850s there were over 16,000 Americans in Australia, and many terms relating to settlement and mining were added to the growing vocabulary (*block, bush, corduroy road, cradle, digger, dirt, landshark, johnny cake, jump, pan out, prospect, rush, section, shanty, squatter, township*, etc.). One must remember that nearly all such words are British after all, and some may have been acquired independently of American contacts. Each country certainly decided which direction their terms would take, and this divergence led to great variation, as in the later, different Australian senses of *block, bush, digger, shanty, squatter, township* in the preceding examples.

During the last century American prestige has moved Australia to accept some Americanisation, mainly by advances in communication from movies, radio, and television, the counterculture of pop music and the drug scene, sports like surfing, direct contacts of students, academics, and businessmen, and alliances in several wars (see Sussex, 1989). Love of the colourful and colloquial smoothed the process of borrowing to the extent that each country could lay claim to many of the other's terms. But there is no point in worrying about who was first with any expession, as did Baker (1943), who took some pains to point out examples of Australian predatings.

The flow of American expressions has continued unabated. In its earlier stages this flow was rather passive, and Americanisms were used only occasionally or in special contexts, seemingly with little likelihood of intruding on existing Australian usage. In an early 1960s address I was wrong in confidently predicting that Americanisms would be "made use of" but unlikely to disturb Australian equivalents in such pairs as *apartment/flat, candy/sweets, cracker/biscuit, dia-*

per/nappy, elevator/lift, fender/mudguard, fries/chips, gas/petrol, grub/tucker, hobo/swagman, hood/bonnet, ranch/station, stag/bucks party, trunk/boot, wrench/spanner. Dozens of Americanisms are enjoying increasing popularity, and Australian English, like other varieties, uses with ease money words like *buck* and *grand, grade* for a school *class, trash* almost as much as *garbage,* and such loans as *campus, crap, gay,* and *screw.* "Such is life," as our most famous bushranger said on the scaffold, and no amount of anti-Americanisation, at present worrying some diehards, is going to change the choice of the people.

Taylor (1989) took the American influence a little further by arguing that Australians are becoming used to spellings like *program, tire* (for a car), *traveling, wagon, -or* for *-our* and *-ize* for *-ise* in some final syllables (*color, flavor, Anglicize, formalize,* etc.) and sometimes *-er* for *-re (theater, meter).* Simplifications like *cook(ery)-book, sail(ing)-boat* have been easily adopted, as are such blends as *scifi, sitcom,* verb-to-noun transfers like *sit-in* or *trade-off,* and the reverse when *impact, source, trial,* and so on are used as verbs. Without realising it, Australians are allowing American pronunciations—for example, *anti-* ending in [taɪ], *schedule* beginning with [sk], *progress* and *project* beginning with [pro]; and *deceive, defer, receive, repair,* and so on, with an [i] vowel in the first syllable. Stress shifts are quite common, so we might hear *add*-dress, *fie*-nance, second-*air*-y, secre-*tair*-y, and so on. Critics of such variations have to be careful; some of these have been Australian practice for decades, and others have been in and out of public approval for just as long.

Aboriginal Influence

One might regard the linguistic impact of the Aboriginal minority in Australia as similar to that of the various and more numerous migrant groups discussed earlier. The reality, however, is that their society and culture began about 40,000 years before white colonisation and migration to Australia began. Over this period European civilisation steadily developed under the influence of trade, invention, technology, education, and other advances, while the world of the Aborigines remained stable and untouched. This divergence made for a huge cultural gap that is proving extremely difficult to bridge. As far as language is concerned, there has been enough interaction for whites to study some of the hundreds of unwritten Aboriginal dialects and for Aborigines to learn enough English to get by. The result is an unbalanced kind of bilingualism.

The white settlers also had a much greater motivation to borrow large numbers of Aboriginal terms than they later had for migrant languages. This motivation was rooted in pragmatism rather than prestige. Many publications have lists of words, a proportion of them surviving in the same way as Maori and Indian languages did in New Zealand and North America. Further loans were necessary to name flora, fauna, and geographical features and to provide an abundance of place names as part of government policy. Inaccuracies, especially in meaning and form, were unavoidable in reports by well-meaning but linguistically unskilled missionaries, government officers, and others. Considerable difficulties, of which there were five general types, were associated with such loans.

1. There is a great variety of English spellings for most Aboriginal terms (e.g., about three dozen exist for *corroboree*), some so different that they could be mistaken for other words altogether. The reason might be cognate terms in dialects, faithful recording of varying pronunciation of different Aborigines, or, more likely, varying perceptions of pronunciation by untrained recorders or British dialect speakers. The *koala, culawine,* and *koolah* are thus the same animal, as are the *yoyo, yahoo,* and *yowie,* a hairy, apelike, mythical creature feared by the Aborigines and allegedly last "sighted" in New South Wales in 1977. With many such groups we simply cannot be sure about the fine linguistic details.

2. Some Aboriginal words can be placed in groups because of a degree of similarity of sense, but it is usually a mistake to regard them as synonyms. If dialectisms for the same referent are different in structure, they could easily become synonymous in the language of the borrowers but remain in Aboriginal dialects as precise names for different members of a class. Thus, the *bettong, euro, pademelon, potoroo, quokka, wallaby,* and *wallaroo* are types of "kangaroo" from the small rat kangaroo to the giants. The word *kangaroo* itself may refer to only one variety of the species, and the whites may have been responsible for popularising it as the class name. Some terms for *club* were *boondi, leeangle, nulla-nulla,* and *waddy,* but each of these no doubt had structural or functional differences. A wooden or bark vessel for carrying necessities could be a *cooliman, pitchi,* or *wirra,* with the shape determined by the tree from which it was peeled; in arid areas a deeper *cooliman* could carry water, not possible for the flatter *pitchi,* which held food. The *woomera* (a throwing stick that added velocity to a spear) might be wide and hollowed out, useful also as a *cooliman,* but in areas of big game it would be slimmer, with less air resistance for the spear thrower. If necessary, anything could double as a club to strike game or another person.

Sources of water were very important, and terms like *billabong, cowal, gilgai,* and *namma* ("hole") had distinctive referents, as do the English *anabranch, lagoon, lake, marsh,* and *pond.* But over time the generalised *waterhole* embraced many of them. Whites described makeshift dwellings by the Aboriginal *gunyah, humpy, mia mia, quamby, wiltja,* and *wurley,* with little concern about exact meanings or regional differences. *Humpy* is still very common for a rough shack and has survived the period of various styles and sizes of bark or slab huts.

3. Some more apparent than real synonymy has been mentioned, but another kind is much more exact when English equivalents coexist with the Aboriginal term. For example, there is *koala, native bear* (less frequently, *Australian* or *monkey bear*); the *dingo* or *warrigal* is the *native dog,* but not *wild dog* (more correctly, a feral animal). The *brolga* is also a *native companion;* the *buln buln,* a *lyre bird;* the *kookaburra,* a *laughing jackass;* and the *budgerigar,* a *love bird* or *shell parrot.*

4. Another likely confusion in so much exchange of terms occurred when Aboriginal pronunciation of an English word was mistakenly reborrowed and assumed to be Aboriginal, or vice versa. Ramson (1964b:50ff) cites *bucklow* or *bacala* ("bullock") and *picanini* as mistakenly Aboriginal, and asserts the true Aboriginality of words like *budgerigar* and *corella* ("parrot"), *gibber* ("stone"),

gin ("woman"), and *waddy* ("club"), some of which have even been endowed with false European etymologies. In quoting a pitiful statement by an Aboriginal youth about to hang, Ramson (1964b:57) pinpoints how pidgin, from the mix of a native dialect and low-class English, including thieves' slang and swearing, can distort both meaning and the source of words form both cultures. As a result of such confused idiom, many Aboriginal terms, familiar to most Australians, are now suspect in origin; for example, *bingy* ("stomach"), *bogey* ("swim"), *cooee* ("call"), *jumbuck* ("sheep"), *yacker* ("work"), and *yarraman* ("horse") could well be Aboriginal attempts at English. *Debbil, peller,* and *plurry* are obvious pidgin for "devil," "fellow," and "bloody," and one might be similarly convinced by *boma* ("gun"), *borak* ("derisive talk" or perhaps "barrack"), *pialler* ("talk," perhaps from *parley*), *yabber* ("talk," perhaps from *jabber*). More research is needed, because one is tempted to conjecture further. What might one read into the "Aboriginal" *badgee* ("angry"), *bombora* ("breaking waves on rocks"), *dhabba* ("painting stick"), *jinki* ("legendary spirit"), *yan* ("go"), *yowi* ("yes"), *yukki* ("exclamation"), *wakaburra* ("club")?

5. Some expressions combine Aboriginal and English words, useful for immediate communication but not always good for the better adjustment of the two cultures: *baal gammon* ("no deceit"), *bora ground* ("ceremonial area"), *bunyip aristocracy* (derogatory name for a failed attempt to create a colonial aristocracy), *finger yabber* ("sign language"), and *piccaninny daylight* ("period before sunrise"). Typically used by English speakers, such words reflect a practice that occurs wherever a host and a new language are coming to terms. An extension of this has been the development of apposite English compounds, some likely to be Australian English creations, such as *blackfellow's buttons* ("australites"), *blackfellow's oven* ("midden"), *black-tracker, digging stick, fire stick,* and *puller* ("didgeridoo player"). These are not nearly as colourful as the Aboriginal *big sick* ("leprosy"), *close-up* ("nearly"), *dream time* ("distant past"), *finger money* ("money for spending"), *flour bag* ("white haired," "old"), *make a light* ("see," "look for"), *sit down* ("stay," "live"), *sorry cuts* ("body cuts to show grief"), *tumble down* ("die," "kill"), *walkabout* ("wandering"), and *white money* ("silver coin"). My father described use of very poor English as *blackfellow talk,* indirectly and rather crudely identifying the presence of a social problem.

The preceding examples were chosen as terms that have been familiar to whites for many decades, and they express something of the closeness of the two peoples in bush settlements. The breakdown of this closeness can be detected when more personal contacts are examined, after the very early days, when no offence seems to have been taken. Aborigines were originally called *Indians,* then *natives;* the latter also described "native" whites, but a further sorting into *black natives, native blacks,* and *white natives* was not popular. Aborigines' words to describe themselves, like *boori, koori,* or *murri,* were not very enduring because the whites seem to have preferred nonspecific names, often smacking of pidgin and the pejorativeness associated with it. There were unpopular Americanisms like *coon, darky, nigger, black, blackboy, blackfellow,* and the local shortening, *Abo. Boong* was a popular, usually friendly name for New Guineans during World War II, but this friendliness is absent in its later use for *Aborigine.*

One denigrating English creation was *charcoal,* used over a century ago by mounted black police and black trackers in reference to Aborigines they were hunting. Such fugitives might also have been called *brumby* ("wild horse"), *myall* ("a black in the wild"), or *warrigal* ("dingo").

Binghi ("brother"), *benjiman* ("husband"), and *kipper,* a probable corruption of *capera* ("circumcised initiate"), were terms that did not have extensive use compared with some white creations. *Jacky* and *Mary,* although little more than labels, were innocent enough forms of address for each sex. *Gin* or *lubra* (in Tasmania) gave women some dignity, but before long we find such denigrations as *black gin* or *black mary.* A white living with a *gin* could be a *combo, gin shepherd,* or a *gin jockey,* and the children from such a union were subject to derogatory names like *bronzewing, creamy,* and *yellow-billy, -boy,* or *-fellow. Black boy* also referred to a *gin* dressed as a boy, apparently as a cover for the station worker or drover with whom she was cohabiting.

Space limitations here prevent further sociolinguistic study of Aboriginal English. Suffice to say that Aboriginal English ranges from the creoles of those living their traditional life in very remote regions, where some decreolisation is now taking place, to the language of those (about 40 percent) living in cities and large towns. Some of the latter would be competent in English, but most of them are barely up to the white nonstandard speech of socially disadvantaged areas. Many Aborigines regard their "black" English as part of their social solidarity and scorn others for speaking *flash.* The children in such a social group can be not only restricted in advancement but also unfairly regarded as deficient cognitively as well as linguistically.

Despite its ubiquitous variety of pronunciation, the homogeneity of Australian English has, in keeping with Labov's "variable rules" (Collins, 1989:4), developed a notion of a "standard form." This concept must also embrace variants in a realistic but liberal way, a principle that applies especially to foreign immigrants and Aborigines who, as we have seen, are under some social, economic, and related pressures to assimilate. To succeed, motivation for assimilation has to be strong, and initiatives must be taken, especially by educators who often see remedial English as something taught in isolation. Rather, remedial English needs to be combined with positive exploitation of well-developed "substandard" forms as a starting point in learning programs moving in the direction of standard.

CONCLUSION

One must have some reservations about conclusions from an essay that had to be both selective in choice of topics and limited in the number of examples to illustrate them. Rather than describe the Australian language, my aim was to demonstrate how historical and social forces could influence the growth of a variety of English as a small, diverse population established a new way of life in a strange environment.

In a longer work one might have moved on to topics that extended those already raised, such as the *bushranging* era, which paralleled and continued beyond the convict years for almost a century. At first there were the more hardened types, as desperate bolters from assigned service threatened Sydney society and settlers when they moved farther out. Few wanted the life of a bandit, but with little chance of survival in the bush, and the hangman or the lash should one surrender or be caught, *taking the bush* became the only way. For a time there was a great sympathy for the *absentees* because their position was appreciated by the citizenry, many of whom had known convict life firsthand. A later development of *bushranging,* from about the mid-nineteenth century, involved convict survivors and some descendants, but it was essentially the risky activity of adventurous, unemployed, and disaffected, wild colonial boys. It was the old story of small beginnings, with a bit of cattle *duffing* ("stealing and obscuring the brand") that "everyone did" in a tit-for-tat way, followed by more serious crimes. In spite of their hard-done-by or persecuted-innocent image, such individuals became a social blight for some decades, *bailing up* ("holding up") without discrimination and applying their excellent riding skills to avoid capture. They also used *bush telegraphs* ("informants"), who supplied food, shelter, and knowledge of the whereabouts of the *traps* and *troopers.* These helpers sometimes betrayed them in bad times—if one of the gang had not himself turned *approver* ("informer") first.

The gun, rope, or gaol saw to the end of most *bushrangers,* but they were followed in the cities by the even less admirable cult of *larrikinism,* usually as members of a *push* ("gang"). The best of them were *flash lairs* or *street louts,* the worst resorted to gangland style thuggery with the club, boot, brick, or razor; and, as elsewhere, they are still with us. One thing that they and the *bushrangers* did was to maintain and add to the colorful idiom of early colonial times, and today we see it perpetuated and increased in various collections of prison slang all over the English-speaking world. As was natural, some of it carried into popular usage.

A better illustration of the growth of Australian terminology by continuing use of dialectisms, adaptation and combination of words, and variation of meaning comes from the study of land settlement and associated industries, such as sheep and wool, cattle grazing, and mining. Work on the language of these, with emphasis on historical development and social interaction, is well advanced (Gunn, 1965).

Apart from the mother lode of British English and the permeation of all Englishes by the high prestige of general, colloquial American, one could not say that there has been a dramatic increase in exchange of terms and usage. Philosophically, we might expect Englishes to draw more closely together in these times of enlightenment about "standards," "correctness," and so on, and the shrinking of what Geoffrey Blainey called the tyranny of distance. Some signs are there, of course, but each variety seems to be satisfied with looking after itself. Australian English is in a very interesting position, having survived the challenges of settling down and various problems rising from contacts with other language speakers; according to some, such problems were engendered by insularity, negativeness, and self-righteous independence. Australians have enlivened their English very effectively, they have developed a reasonable adjustment with a great variety of immigrants, their modified speech and usage has stood the test of time, and, nowadays, there is far less uncritical acceptance of arbitrary "standards" than previously. One can expect that this will continue and that, as Peter Trudgill noted (1984:32), "an increasing tendency towards autonomy" can be expected of Australian English.

WORKS CITED AND OTHER REFERENCES

Andreoni, G. 1967. "Australitalian." *University Studies in History* 5:114–119.

Baker, S. J. 1943. "The Influence of American Slang on Australia." *American Speech* 18:23–26.

_____. 1963. "Australian." In McLeod, ed., pp. 102–130.

_____. 1966. *The Australian Language,* 2nd ed. Sydney: Currawong.

Ball, P., C. Gallois, and V. Callan. 1989. "Language Attitudes: A Perspective from Social Psychology." In Collins and Blair, eds., pp. 89–102.

Barber, C. 1969. *Linguistic Change in Present Day English.* London: Oliver.

Bernard, J.R.L. 1969. "On the Uniformity of Spoken English." *Orbis* 18:62–73.

Bevan, I., ed. 1953. *The Sunburnt Country: Profile of Australia.* London: Collins.

Buchanan, J. 1762. *The British Grammar.* Rpt. 1968 Menston, England: Scolar Press. 97.

Clark, C.M.H. 1962—1987. *A History of Australia.* 6 vols. Melbourne: Melbourne University Press.

Clyne, M. G. 1967. *Transference and Triggering.* The Hague: Nijhoff.

_____. 1970. "Migrant English in Australia." In Ramson, ed., pp. 123–136.

_____. 1976. *Australia Talks: Essays on the Sociology of Australian Immigrant and Aboriginal Languages.* Canberra: Australian National University Press.

_____. 1982. *Multilingual Australia.* Melbourne: River Seine.

Cochrane, G. R. 1989. "Origins and Development of the Australian Accent." In Collins and Blair, eds., pp. 178–186.

Collins, P. 1989. "Sociolinguistics in Australia." In Collins and Blair, eds., pp. 3–20.

_____, and D. Blair, eds. 1989. *Australian English: The Language of a New Society.* Brisbane: Queen's University Press.

Cunningham, P. M. 1827. *Two Years in New South Wales,* 2nd ed. 2 vols, London.

Gimson, A. C. 1962. "Phonetic Change and the R P Vowel System." In D. Abercrombie et al., eds. *In Honour of Daniel Jones.* London: Longman. Pp. 131–136.

Gunn, J. S. 1965. *The Terminology of the Shearing Industry.* Sydney: Australian Language Research Centre, 5–6, University of Sydney.

_____. 1982. "The Australian Bushranging Society." *Journal of the Royal Australian Historical Society* 68(1):59–66.

_____, and B. Levy. 1980. *A Word History of Bushranging.* Sydney: Australian Language Research Centre, 17, University of Sydney.

Haygarth, H. W. 1848. *Recollections of Bush Life in Australia.* London: Murray.

Horvath, B. 1985. *Variation in Australian English: The Sociolects of Sydney.* Cambridge, England: Cambridge University Press.

Hughes, A., and P. Trudgill. 1979. *English Accents and Dialects.* London: Arnold.

Johnston, R. 1967. "Language Usage in the Homes of Polish Immigrants in Western Australia." *Lingua* 18:271–289.

Lang, J. D. 1834. *Historical and Statistical Account of New South Wales*, 2 vols. London.

Langker, R. 1980. *Flash in New South Wales*. Sydney: Australian Language Research Centre, 18, University of Sydney.

——. 1981. *The Vocabulary of Convictism in New South Wales, 1758–1850*. Sydney: Australian Language Research Centre, 19, University of Sydney.

McCarthy, F. D. 1971. *New South Wales Aboriginal Place Names*, 5th ed. Sydney: Museum Publications.

McLeod, A. L., ed. 1963. *The Pattern of Australian Culture*. Ithaca, NY: Cornell University Press.

McNab, K. 1962. "The Nature and Nurture of the First Generation of Native Born Australians." In *Historical Studies: Australia and New Zealand* 10(34):289ff.

Martin, G., ed. 1978. *The Founding of Australia*. Sydney: Hale and Iremonger.

Matthews, W. 1937. "The Vulgar Speech of London in XV–XVIII Centuries." *Notes and Queries* 172:2–5, 21–24, 40–42, 56–60, 77–79, 92–96, 112–115, 130–133, 149–151, 167–170, 186–188, 204–206, 218–221, 241–243.

——. 1937. "Some Eighteenth Century Vulgarisms." *Review of English Studies* 13:307–325.

——. 1938. *Cockney Past and Present*. London: Routledge.

Mitchell, A. G., and A. Delbridge. 1965. *The Pronunciation of English in Australia*, 2nd ed. Sydney: Angus & Robertson.

Nares, R. 1784. *Elements of Orthoepy*. Reprint, 1968. Menston, England: Scolar Press. 56.

Partridge, E. H. "Their Language." In Bevan, ed. Pp. 212–221.

——, and J. W. Clark. 1951. *British and American English Since 1900*. London: Dakers.

Platt, J. 1925. *English Colloquial Idiom in the Eighteenth Century*. Unpublished thesis, University of London, 221B80.

——. 1926. "The Development of English Colloquial Idiom During the Eighteenth Century." *Review of English Studies* 2:70–81, 189–196.

Potter, Simeon. 1969. *Changing English*. London: Deutsch.

Ramson, W. S. 1964a. *The Currency of Aboriginal Words in Australian English*. Sydney: Australian Language Research Centre 3, University of Sydney.

——. 1964b. "Aboriginal Words in Early Australian English." *Southerly* 18(1):50–60.

——, ed. 1970. *English Transported*. Canberra: Australian National University Press.

Ribton-Turner, C. J. 1877. *A History of Vagrants and Vagrancy and Beggars and Begging*. Reprint, 1972. Montclair, NJ: Patterson Smith. No. 138.

Robson, R. L. 1970. *The Convict Settlers of Australia*. Melbourne: Melbourne University Press.

Savage, W. H. 1833. *The Vulgarisms and Improprieties of the English Language*. London.

Shaw, A.G.L. 1971. *Convicts and the Colonies*. London: Faber.

Strang, B. M. 1970. *A History of English*. London: Methuen.

Sussex, R. 1978. "North American English as a Prestige Model in The Australian Media." *Talanya* 5:36–41.

——. "The Americanisation of Australian English: Prestige Models in the Media." In Collins and Blair, eds. Pp. 158–168.

Taylor, B. 1989. "American, British and Other Foreign Influences on Australian English Since World War II." In Collins and Blair, eds. Pp. 225–254.

Tench, W. 1793. *A Complete Account of the Settlement at Port Jackson in New South Wales*. London.

Trudgill, P. ed. 1984. *Language in the British Isles.* Cambridge: Cambridge University Press.

Turner, G. 1960. "On the Origin of Australian Vowel Sounds." *Australian Universities MLA* 13:33–45.

_____. 1966. *The English Language in Australia and New Zealand.* London: Longman.

_____, ed. 1972. *Good Australian English.* Sydney: Reed.

Vaux, J. H. 1819. "A New and Comprehensive Vocabulary of the Flash Language." In *The Memoirs of James Hardy Vaux.* London. Reprint ed., N. McLachlan, 1964. London: Heinemann.

Wakefield, E. G. 1829. *A Letter from Sydney.* London. Reprint Everyman ed. 1929.

Walker, J. 1791. *A Critical Pronouncing Dictionary.* London. Reprint, 1968. Menston, England: Scolar Press. 117.

Ward, R. 1962. "The Nature and Nurture of the First Generation of Native Born Australians." *Historical Studies: Australia and New Zealand* 10.39:289ff.

_____. 1970. *The Australian Legend,* 2nd ed. London: Oxford University Press.

Wilkes, G. A. 1978. *A Dictionary of Australian Colloquialisms.* Sydney: Sydney University Press.

9

The Second Diaspora of English

BRAJ B. KACHRU

The preceding eight chapters of this volume have primarily discussed the socio-linguistic contexts of English in Britain, America, and Australia, traditionally termed the native varieties of the language. This chapter describes English in nonnative sociolinguistic contexts.[1] Let me begin with a question that relates to the speakers of the language, their relationship to the changing sociocultural context of English, and the development of world Englishes.

The question is, "How many people use English around the world?" We actually have no reliable figures in answer to this crucial question. Within the group of English users, moreover, we do not know how to distinguish an English "knower" from a "semiknower" of the language. If we accept the most conservative figures, there are now two nonnative speakers of English for every native speaker. And if we accept an extremely optimistic figure of 2 billion users of English out of the total world population of over 5 billion, roughly every third person is using some variety of English as a nonnative speaker.[2] Whether these statistics are exact or not is not vital. What is significant is that these figures, conservative or optimistic, are indicative of an unprecedented linguistic fact about the spread of the language. The spread involves practically every part of the world, every literate or oral culture, and almost every linguistic area. These figures are also staggering for another reason that I shall return to later.

The major characteristic of this spread is that it has taken place in what one might call diaspora, that is, in sociocultural and historical contexts traditionally not associated with the language. The word *diaspora* is somewhat tricky here, for it has generally been used for the dispersion of religious groups—particularly the Jews—and not often a language. The analogy is, however, applicable to the spread of several languages, especially English. It seems that the original meaning of *diaspora,* which comprises Greek *dia* ("through") and *spora* ("seed" in the sense of "spread seed"), certainly captures the diffusion of English in more senses than one, as I hope will become clearer in this chapter. The "seeds" of the language were "spread" in enormously diverse sociocultural environments, and the resultant varieties of the language show this diversity.

The major method of the diffusion of English has been to transplant it in "un-

English" sociocultural contexts, where it has become a powerful communicative tool. The attitude toward the language has varied from enthusiastic acceptance to extreme hostility in Asia, Africa, and elsewhere.[3]

The diaspora varieties of English are generally associated with colonial expansion outside the British Isles. But that is a limited way of looking at the spread of English. We get a better perspective of the spread of English if we view its diaspora in terms of several phases. The first phase began close to home, in the British Isles. The initial expansion was toward Wales in 1535, when Wales was united with England, and was extended to Scotland in 1603, when the English and Scottish monarchies ceased to be separate. It was not until 1707 that the state of Great Britain was established. The extended state included parts of Ireland as well, and with this expansion, English was no longer the language of only England. This first phase, however, was restricted to the British Isles, and to a sociolinguistic context that had numerous shared characteristics and traditions.

The second phase of dispersion takes us to far-flung parts of the world, to North America (e.g., see Mencken 1919), to Australia, to New Zealand (e.g., see Eagleson, 1982), and to Canada (e.g., see Bailey, 1982). During this phase, English was implanted on two continents. However, these varieties of English were different from the second-diaspora varieties. The American, Australian, and New Zealand varieties were essentially the result of the movement of English-speaking populations from one part of the globe to another. Thus, these varieties only partially entailed change or modification of the linguistic behaviour of local speech communities. And, in terms of numbers, this expansion did not significantly contribute to the numerical superiority of English. When Australia, Canada, the United States, and New Zealand adopted English as the language of new nations, it became one of the major languages of the world, along with Arabic, Spanish, Hindi, French, German, and Russian. However, it was still far from being the global language it is now.

It was the third phase that resulted in the second major diaspora and altered the earlier sociolinguistic profile of the English language. This second diaspora brought English to Asia, to Africa, to Latin America, and to the Philippines. It is this phase of the diaspora that I concentrate on in this chapter.

This second diaspora of English is characterized by various cross-linguistic and cross-cultural features, foremost of which was the creation of new linguistic contexts. The regions where English was transplanted initially had practically no users of English. Thus, in terms of language acquisition, the teaching and learning of English entailed change in the linguistic behaviour of the users of other languages, Asian and African. To begin with, the English-using speech communities in these regions were small, but as time passed and as the colonies stabilized, these communities expanded. This is evident, for example, in the histories of English in Africa, Asia, and the Philippines. A second feature of this diaspora was that it brought English into contact with genetically and culturally unrelated major languages. In Africa, for example, English came in contact with Bantu and Niger-Congo languages, in Asia with Dravidian languages, and in Southeast Asia with Altaic languages. Historically, this was an unprecedented and varied convergence of English with other languages in a multilingual context (known as a language-contact situation) which inevitably left its mark and con-tributed toward the development of regional contact varieties of English.

A third feature of the diaspora was its alteration of the traditions and distinct contexts of the teaching of English. No one "native" model was presented to the new learners. Some teachers of English came from regions where they them-selves had learnt English as a nonnative language. Many missionaries came from Ireland, Wales, Scotland, and even other parts of Europe (e.g., Belgium). They also had received inadequate linguistic training as English teachers. Thus, many learners were not exposed to standard English varieties, as is generally believed. A final feature of this spread was that English came into contact with a variety of major non-Western cultures and sociolinguistic contexts.

In retrospect, we see that the story of the spread of English and its consolida-tion as a world language can be represented by three concentric circles. Figure 9.1 gives graphic representation of this spread. Sociolinguistic, linguistic, and acquisitional factors define these circles, which reflect the type of spread, the range of functions of English in a region, the types of literary creativity and experimentation, the patterns of acquisition, and the depth of penetration of English at various societal levels (Kachru, 1985).

DIMENSIONS OF THE SECOND DIASPORA

The sociolinguistic implications and various dimensions of the second diaspora cannot be fully grasped without seeing them in historical, political, and socio-logical contexts. The major initiator of the diffusion of English was the desire for colonial expansion and an urge to gain strategic control in various parts of the world, first by Britain and later by the United States. But these two motives were sometimes related to yet another two motives: proselytization and cultural imposition. In attaining these nonlinguistic goals, the English language became a primary tool of communication, administration, elitism, and, eventually, lin-guistic control (Kachru, 1986a,b). English acquired an elitist position through the power it provided its users. As the colonial governments established stable foundations, for instance, English acquired vital domains of use. In each part of the colonial empire, the British administrators gave the language status and functional power. What Thomas Babington Macaulay (1800–1859) did in the Indian subcontinent as a senior representative of the Raj (or imperial dominion) in initiating and implementing English education was done by administrators with Macaulay's zeal in other parts of the expanding British empire, such as Africa and Southeast Asia.

It is true that often a segment of the local elite supported such moves. And this local support for English was given for pragmatic reasons. In some colonies the local elite saw English as a window to the scientific and technological develop-ments of the Western world. They wanted to partake of the bounty that the industrial revolution (1750–1850) had made possible for Europe. Additionally, English was considered a great literary resource that opened the door through translations to the rich literary traditions of other European languages, such as

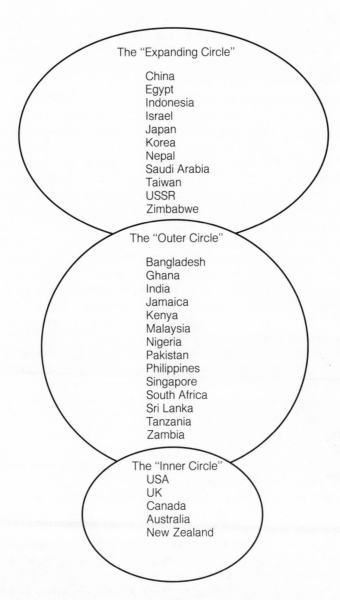

The "Expanding Circle"

China
Egypt
Indonesia
Israel
Japan
Korea
Nepal
Saudi Arabia
Taiwan
USSR
Zimbabwe

The "Outer Circle"

Bangladesh
Ghana
India
Jamaica
Kenya
Malaysia
Nigeria
Pakistan
Philippines
Singapore
South Africa
Sri Lanka
Tanzania
Zambia

The "Inner Circle"
USA
UK
Canada
Australia
New Zealand

Figure 9.1. The spread of English. The circles do not include South Africa and Jamaica. In these countries the sociolinguistic situation is rather complex and an estimate of the English-using population is difficult to make.

French, German, and Russian. There were also some missionary groups that supported the cause of English as the language for proselytization, although a large group of missionaries in Asia and Africa advocated the use of local vernaculars for the spread of Christianity.

Slowly, with the power of the expanding Empire behind it, English became a link language for elite populations in multilingual Asia and Africa. English contributed to the creation of a cross-linguistic and cross-cultural network of people who began to use it in the domains of science, technology, military, pan-regional business, and creative writing (see, e.g., McCrum et al., 1986; Fishman et al., 1978; Kachru, 1982a, 1986a). It is primarily for these reasons that English eventually acquired its present status as a global language. However, the universalization of the language came at a price, primarily that of linguistic and cultural diversification. This diversification increased as the second diaspora of English intensified and increased.

In geographical terms, the second diaspora covers a vast territory. First, it includes those regions where English was introduced during political colonization and became a vital colonial linguistic tool (e.g., South Asia, West Asia, Southeast Asia). Second, it covers those places where historically there are no colonial associations with Britain or the United States, but where English is learnt as an important additional language (e.g., Nepal, Thailand, Vietnam). A partial list of the second-diaspora countries follows.

Africa: Botswana, Cameroon, Gambia, Ghana, Ethiopia, Kenya, Lesotho, Liberia, Malawi, Mauritius, Namibia, Nigeria, Seychelles, Somalia, South Africa, Sudan, Swaziland, Tanzania, Uganda, Zambia, Zimbabwe.

South Asia: Bangladesh, Bhutan, India, Nepal, Pakistan, Sri Lanka, The Maldives.

West Asia: Afghanistan, Bahrain, Israel, Kuwait, Oman, The United Arab Emirates.

Southeast Asia: Brunei, Burma, Hong Kong, Malaysia, Indonesia, The Philippines, Singapore, Thailand, Vietnam.

The Americas and the South Atlantic: Argentina, Ascension Island, Belize, Bermuda, The Falkland Islands, Guyana, Honduras, Nicaragua, Panama, St. Helena, Surinam.

The Caribbean: Anguilla, Antigua and Bermuda, Bahamas, Barbados, The Cayman Islands, Dominica, Grenada, Jamaica, Montserrat, Puerto Rico, St. Christopher and Nevis, St. Lucia, St. Vincent and the Grenadines, Trinidad and Tobago, The Turks and Caicos Islands, The Virgin Islands (American and British).

Oceania: Cook Islands, Fiji, Hawaii, Kiribati, Nauru, Papua New Guinea, The Solomon Islands, Tonga, Tuvalu, Vanuatu, Western Samoa.

Western Europe: The Channel Islands, Cyprus, Malta.

This list does not easily accommodate China, nor does it include what were until recently called the "iron-curtain countries," for example, Russia, Bulgaria, Czechoslovakia, Hungary, Poland, Romania, Yugoslavia, and so on. In these countries the profile of English has suddenly changed, and it is acquiring the status of an important foreign language, replacing Russian.

DIASPORA AND DIVERSIFICATION

The diaspora has naturally resulted in sociolinguistic diversification from two underlying linguistic processes: *nativization* and *acculturation*. Nativization is the linguistic readjustment a language undergoes when it is used by members of another speech community in distinctive sociocultural contexts and language contact situations. A very common linguistic phenomenon in most of the world, nativization involves the approximation of a language to the linguistic and discoursal characteristics of the native (or dominant) language of the area into which it has been transplanted. On the other hand, acculturation focuses on the people learning the transplanted language; it refers to the reflection of their sociocultural identities in a nativized language. It is these two processes that resulted in, for example, the Indianization (Kachru, 1983), Africanization (Bokamba, 1982; Kujore, 1985; Zell and Silver, 1971), and Singaporeanization (Bloom, 1986; Foley, 1988; Platt and Weber, 1980) of English. In the second diaspora, as these two processes of nativization and acculturation intensified, the English language developed several distinct varieties, a number of which are already well institutionalized (see, e.g., Bailey and Görlach, 1982; Kachru, 1982c; Platt and Ho, 1984; Sridhar, 1985; Sridhar and Sridhar, 1986). And now two types of Englishes have appeared: the native transplanted Englishes (e.g., American, Australian, Canadian, New Zealand) and the nonnative Englishes (e.g., West African, South Asian, Southeast Asian). However, a caveat is appropriate here. The term *native,* which I have used with the native varieties, is controversial and problematic in multilingual contexts in which the English language is used as one language among two, three, or more (see Paikeday, 1985).

   In Quirk et al. (1985, see also 1972) the question of varieties of English has been discussed in great detail with a number of descriptive labels. One label that is particularly appropriate to discussion of the second-diaspora varieties of English is "interference varieties." But the concept of interference, as traditionally used, manifests the monolingual's view of a language, in this case English. This is not necessarily the view held in multilingual societies, however, where all the languages in the verbal repertoire of a user are in some sense "interference varieties." There, what the monolingual regards as interference is better seen as the pull of languages toward establishing similarities and the leveling of linguistic structures approximating the dominant language. Although the degree of contact and convergence may vary, it is nevertheless present in all the languages used in such societies. The difference is only of degree, as can be seen in studies of the Balkan linguistic area, the South Asian linguistic area (Emeneau, 1956; D'souza, 1987; Masica, 1976), and the Ethiopian linguistic area (Ferguson, 1976), to name just three such areas. In the native contexts, too, in the "Inner Circle" of English, there have been several levels of "interference," but these have been primarily from the European languages, such as French, Spanish, and German. This interaction of European linguistic and literary trends has resulted in what has been called the "European literature," and in a broader sense, "European civilization."

   With the spread of English and its increased uses in social and literary domains, the creation of new non-Western cultural identities has intensified. These "multicultural" identities of English emerge from a cluster of primarily sociolinguistic features, including speech communities, literary canon, discoursal organization, and demythologization.

Shift of Traditional Interlocutors

English is one of the few languages that is used by a majority of the people who speak it as a second, a third, or an *n*th language. The users come from a wide variety of linguistic and cultural backgrounds: an Indo-Aryan language speaker communicating with a Dravidian language speaker, for instance, or a Japanese with a Taiwanese, or a Nigerian with a Saudi Arabian. Often English is used by groups of nonnative speakers to communicate with other nonnative speakers. There are historical parallels to this situation, but in these cases the imposed language has not affected as many social classes or communication situations as English: Latin in medieval Europe (Kahane and Kahane, 1979; Kahane, 1986), Sanskrit in traditional South Asia, Arabic for religious purposes in the Islamic world, and French in the Francophone countries are some other examples. The traditional position that English is used by nonnative speakers only to communicate with native speakers is thus a linguistic myth.

Shift of Canon

A written language supports a variety of cultural and social traditions, including a literary canon. For example, in the case of Sanskrit the canon includes over 2000 years of history, philosophy, and the types of creativity embodied in the *Mahābhārata* and the *Rāmāyana,* the two celebrated epics originally written in Sanskrit. The canon draws on the Pali, the Prakrtas, and other classical works. In the case of Persian, the canon reflects the impact of Turkish and Arabic, and the Sufi and Islamic canon. In the areas of cultural and linguistic convergence, traditions blend in the same way that Sanskrit did in Southeast Asia (e.g., Indonesia) and Persian in South Asia (e.g., India, Pakistan). When English was implanted in Africa, the Philippines, and Asia, the process—typical of such language and cultural contact situations—was repeated. But with English much more happened than mere repetition of the historically established process of convergence. The language was used as a tool to re-create the local sociocultural traditions. Let me quote here a passage from an Indian metaphysical novelist, Raja Rao (1963:10), and try to show how it entails contextualization at several levels.

> "Today," he says, "it will be the story of Siva and Parvati." And Parvati in penance becomes the country and Siva becomes heaven knows what! "Siva is the three-eyed," he says, "and Swaraj too is three-eyed: Self-purification, Hindu-Moslem unity, Khaddar." And then he talks of Damayanthi and Sakunthala and Yasodha and everywhere there is something about our country and something about Swaraj. Never had we heard *Harikathas* like this. And he can sing too, can Jayaramachar. He can keep us in tears for hours together. But the *Harikatha* he did, which I can

never forget in this life and in all lives to come, is about the birth of Gandhiji. "What a title for a *Harikatha?*" cried out old Venkatalakshamma, the mother of the Post-master. "It is neither about Rama nor Krishna."—"But," said her son, who too has been to the city, "but, Mother, the Mahatma is a saint, a holy man."—"Holy man or lover of a widow, what does it matter to me? When I go to the temple I want to hear about Rama and Krishna and Mahadeva and not all this city nonsense," said she. And being an obedient son, he was silent. But the old woman came along that evening. She could never stay away from a *Harikatha.* And sitting beside us, how she wept! . . .

As I have discussed elsewhere (Kachru, 1982b, 1986a), in this passage it is not so much that the underlying narrative technique is different or collocational rela-tionships are different, but the historical and cultural presuppositions are differ-ent than what has been traditionally the "expected" historical and cultural milieu for English literature. One has to explain Siva and Parvati with reference to the multitude of the pantheon of Hindu gods, and in the context then *three-eyed* (Sanskrit *trinetra*) makes sense: it refers to Lord Siva's particular manifes-tations when he opens his "third eye," located on his forehead, spitting fire and destroying the creation. Damayanthi [Damayanti], Sakunthala [Shakuntala], and Yasodah [Yashoda] bring forth the epic traditions of India immortalized in Kalidasa's [Kalidasa: fifth century A.D.?] play of the same name; and Yasodha, the mother of Krishna, a major character of the Bhagwata Purana (legend). The contemporariness of the passage is in reference to Gandhi (1869–1948), and the political implications of Hindu–Moslem unity and *khaddar* (handspun cloth). The *Harikatha* man is the traditional religious storyteller, usually in a temple, who has woven all this fabric of story.

The same cultural and literary tradition or "ecosystem," to use Thumboo's term (Thumboo, 1985), is found in the following passage of R. K. Narayan's *The Man-eater of Malgudi* (1961:101).

There was Ravana, the protagonist of Ramayana, who had ten heads and twenty arms, and enormous yogic and physical powers and a boon from the gods that he could never be vanquished. . . . Still he came to a sad end. Or take Mahisha, the asura who meditated . . . and . . . secured an especial favour that every drop of blood shed from his body should give rise to another demon in his own image and strengthen . . . the goddess with six arms . . . came riding . . . on a lion which sucked every drop of blood dropped from the demon . . . or think of Daksha, for whom an end was prophesied through the birth of a snake, and he had built himself an island fortress to evade this fate. . . .

This passage is replete with allusions to the epic *Rāmāyana;* here again there is departure from shared European cultural and literary traditions.

One notices greater linguistic demands on a reader who is not part of the extended traditions of English when local aphorisms, proverbs, and idioms are used in English. The message is subtle and at the same time overwhelming for the reader. Let me give some examples in which the collocations, stylistic con-ventions, and interpretations depend on understanding the underlying Vedantic philosophy of India. These are from *The Serpent and the Rope,* a metaphysical novel by Raja Rao: "I do not believe that death is" (p. 9); "Resurrection is not because death is, resurrection is because life is" (p. 110); "God is, and goodness is part of that is-ness" (p. 113); "Water is. So something is. And since is-ness is the very stuff of that something, all you can say is 'is is'" (p. 202). In G. V. Desani's *All About H. Hatterr* (New York: Farrar, Strauss and Young, 1951. Pp. 102–103) the rich storehouse of Sanskritic compounding provides a source for formations such as: "Ruler of the firmament!; Son of the mightiest bird!"; ". . . thy sister my darling, thy name?"; ". . . Son of thy ill-begotten mother! know, I have no sister. Thy accursed name?" In the Nigerian writer Chinua Achebe, the translated proverbs similarly contribute to stylistic identity: "I cannot live on the bank of the river and wash my hands with spittle"; "if a child washed his hands he could eat with kings"; "a person who chased two rats at a time would lose one."

Okara (1964:137) is therefore right when, talking about the African writer in English, he says: "from a word, a group of words, a sentence and even a name in any African language, one can glean the social norms, attitudes and values of a people." Thumboo (1985:219) elaborates Okara's point:

> Okara and others in a similar situation are neither the first nor the last to attempt a language for their tribes. It is not a question of purifying it. English has its history, culture, and environment, a powerful literary tradition from Chaucer to Ted Hughes, with a connotative reach that does not always apply in the Outer Circle. The denotative provides a substantial common base for all Englishes; the connotative will have to be re-constructed to accord with our individual ecosystems.

It is that "re-construction" of the language that we find in the preceding examples and in other localized registers of English in its second diaspora.

In the second diaspora, indeed, English has been used as a tool to present distinct traditions and literary canons unrelated to the traditional ones of English, though this has not always been done consciously. The situation was thus different with American English or Australian English, which made attempts to declare "independence" from what may be called "mother English" (see, e.g., Kachru 1981a). But in spite of an urge for linguistic independence, the first-diaspora varieties were part of the Judeo-Christian tradition and shared the norms of cultural and literary traditions. This was not so for English in Africa, in South Asia, in Southeast Asia, in the Philippines, and so on.

The reasons for this difference are many, but the major reason is that English became a part of an emerging linguistic, cultural, and philosophical ethos in these parts of the world. The process of establishing such a new ethos was slow, but the results are in part visible in the language and in the types of creativity for which English was used (see Smith, 1987). Such uses of English had great impact in the Outer Circle, both integrative and disintegrative. It has been well illustrated in several studies that a distinct African and Asian literary canon was established in the second diaspora of English (see, e.g., Smith, 1981, 1987; Kachru 1982c, and 1983). What we actually find here is not a break from the earlier European literary canon and sociocultural traditions but an expansion of the canon from distinctly unrelated traditions. For this reason a singular designation, *English,* is less appropriate to refer to the language now than is the plural *Englishes* (hence, *World Englishes*), which makes more pragmatic and sociolinguistic sense. McArthur (1986:213) has gone even further and has suggested the term *English "languages."* And so far as the English "literatures" are concerned, the term seems to have been accepted even by those who are unhappy with the pluralization of *English* [see, e.g., the subtitle of Quirk and Widdowson (1985): *Teaching and Learning the Language and Literatures*].

Discoursal Organization

A linguistic convention in discourse and speech acts reflects the conventions of culture: English in England, Scottish in Scotland, White American and African-American in the varieties of American English. This also is true of other native varieties of the language in Australia, Canada, and New Zealand.

What has to be recognized now is that the same phenomenon is repeated in the second-diaspora varieties of the language. In recent studies on contrastive discourse, several features of the diaspora varieties have been highlighted. These include

1. Re-creation of local (e.g., Nigerian, Indian) speech acts, for example, those of abuses/curses, persuasion, greeting. In fiction, such translated speech acts are particularly used to contextualize the characters and occur much more frequently than in the corresponding spoken varieties of English. The following examples from Indian English fiction are illustrative:

   a. Abuses/curses: "you eater of your masters," "you spoiler of my salt," "you donkey's husband," "may thy womb be dead," "you circumcised son of a pig."
   b. Greetings: "bow my forehead," "fall at your feet," "touch your feet."

2. Re-creation of cultural and local symbolism, as in the cultural symbolism associated with words such as *chest, shadow, head, eyes, stomach, mouth* and *heart* in African English as discussed in Chishimba (1983). The same is true, for example, of the words *touch, defile* and *pollute* in Indian English, where *touch* has a sociological and caste connotation and *defile* and *pollute* have ritualistic connotations.

3. Presentation of cultural "meanings" that are essentially not shared with the native speaker of the language. Consider, for example, the use of *caste mark, sacred thread, communal attitude, intermarriage* in Indian English.

In other words, the mutual expectancy between the medium and the message has been altered from the traditional conventions. This is also accomplished by the use of several stylistic devices. Some of the common devices are the use of nativized similes and metaphors, such as Chinua Achebe's use of "like a bushfire in the harmattan," "like a yam tendril in the rainy season," or Raja Rao's use of comparative constructions such as "as honest as an elephant," "as good as kitchen ashes," and "lean as an areca-nut tree" (Kachru 1982b, 1986a).

What are the reasons for this alteration? The major reason is that creativity in English is integral to the national literary traditions. The literary message may be universal, as in, for example, Chinua Achebe's novels, but the contextualization of the text and its formal manifestations are not necessarily shared with other varieties. The text is thus regional and national rather than a part of an extended English-speaking speech community.

Because the speech communities to which these works are addressed are African, South Asian, Southeast Asian, and so on, the discourse strategy adopted must be within the literary and cultural contexts of that community. Chinua Achebe, in his *Things Fall Apart,* very eloquently explains the motivations for nativizing discourse. He provides two alternate texts and explains why (a) is more appropriate than (b), though (b) is closer to Western discourse strategies, whereas (a) is Africanized.

In the following short excerpt, the Chief Priest is explaining to one of his sons the importance of sending him to church. The preferred Africanized version is as follows:

> I want one of my sons to join these people and be my eyes here. If there is nothing in it you will come back. But if there is something then you will bring back my share. The world is like a mask, dancing. If you want to see it well, you do not stand in one place. My spirit tells me that those who do not befriend the white man today will be saying "had we known," tomorrow.

Now, Achebe observes, "Supposing I had put it another way. Like this for instance":

> I am sending you as my representative among those people—just to be on the safe side in case the new religion develops. One has to move with the times or else one is left behind. I have a hunch that those who fail to come to terms with the white man may well regret their lack of foresight.

And Achebe rightly comes to the conclusion that "the material is the same. But the form of the one is in character and the other is not. It is largely a matter of instinct but judgment comes into it too." In other words, the non-Africanized version is not consistent with the linguistic and cultural ecosystem of Africa.

Demythologization Process

The preceding processes—conscious or unconscious—lead to the demythologization of English culture and literature in more than one way. First, they dissociate the language from the sociocultural and historical assumptions used in earlier histories of the English language and literature (cf., e.g., Craig, 1950; Daiches, 1960). Second, they present the Judeo-Christian tradition as only one of the traditions embodied in English literatures and linguistic varieties. And third, they lead to recognition of non-Western literary traditions and use of these traditions in literary creativity. Such creativity draws not only from the European circle of languages, but also from the classical languages and literatures of Asia and Africa (e.g., Sanskrit, Chinese), as is evident from experimentation in

Singapore, India, and the Philippines (see, e.g., Thumboo, 1985). Such experimentation also draws on the rich oral traditions of Yoruba and Swahili, and the mythologies embedded in the literary and oral traditions of Asia and Africa. We find this experimentation in writers such as Raja Rao, Amos Tutuola, and Catherine Lim, of India, Nigeria, and Singapore, respectively.

The preceding discussion makes it clearer that "interference" in the diaspora varieties of English has "meaning" if viewed within the sociolingustic contexts of the diaspora varieties whereas it appears to be "deviation" if seen without that context (Kachru, 1982a).

CREATIVITY, IDENTITY, AND SOCIOLINGUISTIC CONTEXT

The use of modifiers such as *African, Indian,* and *Singaporean* with English is thus one way to express the relationship between creativity, identity, and the changed sociolinguistic context of the English language. It has been shown that the closer the relationship between context and creativity, the greater the identity a variety acquires. The issue of identity, of course, is a double-edged sword. The more non-Western contextualization a variety of English acquires, the greater problems of intelligibility there are for Westerners at each linguistic level (see, e.g., Nelson, 1985).

But the second-diaspora varieties reveal institutionalization in new sociolinguistic contexts in other ways. First, English has been institutionalized by assigning an important role to it in the linguistic repertoire of a speech fellowship. In such repertoires English functions in pluralistic linguistic and cultural contexts. English must, therefore, be viewed as an added member in partnership with other languages. In such sociolinguistic situations, one views language use in terms of domains of function. In the Outer Circle, English has acquired four vital domains of function. It has an instrumental function as a tool for imparting specialized education (e.g., science, technology); a regulative function in the higher courts and in pan-regional and national administration; an interpersonal function as a link language across linguistic, ethnic, and religious groups; and an imaginative and innovative function in developing local literatures in English (e.g., Nigerian writing in English, Indian writing in English).

Another way in which second-diaspora varieties appear institutionalized is in the recognition of the creative potential of the language as part of the national literatures in the countries where these varieties are used. Such identity with English, and such reflection of the attitudes of identity, shows in numerous ways: (1) in the governmental recognition of English in its integrative roles (e.g., as an "associate" official language in India, as the language of administration and education in Singapore, as a language of regional and pan-regional communication in South Asia, Southeast Asia, and West Africa); (2) in the attitudes that educators, literary writers, and historians express about English; and (3) in the histories of literatures of the region.[4]

The governmental attitude and the attitude of academies and learned societies towards the institutionalization of English is further shown in India by the recognition of literature written by Indians in Indian English for annual awards of the National Academy of Letters (Sahitya Academi). In Pakistan the same policy toward English is adopted by the Pakistan Academy of Letters. In other parts of Asia, identical acceptance is given to native English literature (e.g., by the Singapore National Book Development Award, the Southeast Asian Writers Award, and the award of the Cultural Medallion for literature).

Moreover, a considerable body of literature has developed pleading for recognition and acceptance of local creativity in English as part of national literary traditions. In several parts of the globe where English is in its second diaspora, there are now histories of local English literatures written by local scholars. What such recognition shows is that English is viewed as an integral part of a nation's extended literary tradition. In some cases, this tradition dates back over fifteen decades. In South Asia, to take just one example, the first known Indian poetic work in English, entitled *The Shair and Other Poems,* was published in 1830 by Kasiprasad Ghosh, and the first novel, by another Bengali, Sochee Chunder Dutt, was published in 1845.

However, I should hasten to add that there is no paucity of writing strongly denouncing the use of English for literary creativity in Asia or Africa. One of the most articulate among these voices is that of Ngũgĩ wa Thiong'o (1986). Commenting on those who "encountered literature in colonial schools and universities," he says their "entire way of looking at the world, even the world of the immediate environment, was Eurocentric" (1986:93). His book *Decolonizing the Mind* was his "farewell to English as a vehicle for any of my writings. From now on it is Gikuyu and Kiswahili all the way" (1986:xiv).

In India, no one has bid farewell to English in Ngũgĩ's style, but Buddhadeva Bose, a distinguished creative writer and critic, was not presenting only his views when he wrote, "It may seem surprising that Indians, who have always had a firm poetic tradition in their own languages, should ever have tried to write verses in English. That they did so was an outcome of the Anglomania which seized some upperclass Indians in the early years of British rule" (quoted in Lal, 1969: 3–4). However, Bose's view is not a generally accepted one. Iyengar is closer to the generally accepted view when he asks, "How shall we describe Indian creative writing in English?" And he answers, "Of course, it is Indian literature, even as the work of Thoreau or Hemingway are American literature. But Indian literature comprises several literatures . . . and Indian writing in English is but one of the voices in which India speaks. It is a new voice, no doubt, but it is as much Indian as others" (1962:3).

In an earlier section, I mentioned that English is one language among many in a multilingual's code repertorie in Asia, Africa, and the Philippines. In the sociolinguistic contexts of these countries, English has become an integral component in code switching (or alteration), that is, in a speaker's switch from one linguistic code to another in a single utterance. Code switching manifests itself in two ways. One manifestation occurs when an interlocutor switches from one language to another, depending on the context and the participant(s). The following is an example of such code switching from Raja Rao's *The Chessmaster and His Moves* (New Delhi, 1988). Here the alternation is by the narrator between English for exposition and French for the characters' speech:

> "Ça va?" answers Jayalakshmi, adjusting her necklace.
> "Est-ce qu'on va le trouver aujourd'hui?" he continues, the last word said with such heaviness.
> "Si le Seigneur le veut."
> "Mais quel seigneur?"
> "Lui," she said with a mischievous smile, as if thinking of someone far away, very far away.
> "Qui donc?"
> "Son Altesse le lion." Of course she was speaking a lie.
> "Le tigre?"
> "Non," she said, and turned to her father, asking if the mail had come.

Now consider this example of switching into Hindi: "Maji kahan gaye hain?— Acha. Suno. Vo kab arahi hai?—Agaye? Kapada badalke arahi hai? Acha, Padu. Bye-bye" (175). Rao makes no concessions to monolinguals. No clues are given to those who do not know French or Hindi or Sanskrit, and thus linguistic and cultural interpretations of sentences such as the following, wherein Hindi words are borrowed into English, demand much of the reader: "Our alaya, the true home, is forever the Himalaya" (46); "It is all prarabdha, it's written on our foreheads" (49); "For either you touch suffering, and so suffer, or reach to the other side, and be it. One is kashta and the duhkha" (84); "I bhago—I run" (130); "A Brahmin should not touch jhoota, especially, my jhoota" (130); "And so you and your beads, and the sorrow. Duhkh me duhkh mila ja" (108).

The point worth stressing here is that a bilingual or multilingual competence in understanding a text is taken for granted by the author and in the construction of such texts the native speaker of English seems to have become irrelevant. This is evident even in the newspaper headlines and captions of national and international newspapers. Consider the following from South Asia:

1. "Devi Lal leads 'Delhi chalo' padyatra" (*The Statesman,* New Delhi, December 1985).
2. "Lok Adalat settles 20" (*The Times of India,* December 9, 1985).

In these captions, local lexical items are preferred to their easily available English equivalents, *Delhi Chalo* ("march to Delhi"), *padyatra* ("march on foot"); *Lok Adalat* ("peoples' court"). In these newspapers the announcements of death in English are equally culture-specific; one has to understand the context and how the English language is used to convey it. A person leaves "for the heavenly above" (*Hindustan Times,* May 20, 1979) because of "the sad demise." There will, therefore, be, for example "kirtan and ardasa for the peace of the departed soul" (*Hindustan Times,* June 30, 1979). Another way to present such news is that "the untimely tragic death . . . of . . . happened . . . on . . . uthaoni ceremony will take place on . . ." (*Hindustan Times,* June 30, 1979). Cultural and religious pluralism is reflected in another way, too. If the dead person is a Muslim, then "his soyem Fateha will be solemnised on . . ." and "all the friends and relatives are requested to attend the Fateha prayers" (*Dawn,* March 14, 1979). In the case of a Sikh ". . . kirtan and Antim Ardas will be held at . . ." (*The Tribune,* March 15, 1985), or "bhog of Sri Akhand's path in the ever lasting memory of our beloved will be performed on . . ." (*The Tribune,* March 15, 1985). And if it is a "holyman," there will be a "homage on the first nirvana anniversary," and "thousand salutations to His Holiness . . . who became a part of the Param Tatav on . . ." (*The Tribune,* March 15, 1985).

Another way speakers alternate languages is through the use of one language at home, another in the office with one's colleagues, and yet another in the market. We notice this often in Singapore, where the language of home may be Chinese, Tamil, or Malay, that of the office English, while one might use basilect (the variety least like a standard language) for shopping in inexpensive markets. In the metropolitan cities of South Asia and Africa the same situation is present.

Another, more common type of code alteration occurs when, in the stream of discourse, an interlocutor mixes two or more languages within a sentence, a clause, a verb phrase, or a noun phrase in which English is one of the constituent languages. Consider the following examples from different parts of the world:

1. *Kiswahili-English:* "Wambi wakupe *up-to-date image* ya yalitiyotokea *so that you can go ahead with it*" (Tell them to give you an up-to-date image of what happened so that you can go ahead with it.)
2. *Spanish-English:* "*I told him that* pa que la trajera ligero." (I told him that so that he would bring it fast.)
3. *Kannada-English:* "nanu *use* madida *strong language*-u eshto *control*-madock nodde adre nanu *educated*-u, *man of culture*-u, *broadminded*-u. . . ." (I tried so much to control the strong language that I used. But forgetting that I am educated, man of culture and broad-minded. . . .)
4. *Edo-English:*

   DIRECTOR. "*Dial enumber* naa, n'*uniform*'en Mr. Oseni ighe a *approve encountracti* nii ne. *But* khamaa ren ighe ogha ye *necessary* n'o *submit-e photostat copies* oghe *estimate* n'o ka ya *apply* a ke *pay* ere. *You understand?*" (Dial this number, and inform Mr. Oseni that we approved the contract already. But tell him to submit photostat copies of estimate that he applied with before we pay him. You understand?)
   SECRETARY. "*Yes, Sir!* Deghe e irr *office,* ni *dial his house?*" (Yes Sir! If he is not in the office, should I dial his house?)

5. *Chinese-English:* "Zhege jianglai geke laoshi douhui jiaode: ruhe yong *reference,* ruhe yong *bibliography,* shenme shihou yiao *quotation,* yige *point* yinggai ruhe lai *argue* huozhe *counter-argue.* Zhege numen douhui zhu-yide." (How to use reference, how to use bibliography, when it is appropriate to use quotations, how to argue and counterargue a point, all these your instructors will tell you. And these are the things you ought to pay attention to.)
6. *Philippino-English*[5]: "*I'm sorry* saka nag*reduce* ako ngayon e. . . ." (I am sorry but I'm trying to reduce today. . . .)

The use of the strategies of code alteration has serious and often far-reaching linguistic and attitudinal implications that have been discussed within the context of English across languages in Bhatia and Ritchie (1989).

One major implication of code alteration with English is what I have termed the Englishization of the world's languages. This aspect of English in its second diaspora has yet to be explored. What it involves is an investigation of the impact of English on the phonology, grammar, morphology, and lexis of the major languages of the world. But the impact goes beyond these traditionally recognized linguistic levels: it has also contributed to the development of the range of styles and registers of languages across the globe (see, e.g., Bhatia and Ritchie, 1989; Kachru, 1982b).

HIERARCHY OF VARIETIES

The diaspora varieties of English are not homogeneous, nor are their phonological and grammatical intricacies fully documented. But their nondocumentation is not a major limitation on our recognition of their existence. After all, British English and American English existed before these varieties were authenticated by description of their grammatical or phonological characteristics. And even now, after years of aggressive attempts to describe the world's languages, hundreds of languages remain undescribed. But the absence of descriptions really makes no serious difference to the users of such languages. It is true that linguistic descriptions make it easier to compare the range of differences in the varieties of a language and contribute to developing pedagogical aids, but that is a different question from the one I am addressing. It is now also recognized that each nonnative diaspora variety of English has an educated variety and a range of subvarieties. Again, the existence of such subvarieties is not unique to the diaspora Englishes, as these sociolinguistic characteristics are shared with the native varieties of the language.

The differences within the varieties can be vertically categorized in terms of competence in the use of English. Accordingly, using education as a parameter, sociolinguists have divided some nonnative varieties into three groups: *acrolectal, mesolectal,* and *basilectal.* If we view language varieties as a continuum, acrolectal speakers rank highest on the continuum, since they are normally considered the speakers of the educated or standard variety of the language. Mesolectal speakers rank somewhere in the middle, and the speakers of basilect rank the lowest. In terms of social prestige, acrolect is considered highest. But that does not mean that the acrolect (the variety closest to the standard) is necessarily used by the largest number of speakers of a language. It is well established, for example, that although Received Pronunciation (RP) was for a long time recognized by some as the prestige variety of British English, the total number who actually used it did not exceed 3 percent of the British population.

It has been shown in the literature, however, that this hierarchical classification is not without its problems, for it inaccurately implies that a rigid stratification exists among speakers and varieties. In functional terms, each lectal range, a term used for these three lects, does in fact have well-assigned domains of use. But an acrolectal speaker may switch between lects, depending on the context. The following example for Malaysia illustrates this point. In the play *Caught in the Middle,* for example, a major part of the dialogue is in English, but, depending on social context, there is also mixing between three local languages: Bahasa Malaysia, Cantonese, and Tamil. In the following excerpt "Malaysian English" implies "more realistic language in more realistic settings—the home, the pub":

> *Mrs. Chandran:*   Aiee-yah, mow fatt chee ka la (can't do anything about it.) Clean it up, Ah Lan. The rubbish-man will be coming soon, and you know he doesn't take rubbish that isn't nicely packed and tied up.
>
> *Ah Lan (the amah):*   Rubbish is rubbish-lah. Supposed to be dirty, what. Real fussy rubbish-man, must have neat rubbish to take away.

Lloyd Fernando suggests that the Malaysian English humorously injects realism into the play:

> Malaysian English is now a dialect, recognized as such. In some situations, if you don't speak like that, you are regarded as a foreigner. By using it [Malaysian English] the playwright draws us into the magic circle. [*Asia Week,* May 24, 1987, p. 64]

CONTEXTS OF CONFLICT AND RIVALRY

In its second diaspora, English has not been accepted without resistance. There is a long history of linguistic conflict and rivalry. On the one hand, there has always been a group of scholars who accept this historical fact of the intrusion of English as an additional member in the linguistic repertoire with enthusiasm. On the other hand, there are others who continue to consider English an intruder, slowly nibbling away at the linguistic domains that rightfully belong to local languages.

The controversy started when English was first introduced in Africa and Asia several centuries ago and has continued ever since. Furthermore, the positions concerning the continuation of English have not changed much since that period. At present, what we have, on the one hand, is the visible diffusion of English, and, on the other hand, well-articulated slogans for the curtailment of English. One sees these positions about language in Shah (1968) and in Bailey (1990).[6] Even in countries where the educators and politicians adopt the public posture of supporting the curtailment of English, no effort has been made to curtail its "invisible" diffusion and spread.

DIASPORA VARIETIES AND ISSUES OF STANDARDS

Concerns about the standards of English in its second diaspora date back to the period when English was first introduced in the colonies. These concerns were not much different from the concerns expressed earlier about the models for standards in Britain, the United States, or Australia. For example, in 1863, the Very Reverend Henry Alford, D.D., Dean of Canterbury, in his *Plea for the Queen's English,* said, "Look at the process of deterioration which our Queen's English has undergone at the hands of Americans. Look at those phrases which so amuse us in their speech and books, at their reckless exaggeration and contempt for congruity" (see, e.g., Kachru, 1981a).

The case of English in the Asian and African colonies was, however, different in one respect. Since there was no significant population of the native speakers (e.g., British) who were part of the second diaspora of the language, there was no serious input from the native speakers in the stabilization of exonormative standards for the language. Nor were there many societal contexts in which the local English-knowing people and the native speakers interacted in English. In fact, chances for such encounters were minimized as much as possible. Naturally, given the limited local uses of English in the beginning, the main yardstick for standards was intelligibility with the native speakers. This yardstick, however, is misleading in several sociolinguistic contexts and is primarily based on fallacies: that in its second diaspora English is learnt essentially to communicate with the members of what I have called the Inner Circle; that English is primarily studied to teach and understand the American and British sociological and cultural patterns; that the pedagogical models for English are primarily what linguists have termed RP and General American; that the diversity and variation in the Outer Circle is an indicator of linguistic decay; and that innovations and literary experimentation in new literatures in English must follow the norms established in the Inner Circle (see Quirk, 1988, 1989, Kachru, 1991, Cheshire, 1991).

By now it is obvious that the sociolinguistic profile of English outlined in this chapter is significantly different from those in the previous chapters in several important ways. Let me discuss three major points of difference here. The first point concerns the pluricentricity of English, which includes multiple centers in the regions where English is in its second diaspora. Earlier English had only one recognized center for the norms of standard, literary creativity and linguistic experimentation. That center continued to be England during the peak of the colonial period. Then, slowly—and reluctantly—another center was recognized: the United States. But the norm-providing centers of English—as nodes of its creativity and experimentation—have multiplied during the past fifty years. The centers now include non-Western, non-Judeo-Christian, multilingual, and multicultural societies. I have used the terms *multilingual* and *multicultural* with special intent, for these two contexts have serious implications for the creativity and thus development of world varieties of English. The points of pluricentricity and the "shifting" of the center of English are recognized by Steiner (1975:4):

> The first, most obvious point to make is that the linguistic centre of English has shifted. This is so demographically. Great Britain now makes up only a small portion of the English-speaking totality. "Totality," furthermore, is quite the wrong word. The actual situation is one of nearly incommensurable variety and flux. Any map of "world-English" today, even without being either exhaustive or minutely detailed,

would have to include the forms of the language as spoken in many areas of east, west and south Africa, in India, Ceylon, and United States possessions or spheres of presence in the Pacific. It would have to list Canadian English, the speech of Australia, that of New Zealand, and above all, of course, the manifold shades of American parlance. Yet, although such a catalogue would comprise hundreds of mill[ion]s of English-speakers whose idiolects and communal usage would vary all the way from West Indian speech to Texan, or form the cadences of Bengal to those of New South Wales and the Yukon, it would be very far from complete.

Steiner continues (1975:5):

> But this shift of the linguistic centre involves far more than statistics. It does look as if the principal energies of the English language, as if its genius for acquisition, for innovation, for metaphoric response, had also moved away from England. . . .

The second point about the differences between this sociolinguistic profile of English and those of the preceding chapters takes us back to the question of multicultural identities of English in diaspora. This aspect of the English language today has not been well recognized in the literature, but it is an important aspect and has serious implications for understanding the issues of intelligibility, pragmatics, and cross-cultural discourse (Nelson, 1985; Y. Kachru, 1991). The third point, finally, concerns the overused term *native speaker* and the acceptance of this term as a cardinal concept. The diaspora varieties of English raise several theoretical and functional questions concerning this concept (Kachru, 1983; Cheshire, 1991).

CONCLUSION

The importance of the second diaspora to the sociolinguistic profile of English language and literature has been studied seriously during the last two decades. We still do not have more than marginal descriptions of what are termed "new Englishes" (see, e.g., Bailey and Görlach, 1981; Kachru 1982c, 1986a; Platt et al., 1984; Pride, 1982). The expansion of English, particularly in its second diaspora, has not reached its climax, nor are there any indicators as yet that increasing ethnic and linguistic nationalism has arrested the spread of English in a serious sense. What we see is that the present political developments around the world, and particularly those of the 1980s in Eastern Europe and China, have set back the study of Russian. Russian was never even a remote competitor of English, but in recent years Eastern European countries have fully opened their doors to English, so that now the favoured additional language in these parts is English. The leaders of nationalist movements in Asia and Africa have two faces with regard to English: a public anti-English face and a private pro-English face. And so far, numerically and functionally, the spread of English has not been affected. If one country adopts an anti-English attitude, there are two countries that recognize English in their policies. Such language policy shifts occur in both Asia and Africa.

One might ask: What is the future of diaspora varieties? There are, of course, no linguistic crystal balls, but all the sociolinguistic indicators suggest that, in their nativized forms, the diaspora varieties of English will continue to be major contact languages and that creativity in English, especially in its role as a part of national literatures in Asia and Africa, will continue for the foreseeable future.

In the second diaspora of English, a large number of bilingual and multilingual speech communities have adopted and recognized it as a vital additional language. The sociolinguistic implications and effects of such an adoption are that the English language has come out of its traditional Western fold and has acquired many new linguistic conventions and cultural and literary traditions. One has to recognize this unparalleled linguistic change, since the role of English in its social context will be only partially understood if the contexts of convergence and change of the World Englishes are not viewed as appropriate sociolinguistic and pragmatic factors. What is needed is a perspective that is integrative and that considers function as crucial to our understanding of language dynamics.

NOTES

1. This chapter draws heavily on my earlier publications (specifically, Kachru, 1982c, 1983, 1986a, later).

2. The optimistic estimated figure of 2 billion users has been given by Crystal (1985:9). He believes that "if you are highly conscious of international standards, or wish to keep the figures for World English down, you will opt for a total of around 700 million, in the mid 1980s. If you go to the opposite extreme, and allow in any systematic awareness whether in speaking, listening, reading or writing, you could easily persuade yourself of the reasonableness of 2 billion." However, he hastens to settle for a lower figure, saying, "I am happy to settle for a billion. . . ." (See also Strevens, 1982.)

3. See, e.g., Asrani (1964); Bailey (1990); Desai (1964); Mazrui (1975); and Ngũgĩ (1986).

4. See V. K. Gokak, *The Golden Treasury of Indo-Anglican Poetry*, New Delhi: Sahitya Academi, 1970; K.R.S. Iyengar (1962); T. Kandiah, "New Ceylon English" (review article), *New Ceylon Writing*, 1971:90–94; R. Wijesinha, ed., *An Anthology of Contemporary Sri Lankan Poetry in English*, Colombo: The British Council, 1988; T. Rahman, *A History of Pakistani Literature in English*, Lahore, Pakistan: Vanguard, 1991.

5. Several examples of code switching given in this chapter are from "Code-mixing Across Languages: Structure, Function, and Constraints," by Nkonko M. Kamwangamalu, Ph.D. dissertation submitted to the University of Illinois at Urbana-Champaign, 1989. Actual sources of each example and their sociolinguistic and syntactic analyses are given in Kamwangamalu's dissertation.

6. Over the years a vast body of literature, presenting various viewpoints and attitudes on this topic, has developed. Shah's collection and Bailey's paper are just illustrative.

REFERENCES

Asrani, U. A. 1964. *What Shall We Do About English?* Ahmedabad: Navajivan.
Bailey, Richard W. 1982. "The English Language in Canada." In Bailey and Görlach, eds. 1982. Pp. 134–176.

————. 1990. "English at Its Twilight." In Christopher Ricks and Leonard Michaels eds., *The State of the Language.* Berkeley: University of California Press. Pp. 83–94.

————, and Manfred Görlach, eds. 1982. *English as World Language.* Ann Arbor: University of Michigan Press.

Bhatia, Tej K., and William Ritchie, eds. 1989. *Code-mixing: English Across Languages. World Englishes* (special issue) 8(3).

Bloom, David. 1986. "The English Language in Singapore." In Basant K. Kapur, ed., *Singapore Studies: Critical Surveys of the Humanities and Social Sciences.* Singapore: Singapore University Press. Pp. 337–458.

Bokamba, Eyamba G. 1982. "The Africanization of English." In Braj B. Kachru, ed. *The Other Tongue: English Across Cultures.* Urbana: University of Illinois Press. Pp. 77–98.

Cheshire, Jenny, ed. 1991. *English Around the World: Sociolinguistic Perspectives.* Cambridge, England: Cambridge University Press.

Chishimba, Maurice. 1983. "African Varieties of English: Text in Context." Ph.D. dissertation. University of Illinois at Urbana-Champaign.

Craig, Hardin. 1950. *A History of English Literature.* New York: Oxford University Press.

Crystal, David. 1985. "How Many Millions? The Statistics of English Today." *English Today* 1:7–9.

Daiches, David. 1960. *A Critical History of English Literature.* New York: Ronald Press.

Desai. M(aghanbai) P. 1964. *The Problem of English.* Ahmedabad, India: Navajivan.

D'souza, Jean. 1987. "South Asia as a Sociolinguistic Area." Ph.D. dissertation, University of Illinois at Urbana-Champaign.

Eagleson, Robert D. 1982. "English in Australia and New Zealand." In Bailey and Görlach, eds. Pp. 415–438.

Emeneau, Murray B. 1956. "India as a Linguistic Area." *Language* 32:3–16.

Ferguson, Charles. 1976. "The Ethiopean Linguistic Area." In M. Lionel Bender et al., eds. *Language in Ethiopia.* London: Oxford University Press. Pp. 63–76.

Fishman, Joshua A., Robert L. Cooper, and Andrew W. Conrad, eds. 1978. *The Spread of English: The Sociology of English as an Additional Language.* Rowely, MA: Newbury House.

Foley, Joseph, ed. 1988. *New Englishes: The Case of Singapore.* Singapore: Singapore University Press.

Greenbaum, Sidney, ed. 1985. *The English Language Today.* Oxford, England: Pergamon.

Iyengar, K.R.S. 1962, revised 1985. *Indian Writing in English.* New Delhi: Sterling.

Kachru, Braj B. 1981a. "American English and Other Englishes." In Charles A. Ferguson and Shirley B. Heath, eds. *Language in the USA.* Cambridge, England: Cambridge University Press. Pp. 21–43. (Also in Kachru 1986a. Pp. 127–146).

————. 1981b. "The Pragmatics of Non-native Varieties of English." In Smith, ed. 1981. Pp. 15–39.

————. 1982a. "Meaning in Deviation: Toward Understanding Non-native English Texts." In Kachru, ed. 1982c. Pp. 325–350.

————. 1982b. "The Bilingual's Linguistic Repertoire." In B. Hartford, A. Valdman, and C. Foster, eds., *Issues in International Bilingual Education: The Role of the Vernacular.* New York: Plenum. Pp. 25–52.

———— ed. 1982c. *The Other Tongue: English Across Cultures.* Urbana: University of Illinois Press.

————. 1983. *The Indianization of English: The English Language in India.* Delhi: Oxford University Press.

_____. 1985. "Standards, Codification, and Sociolinguistic Realism: The English Language in the Outer Circle." In Quirk and Widdowson, eds. 1985. Pp. 11–30.

_____. 1986a. *The Alchemy of English: The Spread, Functions and Models of Non-native Englishes*. Urbana: University of Illinois Press.

_____. 1986b. "The Power and Politics of English." *World Englishes* 5(2-3):121–140.

_____. 1988. "The Spread of English and Sacred Linguistic Cows." In Lowenberg, ed. 1988. Pp. 207–228.

_____. 1991. "Liberation Linguistics and the Quirk Concern." *English Today* 7(1):3–13.

Kachru, Yamuna. 1991. "Culture, Style and Discourse: Expanding Noetics of English." *South Asian Language Review* 1(2):11–25.

Kahane, Henry. 1986. "A Typology of Prestige Languages." *Language* 62:495–508.

_____, and Renée Kahane. 1979. "Decline and Survival of Western Prestige Languages." *Language* 55:183–198.

Kujore, Obafemi, 1985. *English Usage: Some Notable Nigerian Variations*. Ibadan, Nigeria: Evans Brothers.

Lal, P. 1969. *Modern Indian Poetry in English: An Anthology and a Credo*. Calcutta: Writers Workshop.

Lowenberg, Peter, ed. 1988. *Language Spread and Language Policy: Issues, Implications and Case Studies*. GURT 1987. Washington, DC: Georgetown University Press.

Masica, Colin P. 1976. *Defining a Linguistic Area: South Asia*. Chicago: University of Chicago Press.

Mazrui, Ali A. 1975. *The Political Sociology of the English Language: An African Perspective*. The Hague: Mouton.

McArthur, Tom. 1986. "The Power of Work: Pressure, Prejudice and Politics in Our Vocabularies and Dictionaries." *World Englishes* 5(2-3):209–219.

McCrum, Robert, William Cran, and Robert MacNeil. 1986. *The Story of English*. New York: Viking.

Mencken, H. L. 1919. *The American Language*. New York: Knopf.

Naik, M. K. 1982. *A History of Indian English Literature*. New Delhi: Sahitya Academi.

Narayan, R. K. 1961. *The Man-eater of Malgudi*. New York: Viking.

Nelson, Cecil L. 1985. "My Language, Your Culture: Whose Communicative Competence?" *World Englishes* 4(2):243–250.

Ngũgĩ wa Thiong'o. 1986. *Decolonizing the Mind: The Politics of Language in African Literature*. London: James Currie; Portsmouth, NH: Heinemann.

Okara, Gabriel. 1964. *The Voice*. London: Heinemann.

Paikeday, T. M. 1985. *The Native Speaker Is Dead!* Toronto: Paikeday.

Platt, John, and Heidi Weber, 1980. *English in Singapore and Malaysia: Status, Features, Functions*. Kuala Lumpur: Oxford University Press.

_____, and M. L. Ho. 1984. *The New Englishes*. London: Routledge & Kegan Paul.

Pride, John, ed. 1982. *New Englishes*. Rowley, MA:Newbury House.

Quirk, Randolph. 1988. "The Question of Standards in the International Use of English." In Lowenberg ed., 1988. Pp. 229–241.

_____. 1989. "Language Varieties and Standard Language." *JALT Journal* 11(1):14–25. [Also in *English Today* 21(1990):3–10.]

_____, Sidney Greenbaum, Goeffrey Leech, and Jan Svartvik. 1972. *A Grammar of Contemporary English*. London: Longman.

_____. 1985. *A Comprehensive Grammar of the English Language*. London: Longman.

Quirk, Randolph, and H. G. Widdowson, eds. 1985. *English in the World: Teaching and Learning the Language and Literatures*. Cambridge, England: Cambridge University Press.

Rao, Raja, 1963. *Kanthapura.* London: Allen & Unwin.

Shah, Amritlal B., ed. 1968. *The Great Debate: Language Controversy and University Education.* Bombay: Lalvani.

Smith, Larry E., ed. 1987. *Discourse Across Cultures: Strategies in World Englishes.* Englewood Cliffs, NJ: Prentice-Hall.

_____, ed. 1981. *English for Cross-cultural Communication.* London: Macmillan.

Sridhar, Kamal K. 1985. "Sociolinguistic Theories and Non-native Varieties of English." *Lingua* 68:85–104.

_____, and S. N. Sridhar. 1986. "Bridging the Paradigm Gap: Second Language Acquisition Theories and Indigenized Varieties of English." *World Englishes* 5(1):3–14.

Steiner, George. 1975. "Why English?" Presidential address delivered in 1975. London: The English Association.

Strevens, Peter. 1982. "World English and the World's English—or, Whose Language Is It Anyway?" *Journal of the Royal Society of Arts.* June:418–428.

Thumboo, Edwin. 1985. "Twin Perspectives and Multi-ecosystems: Tradition for a Commonwealth Writer." *World Englishes* 4(2):213–221.

Zell, Hans M., and Helense Silver. Comps. and eds. 1971. *A Reader's Guide to African Literature.* New York: African Publishing Corporation. Pp. 20–59.

AFTERWORD

English: From Village
to Global Village

SUZANNE ROMAINE

Josiah Smith, a Congregationalist minister, confidently asserted just before the turn of this century that the language of Shakespeare would eventually become the language of mankind. Most linguists would be reluctant to hazard such long-range guesses. Although this prognosis was probably uttered from a conviction of cultural and moral superiority rather than from knowledge of the forces of the linguistic marketplace, at the moment many indicators point in favor of Smith's prediction. It is said, for example, that in 1966, 70 percent of the world's mail was already in English and 60 percent of its radio and television broadcasts was also in English. If the medium is the message, as McLuhan (1962) tells us, then the language of his global village is indeed English. Throughout the world, English is now spoken as a mother tongue by 300 million people, and another 300 million use it as a second language. The estimated number of people who are learning English as a foreign language in countries where English has no official status is 1 billion.

In the face of statistics such as these, it is often asserted that the world is becoming more linguistically homogeneous through the increasing spread of a few world languages at the expense of the continuation of many local languages. Although there can be no doubt that the spread of English and the role it plays as a world language are truly remarkable phenomena, the growth of world languages like English is strongly related to colonialism and economic hegemony. Most English speakers take the present position and status of English for granted. Most do not realize that English was very much itself once a minority language initially in all the places where it has since become the mother tongue of millions. It has done so by replacing the languages of indigenous groups such as the American Indian, the Celts, and the Australian Aborigines.

Nevertheless, both the centripetal and centrifugal forces that Rodby refers to in her chapter will always be active. Together I feel they will ensure that there is no overall decline in linguistic diversity. The rise of new varieties of English in the new world has been producing new anglophone countries for the past few centuries. This is itself one consequence of the spread of a language beyond its original mother tongue country.

The rise of these new varieties leads to a continual enriching and renewal of the language and the literatures written in it, since these varieties often export some of their original innovations back to the original users, often to the dismay of the latter. The users of these new Englishes are both first- and second-language speakers. The fact that English is now increasingly used as a second language by nonnative speakers of English is of course another consequence of the spread of English.

These new Englishes, such as Singapore and Indian English, have their own structural norms, their own characteristic features, and even their own communicative styles. This is the price English has to pay on the linguistic marketplace for being a world language. It is a phenomenon that some have called "the Empire strikes back." However, English gets its own back too by exporting its loanwords to the languages of other countries and thereby Englishizing them.

In his chapter Algeo comments on the British attitude that "English is the property of England, lent to others, who should not feel free to do with it as they like." Algeo predicts that "British English is in little danger of disappearing" and that "the two great international branches of English—British and American—which are also at the present time the only two fully institutionalized varieties of the language, will continue to influence each other. Together, they are likely to form the basis for World English."

The value of English on the linguistic marketplace is considerable. Sir Richard Francis, the Director General of the British Council, recognized this when he said recently:

> Nearly half a million students learning English attend British Council schools in 87 countries overseas, and last year our business turnover was 25.3 million in foreign currency—13% larger than the previous year. Britain's real black gold is not North Sea oil, but the English language. . . . It's difficult to quantify a national resource. The value of having, in the post industrial age, people use the language of one's own culture is virtually inestimable.
>
> ["Selling English by the pound." *Times* 24 Oct. 1989, p. 14]

In the same article an economic researcher for the British Tourist Authority said, "we get 550,000 foreign students spending 325 million. A recent Economist Intelligence Unit survey put Britain's total annual earnings from English language teaching in this country at 1 billion."

Sir Richard ignores the fact that English is hardly exclusive to Britain, and therefore, not an exponent of British culture alone. The varieties of English spoken in the major anglophone countries, such as American and Australian English, to name only two, are equally English. Although American English is also widely taught and exported as a model for foreign language learners and competes in many parts of the world with British English, as far as I know, there is not much of a market for Australian English. The reasons for this are fairly obvious.

America's linguistic declaration of independence, for instance, was unparalleled in Australia until the appearance in 1945 of Baker's *The Australian Language,* whose title confidently asserted the autonomy of Australian English in the same way that Mencken's *The American Language* (1919) had attempted to do for American English. Baker (1945:11) wrote, "We have to work out the problem from the point of view of Australia, not from the viewpoint of England and of the judgements she passed upon our language because she did not know it as well as we do."

Still, it was a long time before many Australians were to feel confident about sounding Australian. Although Mitchell (1946) declared there was nothing wrong with Australian speech, his comparison of the Australian accent with that of educated southern British English was for some an unpleasant reminder of the extent to which Australian English deviated from RP (received pronunciation), as described by Jones and other English phoneticians. The Australian Broadcasting Corporation, created in 1932, subsequently recommended Jones' (1917) norms. However, in 1941 its chairman revealed that only two out of 450 applicants for the position of announcer could be selected. Most of those recognized as suitable were Englishmen. Because of Mitchell's influence, so-called educated Australian speech (which Mitchell later termed "cultivated") was subsequently adopted as the style for national broadcasting. This variety of speech, although distinctively Australian, was still close to RP, and quite different from the variety Mitchell terms "broad Australian." Today a cultivated accent is no longer needed for the ABC. Since 1983 it has required only "acceptable styles of educated speech" (Leitner, 1984), and now all questions concerning pronunciation, style, and usage are referred to an Australian dictionary, not a British one.

The upsurge of interest in, rather than embarrassment at, Australian English represents a decided move away from what Phillips (1950) called the "cultural cringe." This is reflected too in the publication of serious scholarly studies of social and regional varieties as well as in popular media. However, even more decisive for the lack of attention given to Australian English as an export model than this belated confidence in it internally is Australia's absence from the political superpower arena. It is political power that makes a language a world language.

Mazrui (1975:73) presents as one of the great paradoxes in the comparative histories of French and English in Africa the fact that French was on the whole intended to be disseminated across the globe as a language of high culture, whereas the English were sometimes arrogantly possessive of their language and much less intent on spreading it. The French were for that reason much less tolerant than the British of local culture. The Germans in Africa and the South Pacific were more like the British; the Germans thought it presumptuous for the colonized to speak German and even proposed that a pidgin German, which they called Kolonial-deutsch, should be spread among the colonized populace. Part of the reason for the paradox noted by Mazrui lies in the fact that, even in the home country, French was seen as liberating. Elitist language policies have always served the interests of the ruling classes. In England, however, there was an almost total lack of attention to any relationship between language and national identity (Grillo, 1989:44). This has been emphasized by Grillo, who misses, however, the equally striking fact that France never succeeded in producing a colony that outstripped the mother country, as the United States, for example, did England. Thus, Mazrui (1975:74): "The British, who did not want their language to become a universal language, are doomed precisely to that fate, while the French are embarked on a determined attempt to stop French from receding in importance."

Not too long after Sir Richard Francis made his comments about the value of the English language as an export, an editorial argued that Britain must do what it could to ensure that it was British English that captured the world market because it could lay claim to being standard English.

However, in a recent interview (*Newsweek* October 8, 1990), then British prime minister, Margaret Thatcher, very generously conceded that Shakespeare belongs as much to Americans as to British in characterizing the "special relationship" that exists between the United States and Britain. Speaking to an American interviewer, she observed:

> the Magna Carta belongs as much to you as it does to us; the writ of habeas corpus belongs as much to you as it does to us. . . . There is such a common heritage as well as the language. Shakespeare belongs as much to you as he does to us. . . . That is what unites us and has united us—rather more than a philosophy, but history as well, and language and mode of thought. . . .

Noah Webster's remarks, cited by Carver, about British English being eclipsed by American English, seem now to give at least some Britons and the British Council pause as they seek to guarantee the supremacy of the British variety of the language, particularly in the lucrative export market for English as a second language. Webster noted over a century ago that "the taste of her [i.e., Britain's] authors is already corrupted, and her language on the decline."

But all this talk about language is really about political power. The position of France and Britain as world powers has eroded. Language is but a symbol of this. The challenge to the hegemony of British English came first from what Kachru calls the inner circle, but increasingly it is coming from the outer circle too, who claim legitimacy for exogamous norms.

Although there seems to be no lack of confidence in exporting native models of English as a foreign language, it is at the same time almost paradoxical to find among all the major anglophone nations enormous linguistic insecurity about standards of English usage. Algeo agrees with me that the complaint tradition is intense on both sides of the Atlantic, and I have recently commented on its manifestations in Australia (Romaine, 1991a). In 1989 Prince Charles angered British schoolteachers by complaining that his staff could not write or speak English properly. Around the same time *The Times Higher Education Supplement* carried a front-page article in which several Oxford professors complained about the low standards of English used by students at Oxford University and suggested the possibility of introducing remedial instruction. Interestingly, these remarks came in the wake of the government's inquiry into the teaching of English, chaired by Brian Cox, which was full of recommendations for tolerance of pupils' local varieties of English. The report of the Cox Committee, however, stressed the need for Standard English as part of a new national curriculum.

A look at Australian media reveals a similar complaint tradition. Australian newspapers, like British and American ones, have complained not only about the inadequacies of local forms of English, but also about the increasing use of Americanisms. One editorial claimed that Australian speech "is far away the worst in the English-speaking world" (*Sunday Mail,* January 22, 1989). Statements such as these echo those expressed by commentators on Australian English from the earliest days of its history. Thus, William Churchill, a member of the American Philological Society who visited Australia in 1911, described Australian speech as "the most brutal maltreatment that has even been inflicted on the mother tongue of the great English-speaking nations" (cited in Delbridge, 1990:67). The *Sunday Mail* article cited earlier singles out as good examples of speech certain actors whose "accents were and never could be anything but Australian (and heaven forbid that they should be)." These he calls cultivated, but from what is said, they are clearly not imitations of RP. However, he singles out for criticism prominent individuals such as the prime minister, Bob Hawke, who is described as a

> brilliant fellow. No dolt gets to be a Rhodes scholar and Prime Minister of Australia. Keating is no slouch. But would you allow them to make announcements in a lift? "level three, four, foive . . . kay? ay? kay . . . sem, ayte, noine, . . . goan deown. . . ." Merciful heavens. The lingual laziness which causes people to make noises like Hawke and Keating is pretty well endemic to both radio and television . . . it's been years since the Nine Network cricket commentators . . . spoke anything but pure pidgin.

The author goes on to suggest naively that "bad speech" could be corrected in a couple of generations by elocution classes in the schools. Interestingly, given the spate of attacks on Americanisms there as well as in Britain, he says he wishes Australians could be taught to copy North American forms of speech. Although most Australians have learned at school to take an anti-American stance in language, especially in spelling, Delbridge (1990:73) observes that by mid-1985 six of Australia's major urban newspapers used the American *-or* spellings for British *-our* ones (e.g., *color/colour*). These cases may be signs of a greater tolerance for Americanisms.

In their introductory chapter Scott and Machan observe how it has been customary for scholars to separate the so-called internal from the so-called external history of the language. Although this seemingly simplified the task of constructing history and, more specifically, of reconstructing linguistic history, scholars now recognize that this idealization has had serious consequences for our understanding of the connections between language and society. It has now been more than two decades since Weinreich, Labov, and Herzog (1968) argued for a research program that would found a theory of language change on the findings and methodology of sociolinguistics. Since then, our knowledge of the social forces that motivate linguistic change has become increasingly sophisticated, so that to ignore them is to run the risk of reinforcing the view that language is impervious to society and that society could be constituted without language.

The prognosis for sociohistorical study of English is bright, as the chapters in this volume attest. Future scholars will be greatly aided by advances in computer technology, which have already led to more powerful concordancing packages, the use of laser scanners to input texts, and so on. One can expect many more data bases such as the Helsinki Corpus of English to provide new topics for research and important findings (see also Smith's mention of the ongoing *Middle English Dictionary* and other such projects).

The papers in this volume provide much evidence of the important ways in which the history of the English language has been shaped by its continually growing contexts of use and its increasing number of users. Scott and Machan, for instance, note in particular that the shift from primary orality to textuality has had profound consequences, a theme that is explored more fully in Toon's chapter. As Toon points out, writing can play an important role in the development of a national variety. Just as instructive, by contrast, are those cases where failure to write in an emerging national language has been decisive in the fate of a language. Thus, the literature of the Anglo-Irish revival as exemplified in the works of poets like Willam Butler Yeats was in English, although it was written in the context of the movement that led to the establishment of the Irish Free State, which promoted the Irish language as a prominently ideologized symbol. Although there were many other reasons that the revival of Irish had limited success, the lack of a national literature in a national language was an important factor. To write in Irish, however, then and now, would be to restrict one's audience. The instrumental value of English outweighed the antipathy the Irish felt toward it as a "colonial" language. This has happened elsewhere too.

For many developing countries the choice of a national language is both a practical and political one. In some parts of Africa, for instance, there were non-colonial languages that presented alternatives to the European metropolitan languages, namely, Arabic, which was widespread among the Muslim community; Hausa, spoken widely in Nigeria and West Africa; and Swahili, spoken in East Africa. However, in many other newly independent colonies it has been difficult to oust the colonial language, either because it had become the language of the indigenous elite, who see it as a way of consolidating their access to the state machinery, and/or because it was the only "neutral" language in the linguistically diverse territories out of which modern states were formed. To favor the language of one local ethnic or other group would be seen as favoritism. In many African countries there was no language but English, although there were trade languages and pidgin varieties of English in Cameroon and Liberia. In 1967, Milton Obote, then president of Uganda, articulated precisely this position, even though he recognized that some sectors of society were likely to regard English-speaking Ugandans as colonial imperialists (Mazrui, 1975:210–211).

Whether to write in a world language is now a nearly universal dilemma. More publications are in English than in any other language. It is for political reasons such as those I have just discussed, however, that African writers like Chinua Achebe and Wole Soyinka have been criticized for choosing to write in English. Achebe, however, does not see his choice of English as cultural betrayal. He is one of the most explicit writers on the subject of how to nativize a language so that it is adapted to serve its new environment (Achebe, 1965:29–30):

> So my answer to the question, Can an African ever learn English well enough to be able to use it effectively in creative writing? is certainly yes. If on the other hand you ask: Can he ever learn to use it like a native speaker? I should say, I hope not. It is neither necessary nor desirable for him to be able to do so. The price a language must be prepared to pay is submission to many kinds of use. The African writer should aim to use English in a way that brings out his message best without altering the language to the extent that its value as a medium of international exchange will be lost. He should aim at fashioning out an English which is at once universal and able to carry out his peculiar experience . . . it will have to be a new English, still in full communion with its ancestral home, but altered to suit its new African surroundings.

Similarly, in Papua New Guinea writers such as Enos, the editor of *Kovave,* also felt they had to use English to reach a wider audience. Thus, Enos (1972:48):

> the diversity of languages forces them [New Guinean writers] to use English (a language that does not really reflect their cultures) as the alternative form which gives them a wider audience than their own group. . . . However, there is a need for creating an acceptable Niuginian English just as there is an American English. . . . On the other hand, Pidgin and Motu must not be disregarded; nor must local languages.

The first classics of Papua New Guinean literature were written in English (e.g., Kiki's *Ten Thousand Years in a Lifetime* and Eri's *The Crocodile*). A locally distinctive form of Papua New Guinean English has already begun to emerge (see Romaine, 1989), as have similar varieties elsewhere, in Singapore and India (see Kachru, this volume). Nevertheless, although English literature has played an important part in the genesis of political consciousness in former British Africa as well as in Ireland, it does not seem to have had that effect in Papua New Guinea, perhaps because the number of people who had access to English has been much smaller until very recently. Writing before independence, Nelson (1972:186–187) says that nationalism would strongly reduce the importance given to English by the educational system. This, however, never happened (see Romaine, 1991b, for further details).

Both India and Malaysia have reduced the role given to English in the formal education system, and Africa and the South Pacific have actually increased it. Postcolonial African governments in fact introduced English at an earlier level in the educational system than the English themselves had done (Mazrui 1975:15).

It is not easy to win a linguistic revolution. In India, for instance, the decision to replace English with Hindi as the national language originally met with riots. It is probably impossible to overthrow the present linguistic hierarchy without making the struggle of far-reaching sociopolitical reform. Mazrui (1975:187) contrasts the case of Zaire with that of other African colonies where there was preindependence nationalist activity that involved a considerable proportion of the population. Because the Belgians kept Zaire in a state of depoliticization, the consciousness of territorial identity was retarded. The comparative success of

Swahili in parts of East Africa owed much to the fact that all movements of nationalist focus have used it as a means of intertribal unity and resistance (e.g. in the Maji Maji war of 1905–1907, when the people of Tanzania violently resisted the German colonial administration). Swahili was also associated with the King's African Rifles, and recruitment was conducted all over East Africa.

I feel there has never been a more exciting time to be a historian of the English language once linguistic history is conceived of in the broad sense that I and others in this volume have characterized it: as a chronicle of changing users and uses. Much more waits to be done.

WORKS CITED

Achebe, C. 1965. "English and the African Writer." *Transition* 4(18):29–30.

Baker, S. J. 1945. *The Australian Language.* Melbourne: Sun Books.

Delbridge, A. 1990. "Australian English Now." In C. Ricks and L. Michaels, eds., *The State of the Language.* Berkeley: University of California Press. Pp. 66–76.

Enos, A. 1972. "Niugini Literature. A View from the Editor." *Kovave: A Journal of New Guinea Literature* 4.

Grillo, R. D. 1989. *Dominant Languages: Language and Hierarchy in Britain and France.* Cambridge: Cambridge University Press.

Jones, D. 1917. *An English Pronouncing Dictionary.* London: Dent.

Leitner, G. 1984. "Australian English or English in Australia—Linguistic Identity or Dependence in Broadcast Language." *English World-Wide* 5:55–85.

Mazrui, A. A. 1975. *The Political Sociology of the English Language: An African Perspective.* The Hague: Mouton.

McLuhan, M. 1962. *The Gutenberg Galaxy.* Toronto: University of Toronto Press.

Mencken, H. L. 1919. *The American Language.* New York: Knopf.

Mitchell, A. G. 1946. *The Pronunciation of English in Australia.* Sydney: Angus & Robertson.

Nelson, H. 1972. *Papua New Guinea: Black Unity or Black Chaos?* Harmondsworth, England: Penguin.

Phillips, A. A. 1950. "The Cultural Cringe." *Meanjin* 9:299–302.

Romaine, S. 1989. "English and Tok Pisin in Papua New Guinea." *World Englishes* (special issue on English in the South Pacific) 8:5–23.

———. 1991a. "Introduction." In S. Romaine, ed., *Language in Australia.* Cambridge, England: Cambridge University Press. Pp. 1–24.

———. 1991b. "The Status of Tok Pisin: The Colonial Predicament." In U. Ammon, and M. Hellinger, eds., *The Changing Status of Languages.* Berlin: Mouton de Gruyter.

Weinreich, U., W. Labov, and M. Herzog. 1968. "Empirical Foundations for a Theory of Language Change." In W. P. Lehmann and Y. Malkiel, eds., *Directions for Historical Linguistics.* Austin: University of Texas Press.

Index